The Coming Storm

To

Richard Parkin

For fifty years of friendship, for being there at all the important times in my life and for supporting me. For the memories and for the laughs along the way.

The Coming Storm

Test and First-Class Cricketers Killed in World War Two

Nigel McCrery

Pen & Sword
MILITARY

First published in Great Britain in 2017 by
Pen & Sword Military
An imprint of
Pen & Sword Books Ltd
47 Church Street
Barnsley
South Yorkshire
S70 2AS

ISBN 978 1 52670 695 9

Typeset in 10pt Dante by
Mac Style Ltd, Bridlington, East Yorkshire

Printed and bound in the UK by CPI Group (UK) Ltd, Croydon, CRO 4YY

Pen & Sword Books Ltd incorporates the imprints of Pen & Sword Archaeology, Atlas, Aviation, Battleground, Discovery, Family History, History, Maritime, Military, Naval, Politics, Railways, Select, Transport, True Crime, and Fiction, Frontline Books, Leo Cooper, Praetorian Press, Seaforth Publishing and Wharncliffe.

For a complete list of Pen & Sword titles please contact
PEN & SWORD BOOKS LIMITED
47 Church Street, Barnsley, South Yorkshire, S70 2AS, England
E-mail: enquiries@pen-and-sword.co.uk
Website: www.pen-and-sword.co.uk

Contents

Contents

1944

1945

Acknowledgments

I wish to thank the following people and organisations who have been of the greatest help in the writing of this book:

The MCC, especially Neil Robinson and Robert Curphey, MCC library and archive. Peter Wynne-Thomas, cricket historian and Nottinghamshire Country Cricket Club archivist and librarian. Alan Clay, historian and researcher. Hal Giblin for his ever-present inspiration. Ashley McCrery, researcher. Richard Steel for his kindness and amazing ability to spot information and medals. Roger Mann for his kindness, and the contribution he made to the book from his amazing cricketing photograph collection. Roddy Fisher, Eton photograph collection. Roger Doherty for his hard work and help. Beverly Matthews, Tonbridge School archive. J. Rudman, the Uppingham School archive. Brian Turner, researcher. Emily Slingsby, Ampleforth College. Katy de la Rivière, Sedbergh School. Gráinne Lenehan, Marlborough College archive. Avril Harrison, Royal School, Armagh. Tom Keyton, Monmouth School. Clara Policella, Alumni Officer, Bedford School, for her time, trouble and speed. Martin Williamson, Cranleigh School archivist and first-class school historian. Dora Nash, the Oratory School, for her time and trouble. Sue Croucher, Epsom College, for kindly taking the time to find photographs of Aubrey Hodges (photos of Hodges copyright Epsom College). Catherine Grove, Charterhouse archivist, for her time and considerable trouble, many thanks. Jackie Wilkie, archivist at Aldenham School for going that extra mile with her help. David Bridges, Taunton School, for his help, speedy replies and additional help. Caroline Bone, Monkton Combe School, for all her time and trouble. Robin Brooke-Smith, Shrewsbury School, for his kind efforts. Alison Lainchbury, librarian and archivist, Leys School, Oxford, for searching so hard for the missing photographs. Simon Cope and Julian Reid, college archivists, Merton College, Oxford, for their persistence. Jane Teal, Christ's College archive, Canterbury, New Zealand, for taking the time and trouble. Sebastian Puncher, Sandhurst Collection, RMA Sandhurst, for his determination. Medals Forum, Second World War Forum, First World War Forum. And lastly to Matt Jones, Jon Wilkinson, Barnaby Blacker, Katie Eaton, Mat Blurton and Katie Noble at Pen & Sword. If there is anyone I have forgotten, please accept my apologies and be assured I will include you in the next edition if you would kindly contact me.

Preface

I promised to write a memorial book for each year that commemorates the 100th anniversary of the First World War. So far I have done rugby, *Into Touch*, first-class cricket, *Final Wicket*, Olympics, *The Extinguished Flame*, rowing, *Hear the Boat Sing*, and football, *The Final Season*. I have now been persuaded to write two about sportsmen killed in the Second World War, this one and *The Final Scrum* due to be published next year. The idea behind these two books is the same as for the books on the First World War. I want to put flesh onto the bones of the lost. They were not just numbers on a casualty roll listed in some long-forgotten newspaper, but real people with family and friends, people who loved and were loved. I can't do all of them so I have selected sportsmen. The lives have filled me with both sadness and interest. Some have been easy to research, others not so much. I am always amazed by people's lives, some modest, some extraordinary, but all fascinating. Thanks to my father I have always loved cricket, so I suppose I have especially enjoyed writing the two books on first-class cricketers killed in both the world wars. I hope you feel the same. If I have made any mistakes – which I am sure with so many biographies I am bound to have done – please feel free to point them out and if I agree I will amend in the next edition. If anyone has any photographs that are missing from this edition I would be pleased to hear from them too. Some photos are not of the best quality either. My policy on this was better a poor photograph than no photograph. Again if you have a better quality one I would be glad to hear from you. It is my personal belief that cricket played before both the First and Second World Wars was the Golden Age. I know some disagree but for me there will never be ages like them. That we lost so much talent, so much promise, before it could be fully developed is one of the saddest legacies of war, whether sporting talent or any other.

N.B. All people identified in group photographs are as you look at the photograph.

Nigel McCrery

1940

Pilot Officer Michael Herbert Anderson
Cambridge University, Free Foresters
Four first-class appearances
RAF 600 Squadron
Died 10 May 1940, aged 23
Right-handed bat/Wicketkeeper

'The First of the Few'

Michael Anderson was born on 11 December 1916 at Devonport, Devon. He was the son of John Slone Anderson and was educated at Clifton College, Bristol, where he was in the first XI. He also represented Lord's School against The Rest at Lord's Cricket Ground in August 1935. The Rest won by five wickets. On 1 October 1935, on leaving Clifton College, Anderson went up to Trinity Cambridge as a pensioner, obtaining his BA in 1938. He later married Priscilla Ann Troughton and they settled in Kingston, Lewes, Sussex.

A decent right-hand bat and above average wicketkeeper, he made four first-class appearances, three for Cambridge University and one for the Free Foresters against Cambridge. He also took part in two minor county matches both for Hertfordshire in 1936 against Norfolk and Lincolnshire. He made his debut for Cambridge against Northamptonshire on 9 June 1937 at F.P. Fenner's Ground, Cambridge. Northamptonshire won the toss and decided to bat making 257. Anderson caught the Northamptonshire tail-ender John Edgar Buswell off the bowling of Norman Walter Dransfield Yardley for eight. Cambridge made 387 during their first innings, John Hanbury Pawle making 105. Anderson made 19 not out. In their second innings Northamptonshire made 174. Anderson caught the New Zealander Kenneth Cecil James off the bowling of Desmond Rought-Rought for zero and stumped Buswell off the bowling of Thomas Fraser also for zero. This left Cambridge 47 to win, Anderson making seven of these as Cambridge won the match by nine wickets.

He played his second first-class match for the Free Foresters against Cambridge on 11 June 1938, once again at F.P. Fenner's, Free Foresters making 636 declared, Edgar Thomas Killick making 124 and Bryan Herbert Valentine 111. Anderson failed to bat due to the declaration. In reply Cambridge made 533, Paul Antony Gibb making 204 and John Ross Thompson 191. In their second innings the Free Foresters made 223. Anderson, batting second, made 60 (his highest first-class score) before being bowled by Bertram Dudley Carris. Running out of time, the match was drawn.

His next match for Cambridge was against Surrey on 15 June 1938 at the Kennington Oval. Surrey won the toss and decided to bat making 512, Edward Walter Whitfield making 198 and Fred Berry 104 not out. Anderson stumped the Surrey opener Laurence Fishlock off the bowling of Michael Kaye for 27. In their first innings Cambridge made 212, Anderson making zero, being caught by the English test cricketer Laurence Fishlock off the bowling of Edward Watts. Following on, Cambridge made 271, Anderson making five before being caught by Frederick Pierpoint off the bowling of Edward Watts once again. Surrey took the match by an innings and 29 runs.

Anderson made his final first-class appearance on 22 June 1938 for Cambridge against Hampshire at the County Ground Southampton. Cambridge won the toss and decided to bat making 330. Anderson opened the batting and was bowled for a duck by Richard Charles Lucy Court. In reply Hampshire made 333, Richard Henry Moore making 128. Anderson took two wickets. He caught Philip Weaver off the bowling of William Rees-Davies for 37 and stumped Clifford Andrews off the bowling of Michael Kaye for 15. Hampshire only needed 93 to take the match and made those quickly, only losing one wicket, that of Arthur Holt, lbw to William Rees-Davies for three. Hampshire won the match by nine wickets.

Anderson also made two minor county appearances for Hertfordshire in June and July 1936 against Norfolk and Lincolnshire.

Anderson joined the Royal Air Force and was commissioned as a pilot officer in 1936 (*London Gazette* 15 December 1936) training as a pilot and later joining 600 squadron flying Blenheims. On 10 May 1940 the invading Nazis ignored Dutch neutrality when their armies crossed their borders and invaded the Low Countries. The Dutch army, small and ill-trained, was no match for the Germans and their new Blitzkrieg. In order to stop the German's rapid advance the RAF carried out several sorties. One of these raids was against Waalhaven airfield by 600 Squadron. Waalhaven airfield played an important part in the German *Fall Gelb*, their plans for the invasion of the Netherlands. The Germans began their bombardment of the airfield at 4am. An hour later, 500 German paratroopers were dropped in and around the airfield and attacked the Dutch positions. The Dutch troops put up a stiff resistance and when the first aircraft full of airborne troops landed the airfield had still not been captured. However with the arrival of reinforcements the airfield was finally captured, as indeed were the airfields at Ypenburg, Ockenburg and Valkenburg, stopping any chance of a counter-attack by the Dutch Air Force. As a result the Dutch requested help from the RAF to bomb the airfields.

Based at RAF Manston in Kent, B-flight of 600 Squadron (City of London) flying the Bristol Blenheim F1 was selected for the attack. With neither the Spitfire nor the Hurricane having the range to operate over the mainland, the Blenheim was converted as a long-distance fighter and equipped with four .303 calibre machine guns. However it was slow, lacked agility and its armament was no match for the German Messerschmitts. Six Blenheims were selected for the assault. Squadron Leader Jimmy Wells decided to lead the attack on Waalhaven himself. Amongst the other crews selected was Pilot Officer Michael H. Anderson, together with his air gunner, Leading Aircraftman Herbert C.W. Hawkins. They flew Bristol Blenheim L1515.

The squadron took off from RAF Manston at 10.30am without the promised fighter escort. Despite this, Wells pressed on. On reaching Waalhaven airfield the squadron attacked. Wells was the first to attack hitting a number of German aircraft. Pilot Officer Hayes: 'I followed him [Wells] and picked out a Junkers-52 which I shot to pieces.' Pilot Officer Haine (in L1517) also claimed he set fire to a number of German aircraft. However before they had a chance to cause real damage they were attacked by twelve Messerschmitt Bf110s of Gruppe 3 of Zerstörergeschwader. The men of 600 squadron were outnumbered, outclassed and quickly picked off.

Blenheim L1335 was the first to be shot down, crashing close to Waalhaven airfield; two men died, Moore and Isaacs. Anderson and Hawkins (L1515) were shot down next, crashing at Spijkenisse, both dying in the crash. Squadron Leader Wells's machine was next (L6616), crashing in the village of Pernis; Wells and Kidd were both killed. Wells's navigator, Sergeant Davis, managed to bale out and survived, making it to British lines. Another Blenheim crashed at the village of Piershil; Pilot Officer Echlin was killed but Flight Officer Rowe survived thanks to the intervention of Dutch soldiers who got him out of the plane and to hospital where he was later made prisoner of war. Haine crash-landed near the village of Herkingen but managed to evade capture, finally making his way back to England. Only one of the Blenheims made it back to base, that flown by Pilot Officer Hayes and corporal Holmes (L1514); this plane was so badly shot up, it was scrapped. For his part in the raid Anderson was mentioned in despatches.

For many years Anderson and Hawkins lay in unmarked graves, their identities unknown. However in the 1980s, a historian, Hans Onderwater, after extensive research established their identity and headstones were finally placed on their graves at Spijkenisse General Cemetery, grave 26. Every May since the war ended, members of 600 Squadron have travelled to the Netherlands to pay their respects to the seven members of the squadron who died that day.

Batting and fielding averages

	Mat	Inns	NO	Runs	HS	Ave	100	50	Ct	St
First-class	4	7	2	92	60	18.40	0	1	3	3

Bowling averages

	Mat	Balls	Runs	Wkts	BBI	BBM	Ave	Econ	SR	4w	5w	10
First-class	4	-	-	-	-	-	-	-	-	-	-	-

Major Colin Cokayne-Frith
Army
One first-class appearance
15th/19th The King's Royal Hussars
Died 18 May 1940, aged 40
Right-handed bat

Held the Germans up long enough for the BEF to escape

Colin Cokayne-Frith was born on 27 March 1900 at St Stephen's House, Canterbury, Kent. He was the son of Lieutenant Colonel Reginald and Pauline Cokayne-Frith. He was educated at Eton where he played in the XI.

On leaving school Firth decided on a career in the Army, going up to Sandhurst. While there he played in the Sandhurst XI against the Royal Military Academy Woolwich.

During the later part of the war Frith served at the front, which he survived. He celebrated the end of the war only forty miles from where he was to be killed during the Second World War.

He made one first-class appearance for the Army against Cambridge University at F.P. Fenner's Ground, Cambridge, on 7 June 1939. Cambridge won the toss and decided to bat making 411. Frith caught John Thompson off the bowling of Henry Hamilton van Straubenzee for 45. In reply the Army made 537. Frith made 54 before being caught by the England Test player Francis George Mann off the bowling of his brother John Pelham Mann. George Sylvester Grimston made 104 and Charles William Christopher Packe (killed 1 July 1944) 145. In their second innings Cambridge made 149. The match was eventually

Cokayne-Frith is buried in Asse (Mollemsebaan) Communal Cemetery. He is buried next to his crewman 556837 Corporal Kenneth Percival Smith.

drawn. Frith played for the Army five times, against the Territorial Army, West Indies, The Royal Navy and the Royal Air Force, but the match against Cambridge University was his only first-class appearance.

Cokayne-Frith was killed together with his tank crew on 18 May 1940 fighting a rearguard action with the 15/19 Hussars during the BEF's retreat to Dunkirk at a place called Assche. The scene was later described:

> As Squadron HQ entered the town, Major Frith's tank was destroyed by an anti-tank gun and he and all his crew were killed. The rest of the force under Captain Mytton then tried to force a way through Assche and after twenty minutes street fighting they succeeded in retaking nearly half the town and in reaching 4th Troop. By now every AFV of this force had been knocked out and the fighting developed into individual actions by small bodies of survivors. By the end Major Frith and his crew were killed. Captain Mytton and SSM Laing were wounded and taken prisoner, and the main body of the squadron was outnumbered and surrounded.

Before dying Frith managed to warn the remaining squadron that he was surrounded. In the words of Second Lieutenant Guy Courage, Frith 'never stood a chance'. Frith was the most senior officer of the regiment to be killed that day. He was later mentioned in despatches for his heroic work throughout the retreat.

Batting and fielding averages

	Mat	Inns	NO	Runs	HS	Ave	100	50	Ct	St
First-class	1	1	0	54	54	54.00	0	1	1	0

Bowling averages

	Mat	Balls	Runs	Wkts	BBI	BBM	Ave	Econ	SR	4w	5w	10
First-class	1	-	-	-	-	-	-	-	-	-	-	-

Captain Patrick (Pat) William Rucker
Oxford University
Seven first-class appearances
D Company, 7th Battalion Royal Sussex Regiment
Died 20 May 1940, aged 40
Left Arm, Medium Pace

Had the honour of bowling the first, first-class
ball following the 1918 Armistice

Patrick Rucker was born on 5 May 1900 at Chislehurst, Kent, the fourth son of Edward Augustus Rucker, sugar broker, and Mary Emmeline (née Farmer). He was educated at Charterhouse, Girdlestoneites House. A decent batsman and fielder he was also a fine left-arm medium bowler and turned out for the first XI playing against Winchester, Harrow, Westminster, Wellington, The Rest against Lord's School, Eton and Public School's against P.F. Warner's XI. He went up to University College, Oxford and made seven first-class appearances all for Oxford University in 1919 and took the honour of bowling the first, first-class ball following the 1918 Armistice.

Rucker made his debut first-class appearance for Oxford against the Gentlemen of England on 12 May 1919 at the University Parks, Oxford. The Gentlemen of England won the toss and decided to bat making 169. Rucker bowled 18 overs and took no wickets for 37. In reply Oxford made 152, Rucker making 17 before being caught by Philip Havelock Davies off the bowling of Humphrey Adam Gilbert. In their second innings the Gentlemen of England made 100, Vincent Price taking eight wickets for 30 runs. This left Oxford needing 120 to take the game, which they did with the loss of only two wickets, Frank William Gilligan for zero and the England test cricketer Donald John Knight for ten. Oxford won by eight wickets.

His second first-class appearance was against the Australian Imperial Forces, once again at the University Parks, Oxford on 29 May 1919. Rucker scored zero in his first innings, bowled Charles Kelleway (who took seven wickets during the innings) once again failing to bat in the second. He also took no wickets for 60 off 17 overs. The match was eventually drawn.

Rucker next turned out for Oxford against P.F. Warner's XI on 5 June 1919 at the University Parks. Rucker scored one not out in his first innings, and 13 in his second, bowled Michael Falcon. He also took one wicket, Michael Falcon (sweet revenge) for 45 runs off 18 overs in the first innings and no wickets for 17 off four overs in the second. He also had the privilege of catching the famous Pelham (Plum) Warner off the bowling of Frank Naumann for 11. Oxford finally won the match by 30 runs.

On 26 June 1919, Rucker made his first appearance against a county side, Surrey, at the Oval. Rucker scored eight before being run out in his first innings and was one not out in his second. He also took four wickets for 107 off 35 overs. The England test cricketer Andrew Sandham caught Gerald Vyvyan Pearse for 14, Henry Starr Harrison for 13, Frederick Charles William Newman lbw for 19, and Walter Hodsoll Gordon Heath for a duck. Surrey won by 47. The match was also noted for the England test cricket Andrew Ducat's 306 not out in the first innings.

Rucker next turned out against the MCC at Lord's on 30 June 1919. Rucker scored five in his first (and only) innings before being bowled by George Cartwright. He also took three wickets for 71 runs off 17 overs during the first innings, the England test cricketer Lionel Tennyson lbw for 30, Harold Marriott for 24 and George Rubens Cox caught Frank Gilligan for 14. In the second innings he took two further wickets, the Surrey opener Lionel Tennyson (once again) stumped Frank Gilligan for 81 and another England test cricketer Nigel Esme Haig lbw for 20. He also caught a further England test cricketer, Ernest Smith, off the bowling of Vincent Price for 27. The match was drawn.

On 3 July 1919 at the Saffrons, Eastbourne, Rucker turned out for Oxford against H.D.G. Leveson-Gower's XI. He scored zero not out in his only innings. He also bowled 8 overs for 23 runs and took one wicket, that of Basil Frederick Clarke, for 16. The match was noted for the two centuries made by Miles Howell, 115 in the first innings and 102 in his second. The match was eventually drawn.

His final first-class match came against the old rivals Cambridge University at Lord's on 7 July 1919. Oxford won the toss and decided to bat making 387, Rucker being caught and bowled by Gordon Armytage Fairbairn for zero, Miles Howell the Oxford opener making 170. Cambridge replied making 280 runs, Rucker bowling 12 overs for 50 runs and taking no wickets. In their second innings Oxford made 168, Rucker making three not out. In reply Cambridge made 230, Rucker bowling a further three overs for 12 runs for no wickets. Oxford won by 45 runs; a nice conclusion to his first-class career.

In 1927 Rucker married Betty Stuart Fairweather in Wycombe, Buckinghamshire.

In 1939 he was commissioned into the 7th battalion Royal Sussex Regiment joining D company. The battalion was formed in late 1939 and based at Dyke Road Barracks, Brighton. It was sent to France on 18 May 1940, travelling to Abbeville then Lens before moving on to Amiens. While still on their troop train the battalion were subjected to attacks from German dive-bombers, losing around 60 men, 25 of which were killed. At 2pm on 20 May the battalion were attacked by a motorcycle battalion of the 1st Panzer Division under the command of Major von Wietershiem. The 7th battalion were only lightly armed with rifles and fifty rounds per man, three Bren guns, one anti-tank gun with ten rounds, and two mortars equipped with smoke bombs. The battalion held out as long as it could, destroying an enemy tank and slowing the German advance, but with ammunition almost spent and casualties mounting the battalion were ordered to surrender at 7.15pm. It was during this action that Captain Pat Rucker was killed. Although at first reported missing in action his death was later assumed to have taken place on that day. Casualties were so high the battalion was disbanded.

Pat Rucker is commemorated on the Dunkirk Memorial, column 63, and at Charterhouse School; 340 Carthusians lost their lives during the Second World War). As a long time member of the MCC, Patrick is also one of the 282 members who are commemorated on a memorial at Lord's, which was unveiled by Field-Marshall Lord Bramall KG GCB OBE MC on 9 August 2005.

His brother Lieutenant Robin Sinclair Rucker was killed serving with the RAF on 12 October 1918. He also went to Charterhouse and was in the first XI. He played an innings of 122 and headed the batting averages in 1915.

Survivors of the 7th battalion made commemorative trips to France up to 2000. Later a memorial to the battalion was erected by the City of Amiens authorities at the site of the battle.

Batting and fielding averages

	Mat	Inns	NO	Runs	HS	Ave	100	50	Ct	St
First-class	7	10	4	48	17	8.00	0	0	2	0

Bowling averages

	Mat	Balls	Runs	Wkts	BBI	Ave	Econ	SR	5w	10
First-class	7	876	462	11	4/107	42.00	3.16	79.6	0	0

A.R.BURBERRY.   T.E.H.LIEBENROOD.   T.N.PENLINGTON.   W.M.A.ANDERSON.   A.R.de BEER.
C.J.WILSON TAYLOR.   P.W.RICKER.   R.B.B.B.COOKE.   D.A.R.B.COOKE   R.A.BURBERRY.
L.R.LEWNS   E.EVELYN

Charterhouse First XI, 1917.

Pilot Officer Reginald Edmund Compton Butterworth
Middlesex, Oxford University, Sir J. Cahn's XI, H.D.G.
Leveson-Gower's XI
Thirty-eight first-class appearances
13 Squadron RAFVR
(Air-Gunner)
Died 21 May 1940, aged 33
Right-hand bat/Right arm fast medium

'And all the brothers were valiant'

Reginald Butterworth was born on 16 August 1906 at Samarang, Java. He was the son of Reginald Butterworth, a merchant and broker, and Cornelia Gertrud Wellenstein. He had an older brother, John, born in 1905 and a sister Dorothy born in 1910.

He was educated at Harrow and was soon playing for the first XI. During the annual match against Eton on 11 July 1924 at Lord's he took five wickets for 66 off 26 overs in the first innings and three wickets for 41 off 23 overs in the second. He also made 42 before being caught by David Fortune Landale off the bowling of Ralph Cobbold during the first innings and 17 not out in the second. Despite Butterworth's best efforts the match was eventually drawn (there is a video of this match on YouTube). Butterworth eventually became head of school.

After leaving Harrow he went up to Christchurch Oxford and was quickly in the University XI. Between May 1926 and May 1939 he made thirty-eight first-class appearances, his debut being against H.D.G. Leveson-Gower's XI on 19 May 1926 at the University Parks, Oxford. Oxford won the toss and decided to bat making 300 in their first innings, Butterworth making the highest score with 79 before being bowled by John Mercer. In reply Leveson-Gower's XI made 202. Butterworth bowled 16 overs for 27 and took two wickets, Robert Lyttleton Lee Braddell for six and John Mercer for seven. He also caught Francis Peter Ryan off the bowling of John Wilfrid Greenstock for zero. In their second innings Oxford also made 202, Butterworth making one not out. In their second innings Leveson-Gower's XI made 132. Butterworth bowled 12 overs for 29 and took no further wickets. Oxford took the match by 168 runs.

Butterworth went on to represent Oxford University against the Australians, Army, Free Foresters, Lancashire, Leicestershire, Harlequins, Surrey, Essex, and MCC, making his final university match against Cambridge on 4 July 1927 at Lord's. Cambridge won the toss and elected to bat making 178. Butterworth bowled 11 overs for 42 runs, taking one wicket, that of Ralph Hamilton Cobbold lbw for three. In reply Oxford University made 149, Butterworth making zero before being bowled by Longfield (Longfield took five wickets during the innings). In their second innings Cambridge made 349, Arthur Kenneth Judd making 124. Butterworth bowled 18 overs for 89 runs and failed to take a wicket. Oxford made 262 in their second innings, Butterworth making 12 before being caught by the England test player Robert Walter Vivian Robins off the bowling of Leonard George Irvine. Errol Reginald Thorold Holmes, another English test cricketer made 113.

A good all-round sportsman Butterworth also played golf for Oxford.

It wasn't until 2 July 1930 that Butterworth played his next first-class match, this time for the MCC against Cambridge at Lord's. He made three and zero and failed to take a wicket. Cambridge took the match by ten wickets. He went on to play for the MCC against the Army, Surrey, and being selected for the MCC tour of Ireland played against Ireland on 4 August 1934 at College Park, Dublin (he played in several other matches but they were not first-class).

Selected to play for Middlesex he made his debut first-class county appearance against Warwickshire at Lord's on 15 May 1935. Warwickshire won the toss and decided to bat making 164. In reply Middlesex made 112, Butterworth, who opened the innings, being caught by Frederick Santall off the bowling of Robert Elliott Storey Wyatt for a duck. In reply Warwickshire made 253 declared, Alfred John William Croom making 101. In their second innings Middlesex made 161. Once again Butterworth opened the innings, being bowled by Joseph Herbert Mayer for two. Warwickshire won by 144 runs. Butterworth went on to play for Middlesex against Kent, Somerset, Yorkshire, Sussex, Northamptonshire, Sussex, Gloucestershire, Lancashire, New Zealand and Nottinghamshire. Butterworth also made three first-class appearances for Sir J. Cahn's XI against Leicestershire, Glamorgan and Ceylon during Sir J. Cahn's XI tour of Ceylon and Malaya between in 1937.

Butterworth made his final first-class appearance for the MCC against Yorkshire. The match took place from 6 May 1939 at Lord's. Yorkshire won the toss and decided to field. The MCC made 92, Butterworth making 11 before being bowled by Ellis Robinson (who took seven wickets in the innings). In reply Yorkshire made 148. In their second innings the MCC made 114, Butterworth making two before being caught by the England test cricketer Arthur Wood (*Wisden* cricketer of the year 1939) off the bowling of the famous England test cricketer Hedley Verity (who was also to lose his life during the war). Verity took no less than nine wickets during the innings. Yorkshire now only had to make 59 which they knocked off quickly for the loss of only one wicket, that of another famous English test cricketer, Herbert Sutcliffe. Yorkshire won by nine wickets.

Butterworth also made fifty-two appearances in matches that were not first-class, playing for G.B. Legge's XI, the Free Foresters, Sir J. Cahn's XI, and others. During his first-class career Butterworth made 1,189 runs including two centuries and six half centuries. He also bowled 3,502 balls taking fifty wickets for 2,079 runs, his best figures being three for eleven. He also made 15 catches.

Living in Chelsea, he married Elisabeth Werner, of Putney.

On 5 March 1940 he was commissioned into the RAF as a pilot officer on probation and posted to 13 squadron RAF Volunteer Reserve as an air gunner flying in Lysanders. During the early stages of the war Lysanders were used as spotters and light bombers. Lightly armed, they made easy targets for the German Luftwaffe. The squadron moved to France on 2 October 1939. Flying with Flight Lieutenant (Pilot) Richard H.N. Graham on a liaison flight he was shot down and killed over St Omer and crashed in St Martin-au-Laert on 21 May 1940.

He is buried in the St Martin au Laert churchyard, grave 2. His name also appears on the MCC Roll of Honour, the Christchurch Oxford Memorial and the Harrow School memorial.

His brother John, a well-known and talented cricketer, also played for Oxford. He was killed at Shooter's Hill, London on 18 March 1941 when serving as a 2nd Lieutenant with the Royal Artillery 160 Battery. He is buried in Greenwich Cemetery, section G, collective grave 74, screen wall panel 1

Batting and fielding averages

	Mat	Inns	NO	Runs	HS	Ave	100	Ct	St
First-class	38	63	2	1189	110	19.49	2	15	0

Bowling averages

	Mat	Runs	Wkts	BBI	Ave	5w	10
First-class	38	2078	50	3/11	41.56	0	0

Corporal Alec Douglas Howie
Army (India)
One first-class appearance
1st Battalion East Surrey Regiment
Died 22 May 1940, aged 26
Right-hand bat/Left arm medium

Heverlee War Cemetery, Leuven, Belgium.

Died defending Dunkirk

Alec Howie was born on 3 September 1913 in Saharanpur, Uttar Pradesh. He was the son of Charles Thomas and Ethel Muriel Howie. After finishing his education, he enlisted into the ranks of the 1st Battalion East Surrey Regiment.

Howie made one first-class appearance playing for the Army against Northern India in the Ranji Trophy. The match was played at the Lawrence Gardens, Lahore, on 4 December 1934. The Army won the toss and decided to bat making 203. Howie made 16 before being caught by George Edmond Brackenbury Abell off the bowling of Mubarak Ali. In reply Northern India made 459 with Abell making 210 and Agha Ahmed Raza Khan 101. Howie bowled three overs for 14 and took no wickets. In their second innings the Army made 204, Howie making 33 before being bowled by Ahmed Khan. Northern India won by an innings and 52 runs.

By the outbreak of the war in September 1939 the 1st Battalion East Surrey Regiment had returned to England. In October they were sent to France with the British Expeditionary Force (BEF) as part of the 11th Infantry Brigade (which also included the 2nd Battalion East Surreys, Lancashire Fusiliers and the 1st battalion Ox and Bucks Light Infantry) attached to the 4th Infantry Division.

In May 1940, the 1st Battalion advanced into Belgium but were driven back by the force of the German Blitzkrieg. Although they managed to hold a line at the River Escaut (the Scheldt) it was only a temporary defence and the battalion was eventually withdrawn to the coast at Dunkirk to be withdrawn back to England. It was during the fighting around the River Escaut on 22 May 1940 that the brave Alec Howie was to lose his life. He is buried in Heverlee War Cemetery, grave reference 3.D.1.

Batting and fielding averages

	Mat	Inns	NO	Runs	HS	Ave	100	50	Ct	St
First-class	1	2	0	49	33	24.50	0	0	0	0

Bowling averages

	Mat	Runs	Wkts	BBI	BBM	Ave	SR	4w	5w	10
First-class	1	14	0	-	-	-	-	0	0	0

Lieutenant William Mark Welch
Free Foresters
Four first-class appearances
1st Battalion Rifle Brigade
Died 25 May 1940, aged 29
Right-handed bat/Right arm medium, right arm off break

'Died so the BEF could escape'

William Welch was born on 12 August 1911 in Brisbane, Australia. He was the son of William Alfred and Jessie Isabella (née Mark) of Brisbane. At some point he was sent to England by his parents to be educated at Harrow. A good all-round sportsman he quickly established himself with the Harrow first XI. In the Eton Harrow match at Lord's on 13 July 1928 Welch almost won the day, the first time Harrow would have beaten Eton since 1908 (most matches were drawn). Winning the toss Eton elected to bat making 126. Welch bowled five overs for three and took two wickets, Cecil Henry Gosling, caught and bowled for 22, and Ian Archibald de Hoghton Lyle, clean bowled for nine. In reply Harrow made 234, Welch making 70 not out, the highest score of the innings. At this stage things were looking good for a Harrow win. In their second innings however, Eton made 415, Ian Stanley Akers-Douglas knocking up an impressive 158. Welch bowled 13 overs for 77 and failed to take a wicket. In reply Harrow made 279, Welch making 36 before being stumped by John Mayhew off the bowling of Arthur Hazlerigg who cut through the Harrow batsmen taking five for 73. Eton finally took the honours by 28 runs (after six draws).

Welch was also first string at racquets, received his colours for rugby, and was a first-class athlete. He was also a sergeant in the Harrow army cadets and later with the Officer Training Corps, being commissioned first into the 28th Battalion London Regiment (Artist's Rifles) before joining the 1st Battalion Rifle Brigade.

Welch made four first-class appearances, all for the Free Foresters, between 1935 and 1939 and all against Cambridge University.

Welch made his debut for the Free Foresters against Cambridge on 8 June 1935 at F.P. Fenner's Ground. Cambridge won the toss and elected to bat making a decent 265, Hugh Tryon Bartlett making 100. Welch did well, bowling 18 overs for 43 and taking five wickets. Hugh Dinwiddy caught Spencer Block for 24; Grahame Wilshaw Parker, lbw for 23; Hugh Bartlett caught John Stephenson for 100; James Grimshaw (KIA 26-9-44) caught Arthur Judd for 11; and finally Frank King clean bowled for a duck. In reply the Free Foresters made 389, Welch making 37 before being caught by James Grimshaw off the bowling of Robert Hunt. In their second innings Cambridge were all out for 195. Welch bowled 15 overs for 49 but failed to take a wicket. This time it was Frederick Brown that did the damage, taking six Cambridge wickets for 67. Welch did however catch the England test cricketer, Norman Yardley, off the bowling of Frederick Brown for a duck. This left the Free Foresters 72 to win, which they did for the loss of three wickets, taking the match by seven wickets.

Welch had to wait a year to make his second first-class appearance, once again against Cambridge, played on 13 June 1936 at F.P. Fenner's. Cambridge won the toss and elected to bat making 228, Hugh Bartlett making 129. Welch took one wicket, that of John Cameron, lbw for 11. The real damage was done by the English test cricketer Frederick Brown (awarded MBE in 1942 for his work in the evacuation of Crete and CBE in 1980 for his services to cricket), who took seven wickets for 88. The Free Foresters made 335 in their first innings, Welch making three before being bowled by Duncan Smart Carmichael (Carmichael took six wickets for 103 during the innings). Cambridge only managed 132 in their second innings before they ran out of time and the match was drawn. Welch bowled four overs for six and failed to take a wicket.

A year later on 12 June 1937 Welch once again represented the Free Foresters against Cambridge, once again at F.P. Fenner's. Cambridge won the toss and this time decided to field. The Free Foresters made 231, Welch making 26 before being caught by Norman Yardley off the bowling of William Michael Eastwood White. In reply Cambridge made 292, John Pawle making 115 not out. Welch bowled ten overs taking one wicket for 27, Allan Frederick Tinsdale White, caught Spencer Block for three. In their second innings the Free Foresters made 257, Welch being run out for zero. Batting again, Cambridge made 105 before running out of time. Welch bowled ten overs for nine and took the wicket of Norman Yardley caught Geoffrey Cuthbertson for 19. The match was drawn.

Welch made his final first-class appearance two years later on 10 June 1939 against Cambridge at F.P. Fenner's. Free Foresters won the toss and decided to bat making 287. Welch made an impressive 104, his highest first-class score before being caught by John Mann off the bowling of Derek Gillespie. In reply Cambridge made 339. Welch bowled ten overs but took no wickets for 58. In their second innings the Free Foresters made 202; Welch failed to bat. The match was once again drawn.

Welch also represented the Harrow Wanderers, the MCC and H.M. Martineau's XI. Welch bowled 476 balls and took eight wickets for 221 runs, his best figures being five for 43; he made 170 runs, his highest score being 104 against Cambridge; he also made one catch.

The 1st Battalion Rifle Brigade was moved to France quickly as reinforcements to help in the defence of Dunkirk and Calais. On 21 May 1940 they were being dispersed in Suffolk villages to help with the defence of England when they received orders to travel to Southampton, boarding SS *Archangel* and disembarking at Calais. Heavy fighting quickly ensued. Lieutenant Welch with B Company was originally posted at the Dunkirk exit. However on 23 May the British, faced by the elite 10th Panzer Division and running low on equipment and ammunition, began to retire to the old Calais walls and on 24 May the siege began. Supported by the Luftwaffe the German attacks were mostly costly failures and by nightfall the Germans reported that about half their tanks had been knocked out and a third of the infantry were casualties. On the night of 24/25 May the defenders were forced to withdraw from the southern *enceinte* to a line covering the Old Town and citadel. The German attacks the following day, the 25th, were all repulsed. It was during the fighting on 25 May that Lieutenant William Welch was killed, while attempting to counter-attack and retake a bridge captured by the advancing Germans. His body was recovered and he is buried in the Calais Southern Cemetery, grave reference plot M, grave 5.

The Coming Storm

Winston Churchill wrote in 1949 that the heroic defence of Calais delayed the German attack on Dunkirk and helped to save the BEF. Three panzer divisions had been diverted by the defence of Boulogne and Calais, giving the Allies time to rush troops to the west of Dunkirk and save thousands of men who were then able to continue the fight.

Batting and fielding averages

	Mat	Inns	NO	Runs	HS	Ave	100	50	Ct	St
First-class	4	5	0	170	104	34.00	1	0	1	0

Bowling averages

	Mat	Balls	Runs	Wkts	BBI	Ave	Econ	SR	5w	10
First-class	4	476	221	8	5/43	27.62	2.78	59.5	1	0

Captain Charles Talbot Orton
Army, Europeans (India)
Four first-class appearances
Royal Warwickshire Regiment
Died 28 May 1940, aged 29
Slow left arm orthodox

Murdered by the SS

Charles Orton was born on 9 August 1910 in Farnham, Surrey. He was the son of Major General Sir Ernest Frederick Orton KCIE CB and of Lady Orton (née Mickleburgh). He was educated at Tonbridge where his talent for cricket was quickly realized and he was soon in the XI.

Deciding on a career in the Army he took a commission into the Royal Warwickshire Regiment. It was while serving with the Army that he played his four first-class matches.

He made his debut for the Army against Oxford University on 22 May 1937 at the University Parks. The Army won the toss and decided to bat making 251. Orton batting in the lower order made seven before being run out. In reply Oxford made 137. Orton bowled five overs for 30 and failed to take a wicket. John William Arthur Stephenson, a right-arm fast-medium bowler (later DSO), took six wickets during the innings. In their second innings the Army made 115. Orton made zero not out. In their second innings Oxford made 230. This time Orton did better, bowling 17 overs and taking two wickets for 63: Eric John Hopkins Dixon (KIA 20 April 1941) caught Francis Edgar Hugonin for six and Michael Moore Walford, caught Harold Eldon Scott for 54. Oxford won the match by six wickets.

His next first-class match was against Cambridge a week later on 29 May 1937 this time at F.P. Fenner's Ground, Cambridge. The Army won the toss and once again decided to bat making a solid 265. Orton made 20 not out. In reply Cambridge made 395, Robert Geoffrey Hunt making 117. Orton bowled 17 overs for 45 and took one wicket, Norman Yardley, caught John Stephenson for 84. In their second innings the Army only managed 146. Orton made six not out. Cambridge only had to make 18 to take the game which they made without losing a wicket. Cambridge took the match by ten wickets. It was Orton's last first-class match in England.

Posted to India, Orton made two further first-class appearances, both in the Bombay Pentangular Tournament playing for the Europeans. The first was against the Parsees on 23 November 1938 at Brabourne Stadium, Bombay. The Europeans won the toss and decided to bat making 142 runs, Orton 13 not out. In reply the Parsees made 235. Orton bowled eight overs for 34 runs and failed to take a wicket. In their second innings the Europeans rallied, making 345, Robert Francis Hugh Philpot-Brookes making 143. Orton made five not out. In reply the Parsees made 233. Orton bowled three overs and failed to take a wicket for 14; he did however catch S.M. Palsetia off the bowling of Henry Lade Murray for four. The Europeans won by 19 runs.

Orton made his final first-class appearance against the Muslims on 29 November 1938, in the semi-final of the Bombay Pentangular at the Brabourne Stadium. The Muslims won the toss and decided to bat making 246, Syed Mushtaq Ali making 157. Orton bowled 12 overs taking seven wickets for 51, his best first-class bowing figures. Syed Mushtaq Ali caught John Edward Tew for 157, Syed Wazir Ali caught Kenneth Stephen Horace Wilson for zero, and bowled Syed Nazir Ali lbw for zero, completing his hat-trick. He then went on to take the wickets of Dilawar Hussain lbw, nine, Khwaja Saeed Ahmed, lbw, three, Khanmohammad Cassumbhoy Ibrahim, lbw, zero and Mohammad Nissar, zero. In reply the Europeans made 172. Orton was bowled by Mubarak Ali for zero. In their second innings the Muslims made 272, Syed Wazir Ali making 112. Orton bowled 15 overs and took two further wickets for 81, Abbas Khan Lodhi, lbw, for ten and Khwaja Saeed Ahmed for 12. In reply the Europeans made 249, Orton making four not out. The Muslims took the match by 97 runs.

Orton also made one minor counties appearance during the 1931 championship, representing Kent's second XI against Norfolk, Norfolk taking the match by nine wickets. He represented the Army on eight occasions, as well as the Yellowhammers, the Catterick Garrison and the Aldershot Command. He later married Margaret Stewart Margot of Hitchin, Hertfordshire.

Returning to England, serving with the second battalion Royal Warwickshire Regiment, and promoted to captain, Orton was sent to France as part of the BEF in September 1939. The battalion was part of the formation of 48th (South Midland) Division 144th Infantry Brigade. In May 1940 they formed part of the rearguard, holding back the German advance and giving the troops held up on the beaches of Dunkirk the chance to escape back to England. Holding the line on the Comines Canal and the Escaut, the battalion were finally overrun and forced to surrender on 28 May 1940. After their surrender, soldiers from the 2nd Battalion Royal Warwickshire Regiment, the Cheshire Regiment, and Royal Artillery, as well as French soldiers, were taken to a barn near Wormhoudt and Esquelbecq where they were massacred by the 1st SS Division Leibstandarte. Fifteen men survived; they were later found by a regular German Army unit who treated their wounds before sending them to PoW camps. Whether he was murdered with his men at Wormhoudt or killed during the defence of the Comines Canal isn't clear. Whatever is the truth, Captain Charles Orton died on 28 May helping to secure the evacuation of the BEF and allowing the war to continue. He is buried in the Dozinghem Military Cemetery, grave reference XVII. A. 30.

Batting and fielding averages

	Mat	Inns	NO	Runs	HS	Ave	100	50	Ct	St
First-class	4	8	6	55	20*	27.50	0	0	1	0

Bowling averages

	Mat	Runs	Wkts	BBI	Ave	5w	10
First-class	4	318	12	7/51	26.50	1	0

Sub-Lieutenant Michael Harrington Matthews
Oxford University
Twenty-Three first-class appearances.
Royal Navy (HMS *Greyhound*)
Died 29 May 1940, aged 26
Right-hand bat, Wicketkeeper

'An Outstanding Man in Every Way'

Michael Matthews was born on 26 April 1914 in Wandsworth. He was the eldest son (he had a younger brother and sister) of the Very Reverend Walter Matthews, Dean of St Paul's (1934-67), and former chaplain to the King who mentions him in his book *Memories and Meanings*, and his wife Margaret Bryan. He was educated at Westminster where he played in the first XI between 1930 and 1933, keeping wicket in his last two years. He played for C.F. Tufnell's XI against Lord's XI on 26 August 1929 at Lord's, C.F. Tufnell's winning by six wickets, Matthews making 27 and 8.

On leaving Westminster in 1933 he was awarded a Westminster classics scholarship going up to Christ Church Oxford where he played first-class cricket for the university.

He made twenty-three first-class appearances for Oxford between May 1934 and July 1937 becoming Oxford's principal wicketkeeper from 1936. He made his debut for Oxford against Yorkshire on 9 May 1934 at the University Parks. Yorkshire won the toss and decided to bat making 351, Morris Leyland making a century. In reply Oxford made 256, Gerald Chalk (killed 17 February 1943) making 135. Matthews made 23 before being caught by the English test cricketer Leonard Hutton (knighted in 1956) off the bowling of another England test cricketer, William Eric Bowes. In their second innings Yorkshire made 161 for two before declaring. In reply Oxford University made 112; Matthews failed to bat. The match was eventually drawn.

Matthews went on to represent Oxford against Lancashire, the Australians, Minor Counties, Gloucestershire, India, Worcestershire, Free Foresters, Leicestershire, the MCC, Sussex, Surrey, H.D.G. Leveson-Gower's XI and Cambridge University.

He made his final first-class appearance for Oxford against Cambridge on 5 July 1937 at Lord's. Cambridge won the toss and elected to bat making 253, Norman Yardley knocking up 101. Matthews took five catches: Yardley off the bowling of Alexander Parkinson Singleton for 101, Mark Tindall off the bowling of Roger Charles MacDonald Kimpton for ten, Peter Malden Studd off the bowling of the England test player Norman Stewart Mitchell-Innes for eighteen, Robert Hunt once again off the bowling of Mitchell-Innes, and finally Thomas William Fraser off the bowling of Mitchell-Innes for one. In their second innings Oxford made 267, John Nelson Grover making 121, Matthews making 13 before being caught by Paul Gibb off the bowling of Bharat Chand Khanna. In reply Cambridge made 173, Matthews catching Desmond Rought-Rought off the bowling of Randle Frederick Hicks Darwall-Smith. Oxford made 160 in reply, taking the match by seven wickets, their first victory for five years.

During his first-class career Matthews scored 393 runs, his highest score being 68 against the Minor Counties in 1936, and he made six catches and 32 stumpings. He also turned out for The Rest against Lord's School, Oxford against Oxford University and B.H. Belle's XI against A.M. Lee's XI.

He graduated with a 2nd in Classic Mods, a 1st in Lit Hum in 1935, and a 1st in Jurisprudence in 1939. He read for the Bar at Gray's Inn and married Loveday Elizabeth Abbott at Wallingford shortly after the outbreak of the war.

Joining the RNVR as a Sub-Lieutenant, he was posted to the destroyer HMS *Greyhound*, the first ship to reach Dunkirk to assist with the evacuation of the BEF. He was killed when a bomb hit his ship on 29 May 1940.

His body was never recovered. He is commemorated on the Portsmouth Naval Memorial, Panel 44, Column 2, and on the memorial at Gray's Inn.

His father made numerous broadcasts during the war and also wrote about his son in his autobiography *Memories and Meanings*:

> On one of the nights when few Londoners had any sleep and many had horrifying adventures fighting fires, rescuing bombed citizens from collapsed houses and searching ruins for the dead and injured – in short one of the really bad nights in hell – I had to 'Lift Up Hearts' in my regular radio broadcast from the Cathedral. I remember thinking 'my little address is quite inadequate and I am on edge because I have been scared.'
>
> So I prayed that my voice would sound calm and confident. Some ten years later, someone who had been acting as a fireman at that time commented 'The last time I heard your voice was after one of the worst nights of the Blitz. I was absolutely done and despairing but you sounded so calm and confident that I was quite pepped up.'
>
> I now come to the great sorrow of our lives, the event after which nothing was quite the same. Our eldest child, Michael Harrington Matthews, Sub-Lieutenant R.N.V.R., was killed on H.M.S Greyhound, the destroyer which was the first to reach Dunkirk, on May 28th, 1940. The little boy who had clung to his mother Margaret in 1916 during a Zeppelin raid crying, 'But you aren't frightened, Mummy, are you?' was shattered by a bomb from a German plane as he stood on the bridge of H.M.S Greyhound in 1940.
>
> Margaret and he were close together. They were in many ways alike and understood each other. Her words when the telegram of death came were characteristic of both: 'Well, poor boy, he can't disappoint himself now.'

His wife Loveday Elizabeth Abbott remarried in 1947, becoming the second wife of Jean Baptiste de Manio, better known as the famous broadcaster, Jack de Manio. She died in 1999.

Batting and fielding averages

	Mat	Inns	NO	Runs	HS	Ave	100	50	Ct	St
First-class	23	33	3	393	68	13.10	0	1	32	6

Bowling averages

	Mat	Balls	Runs	Wkts	BBI	BBM	Ave	Econ	SR	4w	5w	10
First-class	23	-	-	-	-	-	-	-	-	-	-	-

Captain Robert Francis Hugh Philpot-Brookes
Europeans (India)
Two first-class appearances
2nd Battalion Northamptonshire Regiment
Died 28/29 May 1940, aged 27
Right-hand bat

'The Perfect Officer'

Robert Philpot-Brookes was born on 11 August 1912 in Fulham. He was the son of William Robert and Lella Philpot-Brookes of Bexhill-on-Sea. He was educated at King's College School, Wimbledon, where his talent for cricket was quickly appreciated and he was quickly batting in their first XI.

While serving in India Philpot-Brookes played two first-class matches, representing the Europeans. Both matches were played in the Bombay Pentangular Tournament in November 1938 at the Brabourne Stadium, Bombay. He made his debut against the Parsees, commencing on 23 November 1938. The Europeans won the toss and decided to bat making 142, Philpot-Brookes knocking up 23 before being stumped by Khershedji Rustomji Meherhomji off the bowling of Rustonji Jamshedji Dorabji Jamshedji for 23. In reply the Parsees made 235, Jehangir Behramji Khot making 92. The Europeans did better in their second innings making 345, Philpot-Brookes making an impressive 143 before being bowled by S.M. Palsetia (who took seven wickets during the innings). In reply the Parsees made 233, Brookes catching Nairiman Framroze Canteenwala for 32 off the bowling of Albert Frederick Wensley. The Europeans took the match by 19 runs.

Bus House Cemetery, Ypres, Belgium.

Philpot-Brookes made his second and final first-class appearance against the Muslims commencing on 29 November 1938, once again at the Brabourne Stadium, in the semi-final of the Bombay Pentangular. The Muslims won the toss and decided to bat making 246, Syed Mushtaq Ali making 147. Charles Talbot Orton took seven wickets during the innings. In their first innings the Europeans made 172, Brookes making five before being caught by S. M. Kadri off the bowling of Amir Elahi. In their second innings the Muslims made 272, Syed Wazir Ali once again making over a century with 112. In reply the Europeans made 249, Philpot-Brookes making 14 before being caught by Syed Mushtaq Ali off the bowling of Amir Elahi. The Muslims won by 97.

Brookes also represented the Punjab and North-West Frontier Province against the Free Foresters in December 1935. His team won the match by five wickets. He then played by for the Punjab Governor's XI against the Punjab University, once again in December 1935, Punjab University winning by six wickets. Brookes made 55 in the second innings.

Deciding on a career in the Army he was commissioned into the 1st Battalion Northamptonshire Regiment, training and serving in the UK before being posted to India. Transferring to the 2nd Battalion, which formed part of the 17th Infantry Brigade, he travelled to France with the BEF and was killed during a rearguard action a few miles outside Dunkirk holding the Germans back from the beaches and allowing the BEF to escape back to England. For his brave actions on this day, he was mentioned in despatches.

Captain Philpot-Brookes is buried in Bus House Cemetery, grave reference C.3.

Batting and fielding averages

	Mat	Inns	NO	Runs	HS	Ave	100	50	Ct	St
First-class	2	4	0	185	143	46.25	1	0	2	0

Bowling averages

	Mat	Balls	Runs	Wkts	BBI	BBM	Ave	Econ	SR	4w	5w	10
First-class	2	-	-	-	-	-	-	-	-	-	-	-

Lieutenant Peter Thorp Eckersley MP
Lancashire
292 first-class appearances
Royal Naval Volunteer Reserve
Died 13 August 1940, aged 36
Right-handed bat

'The Flying Cricketer'

Peter Eckersley (commonly known as PT) was born on 2 July 1904 at Lowton near Leigh, son of William Eckersley CBE, a master cotton spinner (his grandfather was Charles Eckersley, head of Caleb Wright & Co, a large cotton company), and Eva Mary (née Thorp) of Tyldesley. He was educated at Rugby where he played for the first XI against Brasenose Oxford, Uppingham and Marlborough. He played his club cricket for Leigh Cricket Club, before joining Lancashire in 1923 at the tender age of 19, playing for them until 1935. He was made captain at 24 and remained in that position for the last seven years of his career. Under his direction Lancashire took the county champions twice with some of their greatest players such as Paynter, Duckworth, Hopwood, McDonald and the Tyldesleys performing at their peak.

Going up to Trinity Cambridge he made 292 first-class appearances. His debut wasn't for his university but for Lancashire against Cambridge. The match took place on 9 May 1923 at F.P. Fenner's. Lancashire won the toss and elected to field. Cambridge made 171 runs. In reply Lancashire made 234, Eckersley being caught by Claude Thesiger Ashton off the bowling of Philip Alan Wright for zero (Wright took six wickets during the innings). In their second innings Cambridge made 281, the New Zealand test player Thomas Coleman Lowry making 161. In their second innings Lancashire made 129, Eckersley failed to bat. The match was drawn.

Between October 1926 and February 1927 Eckersley was chosen to represent the MCC during their tour of India and Ceylon making twenty-six appearances during the tour. Returning to county cricket in April 1927 he went on to play against most county sides. In all he played in 226 county championship matches. He also played for the Gentlemen against The Players, L.H. Tennyson's XI against Jamaica, and for Lancashire against South Africa, New Zealand, India and West Indies. In 1930 he travelled with Sir J. Cahn's XI during their tour of South America.

Eckersley made his final first-class appearance for an England XI against the Australians on 31 August 1938 at Stanley Park, Blackpool, during Australia's tour of England between April and September 1938. Australia won the toss and decided to field. England made 132, Eckersley making two before being lbw off the bowling of William Joseph O'Reilly (*Wisden* cricketer of the year 1935), Francis Anthony (Frank) Ward taking six wickets during the innings. In their first Innings Australia made 174. In their second innings England made 99. This left Australia only 58 runs to win, which they did, taking the match by ten wickets.

During his first-class career Eckersley made 5,629 runs, his highest score being 102 against Gloucestershire at Bristol in June 1927. He made twenty-five fifties, took 141 catches, and

The Coming Storm

Memorial window, Chowbent Unitarian Chapel in Atherton.

" Pro Patria "
Lᵗ (A) Peter Thorp Eckersley R.N.V.R., J.P., M.P.
A trustee of Chowbent Chapel, born 2ⁿᵈ July 1904.
killed flying on active service 13ᵗʰ August 1940.
Devoted remembrance from his Wife,
Mother and Sister.

bowled 383 balls taking seven wickets for 348 runs. He also made 34 appearances for the Minor Counties, playing for Lancashire's second XI.

Eckersley worked for a while as a director for G.W. Smith & Co, coach builders, in Stockport. In June 1928 he was adopted as the prospective candidate for Newton le Willows, however gave up these early attempts to enter politics to captain Lancashire. Resuming his political career he was elected MP for the Exchange Division of Manchester and in February 1940 was appointed private secretary to the Board of Trade. He also found time to meet and marry Audrey E. J. Eckersley, of Ashley, Cheshire. They had two sons.

Eckersley had always been a keen flyer and was chairman of the Lancashire Aero Club, which he joined together with his wife. Often flying his own plane to various fixtures he became known as the 'Flying Cricketer'. On the outbreak of the Second World War he took a commission into the Fleet Air Arm and commenced training. While flying with 758 Squadron, then stationed at HMS *Raven* (now Southampton Airport), Eckersley together with Airman Sidney John Snow, while flying in a Percival Proctor training plane (P6113), was involved in an accident, crashing near Eastleigh, Hampshire, both men being killed. He was the fourth MP to be killed during the war.

He was later buried in Tyldesley Cemetery, section G, grave 340. There is a stained glass window dedicated to his memory in the Chowbent Unitarian Chapel in Atherton.

Batting and fielding averages

	Mat	Inns	NO	Runs	HS	Ave	100	Ct	St
First-class	292	339	51	5629	102*	19.54	1	141	0

Bowling averages

	Mat	Runs	Wkts	BBI	Ave	5w	10
First-class	292	348	7	2/21	49.71	0	0

2nd Lieutenant Harold Gordon Jameson
Cambridge University
Two first-class appearances
Royal Marines
Died 26 August 1940, aged 22
Right-handed bat/right arm fast medium

I will give him the morning star

Harold Jameson was born on 25 January 1918 in Dundrum, County Dublin, the son of William L. and G. Marjorie Jameson. He was educated at the Monkton Combe School before going up to Cambridge.

Jameson made two first-class appearances, both for Cambridge University and both in May 1938. He made his debut on 11 May 1938 at F.P. Fenner's against Australia. Cambridge won the toss and decided to bat making 120. Jameson made zero before being clean bowled by Mervyn George Waite. Waite took five wickets for 23 off 16 overs. William O'Reilly also took five wickets this time for 55 off 21 overs. In reply Australia made an impressive 708

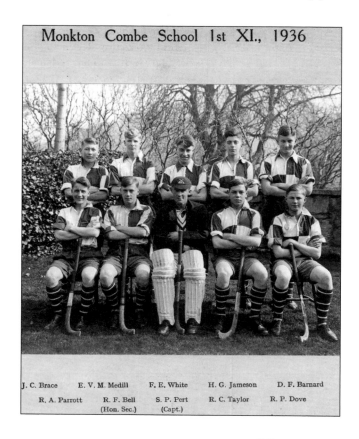

Monkton Combe School 1st XI., 1936

J. C. Brace E. V. M. Medill F. E. White H. G. Jameson D. F. Barnard
R. A. Parrott R. F. Bell (Hon. Sec.) S. P. Pert (Capt.) R. C. Taylor R. P. Dove

THE NEWS FROM HOME

Yet another part of our far-flung line that the "Bath Weekly Chronicle and Herald" reaches is an outpost "somewhere in India" where 2nd. Lieut. J. L. Jameson, R.A., is stationed. Every week his father, the Rev. W. L. Jameson, headmaster of Monkton Combe Junior School, posts it to his son, and here he is reading it. The paper is afterwards passed on to many other readers who are eager to have any news from home. An old Monktonian, Lieut. Jameson has been in the Army for 18 months.

for five. John Henry Webb Fingleton made 111, Don Bradman made 137, Clayvel Lindsay (Jack) Badcock 186 and Arthur Lindsay Hassett 220 not out. Jameson bowled 29 overs taking no wickets for 127. In their second innings Cambridge made 163. Jameson made four before being bowled by Frank Ward. Ward took six wickets during the innings for 49. Australia won by an innings and 425 runs.

His second was against Essex on 25 May 1938 again at Fenner's. Cambridge won the toss and decided to bat making 218. Jameson made one before being bowled by Raymond Smith. The England Test cricketer Morris Stanley Nichols (*Wisden* cricketer of the year 1934) took five wickets for 40 off 26 overs. In reply Essex made 385. James bowled 17 overs taking two wickets for 68, Alan Braden Lavers caught by Paul Gibb for 32 and Thomas Henry Wade lbw for two. John Vernon Wild took five wickets for 96. In their second innings Cambridge made 236. Jameson made two not out. Nichols took five wickets for 37. In their second innings Essex made 73 for one. Jameson bowled four overs taking no wickets for nine. Essex won by nine wickets.

During the war Jameson was commissioned into the Royal Marines as a second lieutenant. He was killed on 26 August 1940 during an air raid on Fort Cumberland which was then being used as an overflow base for the Royal Marines. Seventy-eight bombs were dropped on the fort, only one of which caused loss of life; it hit a perimeter room killing eight marines including Jameson. The memorial to the men who lost their lives was erected on the spot where they died.

Jameson was buried in Haslar Royal Navy Cemetery, grave reference G.9.

Batting and fielding averages

	Mat	Inns	NO	Runs	HS	Ave	100	50	Ct	St
First-class	2	4	1	7	4	2.33	0	0	0	0

Bowling averages

	Mat	Balls	Runs	Wkts	BBI	Ave	Econ	SR	5w	10
First-class	2	300	204	2	2/68	102.00	4.08	150.0	0	0

Lieutenant Michael Desmond Ponsonby Magill
Oxford University, Free Foresters, Army
Oxford and Cambridge University
Six first-class appearances
1st Battalion Royal Berkshire Regiment
5 September 1940, aged 24
Right-hand bat/Right arm fast medium

As great a sportsman as he was an officer

Michael Magill was born on 28 September 1915 in Sevenoaks, Kent. He was educated at Eton where he played in the XI. Going up to Brasenose College Oxford he made six first-class appearances, three for Oxford University, two for a combined Oxford and Cambridge side, and later one for the Army against Cambridge University.

He made his debut for Oxford University against the Minor Counties on 11 May 1938 at the University Parks. Oxford won the toss and decided to bat making 217. Magill made zero before being caught by the England test cricketer William Howard Vincent 'Hopper' Levett off the bowling of Fred Berry. Berry took six wickets for 81. In reply the Minor Counties made 175. Magill bowled 23 overs taking five wickets for 57: the Minor Counties opener Basil William Roughton-Roughton lbw for four, Dennis Wilfred Stokes bowled for one, Eric Harry Edrich caught Hector Gordon Jelf for 25, William Lovell-Hewitt clean bowled, and Thomas Stanislaus Alfred Charles Joseph Maxwell bowled for six. In their second innings Oxford made 319 for four declared. Magill failed to bat. Edward Desmond Russell Eagar made 147. In reply Minor Counties made 131. Magill bowled 12 overs taking two wickets for 21, Stokes bowled for seven and Lovell-Hewitt bowled for two. Oxford University won by 230 runs.

His next appearance for Oxford was against Leicestershire on 18 May 1938 at the University Parks. He made 80 and 40 not out, and bowled 19 overs taking no wickets for 40. The match was drawn.

He was selected to tour Jamaica with a mixed Oxford and Cambridge team making his first appearance for them on 10 August 1938 at Sabina Park, Kingston. Magill made 15 and one. He also bowled five overs taking no wickets. The match was drawn. He played again on 20 August 1938 at Sabina Park making three and ten, bowling six overs, taking no wickets, but hung onto a catch from Frank Smith off the bowling of David Clement Wilson for eight. Jamaica won by an innings and 74 runs.

 Magill made his final first-class appearance for the Army against Cambridge University on 7 June 1939 at F.P. Fenner's. Cambridge won the toss and decided to bat making 411 for eight declared. Magill bowled 16 overs taking no wickets for 57. In reply the Army made 537. Magill made 11 before being lbw off the bowling of Bertram Carris. George Grimston made 104 and Charles Packe 145. In their second innings Cambridge made 149. The match was drawn.

He made five appearances for the Army, against the West Indies, Territorial Army, Cambridge University, Royal Navy and the Royal Air Force, and one appearance in the Minor Counties Championship for Berkshire against Dorset on 2 August 1939.

During the war he was commissioned into the 1st Battalion The Royal Berkshire Regiment becoming a lieutenant. He was killed during a training accident in Filey, Yorkshire, when he stood on a mine. He is commemorated at Darlington crematorium Yorkshire, panel 3.

Batting and fielding averages

	Mat	Inns	NO	Runs	HS	Ave	100	Ct	St
First-class	6	9	2	160	80	22.85	0	3	0

Bowling averages

	Mat	Runs	Wkts	BBI	Ave	5w	10
First-class	6	291	7	5/57	41.57	1	0

Sergeant Clement Patrick Stephen Wareham
Wellington
Two first-class appearances
5th Field Regiment New Zealand Artillery
Died 30 September 1940, aged 29

'Taken by a Tragic Accident'

Clement Wareham was born on 23 March 1911 (although some records give a different date) in Wellington, New Zealand. He was the son of Joseph and Emily Wareham, also of Wellington. He was educated at Wellington College, New Zealand, playing in their first XI. He was also a fine golfer, being a member of the Karori Golf Club. He made two first-class appearances, both in December 1934 in the Plunket Shield.

He made his debut appearance for Wellington against Otago, commencing on 24 December at the Basin Reserve, Wellington. Otago won the toss and elected to bat. Otago made 255, Cedric James Elmes making 94 and the Wellington bowler Edward Denis Blundell taking six wickets for 84 during the innings. In reply Wellington made 242, Wareham making six before being caught by James Bernard Clark off the bowling of Frederick Theodore Badcock, John Rider Lamason making 103. Badcock took six wickets for 98 runs. In their second innings Otago made 133, this time Blundell taking five wickets for 48. Welling made 148 in their second innings, taking the match by eight wickets. Wareham failed to bat.

He made his second appearance for Wellington against Canterbury on 31 December, this time at Lancaster Park, Christchurch. Canterbury won the toss and decided to bat making an impressive 323. Francis William James Bellamy making 113 and the New Zealand test cricketer, Walter Arnold Hadlee, 103. In reply Wellington made 155, Wareham being bowled by Stephen Garland Lester for one. Following on, Wellington made 241, Wareham being bowled by Stanley Andrews for a duck. This only left Canterbury 74 runs to take the match, which they did without losing a wicket. Canterbury won by ten wickets.

During the war Wareham enlisted into the 5th Field Regiment, New Zealand Artillery, later being promoted to sergeant. Sailing to England he played in two further matches (neither first-class) both for the New Zealand Expeditionary Force. The first was a one-day match against Australian Imperial Forces, played on 24 August 1940 at the Officers Club Services Ground, Aldershot. Wareham made 50 and New Zealand won by 66 runs.

His next match was against Aldershot Command, played on the 31 August 1940 on the same ground, again a one-day match. Aldershot won the toss and elected to bat making 248, the England test player Bryan Valentine making 91. In reply New Zealand made 162, Wareham making another 50. The match was drawn.

Posted to Moat Park, Maidstone, with his battery, Wareham was knocked down and killed by a lorry in a tragic accident. He is buried in Lenham Cemetery, section B, grave 1039.

Batting and fielding averages

	Mat	Inns	NO	Runs	HS	Ave	100	50	Ct	St
First-class	2	3	0	7	6	2.33	0	0	0	0

Bowling averages

	Mat	Balls	Runs	Wkts	BBI	BBM	Ave	Econ	SR	4w	5w	10
First-class	2	-	-	-	-	-	-	-	-	-	-	-

Air Vice Marshal Charles Hubert Boulby Blount CB OBE MC
Ten first-class appearances
Royal Air Force
Died 23 October 1940, aged 46
Right-hand bat/Right arm slow

Great Uncle of James Blunt, the popular singer

Charles Blount was born on 26 October 1893 at Kamptee (now Kamthi), Maharashtra, India. He was the son of Major Charles Hubert Blount who served with the 20th Battery, Royal Field Artillery, and died of dysentery at Wymberg, Cape Town, during the Second Boer War, and Mary Elizabeth Bell. He was educated at Harrow where he was soon in the First XI. In 1910 he played as wicketkeeper and in 1912 was made captain, making 137 runs in Harrow's second innings.

Blount made ten first-class appearances for the Combined Services and RAF between August 1920 and July 1930. He made his debut against the Gentlemen-of-England on 21 August 1920 at Lord's. The Gentlemen-of-England won the toss and decided to bat making 225. In reply the Combined Services made 150, Blount making 11 before being caught by Mervyn Llewellyn Hill off the bowling of Reginald Sawdon Swalwell, George Aubrey Faulkner taking six wickets during the innings. In their second innings the Gentlemen of England made 103. Combined Services made 181 in their second innings, Blount making ten before being bowled by Faulkner, who took a further four wickets during the innings. The Combined Services took the match by five wickets. He went on to represent the Combined Services against Australia, Essex and South Africa.

Blount made his debut for the RAF against the Royal Navy on 10 August 1927 at the Oval. The Royal Navy won the toss and decided to bat making 347, Gerald Seymour Tuck making 96. Blount bowled nine overs, taking one wicket for 37. Reginald Alexander Dallas Brooks stumped Gerald Edward Livock for 28. He also caught the Royal Navy opener Robert John Shaw off the bowling of Reginald Edgar Gilbert Fulljames for 41. In reply the RAF made 321, Blount making 35 before being caught by Robert Hearfield Stephenson off the bowling of Brooks. Brooks took eight wickets during the innings. In their second innings the Royal Navy made a poor 81, Blount bowling 12 overs for 16 and taking three wickets, Reginald Brooks lbw for 26, Thomas Edgar Halsey (later Sir Thomas Halsey DSO) lbw for 19 and Arthur Stanley Cantrell caught Cyril Bertram Cooke for zero. In their second innings the RAF made108, Blount making 37 before being bowled by Halsey. The RAF won by six wickets. He represented the RAF against the Army and Navy on several more occasions.

He made his final first-class appearance for the RAF against the Army on 5 July 1930 at the Oval. The RAF won the toss and decided to bat making 118. Blount made four before being caught by William Alexander Camac Wilkinson off the bowling of John Erskine Scott

Walford, who took six wickets during the innings. In reply the Army made 302, Leoline Williams making 107. Blount bowled 12 overs taking one wicket for 57. Frederick George Arnold caught Victor Croome for 15. He also caught Edward Stephen Bruce Williams off the bowling of Reginald Fulljames for 20. In their second innings the RAF made an impressive 336, Blount making his best first-class score of 110 before being bowled by Ernest Desmond Dynes.

During his first-class career Blount made 575 runs, his highest score being 110, four fifties and took nine catches. He also bowled 542 balls and took 12 wickets for 303 runs, his best figures being three for 16. As well as his first-class career he made six minor county appearances for Sussex, against Bedfordshire, Cambridgeshire and Hertfordshire. He also represented I Zingari and the Free Foresters.

On leaving Harrow Blount decided on a career in the Army and went up to the Royal Military College Sandhurst before being commissioned into the Queen's (Royal West Surrey) Regiment in September 1913. In October 1914 he was promoted to lieutenant and in March 1916, captain. Learning to fly in a Maurice Farman biplane he transferred to the Royal Flying Corps, being awarded the Military Cross on 14 November 1916 for bravery. He took command of a flight of number 34 Squadron flying BE2s, later commanding the squadron in June 1917. He was promoted to major and joined the newly formed RAF on 1 April 1918. He was also awarded the Silver Medal of Military Valor, an Italian decoration. In August 1919 he became a squadron leader, taking command of 4 Squadron at Farnborough flying Bristol F2 Fighters. In June 1924 he was appointed OBE. In 1925 he was promoted to wing commander, taking command of 7 Squadron at Bircham Newton flying Vickers Vimys and Virginias. He later commanded 70 Squadron and was promoted to group captain in 1932, serving in Iraq. He became an air commodore in 1937 and Air Vice Marshal in 1939. In September 1939 Blount became AOC of the air component of the BEF, returning to England in May 1940.

Blount was killed in an air accident five months later in October 1940, when a scheduled flight from Hendon Aerodrome to Belfast crashed near the airfield shortly after take-off killing all on board. Blount was later buried in the south-west corner of the churchyard at St Mary the Virgin's Church, Essendon. He is commemorated on the Felixstowe War Memorial, where the death of his younger brother, John Hillier Blount, who was also killed in an air accident in 1918, is commemorated. His name is also recorded on the roll of honour at Lord's.

Blount's half-brother, Captain Greville Blount, Royal Horse Artillery, was killed in 1914. He was the great-grandfather of the singer James Blunt.

Batting and fielding averages

	Mat	Inns	NO	Runs	HS	Ave	100	50	Ct	St
First-class	10	17	0	575	110	33.82	1	4	9	0

Bowling averages

	Mat	Balls	Runs	Wkts	BBI	Ave	Econ	SR	5w	10
First-class	10	542	303	12	3/16	25.25	3.35	45.1	0	0

Second Lieutenant Robert Prynne Nelson
Middlesex–Cambridge University–Northamptonshire–MCC
Seventy-seven first-class appearances
Royal Marines (Siege Regiment)
Died 29 October 1940, aged 28
Left-hand bat/Slow left arm orthodox

'A lover of cricket, he maintained in his life the spirit of the game'

Robert Nelson was born on 7 August 1912 in Fulham. He was the son of Robert and Mary Susanna Nelson of Harpenden, Hertfordshire. He was educated at St George's School, Harpenden, where he later became a master. While there he played for the school XI from the age of 12, knocking up a good few runs and never missing a season. From school he went up to Gonville and Caius College Cambridge.

He made seventy-seven first-class appearances, making his debut for Middlesex against Hampshire in the county championship on 11 May 1932 at Lord's. Hampshire won the toss and decided to bat making 70. In reply Middlesex did little better, making 76, Nelson making one before being bowled by the English test cricketer Alexander Stuart Kennedy. In their second innings Hampshire made 71, Middlesex made 18, Nelson failing to bat, and the match was drawn. Nelson went on to represent Middlesex against Cambridge University, Northamptonshire, Worcestershire, the visiting Indians, Leicestershire and Surrey.

Going up to Cambridge he was soon playing for the University making his debut against Yorkshire at F.P. Fenner's Ground on 2 May 1934. Cambridge University won the toss and elected to bat making 248, Nelson making four before being caught by Arthur Wood off the bowling of another English test cricketer Morris Leyland. In reply Yorkshire made 495, the England test cricketer Herbert Sutcliffe making 152 and the England test cricketer Wilfred Barber 103. Nelson bowled 17 overs for 60 and failed to take a wicket. In their second innings Cambridge made 260, Nelson making 21 before being caught by Arthur Brian Sellers off the bowling of the England test cricketer Leonard Hutton (later Sir) and Roger de Winton Kelsall Winlaw making 104. Only needing 14 to win, Yorkshire knocked them off quickly without loss, winning the match by ten wickets.

Nelson went on to play for Cambridge against Somerset, Free Foresters, Warwickshire, Nottinghamshire, the Army, the Indians, Essex, Sussex, Surrey, MCC and Oxford University.

Going on to play for Northamptonshire he made his debut against New Zealand on 2 June 1937 at the County Ground, Northampton. New Zealand won the toss and decided to bat making 334. Nelson bowled four overs for 27 and failed to take a wicket. In their first innings Northamptonshire made 185, Nelson, who opened for them, making three before being caught by William Nicol Carson off the bowling of John Angus (Jack) Dunning, who took six wickets during the innings. In their second innings New Zealand made 280 before declaring. Northampton chose to bat making 308, Nelson making 69 before being run out and the English test cricketer Dennis Brookes making 102 not out. The match was eventually drawn.

Nelson went on to represent Northamptonshire against, Nottinghamshire, Cambridge, Australia, Lancashire, Somerset, Leicestershire, Derbyshire, Worcestershire, Warwickshire, Glamorgan, Yorkshire, Hampshire, Sussex, Essex and the West Indies.

He played his final first-class match for Northamptonshire against Somerset at the County Ground, Taunton, in the county championship on 30 August 1939, by which time Nelson had been made captain (1938-39). Northamptonshire won the toss and elected to bat making 138. Nelson made one before being caught by Walter Thomas Luckes off the bowling of William Harry Russell Andrews. In reply Somerset made 380, Nelson bowling five overs for 14 for no wicket. In their second innings Northamptonshire made 150, Nelson making the top score of 42 before being caught by Thomas Ronald Garnett off the bowling of Herbert Francis Thomas Buse. Somerset won by an innings and 92 runs.

Nelson also made three first-class appearances for the MCC against Yorkshire: 30 April 1938, draw, Surrey; 4 May 1938, MCC, victory by five runs; and Cambridge University, 29 June 1938, match drawn. Nelson also made seven minor counties championship appearances all for Hertfordshire. He also played for The Rest, Public Schools, Etceteras, Berkhamsted, A.F. Skinner's, the British Empire XI and the Club Cricket Conference.

During his first-class career Nelson made 3,394 runs including two centuries, his highest score being 123 against Sussex. His other century was made against Essex when he knocked up 110. He made 24 half centuries and took 34 catches. He also bowled 5,367 balls taking 62 wickets for 2,208 runs, his best figures being three for seven.

During the war Nelson took a commission with the Royal Marines as a second lieutenant. He was killed on 29 October 1940 when Italian bombers escorted by German fighters bombed the local area at around 2040 hours. Twenty-two buildings were seriously damaged, twenty-seven buildings slightly damaged, there was one casualty, Lieutenant Nelson, and five other ranks were wounded. A local resident later made a note in his diary: 'The bombs fell in Cornwall Road, Cemetery Road, and near the railway bridge in Telegraph Road. My uncle Leslie can remember seeing an Italian aircraft flying by after dropping a bomb in front of the Officers' Mess at the RM depot, and on the railway line south of Cornwall Road. There was some damage to the railway bridge, and houses in Telegraph Road were badly damaged. The officer killed at the RM depot was Temporary 2nd Lieutenant R.P. Nelson.'

He is buried in Deal Cemetery, plot C, block 8, grave 4750. On his gravestone his family had engraved, 'a lover of cricket, he maintained in his life the spirit of the game.'

Batting and fielding averages

	Mat	Inns	NO	Runs	HS	Ave	100	50	Ct	St
First-class	77	136	12	3394	123*	27.37	2	24	35	0

Bowling averages

	Mat	Balls	Runs	Wkts	BBI	Ave	Econ	SR	5w	10
First-class	77	5367	2208	62	3/7	35.61	2.46	86.5	0	0

Lieutenant Geoffrey Bevington Legge
England, Kent, Oxford University
Five tests, 147 first-class appearances
Royal Naval Air Service
Died 21 November 1940, aged 37
Right-hand bat/Leg break

'The first test cricketer to be killed in the war'

Geoffrey Legge was born on 26 January 1903 in Bromley, Kent. He was the eldest son of Henry B. Legge, a 'paper agent', and his wife Edith of Sundridge Avenue, Bromley. Legge was educated at Malvern where he was captain of the cricket XI in 1922. In *Wisden*'s annual review of public school cricket Legge's batting was praised saying he had 'beautiful off-side strokes' and that he was 'an excellent captain who knew how to get the best out of his bowlers, and had a sound control of his eleven in the field.'

On leaving school he went up to Brasenose Oxford. He was to go on to play in five tests and made 147 first-class appearances.

Legge made his debut in first-class cricket for Kent against Northamptonshire on 14 May 1924 at the Bat and Ball Ground, Gravesend. Kent won the toss and elected to bat making 206, Legge making three before being bowled by the England test cricketer Edward Winchester Clark. In reply Northampton made 193. In their second innings Kent made a very poor 67, Legge being bowled by Albert Edward Thomas for two. In their second innings Northamptonshire only managed 53, with the two English test cricketers Alfred Freeman and Frank Edward Woolley both taking five wickets during the innings. Kent won by 27 runs.

Going up to Oxford, Legge wasn't chosen to represent the university at once. Playing in trial matches in both 1923 and 1924, he did not perform well and wasn't selected. Trialling again in 1925, he once again failed to impress and wasn't selected for the first three first-class matches against Middlesex, Lancashire and Leicestershire. However he did finally make his debut for Oxford against Worcestershire at the University Parks, Oxford on 20 May 1925. Oxford University won the toss and decided to bat. It was a turning point for Legge's career. Oxford made 364, Legge making 120 (in two hours) before being caught by Maurice Frederick Stewart Jewell off the bowling of the England test cricketer Charles Frederick Root who took five wickets during the innings. In reply Worcestershire made 379, Herbert Oxley Hopkins making 122, Legge catching Charles Root off the bowling of John Lindsay Guise for two. In their second innings Oxford made 272, Legge making 40 before being bowled by William Herbert Taylor. Claude Hilary Taylor, the Oxford opener, making 105 not out, batting throughout the innings. Charles Root took six wickets during the innings. In their second innings Worcestershire made 194 and the match was drawn. The selection was justified as Legge topped the Oxford batting averages for the season. Legge's place in the Oxford team was now secure. Top of the averages again in 1926, despite matches being abandoned due to the general strike, Legge, who had a taste for fast cars and was a member of the Oxford motor racing team, was involved in a car crash in which he injured his hand, *Wisden* announcing that it was 'A most unfortunate affair'.

He went on to play against Harlequins, Army, Free Foresters, Essex, Gloucestershire, MCC, Cambridge University, H.D.G. Leveson-Gower's XI, Australia and Ireland.

Leaving Oxford, he resumed his career with Kent (he had played one match for them in 1925) turning out against Gloucestershire on 14 July 1926 at Fry's Ground, Bristol. Gloucestershire won the toss and decided to bat making 241, the England test cricketer Harry Smith making 123. The Kent bowler George Christopher Collins took five wickets during the innings. In reply Kent made 185, Legge making nine before being bowled by Percy Thomas Mills. The Gloucestershire and England bowler Charles Warrington Leonard Parker took seven wickets during the innings. In their second innings Gloucestershire made 210, Legge catching Bernard Sydney Bloodworth off the bowling of the England test cricketer Harold Thomas William Hardinge for two. Alfred Freeman took six wickets during the innings. In their second innings Kent made 267, Legge making eight before being caught by John George William Thomas Bessant off the bowling of Charles Parker for eight. Harold Hardinge made 116 and William Leggatt 92. Kent took the honours by four wickets. Legge made two more appearances for Kent during the 1926 season, both against Surrey, both matches were drawn.

During the following season,1927, Legge made more than 900 runs at an average of more than 30 runs per innings, scoring two centuries. It is also interesting to note that despite being a strong batsman, he batted as low as number seven. During the winter of the 1927-28 season Legge was selected by the MCC to tour South Africa. During the tour Legge equalled his best first-class score, making 120 against the Orange Free State. This together with several other good scores led to his selection for the first test. However it didn't go well and he failed to score in his only innings, although England went on to win by ten wickets. As a result Legge lost his place in the next test and did not regain it.

During the 1928 season Legge took over the captaincy of Kent, taking them to second place in the county championship behind Lancashire (Tich Freeman taking more than 300 first-class wickets, a record for a single season that is likely never to be broken). Legge scored 891 runs during the season despite appearing regularly, down on previous seasons. During the 1929 season this rose again to 929 runs and for a while it looked like they were in with a chance of winning the county championship, something they had failed to achieve since 1913. However poor results in later matches left them eighth.

Legge married, on 19 September 1929, Rosemary Frost from Baston Manor, Hayes, Kent. Following his marriage he was selected for England's tour of New Zealand. He played in all four tests, making little impact in the first three. He made 36 in the first test at Lancaster Park on 10 January 1930, England winning by eight wickets; 39 and 9 in the second on 24 January 1930 at the Basin Reserve, Wellington, match drawn; 19 in the third on 14 February 1930 at Eden Park, Auckland, match drawn. However in the fourth, also played at Eden Park on 21 February 1930, Legge made 196, part of England's impressive total of 540. Despite this the match was still drawn. It was to be Legge's final test.

The 1930 season wasn't a good one for Legge. He failed to make a single 50 and ended it with an average of 14. At the end of the season he gave up the captaincy for 'business reasons'.

Legge made his final first-class match for Kent against New Zealand on 26 August 1931 at the St Lawrence Ground, Canterbury. New Zealand won the toss and decided to bat making 326, John Mills making 163. In reply Kent made 437, Legge making one before being run out. The England test cricketers Frank Woolley made 224 and Leslie Ames 115. In their second innings New Zealand made 159, leaving Kent 49 to win. Kent did this quickly, losing only one wicket and taking the match by nine wickets. Legge didn't bat in the second innings.

During an impressive career Legge played in five tests, scoring 299 runs, his highest score being 196 against New Zealand. In 147 first-class appearances he scored 4,955 runs including seven centuries and sixteen fifties, bowled 179 balls taking eight wickets for 181 runs, and made 123 catches. Legge also made seven minor county appearances, for Kent Seconds against Wiltshire, Surrey and Norfolk, and played for The Rest, West Kent, the MCC and GB Legge's XI.

A keen flyer, Legge purchased his own plane flying to many business engagements in the UK and Europe. At the beginning of war Legge joined the Royal Navy's Fleet Air Arm, being promoted to lieutenant commander. He was killed in a flying accident on 21 November 1940 while flying a Proctor from Lee-on-Solent back to his base, HMS *Vulture*, the RNAS station at St Merryn, Cornwall when the weather closed in. He is buried in St Merryn Churchyard, grave one.

Batting and fielding averages

	Mat	Inns	NO	Runs	HS	Ave	100	50	6s	Ct	St
Tests	5	7	1	299	196	49.83	1	0	0	1	0
First-class	147	210	11	4955	196	24.89	7	16		122	0

Bowling averages

	Mat	Inns	Balls	Runs	Wkts	BBI	BBM	Ave	Econ	SR	4w	5w	10
Tests	5	1	30	34	0	-	-	-	6.80	-	0	0	0
First-class	147		179	181	8	3/23		22.62	6.06	22.3		0	0

Pilot Officer George Gibson Macaulay
England, Yorkshire
Eight tests, 468 first-class appearances
RAF Volunteer Reserve
Died 13 December 1940, aged 43
Right-hand bat

'The finest of cricketers'

George Macaulay was born on 7 December 1897 in Thirsk, Yorkshire. He was the son of Charles Harold a well-known local cricketer (as indeed were his uncles) and Ellen Macaulay. He was educated at Barnard Castle where he played in the school XI. On leaving school he became a bank clerk and worked in Wakefield. He played football and cricket for both Wakefield and Ossett and served with the Royal Field Artillery during the First World War. After being demobbed he continued to work as a bank clerk in London and later Herne Bay, Kent, playing club cricket in his spare time.

It was while playing in one of these local matches that Macaulay was spotted by Sir Stanley Christopherson, a well-known former Kent player. The word must have got out because the former Yorkshire cricketer Harry Hayley made a special effort to see him play and was impressed enough to recommend him for a trial with Yorkshire. As a result Macaulay played in two trial matches at the beginning of the 1920 season. In his first match Macaulay took six wickets for 52 in a one-day game and four wickets for 24 and 19 for two in a two-day game. It was good enough for Yorkshire who were at the time desperate to improve their bowling attack and needed good quality pacemen. Based on this they decided to give him a try. It wasn't a bad decision; Macaulay went on to play for England in eight tests and between 15 May 1920 and 19 June 1935 made a remarkable 468 first-class appearances, almost exclusively for Yorkshire.

Macaulay made his first-class debut for Yorkshire against Derbyshire in the county championship on 15 May 1920 at Bramall Lane, Sheffield. Derbyshire won the toss and decided to bat making 103. Macaulay bowled nine overs and took his first first-class wicket for 14. His wicket was the Derbyshire opener Leonard Oliver, caught Emmott Robinson for 25. In reply Yorkshire made 419; Macaulay made 15 not out. Roy Kilner knocked up 206. Yorkshire declared. In their second innings Derbyshire made 93, Macaulay bowled nine overs and failed to take a wicket for 32. Yorkshire took the match by an innings and 223 runs.

Continuing to play for Yorkshire he met with varied success. He had his first five-wicket success for 50 against Gloucestershire, followed by taking six wickets for 47 against Worcestershire. He continued to play for Yorkshire until mid-June when he was dropped after a poor match against Surrey. In his first ten first-class matches he took 24 wickets at an average of 24.35, managing a top score of 15 with his bat. *Wisden* commented that 'he had neither the pace nor the stamina required' and accused him of trying to bowl at speeds beyond his capability. Two Yorkshire legends, George Herbert Hirst (1871-1954) and Wilfred Rhodes (1877-1973), persuaded him to reduce his pace and concentrate on bowling a good length while trying to spin the ball. Advice from men like Hirst and Rhodes was not to be ignored and he set himself to practising through the winter of 1920–21 in readiness for the following season.

Bowling a mixture of medium pace and his new style of off-spin, his efforts paid off. During the 1921 season Macaulay made 27 appearances for Yorkshire. In his fourth match he took six wickets for ten runs as Warwickshire were bowled out for 72 in the first innings and four further wickets for 55 runs during Warwickshire second innings. This was the first time Macaulay had taken ten wickets in a match. It was followed by taking six runs while bowling Derbyshire out for 23 and ten wickets against Surrey. During the season Macaulay took 101 first-class wickets at an average of 17.33, placing him third in the Yorkshire bowling averages. He also knocked up 457 runs including his first first-class century, making 125 not out against Nottinghamshire. His place in the Yorkshire team was now secure. In 1922 he helped Yorkshire win the first of four county championships in a row.

His continual fine performances got him selected for the MCC winter tour of South Africa. Macaulay played in eight first-class matches while touring South Africa in 1922-23, taking 29 wickets, his best figures being six for 18 against Pretoria, and a further eight wickets against Transvaal. After England lost the first test due to, as *Wisden* put it, 'a weakness in bowling', Macaulay was called up to replace Greville Stevens (1901-70) who played for Middlesex and Oxford.

Macaulay made his test match debut in the second test against South Africa on 1 January 1923 at Newlands, Cape Town. South Africa won the toss and decided to bat making 133. Macaulay bowled thirteen overs in the first innings, taking two wickets for 19 runs. George Alfred Lawrence Hearne caught Percy George Herbert Fender for zero. Macaulay took his wicket with his first test ball. He was only the fourth player to take a wicket with his maiden delivery in test cricket: Eiulf Peter 'Buster' Nupen, who Macaulay caught and bowled for two. In reply England made 183, Macaulay making 19 before being bowled by James Manuel Blanckenberg. In their second innings South Africa made 242, Macaulay bowling 37 overs for 64 runs taking five wickets: the South African opener Robert Hector Catterall for 78; Herbert Wilfred Taylor, caught Vallance William Crisp Jupp for 68; William Victor Stone Ling, caught Percy Fender for two; William Henry Brann, lbw for four; and Cyril Matthew Francois caught and bowled. In their second innings England managed 173, Macaulay making one not out. England took the match by one wicket. *Wisden* later commented that 'Macaulay bowled very finely in this match. He hit the winning run, batting at number eleven, to seal a one-wicket win for England.' In the third test Macaulay only took one wicket and the match was drawn. In the fourth test Macaulay took two wickets, one per innings, and the match was once again drawn. In the fifth and final test Macaulay took five wickets, England winning by 109. Despite England winning the series two to one, the *Wisden* correspondent for the tour was not impressed by the English performances, noting that no really effective bowlers had emerged.

Macaulay's form throughout the 1923 season was excellent. He took 166 wickets at an average of 13.84, coming third in both the Yorkshire and national bowling averages. His form was probably best demonstrated in the match against Glamorgan, played on 5 May 1923 at Cardiff Arms Park when he took seven wickets for 13 during Glamorgan's first innings (Glamorgan were bowled out for 63). Yorkshire won the match by nine wickets. During the same season he took a hat-trick against Warwickshire, on 23 May 1923 at Edgbaston, dismissing George William Stephens (12), John Abbotts Smart (0) and Frederick Reginald Santall (0) while at the same time taking five wickets for 42 runs. Macaulay took four hat-tricks during his career. The *Wisden* editor Sydney Pardon was not convinced. He wrote, 'I think Macaulay is the most likely bowler who has not yet played in test matches at home, but whether he has the right temperament for such nerve-taxing cricket is a question.' He did despite this choose Macaulay as one of his 'Cricketers of the Year' for 1924, praising his stamina, spin and ability to bowl on all kinds of pitches, finishing however with, 'His fault is that he is apt to become depressed and upset when things go wrong. His friends wish that he had a little more of Roy Kilner's cheerful philosophy.' In 1924, Macaulay further increased his total of wickets to 190 and lowered his bowling average to 13.23, placing him first in the national averages.

He was selected to play in the third test against South Africa on 12 July 1924 at Headingley. Although England did well, taking the match by nine wickets, Macaulay's performance was disappointing. He failed to score in his one innings and only took two wickets. He had to wait two years before being selected again, this time against Australia, played at Headingley on 10 July 1926. Once again he failed to live up to expectations, taking only three wickets, however he did much better with the bat. He made 76 runs in the first innings before being caught and bowled by Clarence Victor Grimmett. It was his only innings and the match was drawn.

It was seven years before he was called up again, this time taking part in two tests against the West Indies. In the first, played at Lord's on 24 June 1933, Macaulay made nine in his only innings and took five wickets, England winning by 27 runs. In the second, played at Old Trafford on 22 July 1933, Macaulay failed to take a wicket in the first innings and due to injury failed to bowl during the West Indies second innings (he also failed to bat due to injury). It was to be Macaulay's last test match.

Macaulay continued to play first-class cricket for Yorkshire until June 1935. He played his final first-class match on 19 June 1935 for Yorkshire against Leicestershire at Headingley in the county championship. Leicestershire won the toss and decided to bat making 153. Macaulay bowled 21 overs taking one wicket for 39, Haydon Arthur Smith for a duck. In reply Yorkshire made a not very impressive 93, Macaulay being bowled for zero by Haydon Smith (sweet revenge). In their second innings Leicestershire were bowled out for 55, Hedley Verity taking eight wickets for 27 runs. Macaulay failed to bowl. In their second innings Yorkshire made 75 runs before the weather closed in and the match was drawn. It was the end of a magnificent first-class career for one of Yorkshire's cricketing legends (he did however continue to play in the Lancashire League mainly for Todmorden until shortly before the war).

During his career George Macaulay played in eight tests making 112 runs with a top score of 76. He bowled 1,701 balls taking 24 wickets for 662 runs, his best figures being 5/64. He also took five catches. During his first-class career he made 468 appearances making 6,055 runs including three centuries and twenty-one fifties, his highest score being 125 against Nottinghamshire. He also bowled 89,997 balls taking 1,837 wickets for 32,441 runs, his best figures being 8/21. He also took 373 catches.

In 1940 Macaulay was commissioned as a pilot officer into the RAF Volunteer Reserve. He was posted to Church Fenton. During this time he also met and married Edith K. Macaulay. He was later transferred to the Shetland Islands where he was stationed at Sullom Voe. The wet cold weather didn't suit him and he became ill. What seemed to be a bad cold soon turned to pneumonia and he died on 13 December 1940. He was buried a few days later in Lerwick New Cemetery, terrace 9 grave 35.

Batting and fielding averages

	Mat	Inns	NO	Runs	HS	Ave	100	50	6s	Ct	St
Tests	8	10	4	112	76	18.66	0	1	0	5	0
First-class	468	460	125	6055	125*	18.07	3	21		373	0

Bowling averages

	Mat	Inns	Balls	Runs	Wkts	BBI	BBM	Ave	Econ	SR	4w	5w	10
Tests	8	13	1701	662	24	5/64	7/83	27.58	2.33	70.8	1	1	0
First-class	468		89877	32441	1837	8/21		17.65	2.16	48.9		126	31

P/JX 220456 Ordinary Coder Montague Valentine Bennett
Minor Counties
One first-class appearance
Royal Navy (HMS *Acheron*)
Died 17 December 1940, aged 28
Fast Medium

'Gone too soon'

Montague Bennett was born on 19 February 1912 at Glentham, Lincolnshire. He was the son of Reuben and Gertrude Ellen (née Burrell). Bennett, playing mainly for Lincolnshire in the minor counties championship, made sixty-five appearances for them between 7 June 1932 and 15 August 1939, although he made his debut for Lincoln against Warwickshire's second XI on 7 June 1932 at London Road, Grantham. Lincoln won the toss and elected to bat making 227 runs, Bennett making 25 before being run out. In reply Warwickshire made 165, Bennett taking five wickets off 16 overs for 36. In their second innings Lincoln made 104. Bennett made two before being caught by Charles Frederic Roy Cowan off the bowling of Geoffrey Elson. In reply Warwickshire made 167, this time Bennett failed to take a wicket off nine overs for 23. Warwickshire won by two wickets.

Glentham Memorial, West Lindsey, Lincolnshire.

Bennett's one and only first-class game was played for the Minor Counties against Cambridge University on 18 May 1935 at Fenner's. Minor Counties won the toss and decided to bat making 195, Bennett making 16 not out. In reply Cambridge made 163, Bennett failing to take a wicket off nine overs for 27. In their second innings Minor Counties made 141, Bennett making six before being caught by Grahame Parker off the bowling of the West Indian test bowler John Hemsley Cameron. In reply Cambridge made 174, Bennett bowling 14 overs and taking two wickets for 60, Mark Tindall caught and bowled for five and Hugh Tyron Bartlett (*Wisden* cricketer of the year 1939) for 72. Cambridge University won by four wickets.

During the war, Bennett served as an ordinary coder with the Royal Navy, serving on HMS *Acheron* being part of the Destroyer Flotilla of the Home Fleet at Scapa Flow before being deployed to the North Western Approaches and later taking part in the Norway landings and later their evacuation. Moving on to duties in the North Sea, *Acheron* was attacked by German dive bombers and damaged. While undergoing repairs in the Portsmouth Dockyard she was attacked again, this time two of the crew were killed and three injured. As a result her repairs had to continue until October 1940. By 2 December the repairs were completed and her sea trials began. On 17 December while she was sailing off the Isle of

HMS *Acheron*.

Man at night in heavy seas *Acheron* hit a mine, laid, it is thought, by the German Luftwaffe. The ship sank within four minutes taking 196 crew and dockyard workers with her. There were only nineteen survivors. Alas Montague Valentine Bennett wasn't amongst them. Her sinking was not made public until 27 December 1940.

Bennett's body was never recovered and he is commemorated on panel 41, column 1, Portsmouth Naval Memorial, Hampshire. He is also commemorated on the Glentham Memorial, West Lindsey, Lincolnshire.

Batting and fielding averages

	Mat	Inns	NO	Runs	HS	Ave	100	50	Ct	St
First-class	1	2	1	22	16*	22.00	0	0	2	0

Bowling averages

	Mat	Balls	Runs	Wkts	BBI	Ave	Econ	SR	5w	10
First-class	1	138	54	2	2/27	27.00	2.34	69.0	0	0

1941

Major Cyril Penn Hamilton
Army, Kent
Eight first-class appearances
25 Field Regiment, Royal Artillery
Died 10 February 1941, aged 31
Right-hand bat/Right arm slow

'A very fine sportsman'

Cyril Hamilton was born in Adelaide Australia on 12 August 1909. Returning to England he was educated at Wellington, Lynedoch House, between 1923 and 1927 being, much to his surprise, head of his dormitory in 1927. A keen actor he took part in several college plays. His talent for cricket was quickly realized too and he was soon in the first XI. He took part in matches against Marlborough, Westminster, Charterhouse and Haileybury. He also played rackets for his school. Deciding on a carrier in the Army he won a cadet scholarship, going up to Woolwich and later joining the Royal Artillery. He continued to play cricket, turning out for the Royal Artillery Subalterns against the Royal Military Academy Woolwich. He made zero and nine, took two wickets and two catches. The Subalterns won by five wickets.

Hamilton went on to make eight first-class appearances between 22 June 1932 and 23 May 1936, mostly for the Army, but he also tuned out for Kent and for the Gentlemen against the Players.

Hamilton made his first-class debut for the Army against the South Americans in the British Isles on 22 June 1932 at the Officers Club Service Ground, Aldershot. The South Americans won the toss and decided to bat and made 303, Robert Livingstone Stuart making 133. Hamilton managed to catch Ernest Nevile Dennett Ayling off the bowling of Montagu Brocas Burrows for 29. In reply the Army made 208, Hamilton making the highest score of the innings, 46, before being caught by Robert Stuart off the bowling of Cyril Edgar Ayling. In their second innings the South Americans made 100. In reply the Army made 196, Hamilton making zero before being run out. The Army took the match by five wickets.

Hamilton went on to play against the RAF, the West Indies, the Gentlemen, Cambridge University and Kent (in the county championship).

Hamilton made his final first-class appearance for the Army against Cambridge University on 23 May 1936 at F.P. Fenner's. Cambridge won the toss and decided to bat making 238, Norman Yardley making 101. Hamilton caught Allan White off the bowling of John Henry Hamlyn Whitty (died 23 October 1944) for 21. In reply the Army made 151, Hamilton knocking up the highest score of the innings of 41 before being stumped by Stewart Cathie 'Billy' Griffith off the bowling of John Cameron. In their second innings Cambridge made 109. In their second innings the Army made 191, Hamilton making 24 before being stumped once again by Billy Griffith off the bowling of the Indian test cricketer Jahangir Khan (Khan took five wickets for 55 during the innings). Cambridge won by five runs.

Hamilton also made a minor county appearance for Kent Seconds and played for the Royal Artillery, the MCC, Gezira Sporting Club, United Services and Egypt. During his eight first-class matches Hamilton scored 475 runs, making two centuries, his highest score being 121 against the West Indies (his other century was against the RAF: 105), and one fifty (for the Gentlemen against the Players). He bowled 241 balls, taking six wickets for 203, his best figures being five for 83. He also made eight catches. A fine all-round athlete he also won both the Army and the Amateur squash championships and played rackets for Woolwich.

During the war Hamilton served with the 25 Field Regiment, Royal Artillery, being posted to the Western Desert. He was killed in action on 10 February 1941 in Libya (some records say Eritrea). He is buried in the Keren War Cemetery, grave reference 5. C. 5. He is also commemorated in the Church of St Peter and St Paul in the village of Shropham, Norfolk.

Batting and fielding averages

	Mat	Inns	NO	Runs	HS	Ave	100	50	Ct	St
First-class	8	13	1	475	121	39.58	2	1	8	0

Bowling averages

	Mat	Balls	Runs	Wkts	BBI	Ave	Econ	SR	5w	10
First-class	8	241	203	6	5/83	33.83	5.05	40.1	1	0

Civilian George Jasper Groves
Nottinghamshire
Seventeen first-class appearances
Civilian journalist
18 February 1941, aged 72
Right-handed bat

The oldest first-class cricketer to be killed in the war

George Groves was born on 19 October 1868 in Nottingham, the son of George T. Groves who played for the Gentlemen of Sheffield and Longsight and against the visiting Australians twice in May 1880. Interestingly Longsight played with eighteen men against the Australians eleven. Despite this Australia still managed to win the first match by ten wickets, Groves making eight runs. The second match, a one day game was drawn due to the weather (there was no play).

On leaving school Groves became a journalist reporting mainly on sporting events, specializing in cricket and horse racing. He married Florence who came from 9 Tangier Road, Richmond, Surrey.

Groves played seventeen first-class matches between August 1899 and August 1900, all in the county championship except the match against the MCC.

He made his debut for Nottinghamshire against Surrey at the Kennington Oval. Nottinghamshire won the toss and decided to bat making 300. Groves made 42 (the second highest score of the innings) before being caught by the England test cricketer Thomas Richardson (*Wisden* cricketer of the year 1897) off the bowling of the England test cricketer Thomas Walter Hayward (*Wisden* cricketer of the year 1895). The England test cricketer Arthur Owen Jones (*Wisden* cricketer of the year 1900) made 129. The England test cricketer William Henry Lockwood (*Wisden* cricketer of the year 1899) took five wickets for 84. In reply Surrey made 493, Harold Cooper Pretty making 124. In their second innings Nottinghamshire made 301. Groves only managed four before being bowled by the England test cricketer Walter Scott Lees (*Wisden* cricketer of the year 1906). Lockwood took a further six wickets for 83. In reply Surrey made 88 for four. The match was drawn.

Groves went on to play against many other sides, his final first-class appearance being against Lancashire in the County Championship on 23 August 1900 at Old Trafford. Nottinghamshire won the toss and decided to bat making 128. Groves made 15 before being stumped by Charles

The bombed remains of the *Sporting Chronicle*'s offices where Groves was killed along with twenty-seven other civilians on the night of 18 February 1941.

Smith off the bowling of Sidney Webb. The England test cricketer John Briggs took seven wickets for 53. In reply Lancashire made 237. Groves caught the England test cricketer John Thomas Tyldesley (*Wisden* cricketer of the year 1902) off the bowling of William Bennett Goodacre for 12. In their second innings Nottinghamshire made a poor 57. Groves made nine before being caught by Charles Robert Hartley off the bowling of Sidney Webb. Lancashire won by an innings and 52 runs.

During his first-class career Groves made 584 runs including two fifties, his highest score being 56 against Kent. He was not a bowler but he took twelve catches.

Groves was also a fine footballer. Playing as an amateur from around 1888 he represented Heeley, later playing for Sheffield United. In 1891 he signed with the club playing with them full time until 1896. Moving to London he also made the odd appearance for Woolwich Arsenal.

On retirement Groves retired to Newmarket where he continued to write for the *Sporting Chronicle*. He was killed (together with twenty-seven other civilians) while working in the *Chronicle*'s office at Eton House when the Germans bombed Newmarket High Street on 18 February 1941. He is buried in East Sheen cemetery, grave 134.

Batting and fielding averages

	Mat	Inns	NO	Runs	HS	Ave	100	Ct	St
First-class	17	29	4	584	56*	23.36	0	12	0

Bowling averages

	Mat	Balls	Runs	Wkts	BBI	BBM	Ave	Econ	SR	4w	5w	10
First-class	17	10	6	0	-	-	-	3.60	-	0	0	0

2nd Lieutenant John Compton Butterworth
Middlesex, Oxford University
Three first-class appearances
160 Battery, 54 Heavy Anti-Aircraft Regiment, Royal
Artillery
Died 18 March 1941, aged 35
Right-hand bat

'Died defending London'

John Butterworth was born on 17 August 1905 in Samarang, Java. He was the son of Reginald and Cornelia Gertrud Butterworth of St Pancras. He was educated at Harrow where his talent for cricket put him in the first XI. He played in the annual Eton Harrow match at Lord's on 13 July 1923 together with his younger brother Reginald. John was run out in his first innings for thirteen and clean bowled in his second for twelve. His brother did better making 56 in his first innings and 22 in his second. The match was noted for the impressive 159 made by Eton opener Edward William Dawson and another century made by Ralph Cobbold, Eton making a total of 502 runs. The match was eventually drawn. Both John and his brother Reginald played for Harrow against Eton the following year, this time with more success, John making 72 (the highest score of the innings) and Reginald 42. In their second innings John made 40 not out and Reginald 17 not out. The match was again drawn.

John Butterworth also played against Charterhouse and Winchester, and for Lord's Schools against The Rest at Lord's on 4 August 1924, again with his brother Reginald. The Rest won by five wickets. On leaving school he went up to Magdalen College Oxford.

John Butterworth played in three first-class matches between 1925 and 1926. He made his debut for Middlesex against Oxford University at the University Parks, Oxford on 2 May 1925. Middlesex won the toss and elected to bat making 312. Butterworth, who opened with Henry William Lee, made four before being bowled by Walter Nelson McBride. In reply Oxford made 202. In their second innings Middlesex made 13 before being bowled by Claude Taylor, Middlesex making 37 before declaring. Oxford made 47 in their second innings and the match was drawn.

Playing once again with his brother Reginald, John Butterworth made his debut for Oxford University against the Free Foresters on 5 June 1926 again at the University Parks. Oxford won the toss and decided to bat making 275. John Butterworth, opening for Oxford, made eight before being caught by Mark Patten off the bowling of England test cricketer Nigel Haig. Reginald, batting number eight, did little better, also making eight before being bowled lbw by Haig. In reply the Free Foresters made 450, Reginald taking two catches and bowling the England test cricketer Francis Mann for 44, caught George Abell. In their second innings Oxford made 253, Butterworth being bowled by Nigel Haig for three. Reginald was bowled by John Heathcoat-Amory also for three. In their second innings the Free Foresters made 25. The match was drawn.

Butterworth made his final first-class appearance for Oxford against the MCC just over a week later, on 16 June 1926 at Lord's. The MCC won the toss and decided to bat making

242. In reply Oxford made 139. Butterworth opened, making five before being stumped by the England test cricketer Ronald Thomas Stanyforth off the bowling of another England test cricketer Nigel Haig. Haig took five wickets during the innings. In their second innings the MCC made 303. In reply Oxford made 22, Butterworth making 16 not out. The match was drawn.

During the war John Butterworth was commissioned into the Royal Artillery, being attached to 160 Battery, 54 HAA Regiment. He was killed at Shooters Hill, London, during the Blitz on 18 March 1941 when a bomb exploded close to his battery. He is buried in Greenwich Cemetery, section G. coll, grave 74, screen wall, panel 1. He is also commemorated on the Harrow memorial.

His brother Reginald was killed while serving with the RAF Volunteer Reserve, 13 Squadron, on 21 May 1940.

Batting and fielding averages

	Mat	Inns	NO	Runs	HS	Ave	100	50	Ct	St
First-class	3	6	1	49	16*	9.80	0	0	1	0

Bowling averages

	Mat	Balls	Runs	Wkts	BBI	BBM	Ave	Econ	SR	4w	5w	10
First-class	3	-	-	-	-	-	-	-	-	-	-	-

Sergeant Lawrence Charles Eastman
Essex/Otago
451 first-class appearances
Civilian ARP Warden
Died 17 April 1941 (in the Blitz), aged 43
Right-hand bat/Right arm medium leg break

Died doing his duty to the end

Laurie Eastman was born on 3 June 1897 at Enfield Wash, Middlesex. He was educated at the Leyton Technical Institute and fought during the First World War serving as a sergeant with the 22nd London Regiment. He apparently won both the DCM (some records say DSM) and the Military Medal for bravery; however I have been unable to trace either of these awards to him.

Eastman made a remarkable 451 first-class appearances, mostly for Essex in the County Championship (408 appearances) between July 1920 and August 1939. He also turned out for Otago, The Rest and Sir T.E.W. Brinckman's XI.

He made his debut for Essex against Gloucestershire on 7 July 1920 in the County Championship at Fry's Ground, Bristol. Gloucestershire won the toss and decided to bat making 175. Eastman bowled 24 overs taking five wickets for 53: the England test cricketer Harry Smith caught Sidney Haddon for 38, Philip Francis Cunningham Williams bowled for five, Foster Gotch Robinson caught by the England test cricketer Charles Albert George (Jack) Russell (*Wisden* cricketer of the year 1923) for one, Arthur William Frederick Roper caught Percy Toone for two, and William Kerr McClintock bowled for six. In their first innings Essex made 146. Eastman failed to bat. The match was drawn but it was a fine debut for the young Eastman.

Between 1922 and 1926 Eastman became Assistant Secretary of Essex County Cricket Club.

Eastman made his final first-class appearance for Essex against Middlesex in the County Championship on 16 August 1939 at Southchurch Park, Southend-on-Sea. Middlesex won the toss and decided to bat making 215. In return Essex made 196. Opening for Essex Eastman made two before being lbw to the England test cricketer Cedric Ivan James (Big Jim) Smith (*Wisden* cricketer of the year 1935). Smith took five wickets for 48. In their second innings Middlesex made 183. In reply Essex made 197. Playing further down the order Eastman made four before being lbw to Smith. The England test player James Morton Sims took eight wickets for 62. Middlesex won by five runs.

During his career Eastman made 13,385 runs, including seven centuries and sixty-one fifties, his highest score being 161 against Derbyshire. He also bowled 63,136 balls taking 1,006 wickets making thirty five-wicket hauls and three-ten wicket hauls, his best figures being seven for 28. He made 260 catches.

He also made five appearances for Otago in the Plunket Shield.

On 16 April 1941 the Germans launched one of their heaviest attacks on London. Starting at 9 pm, 685 aircraft continued their work until dawn. Among the public buildings damaged were St. Paul's Cathedral, the Houses of Parliament, the Admiralty, the Law Courts and the National Gallery. Serious fires were also caused at Selfridges, Bessborough Gardens, Westminster, and the Kidbrooke RAF stores depot. Over two thousand fires were started and over one thousand people killed. Eastman, serving as an ARP warden, was on duty during the raid and was seriously wounded when a bomb dropped close to him. He was rushed to Harefield Hospital but nothing could be done and he died there on 17 April 1941.

Batting and fielding averages

	Mat	Inns	NO	Runs	HS	Ave	100	Ct	St
First-class	451	693	50	13385	161	20.81	7	259	0

Bowling averages

	Mat	Runs	Wkts	BBI	Ave	5w	10
First-class	451	26940	1006	7/28	26.77	30	3

Sub-Lieutenant Eric (Budgie) John Hopkins Dixon
Northamptonshire, Oxford University
Forty-Nine first-class appearances
Fleet Air Arm
Died 20 April 1941, aged 25
Right-handed bat

'Some of his record statistics still stand today'

Eric Dixon, known to his friends as 'Budgie', was born on 22 September 1915 in Oakfield, Horbury, Yorkshire. He was the son of John Kemp Smith Dixon and Elfrida (née Hopkins). His father was a manager at Henry Richardson & Company of York. He had one sister. He was educated at Queen Elizabeth Grammar School, Wakefield, before winning an exhibition to St Edward's School, Oxford. While there he played in the first XI, making appearances against Eastbourne College, Bromsgrove and Eastern Canadian Schools. He also represented the Young Amateurs against the Young Professionals at Lord's on 9 and 10 August 1935 at Lord's. Dixon went on to make forty-nine first-class appearances between 20 May 1936 and 30 August 1939 for Oxford University and Lancashire.

Selected to play for Oxford University, he made his first-class debut for them in a university match against Lancashire on 20 May 1936 at the University Parks, Oxford. Oxford won the toss and decided to bat making 368. Dixon contributed 49 before being stumped by the England test cricketer George Duckworth off the bowling of Leonard Wright Parkinson. John Grover made 119. In reply Lancashire made 377, the England test cricketer John Leonard Hopwood making 111. In their second innings Oxford made 250, Dixon knocking up 29, Roger Kimpton making 102. In their second innings Lancashire made 47. The match was drawn.

Dixon went on to make thirty-nine appearances for Oxford, later captaining the side. He also played in the match against Australia captained by the legendary Don Bradman, Australia making 679 including three centuries, made by John Fingleton 124, Stanley Joseph McCabe 110, and Lindsay Hassett 146. Australia took the match by an innings and 487 runs. Dixon made 17.

He also made two first-class appearances for Oxford and Cambridge University during their tour of Jamaica in July and August 1938.

His final appearance was against Cambridge University at Lord's on 1 July 1939. Oxford won the toss and decided to bat making 313, Dixon making the highest score of the innings with 75 before being bowled by Alexander 'Alan' Campbell Shirreff. In reply Cambridge made 157. In their second innings Oxford made 273 before declaring. Dixon didn't bat. Cambridge made a stand, making 384, Patrick John Dickinson making a century. Despite this Oxford still took the match by 45 runs.

On leaving Oxford, Dixon began to represent Northamptonshire, making his debut for them on 26 July 1939 at Stanley Park, Blackpool against Lancashire. Northampton won the toss and decided to bat making 368. Dixon, opening for Northamptonshire, made 20 before being bowled by Albert Edward Nutter. In reply Lancashire made 198, Dixon catching

William Edward Phillipson off the bowling of William Edward Merritt for 11. The weather closed in and the match was drawn.

Dixon went on to play for Northamptonshire against Somerset, Leicestershire, Derbyshire, Warwickshire and Glamorgan.

He made his final first-class appearance against Somerset on 30 August 1939 at the County Ground, Taunton. Northampton won the toss and decided to bat making 138. Dixon, opening the batting, made two before being bowled by William Andrews. In reply Somerset made 380. In their second innings Northampton made 150, Dixon making five before being caught by the England test cricketer Arthur William Wellard (*Wisden* cricketer of the year 1936) off the bowling of William Andrews. Somerset won by an innings and 92 runs.

During his first-class career Dixon made 2,356 runs, including two centuries, his highest score being 123 against Somerset (his other century was against Yorkshire), twelve fifties, and nineteen catches. He also made six minor county appearances for Yorkshire Second XI, and represented N.S. Mitchell-Innes' XI, Craven Gentlemen and E.J.H. Dixon's XI.

On leaving St Edward's in September 1939 he became a teacher at Summer Fields. He married Avice Margaret Harrison in 1940. After only a term at Summer Fields he was called up, being commissioned into the Fleet Air Arm as a Sub-Lieutenant with 806 Squadron. He went missing while flying from HMS *Formidable* off the coast of Libya on 20 April 1941. He was mentioned in despatches for his work while serving with the Fleet Air Arm.

The St Edward's records states, 'During his six years at SES he never altered in character or lost his simplicity of outlook. The years brought increasing success and responsibility, at the organ, on the cricket field, as a prefect, but these things left him unchanged and he still got from life, laughter and beauty and an ever-growing number of friends. He was an Exhibitioner, a School Prefect, he played the organ and above all was one of the best cricketers the school ever produced, both before and since. Some of his record statistics still stand today.'

He is commemorated on the Lee-on-Solent Memorial, bay 2, panel 6, and on the memorials at Queen Elizabeth Grammar School Wakefield, St Edward's and Summer Fields.

He left £174-1-9. Probate was granted to his widow. She remarried in 1949 and died in 2004.

Batting and fielding averages

	Mat	Inns	NO	Runs	HS	Ave	100	Ct	St
First-class	49	86	4	2356	123	28.73	2	19	0

Bowling averages

	Mat	Balls	Runs	Wkts	BBI	BBM	Ave	Econ	SR	4w	5w	10
First-class	49	31	29	0	-	-	-	5.61	-	0	0	0

Captain Arthur Wellesley (Dooley) Briscoe MC
South Africa, Transvaal
Two tests, thirty-five first-class appearances
Transvaal Scottish Regiment South African Forces
Died 22 April 1941, aged 30
Right-hand bat

'took part in the first action involving South African ground troops'

Arthur Wellesley (Dooley) Briscoe was born on 6 February 1911 in Johannesburg. He was the son of Arthur and Rhoda Briscoe. He was educated at the King Edward VII School (KES) in Johannesburg and was soon in the school XI going on to represent Transvaal and Natal School Boys against the Marylebone Cricket Club. The schoolboys were allowed fifteen players to the MCC eleven. The match was played on 13 December 1927 at Walter Milton Oval, University of Witwatersrand, Johannesburg. The MCC won the toss and elected to bat making 312, the England test cricketer Bob Wyatt (*Wisden* cricketer of the year 1930) making 136 not out. In reply the Natal School Boys made 199, Briscoe making 28 before being caught by the England test player Harry Elliott off the bowling of another England test cricketer, George Geary. Geary took seven wickets during the innings. In their second innings the MCC made 206 and the match was drawn.

Briscoe made two test appearances for South Africa and played thirty-five first-class matches between 27 November 1931 and 5 January 1940 mostly for the Transvaal. He made his debut for the Transvaal against Natal on 27 November 1931 at Kingsmead, Durban. Natal won the toss and elected to bat making 208. In reply Transvaal made 238, Briscoe making 23 before being lbw off the bowling of Arthur Phillips Woods. In their second innings Natal made 385, Herbert Frederick Wade making 154. In their second innings Transvaal made 241, Briscoe making 33 not out, Manfred John Susskind knocking up 124. The match was drawn. Briscoe went on to represent Transvaal on thirty-three occasions.

He also made two test appearances for South Africa, the first against Australia during their 1935-36 tour of South Africa. The second test was played between 24 and 28 December 1935 at the Old Wanderers, Johannesburg. South Africa won the toss and decided to bat making 157, Briscoe making 15 before being bowled by Bill O'Reilly. In reply Australia made 250, Briscoe catching William Albert Stanley Oldfield off the bowling of Bruce Mitchell for 40. In their second innings South Africa made 491, Briscoe making 16 before being bowled by Ernest Leslie McCormick. The outstanding innings came from Arthur Dudley Nourse who made 231. In reply Australia made 274, Stan McCabe making 189 not out. The match was drawn.

Briscoe made his second test appearance against England during the second test. The match was played between 31 December 1938 and 4 January 1939 at Newlands, Cape Town. England won the toss and decided to bat making an impressive 559 including several notable innings. Leslie Ethelbert George Ames who made 115, Walter Reginald 'Wally' Hammond 181 and Bryan Valentine 112. In reply South Africa made 286, Briscoe making two before being lbw off the bowling of Thomas William John Goddard, Dudley Nourse making 120.

Hedley Verity took five wickets during the innings. Following on, South Africa managed 201. Briscoe failed to bat and the match was drawn.

Briscoe played his final first-class match against Griqualand West on 5 January 1940 at De Beers Stadium, Kimberley. Griqualand West batted first, making 156. In reply Transvaal made 176, Briscoe making five before hitting his own wicket off the bowling of Frank Cotty. In their second innings Griqualand West made 68, Briscoe catching Frederick Wilmot Whelan off the bowling of Roy Neville Edwin Peterson for 17. Transvaal only needed to make 49 which they did quickly, taking the match by eight wickets.

During his career Briscoe played in two test matches, making a total of 33 runs, his highest score being 16 against Australia. During his first-class career he made 2,189 runs including six centuries, against Border 140, North Eastern 172, Orange Free State 175, and The Rest 100. His highest score was 191 against Griqualand West. He also made ten fifties.

He married Stella Briscoe of Johannesburg before being commissioned into the Transvaal Scottish Regiment South African Forces and serving with cricketing friends Bruce Mitchell and Ronnie Grieveson. After being inspected by General Smuts they sailed to Mombasa on 16 July 1940 and commenced their training in Nairobi. On 6 September 1940 the 1st Transvaal Scottish was transferred to the 2nd East African Brigade under British command and took part in the first action involving South African ground troops in the Second World War, near Liboi when a column was attacked by a force of Banda and Italian Colonial troops.

Continuing to serve in Somaliland and Abyssinia against the Italians, he was awarded the Military Cross for bravery in the field at Huberta and Ionte (*London Gazette* 21 October 1941). Always in the thick of things, he was eventually killed in action on 22 April 1941.

He is buried in Addis Ababa War Cemetery, grave reference 2. E. 2.

Batting and fielding averages

	Mat	Inns	NO	Runs	HS	Ave	100	50	6s	Ct	St
Tests	2	3	0	33	16	11.00	0	0	0	1	0
First-class	35	56	8	2189	191	45.60	6	10		15	0

Bowling averages

	Mat	Inns	Balls	Runs	Wkts	BBI	BBM	Ave	Econ	SR	4w	5w	10
Tests	2	-	-	-	-	-	-	-	-	-	-	-	-
First-class	35		18	19	0	-	-	-	6.33	-	0	0	0

Sergeant WX 4544 Percival Barnes 'Barney' Wood
Western Australia
One first-class appearance
2/16 Batt's Australian Infantry
Died 9 June 1941, aged 39
Right-hand bat/Right arm medium pace

'He was a sportsman who was popular wherever he competed'

Percival Barnes 'Barney' Wood was born on 22 December 1901 in Wellington New Zealand (he later moved to Australia with his family). He was the son of Robert Ellis Wood and Nellie Elizabeth of Berwick, Victoria, Australia. He was educated at Melbourne Grammar School becoming one of their star athletes, cricket players and Australian Rules footballers. On leaving school Wood played his football as a defender for Melbourne Football Club in the WAFL. He appeared in five games during the 1928 VFL season before moving to Western Australia where he spent some time playing for Perth Football Club. A keen motorist Wood was also the holder of several Transcontinental Motoring records established with Dr Alan MacKay in 1926 while driving an Essex Super Six. He also won a Victorian amateur welterweight boxing title.

Wood played his cricket for Melbourne Cricket Club, appearing for them during the 1927 season against Auckland, Waikato, Hawke's Bay, Wanganui, Taranaki, Wellington, Canterbury, Southland, Otago and New Zealand. He also made thirty-one appearances for Melbourne in Victoria Premier cricket matches between January 1922 and January 1927.

Wood made one first-class appearance for Western Australia against the visiting South Africans. The match was played on 19 March 1932 at the Western Australia Cricket Association Ground, Perth. Western Australia won the toss and decided to bat making 183, Wood making six before being caught by Horace Brakenridge 'Jock' Cameron off the bowling of Cyril Leverton Vincent. In reply South Africa made 488, Bruce Mitchell making 125 and Denijs Paul Beck Morkel 150 not out. Wood bowled four overs and failed to take a wicket for 16. He did however catch Bruce Mitchell off the bowling of Mervyn Inverarity for 125. In their second innings Western Australia only managed 63 all out. Wood made two before being caught by Xenophon Constantine 'Xen' Balaskas off the bowling of Morkel. Morkel took eight wickets for thirteen off eight overs during the innings. South Africa took the match by an innings and 242 runs.

At the outbreak of the war, Wood originally joined the RAF. However, tired of being held in reserve all the time and keen to see some action, he transferred to the infantry joining 2/16 Battalion Australian Infantry. Quickly promoted to sergeant he served in the Middle East where he was killed in action when his unit were hit by mortar fire during the battle of the Litani River on 9 June 1941.

His local paper later reported the loss:

POPULAR SPORTSMAN
Death of Sergeant B. Wood.

Advice has been received by Mr O. Williams from the relatives of Sergeant Barney Wood that he has been killed in Syria. The late Sergeant Wood was an outstanding sportsman in a wide sphere. He played league football and first grade cricket with the Melbourne Club in Victoria before coming to Perth. Then he played cricket with West Perth and football with Perth. He gained State cricket honours when he played against South Africa at the W.A.C.A. ground in 1932 and was regarded as a fine all-round cricketer. In golf circles he was also prominent and became captain of the Royal Perth Club. He was a sportsman who was popular wherever he competed.

He is buried in Sidon War Cemetery, grave reference, 3. C. 1.

Batting and fielding averages

	Mat	Inns	NO	Runs	HS	Ave	100	50	Ct	St
First-class	1	2	0	8	6	4.00	0	0	1	0

Bowling averages

	Mat	Runs	Wkts	BBI	BBM	Ave	SR	4w	5w	10
First-class	1	16	0	-	-	-	-	0	0	0

Pilot Officer Donald Frederick (Fezard) Walker
Hampshire
Seventy-Three first-class appearances
RAVR 58 Squadron
Died 18 June 1941, aged 28
Left-hand bat

'Sound in defence, with unlimited patience...'

Donald Frederick (some records call him Fezard) Walker was born on 15 August 1912 in Wandsworth. He was the son of James Fezard Walker and Ethel Maud (née Lawrence) of Parkstone, Dorset. He was educated at King's College School, Wimbledon. A left-handed batsman his talent as a cricketer was quickly recognized and developed and he was soon playing in the school's first XI. He made appearances against University College School, Epsom College and Beaumont College. He also represented The Rest against Lord's School on two occasions. He averaged 30.62 in 1928 and in his last year he headed the batting with 23.20. He also became a fine bowler, an outstanding fielder and a talented wicketkeeper. He was so good that he was given a trial for Surrey's second XI against Devon on 1 July 1933 at the Oval. Surrey won the toss and elected to bat making 455. Walker made a solid 30 in his first innings before being caught by Leslie John Louis Turl off the bowling of William Thomas French. In their first innings Devon made 179. Being forced to follow on, they made 253, Walter William Hoare making 140 not out. The match was drawn.

This, combined with his considerable success at club cricket, led to an approach by Hampshire County Cricket Club who persuaded him to turn professional.

Between 19 May 1937 and 26 August 1939 Walker made seventy-three first-class appearances, seventy in the county championships, one university match against Cambridge, one against New Zealand in the British Isles (1937), and one against the West Indies in England (1939).

He made his debut for Hampshire against Lancashire on 19 May 1937 at Old Trafford in the county championship. Hampshire won the toss and decided to bat making 280, Walker making two before being bowled by the England test cricketer Richard Pollard, and Arthur Ernest Pothecary making a century. In reply Lancashire made 224, Walker catching the Lancashire opener and England test cricketer Edward Payne off the bowling of Gerald Hill for 54. In their second innings Hampshire made 161, Walker making one before being caught by Frank Bramley Watson off the bowling of Reginald Henry Parkin. Not the best of starts. The match was drawn.

Altogether during the 1937 season Walker scored 847 runs. This includes the 235 he put on with Gerry Hill for a fifth wicket stand against Sussex at the United Services Recreation Ground, which remains a Hampshire record to this day (Hill 161, Walker 123).

The following season, 1938, he made 925. In 1939 he did even better with 1,117 runs, including three centuries, average 29.39.

Walker made his final first-class appearance in the county championship against Yorkshire on 26 August 1939 at Dean Park, Bournemouth. Yorkshire won the toss and decided to field. Hampshire made 116, Walker being caught by Arthur Wood off the bowling of the England test player Thomas Francis Smailes for a duck. Hedley Verity took six wickets during the innings. In reply Yorkshire made 243. In their second innings Hampshire matched their first innings score, making 116, Walker making six before being bowled by Smailes. Yorkshire won the game by an innings and eleven runs.

During his career Walker made 3,004 runs, including four centuries, against Surrey 108, Sussex 123, Sussex 107, and Nottinghamshire 147 – his highest first-class score. He also made fifteen fifties, seventy-five catches and one stumping.

He played for the RAF while serving with them. *Wisden* said of him, 'Sound in defence, with unlimited patience, Walker brought off good strokes all round the wicket and generally gave every indication of a successful career.' Like many top sportsmen he played other sports to a high level, captaining Dorset at Rugby as well as an RAF XV.

During the war, Walker was commissioned into the RAF and trained as a pilot joining 58 Squadron flying Whitley bombers out of Linton-on-Ouse as part of Bomber Command. On 18 June 1941, while flying Whitley Bomber number N1462 on his return from a raid on Cologne, his aircraft was attacked by a German night fighter and shot down north of the Dutch village of Best. Walker and his four-man crew were all killed. They are buried at Eindhoven (Woensel) General Cemetery in the Netherlands, grave reference plot JJ, grave 21.

Batting and fielding averages

	Mat	Inns	NO	Runs	HS	Ave	100	Ct	St
First-class	73	126	11	3004	147	26.12	4	75	1

Bowling averages

	Mat	Balls	Runs	Wkts	BBI	BBM	Ave	Econ	SR	4w	5w	10
First-class	73	18	22	0	-	-	-	7.33	-	0	0	0

Major Robert Alexander Tamplin Miller
Sussex
Twelve first-class appearances
General List
Died 10 July 1941, aged 45
Right-handed bat/wicketkeeper

A fine wicket keeper and hard hitting captain

Robert Miller was born on 12 November 1895 in Lockwood, Travancore, India, the son of Robert Tamplin and Ellen Marion Miller. He was educated at Uppingham where he was in the XI captaining the side. He also played for The Rest against Lord's School and Public Schools against the MCC.

With the First World War at its height on leaving school he went straight into the army taking a commission into the Royal Warwickshire Regiment. He managed to battle his way through the whole Great War coming out unscathed with the rank of major.

After the war he appeared in twelve first-class matches for Sussex, nine in the county championship, two against Australian Imperial Forces in the British Isles and one a university match, all played in 1919.

He made his debut for Sussex against Somerset on 21 May 1919 at the County Ground, Taunton. Somerset won the toss and decided to bat making 243. Playing as wicketkeeper he caught two and stumped one: Arthur Ernest Sydney Rippon off the bowling of George Arthur Stannard for 26, and Albert Dudley Eric Rippon off John Herbert Vincent for 60 (the Rippons were twin brothers). He stumped James Bridges off the bowling of Vincent for 34. George Rubens Cox took five wickets for 51 off 15 overs. In reply Sussex made 242. Miller made 33 before being bowled by James Bridges. Bridges took five wickets for 84. In their second innings Somerset made 103. Miller stumped Bridges off the bowling of Vincent for 14. In their second innings Sussex made 104. Miller made a duck before being caught by Bridges off the bowling of the England test cricketer John Cornish (Jack) White (*Wisden* cricketer of the year 1929). The match was eventually drawn.

Miller next played against Gloucestershire (lost by 24 runs), Nottinghamshire (lost by an innings and 175 runs), Australian Imperial Forces (draw), Essex (Essex won by six wickets), Surrey (lost by an innings and 189 runs), Kent (lost by an innings and 123 runs), Oxford University (won by an innings and 125 runs), Hampshire (lost by 64 runs), Lancashire (lost by three wickets), and Yorkshire (won by five wickets).

He made his final first-class appearance for Sussex against the Australian Imperial Forces on 4 August 1919 at the County Ground, Hove. Sussex won the toss and decided to bat making 120. Miller made two before being bowled by the Australian test cricketer Jack Morrison Gregory (*Wisden* cricketer of the year 1922). Gregory took six wickets for 38 off 23 overs. In reply Australia made 300. The Australian opener Carl Bleackley Wills made 127 before he was run out. Miller stumped Gregory and Edmund James Long, both off the bowling of Cox. In their second innings Sussex made 126. Miller made one before being lbw to Charles Samuel Winning. The Australian test cricketer Herbert Leslie Collins took six wickets for 27 off 17 overs. The Australian Imperial Forces won by an innings and 54 runs.

During his career Miller made 191 runs, his highest score being 39 against Oxford University. He also made nine catches and eleven stumpings.

Trying his luck at farming in Kenya things didn't work out as he had hoped and on 3 May 1935 he was declared bankrupt. During the Second World War he was placed on the General List and travelled to Aden, dying on 10 July 1941 near Maala, South Yemen. He is buried in Maala Cemetery, grave reference H. 43.

Batting and fielding averages

	Mat	Inns	NO	Runs	HS	Ave	100	50	Ct	St
First-class	12	22	2	191	39	9.55	0	0	10	10

Bowling averages

	Mat	Balls	Runs	Wkts	BBI	BBM	Ave	Econ	SR	4w	5w	10
First-class	12	-	-	-	-	-	-	-	-	-	-	-

Flying Officer Gerald Henry Seeley
Worcestershire
One first-class appearance
21 Squadron RAFVR (Air Gunner)
Died 23 July 1941, aged 38
Right-hand bat

'One of the finest athletes the school has ever had'

Gerald Seeley was born on 9 May 1903 in Port Blair in the Andaman Islands. On returning to England the family moved to Malvern. Seeley was educated at Marlborough where he excelled at athletics and was soon in the school's first XI. On 27 July 1921 Seeley, a keen batsman, knocked up an impressive 122 against Rugby at Lord's, as well as taking an equally impressive five wickets for 59 runs.

Gerald Seeley made one first-class appearance for Worcestershire in the county championship against Nottinghamshire at the County Ground, New Road, Worcestershire, on the 13 August 1921. Nottinghamshire won the toss and decided to bat making 132, Humphrey Gilbert taking six wickets for 56 during the innings. In reply Worcestershire made 196, Seeley batting number seven, making seven before being lbw to the England test cricketer John Richmond Gunn. In their second innings Nottinghamshire made 222, Gilbert taking a further seven wickets for 60. Worcestershire went on to make 159 in the second innings, Seeley failing to bat. Worcestershire won by eight wickets.

During the Second World War Seeley joined the RAF Volunteer Reserve, being commissioned to Pilot Officer on 23 July 1940 and later Flying Officer on 6 June 1941. Trained as an air gunner he was posted to 21 Squadron, a light bomber squadron which flew Blenheim IVs. Operations were initially limited to reconnaissance missions. In May 1940, with the German attack on the Low Countries and France, 21 Squadron began daylight attacks on advancing German forces, flying its first mission of the campaign on 11 May 1941 when eleven Blenheims unsuccessfully attacked a bridge at Maastricht. Two Blenheims were shot down and eight damaged. After that the squadron were moved to Lossiemouth and joined Coastal Command between June 1940 and December 1941, where they operated as an anti-shipping unit off the coast of Norway, alternating between Lossiemouth and Watton. Seeley died on 23 July 1941 when his aircraft was lost at sea off Ostend. His body was

G.H. Seeley Crosley A.S. Horwood

recovered and laid to rest at the Oostende New Communal Cemetery, plot 9, row 4, grave 12. He is also commemorated at the Worcestershire County Cricket Club and on the Malvern War Memorial.

Batting and fielding averages

	Mat	Inns	NO	Runs	HS	Ave	100	50	Ct	St
First-class	1	1	0	7	7	7.00	0	0	0	0

Bowling averages

	Mat	Balls	Runs	Wkts	BBI	BBM	Ave	Econ	SR	4w	5w	10
First-class	1	-	-	-	-	-	-	-	-			

Wing Commander Grahame Lawrence Cruickshanks DFC
Eastern Province
Two first-class appearances
RAF 214 Squadron (Pilot)
Died 8 September 1941, aged 28
Left-handed bat/Wicketkeeper

'A wonderful and experienced pilot'

Cruickshanks DFC far right.

Grahame Cruickshanks was born on 2 March 1913 in Port Elizabeth, Eastern Cape Province. He was one of four sons of Alexander Craighead Cruickshanks and Agnes. He was educated at Grey High School in Port Elizabeth, where he excelled at cricket, becoming a regular member of the first XI as the school's opening bat. He also played football for the school. On leaving school he worked for Shell in South Africa. During that time he made his two first-class appearances, both for Eastern Province in the Currie Cup and both in December 1931.

He made his debut against Natal on 21 December at the Old Wanderers Top Back Ground, Johannesburg. Natal won the toss and decided to bat making 163, Cruickshanks catching Harold Redmayne Fawcett off the bowling of Arthur Lennox Ochse for 21. In their first innings Eastern Province made 190, Cruickshanks scoring five before being lbw to Arthur Philipps Woods. Eastern Province's batting would have collapsed had it not been for an innings of 122 by Hubert Dainton Freakes who batted throughout the innings. In their second innings Natal made 237, Cruickshanks bowling two overs for 12 and taking one wicket, that of Dudley Nourse, caught Dudley Arthur Theophilus for 85. In their second innings Eastern Province were all out for 48, Cruickshanks lbw to Harold Fawcett for a duck. Richard Edwyn Davies took six wickets for 21 off six overs. Natal took the match by 162 runs.

Cruickshanks made his second and final first-class appearance against the Orange Free State on 23 December 1931 at the Old Wanderers, Pirates Lower Back Ground. Eastern Province won the toss and decided to bat making 256, Cruickshanks making three before being caught and bowled by Louis Ewald de Villiers, De Villiers taking six wickets during the innings. In reply the Orange Free State made 403. Cruickshanks bowled four overs and took no wickets for nine runs. In their second innings Eastern Province made 336, Cruickshanks making 19 before being lbw to Alfred Bernard Machin. The match was drawn.

Leaving South Africa for England in 1933 to join the RAF, he was sent for pilot training in Egypt joining No. 14 Squadron, RAF in Transjordan. Just before leaving South Africa he married Phyllis (Billie), of Durban. They had one son who was born in Egypt.

While in Egypt between 13 April 1935 and 22 April 1938 Cruickshanks made five appearances for Egypt's national cricket team, all against H.M. Martineau's XI (non-first-class).

In 1938 he returned to England and became an instructor, later playing cricket twice for the RAF, both times in July 1939 (again not first-class), the first against the Navy (drawn) and the second against the Army which the RAF won by six wickets. Not entirely settled, he later wrote, 'Life in England is changeful, in nine months we have lived in nine different houses and have made three big changes, but hope to be comfortably settled soon.'

One thing he did enjoy however, was training the flying pupils, many from his home country of South Africa and Rhodesia, calling them 'first-class men'.

During the war he became operational, taking part in many raids on some of the most heavily defended targets in Germany and Europe. With No. 9 Squadron he was promoted to temporary squadron leader (*LG* 20 September 1940) before taking over command of No. 214 (Federated Malay-Wellington Mk IIs) Squadron RAF (part of No. 3 Group RAF). By August 1941 he had been promoted to wing commander and had been awarded the Distinguished Flying Cross for continuous good work and leadership ability. He was shot down and killed on 8 September 1941 while returning in a Wellington Mark I from a raid on Berlin. He had taken off from Stradishall. His crew consisted of:

Sergeant Leonard Tyne Chapman, 929858, wireless operator/air gunner, RAF Volunteer Reserve, KIA 8 September 1941, aged 27

Wing Commander Grahame Lawrence Cruickshanks DFC, 34191, pilot, RAF, KIA 8 September 1941

Squadron Leader William Davies, 74467, RAF Volunteer Reserve, KIA 8 September 1941, aged 42

Flying Officer William Esplen, 82979, wireless operator/air gunner, RAF Volunteer Reserve, KIA 8 September 1941, aged 33

Flight Lieutenant Keith James Falconer DFC, 84730, observer, RAF Volunteer Reserve, KIA 8 September 1941, aged 33

Sergeant Arthur Norman Page, 1376222, RAF Volunteer Reserve, KIA 8 September 1941, aged 26

Cruickshanks, together with his entire crew, are buried in the Berlin 1939-1945 cemetery, grave reference, 4. A. 1.

His younger brother, Clive Cruickshanks, also played cricket for Eastern Province.

Batting and fielding averages

	Mat	Inns	NO	Runs	HS	Ave	100	50	Ct	St
First-class	2	4	0	27	19	6.75	0	0	1	0

Bowling averages

	Mat	Balls	Runs	Wkts	BBI	BBM	Ave	Econ	SR	4w	5w	10
First-class	2	-	-	-	-	-	-	-	-	-	-	-

Captain Charles Richard Spencer
Oxford University-Glamorgan
Four first-class appearances
Royal Marines
29 September 1941, aged 38
Right-handed bat/Wicketkeeper

'Tragic end to a brave man and fine cricketer'

Charles Spencer was born on 21 June 1903 at Llandough, Glamorgan. He was the son of Charles St David Spencer a well-known Cardiff solicitor and Anna Isabella of Hailsham, Sussex. He was educated at Clifton College where he played for the first XI during the 1922 season playing against Downside (draw), Rugby (won by innings and 51 runs), Cheltenham College (lost by six wickets), and Tonbridge (won by innings and 13 runs). On leaving school he went up to Magdalen College Oxford. Spencer made four first-class appearances three for Oxford University and one for Glamorgan between June 1923 and August 1925.

He made his debut first-class appearance for Oxford University against the West Indies during the tour of the British Isles on 6 June 1923 at the University Parks, Oxford. Oxford won the toss and decided to bat making 390. The side also contained Douglas Jardine of Bodyline fame. Greville Thomas Scott Stevens the England test cricketer made 182 and John Guise 120. Due to an early declaration Spencer failed to bat. In reply the West Indies made 388. In their second innings Oxford made 178, Spencer making 11 not out. In reply the West Indies made 183, George Challenor making 100 not out. The West Indies won by eight wickets.

He next turned out for Oxford against H.D.G. Leveson-Gower's at the Saffrons, Eastbourne on 30 June 1923. Oxford won the toss and elected to bat making 256, Spencer batting last, making seven not out. In reply H.D.G. Leveson-Gower's XI made 305. In their second innings Oxford made 182, Spencer making 17 before being caught by Francis Bernard Ross Browne off the bowling of Ernest Smith. H.D.G. Leveson-Gower's XI made 134 in reply. Spencer caught Miles Howell off the bowling of Thomas Barkley Raikes for 16. H.D.G. Leveson-Gower's XI took the match by three wickets.

He made his third first-class appearance for Oxford against Middlesex at the University Parks on 3 May 1924. Middlesex won the toss and decided to bat making 364, Raikes taking five wickets. In reply Oxford made 196, Spencer making seven before being lbw to Archibald John Burgess Fowler. In reply Middlesex made 167. Oxford fought back making 218, Spencer making four before being lbw to the England test cricketer Greville Stevens. Middlesex won by 117 runs.

Despite making three appearances for Oxford, Spencer was never awarded his Blue.

He made his final first-class appearance for Glamorgan against H.D.G. Leveson-Gower's XI at St Helen's, Swansea on 1 August 1925. Glamorgan won the toss and elected to bat making 214, Spencer being caught by the England test cricketer John William Hitch off the bowling of Harold Lawrence Hever for zero. In reply H.D.G. Leveson-Gower's XI made 141, Spencer stumping Archibald Fowler off the bowling of Francis Peter Ryan for four.

Ryan took six wickets during the innings. During Glamorgan's second innings they made 193 before running out of time. The match was drawn.

On leaving Oxford Spencer became a teacher at Stowe. During the war Spencer took a commission into the Royal Marines rising to the rank of captain. Captain Spencer died on 29 September 1941. His body was discovered on a footpath in Park Road South, Havant. His service revolver was found by his body and it was found that he had committed suicide. The local papers covered the story.

Portsmouth Evening News – Tuesday, 30 September 1941

Shot Officer: Inquest Fixed. Captain Charles Spencer, Royal Marines, who was found shot on the footpath in Park Road South, Havant, about daybreak yesterday, was 38 and unmarried. On Sunday night he had supper at a local hotel and chatted with one of his fellow officers. He left the hotel about nine o'clock to catch a bus, which would have taken him to his destination within half an hour. His body was still warm when found. A Service revolver was close by. An inquest will be held by the South Hants Coroner to-morrow afternoon.

Portsmouth Evening News – Wednesday, 1 October 1941

OFFICER'S SUICIDE. Verdict 'Suicide while balance of mind disturbed' was returned at Havant inquest this afternoon on Capt. Charles Richard Spencer (38), single, who was found shot in Park Road South, Havant, Monday.

He was later buried in Haslar Royal Naval Cemetery, grave reference G. 9. 16.

Batting and fielding averages

	Mat	Inns	NO	Runs	HS	Ave	100	50	Ct	St
First-class	4	6	2	46	17	11.50	0	0	1	1

Bowling averages

	Mat	Balls	Runs	Wkts	BBI	BBM	Ave	Econ	SR	4w	5w	10
First-class	4	-	-	-	-	-	-	-	-	-	-	-

Pilot Officer Kenneth Farnes
England, Cambridge, Essex
Fifteen tests, 168 first-class matches
RAF Volunteer Reserve
Died 20 October 1941, aged 30
Right-hand bat/Right arm fast

'more striking perhaps than any other characteristic
about him was his love of life'

Kenneth Farnes was born on 8 July 1911 at Leytonstone, Essex. He was the second son of Sidney Heath Farnes and Florence Susanna Georgiana. He was educated at the Royal Liberty School in Gidea Park, London. Farnes' father was a prominent cricketer in his own right. While at school he captained the first XI and his talent was developed by the school's headmaster, Mr S.B. Hartley. Whilst playing for Gidea Park he bowled against Mr P. Perrin, a test selector and former Essex player. Perrin was so impressed by Farnes' bowling that he brought him to the notice of the county authorities. As a result at the tender age of 19 Farnes made his debut first-class appearance in the county championship for Essex against Gloucestershire. He was to go on to make 168 first-class appearances, seventy-seven of them in the county championship.

The match was played on 29 June 1930 at the County Ground, Chelmsford. Essex won the toss and decided to bat making 195, Farnes making eight before being bowled by the England test cricketer Thomas Goddard (*Wisden* cricketer of the year 1938), the England test cricketer Charles Parker taking five wickets during the innings. In reply Gloucestershire made 236. Farnes bowled eleven overs, failing to take a wicket for 60. In their second innings Essex made 186, Farnes making one before being bowled by Parker once again, Goddard taking five wickets and Parker a further four during the innings. In their second innings Gloucestershire made 146. Farnes bowled four overs for 16 and failed to take a wicket. He continued to play for Essex and against Kent took five wickets for 35 in one innings.

Farnes went up to Cambridge University and made his debut for Cambridge against Yorkshire in a university match played at F.P. Fenner's on 13 May 1931. Cambridge won the toss and decided to bat making 179. Farnes made a duck before being bowled by Emmott Robinson. The England test cricketer Hedley Verity (who was also to die in the Second World War, 31 July 1943) took five wickets during the innings. In reply Yorkshire made 376, the England test cricketer Herbert Sutcliffe making 173 not out batting throughout the innings. Farnes bowled 24 overs taking one wicket for 88 runs, the England test cricketer Morris Leyland lbw for 41. In their second innings Cambridge made 93, Farnes failed to bat. The match was drawn.

Farnes now began playing for both Essex (out of term) and Cambridge (in term). In his final year at Cambridge, 1933, he took 41 wickets for the university at a bowling average of 17.39 runs.

On leaving Cambridge with honours in the historical and geographical triposes he took up a teaching position at Worksop College, becoming housemaster of Pelham in 1934 and remaining at the college until 1940 when he was commissioned into the RAF. While teaching at the college he continued to play cricket for Essex. His form remained strong and he was called up for the first test against Australia, played at Trent Bridge, Nottingham on 8 June 1934. Australia won the toss and decided to bat making 374. Farnes bowled 40 overs taking five wickets for 102, including Arthur Gordon Chipperfield, caught Leslie Ames for 99, one short of his century. In reply England made 268, Farnes bowling Clarence Grimmett (who also took five wickets during the innings) for one. In their second innings Australia made 273, Farnes bowling 25 overs and taking a further five wickets for 77. In reply England made 141, Farnes being caught by Albert Oldfield off the bowling of William O'Reilly for a duck. Australia won by 238 runs.

Farnes was selected for the second test against Australia. This time despite England taking the test by an innings and 38 runs, Farnes was not so successful, bowling 16 overs and failing to take a wicket. Due to injury he wasn't selected for the next two tests against Australia. Farnes played in fifteen tests altogether, against Australia, West Indies and South Africa.

Farnes was a tall man, standing 6 foot 5 in his stockinged feet, and superbly fit. As a bowler he achieved considerable pace from a short run-up, and sharp lift from a good length. His height also made him a dangerous fielder, able to take difficult catches at slip. Although his batting was poor and he was a confirmed tail-ender, he achieved a first-class score of 97 not out against Somerset at Taunton in 1936, just missing out on his maiden century.

In 1939 he was made *Wisden* cricketer of the year and in 1940 published his autobiography, *Tours and Tests*.

Farnes made his final first-class appearance for Essex against Northamptonshire on 26 August 1939 at the Vista Road Recreation Ground, Clacton-on-Sea. Essex won the toss and decided to bat making 206. Farnes made two before being stumped by the New Zealand test cricketer Kenneth James off the bowling of Eric James Herbert. In reply Northampton made 173, Farnes bowling 17 overs for 79 and taking two wickets, Robert Nelson, caught Reginald Minshall Taylor for 29, and Bill Merritt, caught Alfred Victor Avery for three. In their second innings Essex made 304, Farnes failing to bat. In their second innings Northamptonshire made 127, Farnes taking six wickets for 47. It was a glorious and fitting final innings for him.

During his career he made fifteen test appearances scoring 58 runs, his highest score being 20. He also bowled 3,932 balls and took 60 wickets for 1,719 runs, including taking five wickets on three occasions and on one occasion taking ten wickets. His best figures were six for 96. He also made one catch. In first-class cricket he scored 1,182 runs, his highest score being 97. He also bowled 32,327 balls, taking 690 wickets for 14,805 runs. He took five wickets in an innings on forty-four occasions and eight wickets in an innings once. He made eighty-four catches.

During the Second World War he joined the RAF Volunteer Reserve, training as a pilot in Canada. He was commissioned from sergeant to pilot officer on 1 September 1941. He was killed in a tragic accident not long after returning from Canada during a night flight near Chipping Warden in Oxfordshire on 20 October 1941.

He is buried in Brookwood Military Cemetery, grave reference 21. A. 11. Worth a visit and a few flowers if you're passing.

In 1941 the college paper *The Worksopian* published the following tribute to one of their finest old boys:

Kenneth Farnes

It is with the feeling of deeply personal loss that we record the death in action with the RAF of Pilot-Officer Kenneth Farnes. He went up to Cambridge University in 1930 and besides gaining Blues for cricket and putting the weight, took sound honours in the historical and Geographical Triposes. Appointed to Worksop College in 1933, he became Housemaster of Pelham in 1934, staying with us until 1940, when he joined the RAF. This summer he won his 'wings' in Canada, passing out top of his group, and had only been back in England a few weeks when his tragic death occurred.

His cricketing career is too well-known to need more than a brief recapitulation here. He stood easily in the forefront of the fast-bowlers of his generation, not only because of his magnificent natural gifts but because of his determination. It was this determination that transformed him from the looselimbed, promising youngster we knew at Fenner's to the mature man with the classically perfect action we saw at Trent Bridge; which raised his fielding from mediocrity to excellence and which changed him from being a mere slogger into an able, hard-hitting batsman who made plenty of runs in the best of company. Despite his well-deserved success and popularity, he never became swollen headed; his innate modesty - almost shyness - prevented him from the usual fault of the outstanding athlete. Even in his own book on cricket, *Tours and Tests*, he tells us little of himself, nothing of the varied interests of his mind. And yet that mind was well-stocked with varied interests; he painted and sketched with much more than ordinary talent; his knowledge and appreciation of Art were sound and keen; his reading was wide, and his literary enthusiasms unusual, his chief love being the stylists, amongst whom he reverenced above all George Moore.

Yet, more striking perhaps than any other characteristic about him was his love of life, his enjoyment of fun, his quickness of response, his gusto. His House, the School, and most of all the Common Room, will be eternally poorer for the loss of him.

Batting and fielding averages

	Mat	Inns	NO	Runs	HS	Ave	100	50	6s	Ct	St
Tests	15	17	5	58	20	4.83	0	0	0	1	0
First-class	168	201	59	1182	97*	8.32	0	2		84	0

Bowling averages

	Mat	Inns	Balls	Runs	Wkts	BBI	BBM	Ave	Econ	SR	4w	5w	10
Tests	15	27	3932	1719	60	6/96	10/179	28.65	2.62	65.5	6	3	1
First-class	168		32397	14805	690	8/38		21.45	2.74	46.9		44	8

Flight Lieutenant Alec Percy Stanley Wills
Combined Services
One first-class appearance
RAF 243 Squadron (Pilot Instructor)
Died 7 November 1941, aged 30
Right-hand bat

'An accident took a fine life'

Alec Wills was born on 11 March 1911 at Guykit, Trincomalee, Ceylon. He was educated at Haileybury where he was quickly in the first XI. On leaving school he was commissioned into the RAF as a pilot officer being promoted to flight lieutenant on 29 August 1933.

On 17 August 1936 Wills was selected to play for the RAF against the Navy at Lord's. It was a non-first-class match. The Royal Navy won the toss and decided to bat making 320. Wills bowled 19 overs taking six wickets for 71. In reply the RAF made 94, Wills making 14 not out. Forced to follow on, the RAF made 196, Wills making the top score of 59 before being bowled by Robert Stephenson. The Royal Nay won by an innings and 30 runs.

On 30 July 1937 Wills represented the RAF once again, this time against the Army at the RAF Cricket Ground, Aylesbury (again a non-first-class match). The match was eventually drawn, with Wills doing great execution with the ball taking five wickets for 60 off 28 overs during the first innings. He also made nine runs before being bowled by Godfrey James Bryan in the first innings and failed to bat in the second. The match was drawn.

He next represented the RAF against the Royal Navy, once again a non-first-class match. The RAF won the toss and elected to bat making 220, Wills making three before being caught by Charles Justly Probyn Pearson off the bowling of Richard Peter Borgnis. In reply the Royal Navy made 197. Wills took three wickets off 18 overs for 36 runs. In their second innings the RAF made 183, Wills making seven before being bowled by John Archie Coachafer. In reply the Royal Navy made 149, Wills taking four wickets from 15 overs for 43. The RAF took the match by 57 runs.

Wills made one first-class appearance, for the Combined Services against New Zealand. The match took place on 18 August 1937 at the United Services Ground, Portsmouth. The Combined Services won the toss and decided to bat making 180, Wills zero not out, Richard Borgnis making 101. In reply New Zealand made 189. Wills bowled two overs and took no wicket for 13. In their second innings the Combined Services made 148, Wills made three not out. In their second innings New Zealand made 140, taking the match by nine wickets.

Still serving with the RAF at the outbreak of the war he was posted to Malaya as a pilot instructor with 243 Squadron. He was killed in an accident on 7 November 1941 while flying a Tiger Moth when it was struck from behind at Kallang by a landing Buffalo of 243 Squadron flown by Sergeant C.F. Powell.

He was buried in Kranji War Cemetery, grave reference 37. D. 7.

Kranji War Cemetery, Singapore.

Batting and fielding averages

	Mat	Inns	NO	Runs	HS	Ave	100	50	4s	6s	Ct	St
First-class	1	2	2	3	3*	-	0	0	0	0	0	0

Bowling averages

	Mat	Balls	Runs	Wkts	BBI	BBM	Ave	Econ	SR	4w	5w	10
First-class	1	48	36	0	-	-	-	4.50	-	0	0	0

Sergeant 48080 Christiaan Frederick Beyers Papenfus
Orange Free State
Five first-class appearances
21 Squadron South African Air Force
Died 18 November 1941, aged 25

'Died during his duty to the end'

Christiaan Papenfus was born on 10 December 1915 in Barberton, Transvaal. He made five first-class appearances, all for the Orange Free State, between December 1936 and February 1940.

He made his first-class debut for the Orange Free State in the Currie Cup against Natal on 16 December 1936 at the Ramblers Cricket Club Ground, Bloemfontein. The Orange Free State won the toss and decided to bat making 235, Papenfus batting in the lower orders making two not out. The Natal bowler Leslie William Payn took eight wickets during the innings for 89 and the Orange Free State opener Cecil James Kaplan made 111. In reply Natal made 337, with Desmond Robert Fell making 106. Papenfus bowled twelve overs taking two wickets for 46, Noel Vivian Bellville lbw for six, and Fell, caught Alan Richard Newton for 106. In their second innings the Orange Free State made 320, Murray Godfrey Francis making 117 and Papenfus twelve not out. In their second innings Natal made 128. Papenfus bowled four overs taking no wickets for 21. The match was eventually drawn.

Papenfus's next first-class match for the Orange Free State was also against Natal, played on the 19 December 1939, again at the Ramblers Ground, this time Natal taking the honours by seven wickets, Papenfus making three runs and taking four wickets. He next turned out against Border on 26 December 1939 this time at the South African Railways Club Old Ground, Bloemfontein. Despite Papenfus taking eight wickets, five in Border's first innings (he also made two runs), Border won by 191 runs.

His next match was against Eastern Province on 30 December 1939 at St George's Park, Port Elizabeth. Papenfus took three wickets and made a single run, Orange Free State taking the match by 226 runs.

Papenfus made his final first-class appearance against North Eastern Transvaal on 2 February 1940 at Berea Park, Pretoria. North Eastern Transvaal won the toss and elected to bat making 219. Papenfus bowled 24 overs taking six wickets for 88. In reply the Orange Free State made 173, Papenfus making one before he was bowled by William Andrew Henderson. In their second innings North Eastern Transvaal made 329, Papenfus bowling 22 overs and taking two wickets for 89. He also caught Robert Carey Hicks off the bowling of Geoffrey Frank Kennedy Jackson for 47. In their second innings the Orange Free State made 292 Papenfus making his best ever first-class score of 60 before being caught by Arnoldus Christiaan Vlok off the bowling of Lennox Sydney Brown. Lindsay Thomas Delville Tuckett made 101. Despite Papenfus's and Tuckett's best efforts North Eastern Transvaal won by 83.

During the war Papenfus joined 21 Squadron South African Air Force serving as a sergeant and flying as crew in Maryland medium bombers. 21 Squadron was formed in

Knightsbridge War Cemetery, Acroma, Libya.

Nakuru Kenya on 8 May 1941. The squadron began operations on 24 September 1941. Its brief was to attack Axis bases and airfields. During this period it lost two aircraft in a collision on 30 October and two were shot down by Italian fighters early in November. One of these was shot down on 18 November and was the bomber Papenfus was flying in. The entire crew was killed.

He is buried in Knightsbridge War Cemetery, Acroma, collective grave 8, G. 5.

Batting and fielding averages

	Mat	Inns	NO	Runs	HS	Ave	100	50	Ct	St
First-class	5	9	3	81	60	13.50	0	1	3	0

Bowling averages

	Mat	Runs	Wkts	BBI	Ave	5w	10
First-class	5	497	25	6/88	19.88	2	0

Major Geoffrey Martin Warren
Roshanara Club
One first-class appearance
6th Royal Tank Regiment RAC
Died 21 November 1941, aged 33
Wicketkeeper

'Died while Prisoner of War'

Geoffrey Warren was born on 3 March 1908 at Alresford, Hampshire. He was the son of Lieutenant Colonel Percy Bliss Warren, Indian Army, and Margaret Ellen (née Martin). He was educated at Wellington. Deciding on a career in the army he went to Sandhurst, being commissioned into the Royal Tank Corps in 1928. Posted to India in 1930 he served there until 1935. Always a keen cricketer he was secretary of Ironsides Cricket at the outbreak of war.

He made one first-class appearance for the Roshanara Club against the Viceroy's XI, played on 6 February 1933 at the Roshanara Club Ground, Delhi. The Viceroy's XI won the toss and elected to bat making 264. Warren playing as wicketkeeper caught Thomas Longfield off the bowling of Shahabuddin for 53. Shahabuddin took five wickets during the innings. In reply the Roshanara Club made 140, Warren batting last making one not out. In their second innings the Viceroy's XI made 276, Warren stumping Wilfred William Hill Hill-Wood off the bowling of the Indian test cricketer, Cottari Subbanna Nayudu for 56. Opening the batting in the Roshanara Club's second innings, Warren made three before being bowled by Eustace Howard Hill. The Viceroy's XI won by 215 runs.

Warren later married Margaret Rosemary of Walton, Somerset.

Returning to England, he became an instructor at Lulworth from 1937 to 1940. In November 1940 he was sent to the Middle East as a squadron commander. During the spring of 1941 he served in Greece as second in command of the 6th Battalion Royal Tank Corps. He took part in the advance into Libya in the November and was fatally wounded at Sidi Rezegh, dying on 21 November 1941 in enemy hands.

He is buried in the Knightsbridge War Cemetery, Acroma, grave reference 1. D. 19. There is a photograph of him in the Wellington school roll of honour 1939-45.

Batting and fielding averages

	Mat	Inns	NO	Runs	HS	Ave	100	50	Ct	St
First-class	1	2	1	4	3	4.00	0	0	1	1

Bowling averages

	Mat	Balls	Runs	Wkts	BBI	BBM	Ave	Econ	SR	4w	5w	10
First-class	1	-	-	-	-	-	-	-	-	-	-	-

Major John Devitt Elrick Gartly
Transvaal
Three first-class appearances
3rd Battalion Transvaal Scottish, SA Forces
Died 22 November 1941, aged 33
Wicketkeeper

'A brave son of country'

John Gartly was born on 8 January 1908 in Johannesburg, the son of William and Elizabeth. He was educated at King Edward VII School, Johannesburg.

He played in three first-class matches between March and December 1932, his debut being on 26 March 1932 at Newlands, Cape Town for Transvaal against Western Province. Transvaal won the toss and elected to bat making 217,

Gartly making two before being caught by the South African test cricketer Gerald Edward Bond off the bowling of Alfred Samuel Bensimon. In reply Western Province made 391, the South African test player Arthur William 'Dave' Nourse making an impressive 160 not out. In their second innings Transvaal made 295, Gartly making nine before being caught by Frank Clarke Martin off the bowling of Bensimon. The South African test player Fred Susskind made 110. In reply Western Province made 122, taking the match by six wickets. Gartly stumped the South African test player and Western Province opener Stanley Keppel Coen off the bowling of Hilton Robert Vivian Hoar for 33.

He next represented Transvaal against Western Province again, this time on the 24 December 1932 at Newlands. Western Province won the toss and decided to bat making 246. In reply Transvaal made 90, Gartly lbw to the South African test cricketer Robert James Crisp for nine, Crisp taking five wickets for twenty-five during the innings. In their second innings Western Province made 220, Lennox Brown taking five wickets for 67. In reply Transvaal made 377. Gartly failed to bat but the South African test cricketer Sydney Harry Curnow batted throughout the innings making 192 not out. Transvaal won by six wickets.

Gartly made his final first-class appearance for Transvaal against Natal on 29 December 1932 at Green Point, Cape Town. Natal won the toss and decided to field. Transvaal made 307, Gartly making ten before being caught by Ivan Julian Siedle off the bowling of Richard Davies. The two Transvaal openers did a little better, Curnow making 105 and another South African test cricketer, Eric Alfred Burchell Rowan, making 103. The Natal bowler Richard Davies took five wickets during the innings. In reply Natal made 143, the Transvaal bowler Lewis Henry Clayton taking five wickets. In their second innings Transvaal made 177, Gartly made eight not out. Transvaal declared. In reply Natal dug in and made 149. The match was drawn.

During the war, Gartly served with the 3rd Battalion Transvaal Scottish rising to the rank of major. Third Transvaal Scottish took part in the East African campaign in Ethiopia, in particular the three-day attack on Mega. After this the battalion was sent to Egypt to take part in Operation Crusader where it suffered heavy losses at the battle of Sidi Rezegh in November 1941. One of these casualties was Major John Devitt Elrick Gartly who died of wounds on 22 November 1941.

He is buried in Knightsbridge War Cemetery, Acroma. Grave reference 5. D. 18.

His brother Captain D.C. Gartly died on 20 April 1945 serving with the South African Engineering Corps, 5 Field Squadron.

Batting and fielding averages

	Mat	Inns	NO	Runs	HS	Ave	100	50	Ct	St
First-class	3	5	1	38	10	9.50	0	0	2	1

Bowling averages for nine

	Mat	Balls	Runs	Wkts	BBI	BBM	Ave	Econ	SR	4w	5w	10
First-class	3	-	-	-	-	-	-	-	-	-	-	-

221538 Private Geoffrey Charles Hart-Davis
Natal
Two first-class appearances
2nd Battalion Transvaal Scottish, SA Forces
Died 9 December 1941, aged 36
Wicketkeeper

'Killed by his own side'

Geoffrey Hart-Davis, better known to his friends as Jumbo, was born on 15 September 1905 (some records have 1907) at Alskeigh, Lidgetton, Natal. He was one of four sons, Walter, Jack and Philip, born to Sidney Davis and Catherine Raw.

Hart-Davis made two first-class appearances in 1927, his debut being for Natal against the MCC on 30 November 1927 at the City Oval, Pietermaritzburg during the MCC's tour of South Africa, which took place between 12 November 1927 and 18 February 1928. Natal won the toss and decided to bat making 171 runs, Hart-Davis making six before being caught by George Ernest Tyldesley off the bowling of Greville Stevens. In reply the MCC made 333, Tyldesley making 161. Hart-Davis took two wickets, catching Herbert Sutcliffe off the bowling of Francis John Smith for a duck and Greville Stevens off the bowling of Clifford Earl Tutton for 18. The match was drawn.

His second first-class appearance was again against the MCC, on 3 December 1927, this time at the Kingsmead, Durban. The MCC won the toss and decided to bat making 354 before declaring, Hart-Davis catching the MCC opener Percy Holmes off the bowling of Tutton for 42. In reply Natal made 192, Hart-Davis making two before being bowled by William Ewart Astill. Forced to follow on, Natal made 167, Hart-Davis failing to bat. Again the match was drawn.

At some point Hart-Davis married his long-time girlfriend Margaret Mary Bond. During the war he served with the 2nd Battalion, Transvaal Scottish, serving under the 6th South African Infantry Brigade of the 2nd South African Division. During the early part of the North African Campaign Hart-Davis was taken prisoner of war by the Germans. Taken to the cargo ship *Sebastiano Veniero* for shipment to Europe he was boarded with several thousand British and Dominion prisoners of war. During the journey the ship was attacked by the British Submarine HMS *Porpoise* a few miles south of the Peloponnese, badly damaging her. Despite the Germans managing to beach the ship at Methoni in Greece over 300 PoWs were killed, including the unfortunate Hart-Davis. HMS *Porpoise* was herself sunk later in the war with the loss of all hands.

Hart-Davis's body was later recovered and he was laid to rest at Halfaya Sollum War Cemetery, grave reference 14. F. 2.

Batting and fielding averages

	Mat	Inns	NO	Runs	HS	Ave	100	50	Ct	St
First-class	2	2	0	8	6	4.00	0	0	3	0

Bowling averages

	Mat	Balls	Runs	Wkts	BBI	BBM	Ave	Econ	SR	4w	5w	10
First-class	2	-	-	-	-	-	-	-	-	-	-	-

Private William Frederick Baldock
Somerset
Ten first-class appearances
2nd (Selangor) Battalion Federated Malay States Volunteer
Force
Died 30 December 1941, aged 41
Right-handed bat

'Murdered by the Japanese'

William Baldock was born on 1 August 1900 at Wellesley Park, Wellington, Somerset. He was the son of Colonel W. S. Baldock and Mary (née Elworthy). He was educated at Twyford and Winchester, as was his father (1861) and his brothers, Frank (1915-20) and Thomas Arthur (1917-22). A good all round athlete he was soon in the school XI, being a contemporary with D.R. Jardine and C.T. Ashton. He was also in his house's winning team for Chawker Pot. He went up to Oriel Oxford in 1919 and was tried in the freshmen's match of 1920, but never played in a university side. He obtained a diploma in forestry in 1921 before obtaining his degree in 1922. Although he failed to win his blue he did begin to play first-class cricket for Somerset, going on to make ten first-class appearances for them.

His father had played first-class cricket for Hampshire and his grandfather played eight first-class matches for the Gentlemen of Kent. His link with Somerset came from his father-in-law John Daniell, who played 304 first-class matches, mostly for Somerset as their captain.

Baldock made his first-class debut for Somerset against Oxford University at the University Parks in a university match on 2 June 1920. Somerset won the toss and decided to bat making 148. Baldock was lbw by the Oxford bowler Reginald Henshall Brindley Bettington for a duck. Bettington went on to take seven wickets for 47 off 16 overs during the innings. In reply Oxford made 185. In their second innings Somerset made 152, Baldock making five before being stumped by Frank Gilligan, again off the bowling of Bettington, who took a further five wickets for 42 off 23 overs. In their second innings Oxford made 116, Oxford taking the match by two wickets.

Baldock made his first county appearance for Somerset against Leicestershire on 16 July 1921 at the Bath Grounds, Ashby-de-la-Zouch. Somerset won the toss and elected to bat making 128, Baldock making 11 before being caught by Astill (Astill also taking five wickets during the innings) off the bowling of Frank Bale. In reply Leicestershire made 249. In their second innings Somerset made 97, Baldock being caught and bowled by Astill who took a further six wickets during the innings and reaching his 100th wicket in first-class cricket. Leicestershire took the match by an innings and 24 runs.

Baldock went on to play against Sussex, India in the British Isles, Lancashire, Surrey, Northamptonshire, Middlesex and Cambridge University. He made his final first-class appearance for Somerset against Surrey on 1 July 1936 at the County Ground, Taunton. Surrey won the toss and decided to bat making 196, the Somerset and England bowler Arthur Wellard taking five wickets. In reply Somerset made a very poor 38, Baldock being caught by Edward William John Brooks off the bowling of Edward Alfred Watts for zero. The match was drawn.

Although this was the end of Baldock's first-class career he went on to play several times for the Somerset Stragglers, as well as V.H. Northrop's XI and J.H.P. Brain's XI. During his first-class career Baldock made 238 runs, his highest score being 63 against the visiting Indians. He also made two catches.

He married Joan Clinton, daughter of John Daniell of Holway Farm House, Taunton, and they had one son, John, who was born on 21 April 1940. Alas William never got to meet his son.

In 1922 Baldock was appointed by the Colonial Office to a post in the Forestry Service and was sent out to Tanganyika. He remained there for seventeen years, taking holidays in England when he took the opportunity to turn out for Somerset. In 1939 he was transferred to Malaya as a conservator of forests. In 1940 he enlisted into the ranks of the 2nd Battalion Malaya Volunteer Defence Force. When the Japanese attacked, on 16 December 1941, Baldock acted as intelligence officer to 29 Brigade. He was captured by the Japanese and on 30 December 1941, in the Jabor Valley, Terengganu, was murdered by them. His body was never recovered and he is commemorated on column 391 of the Singapore Memorial. He is also commemorated in the War Cloister at Winchester College, inner D 2, and Oriel College Oxford. His son John also went to Winchester (house E 1953-58).

Batting and fielding averages

	Mat	Inns	NO	Runs	HS	Ave	100	50	Ct	St
First-class	10	16	2	238	63*	17.00	0	1	2	0

Bowling averages

	Mat	Balls	Runs	Wkts	BBI	BBM	Ave	Econ	SR	4w	5w	10
First-class	10	-	-	-	-	-	-	-	-	-	-	-

1942

41419 Major Vivian Alexander Chiodetti
Hyderabad (India)
One first-class appearance
2nd Battalion Manchester Regiment attached
3rd Burma Rifles
Died 17 January 1942, aged 38

Rangoon Memorial, Burma.

'The only Indian first-class cricketer to have
been killed while serving in the armed forces'

Vivian Chiodetti was born on 31 May 1905 in Rawalpindi. He was educated at the Bishop Cotton School, Shimla (it is one of the oldest boarding schools for boys in Asia, having been founded on 28 July 1859, by Bishop George Cotton). On leaving school in 1925 he enlisted into the British Army and was commissioned into the Manchester Regiment in 1928.

There is a piece in a local paper from 1 October 1936 regarding Chiodetti. When the London, Midland and Scottish Railway Company decided to name a locomotive of the Royal Scot Class *The Manchester Regiment*, the naming ceremony took place at Victoria Station, Manchester, and a guard of honour was provided by the depot under the command of Lieutenant V.A. Chiodetti.

While he was on leave in December 1931 he made his one and only first-class appearance, in the semi-final of the Moin-ud-Dowlah Gold Cup, playing for Hyderabad against the Aligarh Muslim University, Past and Present. The match took place between 4 and 6 December 1931 at the Gymkhana Ground, Secunderabad. Aligarh won the toss and elected to bat making 274. In reply Hyderabad made 176, Chiodetti making 15 before being bowled by Habibullah. In their second innings Aligarh made 263. In reply Hyderabad made 311, Chiodetti making the highest score of the innings with 73 before falling lbw to Abdus Salaam. Aligarh took the match by 50 runs.

In September 1938 he was posted to the Burma Defence Force with the 3rd Burma Rifles with the rank of acting major. He was killed as he led C Company of the 3rd Battalion into action immediately after reaching Tavoy by ship at 1800 hours on 17 January 1942.

He has no known grave and is commemorated on the Rangoon Memorial to the Missing, Burma face 17. The museum at Lord's tells the Chiodetti story.

Batting and fielding averages

	Mat	Inns	NO	Runs	HS	Ave	100	50	Ct	St
First-class	1	2	0	88	73	44.00	0	1	0	0

Bowling averages

	Mat	Balls	Runs	Wkts	BBI	BBM	Ave	Econ	SR	4w	5w	10
First-class	1	-	-	-	-	-	-	-	-	-	-	-

Captain Richard Geoffrey Tindall
Oxford University
Eighteen first-class appearances
2nd Battalion King's Royal Rifle Corps
Died 22 January 1942, aged 29
Right-hand bat/Right arm fast

'no mourning'

Richard Tindall was born on 20 February 1912 at Sherborne, Dorset. He was the eldest son of Kenneth Bassett, headmaster of West Downs School, Winchester, from 1922, and Theodora Mary, daughter of the Reverend William James Boys. They resided in Winchester. He was educated at Hawtreys, Westgate-on-Sea, before going up to Winchester into Mr Robinson's House. A fine athlete he was in the first XI playing against Charterhouse (draw), Harrow (lost by three wickets), Marlborough (draw) and Eton (lost by seven wickets, Tindall being their top scorer in both innings with 68 and 55). He also played full back for 2nd XI soccer, rowed in the Challenge IVs and got his fives colours, as well as being head of house.

On leaving Winchester in 1930 he went up to Trinity Oxford and while there made eighteen first-class appearances for his university between May 1933 and July 1934. He made his debut on 3 May 1933 against Yorkshire at the University Parks. Oxford won the toss and decided to bat making 277. Tindall made seven before being lbw to Arthur Cecil Rhodes. Joseph Stanley Douglas took six wickets during the innings. The weather closed in and Yorkshire failed to bat. The match was drawn.

Tindall went on to play against Gloucestershire, West Indians in England, Worcestershire, Lancashire, Leicestershire, Free Foresters, Sussex, Surrey, H.D.G. Leveson-Gower's XI, MCC, Cambridge University and Australia in the British Isles. He made his final first-class appearance on 9 July 1934 against Cambridge at Lord's. Oxford won the toss and decided to bat making an impressive 415, the England test cricketer David Charles Humphery Townsend making 193 and Gerald Chalk 108. Tindall made 27 before being caught by John Hanbury Human off the bowling of James William Travis Grimshaw. Jack Gale Wilmot Davies took five wickets during the innings for 43 off 14 overs. In reply Cambridge also made an impressive score, 400, Anthony William Allen making 115. Tindall bowled 29 overs taking two wickets for 90. He caught and bowled Hugh Bartlett for 12 and Adam Gordon Powell for 11. Oxford made 182 in their second innings, Tindall lbw to Jack Davies for 15. In their second innings Cambridge University made 94. The match was drawn.

During his first-class career Tindall scored 610 runs, his highest score being 113. He also made two fifties. He bowled 3,020 balls taking 50 wickets for 1,581 runs, his best figures being five for 73. He also made 11 catches. He played forty-nine minor county matches for Dorset between 1931 and 1939 as well as turning out regularly for Old Wykehamists, helping them to win the Dunn Cup. He also played golf well and won a blue for soccer in 1934 playing at fullback in the Oxford team which beat Cambridge 3-0 at Stamford Bridge. He gained a third in classical moderations and modern greats.

On leaving Oxford in 1934, he joined the staff at Eton College, as a sports coach. He was also a captain in the Eton OTC. During the war Tindall was commissioned into the King's Royal Rifle Corps, becoming a captain in April 1940. On 23 September 1941 Tindall left with the rest of the 1st Armoured Division for North Africa. On 27 December the battalion was posted to Libya. Tindall was by now second-in-command of D Company. By 6 January 1942, after driving for over 700 miles, the battalion had reached the front line near Antelat, forty miles north-east of Agedabia and were in action immediately. On 21 January the Germans attacked. With few anti-tank guns to stop them and with little air support the British were forced to retreat.

Tindall was killed during a German air raid at Agedabia on 22 January 1942. His body was never recovered or identified and he is commemorated on the Alamein Memorial, column 65.

A memorial service for Tindall was held in Eton College Chapel on Friday, 6 March 1942, at 1515. The notice in *The Times* stated, 'no mourning'. He is also commemorated at Winchester College War Cloister, inner E2, and the Trinity College Oxford Memorial.

He was the brother of Mark Tindall who also served with the KRRC was killed in a training accident in August 1942.

Batting and fielding averages

	Mat	Inns	NO	Runs	HS	Ave	100	50	Ct	St
First-class	18	30	3	610	113	22.59	1	2	11	0

Bowling averages

	Mat	Balls	Runs	Wkts	BBI	Ave	Econ	SR	5w	10
First-class	18	3020	1581	50	5/73	31.62	3.14	60.4	2	0

Flight Lieutenant David Frank Walker
Oxford University, MCC, Sir P.F. Warner's XI
Thirty-Seven first-class appearances
608 Squadron RAF Volunteer Reserve
Died 7 February 1942, aged 28
Right-hand bat/Slow left arm orthodox

'An athlete and a gentleman'

David Walker was born on 31 May 1913 in Loddon, Norfolk. He was the son of Reginald Hope and Kathleen Walker, also of Loddon. He was educated at Uppingham where he was quickly in the XI playing against Rugby, Haileybury, Repton, Brasenose College Oxford, Oundle, Shrewsbury, and topping the batting averages in his three seasons with his school (1930-32). Only one match was lost when he was captain in his last two years. He also turned out for Norfolk in the Minor Counties. Walker played for Norfolk for nine seasons, finally hanging up his bat in August 1939, making his final appearance against Durham. During this time he scored 4,034 runs at an average of 62. He also topped the county averages on no less than seven occasions and on three occasions headed the minor counties competition. His highest score came in 1939 when he made an innings of 217 against Northumberland. He shared in a Minor Counties record first-wicket partnership of 323 with Harold Theobald (1896-1982). He was the most successful batsman ever to play for Norfolk.

Between May 1933 and September 1938 Walker made thirty-seven first-class appearances for Oxford University (captain 1935), the MCC and Sir P.F. Warner's XI. On leaving school he went up to Brasenose Oxford and was soon playing for the University XI. He made his first-class debut for Oxford University against Yorkshire on 3 May 1933 at the University Parks. Oxford won the toss and decided to bat making 277. Walker, opening for Oxford, made 67 before being caught by the England test cricketer George Macaulay (died 13 December 1940) off the bowling of Stanley Douglas, Douglas taking six wickets during the innings for 59 runs. Due to the weather Yorkshire failed to bat. The match was drawn.

Walker went on to play for Oxford against Gloucestershire, West Indies in England, Minor Counties, Lancashire, Leicestershire, Sussex, Surrey, H.D.G. Leveson-Gower's XI, MCC, Cambridge University, Worcestershire, Australia in the British Isles, Free Foresters and South Africa in the British Isles.

Walker made his final appearance for Oxford against the old enemy Cambridge on 8 July 1935 at Lord's. Cambridge University won the toss and elected to bat making 302. In reply Oxford made 221. Walker opening for Oxford made fifteen before being caught by James Grimshaw off the bowling of the Indian test cricketer Mohammad Jahangir Khan. The West Indies test cricketer John Cameron took seven wickets for 73 off 25 overs. During their second innings Cambridge made 223, Antony Ronald Legard taking seven wickets for 36 off 25 overs. Oxford made 109 during their second innings, Walker making four before being caught by the England test cricketer Billy Griffith off the bowling of Jahangir Khan. Cambridge took the match by 195 runs. A first-class sportsman he also won his blue for hockey.

He went on to make two first-class appearances for the MCC, against Yorkshire (Yorkshire won by eight wickets) and Kent (Kent won by five wickets), both matches played in 1936.

He made his final first-class appearance for Sir P.F. Warner's XI against England Past and Present on 7 September 1938 at the Cheriton Road Sports Ground, Folkestone. Warner's XI won the toss and decided to field. England Past and Present made 256, Alfred Vardy Pope taking six wickets for 70 off 23 overs. In reply Warner's XI made 173, Walker making 23 before being caught by Wally Hammond off the bowling of Douglas Vivian Parson Wright. Wright took six wickets during the innings for 72 runs off 21 overs. In their second innings England Past and Present made 329. In their second innings Warner's XI made 39 without losing a wicket before they ran out of time. The match was drawn.

During his first-class career Walker made 1,880 runs, his highest score being 118 against Worcestershire. He also made 107 against Gloucestershire and twelve scores over fifty. He bowled 427 balls taking six wickets for 299 runs, his best figures being two for 36, and he took 18 catches.

On leaving Oxford he was appointed cricket master at Harrow, which he left in September 1939 for an educational post under the Sudan Government. He joined the RAF, becoming a sergeant before being commissioned as a pilot officer on probation on 9 July 1938. He trained as a pilot in Rhodesia before returning to England in August 1941 and joining 608 Squadron flying Lockheed Hudsons. Walker's Hudson, AM876, took off from Wick at 1133 hrs on 6 February 1942 for an operational flight to attack German shipping. His crew consisted of Sergeant Douglas Bennett, Sergeant Thomas Birtwhistle and Pilot Officer John Watterson Kelly. During this operation the Hudson was damaged by anti-aircraft fire, crashing or ditching into a Norwegian fjord. Local fisherman reached the crash site quickly and appear to have rescued Walker alive as Walker is listed as dying the following day. Only three months before, he had married Monica Walker of Gorleston, Great Yarmouth, Norfolk.

Walker is buried in Trondheim (Stavne) Cemetery, grave reference A IV British. K. 6. His fellow crew member Douglas Bennett, whose body was recovered, is buried in the same cemetery. The bodies of the other two crew, Birtwhistle and Kelly, were never recovered and are commemorated on the Runnymede Memorial.

Batting and fielding averages

	Mat	Inns	NO	Runs	HS	Ave	100	Ct	St
First-class	37	66	2	1880	118	29.37	2	18	0

Bowling averages

	Mat	Balls	Runs	Wkts	BBI	Ave	Econ	SR	5w	10
First-class	37	427	299	6	2/36	49.83	4.20	71.1	0	0

Pilot Officer Frank Leslie Oliver Thorn
Victoria
Seven first-class matches
23 Squadron Royal Australian Air Force
Died 11 February 1942, aged 29
Right-handed bat/Right arm medium

His plane and remains were found sixty-six years later

Frank Thorn was born on 16 August 1912 at St Arnaud, Victoria, Australia, one of five sons born to James Alfred and Beatrice Thorn. Frank was brought up in Thornbury, a suburb of Melbourne. On leaving school he worked for the Black and White Whisky company. A decent cricketer he played club cricket for Northcote. He must have impressed because he went on to make seven first-class appearances for Victoria between 1937 and 1939.

He made his debut first-class appearance for Victoria against Western Australia on 29 November 1937 at the Melbourne Cricket Ground. Western Australia won the toss and decided to bat making 137. Thorn bowled 11 overs taking one wicket for 32. In reply Victoria made 207. Thorn batting in the lower orders made three before being run out bowled Anthony Zimbulis. Zimbulis took five wickets during the innings for 80. In their second innings Western Australia made 265, John Adrian Shea making 110. Thorn bowled a further 11 overs taking one wicket for 44. In their second innings Victoria made 198 for five. Thorn failed to bat. Victoria won by five wickets.

Thorn made his next appearance against South Australia three months later on 4 February 1938 at the Adelaide Oval in the Sheffield Shield. Thorn took three wickets and made no runs. South Australia won by 125.

It was a further ten months before Thorn made his third appearance, this time against Tasmania on 26 December 1938 at the North Tasmanian Cricket Association Ground, Launceston. Thorn made zero in his only innings but did manage two wickets for 44. The Victoria player Percy Beames made 226 not out. The match was drawn.

He made his fourth first-class appearance against Tasmania a few days later on 30 December 1938, this time at the Tasmania Cricket Association Ground, Hobart. Thorn's bowling in this match was outstanding. He took ten wickets, five in the first innings and five in the second. He failed to bat. The Victoria batsman Hector Oakley made 162 and Beames made 169 not out. Victoria won by ten wickets.

His fifth match came against South Australia on 24 February 1939 at the Adelaide Oval in the Sheffield Shield. Thorn made three runs and took two wickets. The Victoria batsman Lindsay Hassett (*Wisden* cricketer of the year 1949, MBE 1953 for services to cricket) made 102. The match was drawn.

His next match was against Western Australia on 4 March 1939 at the Western Australia Cricket Association Ground, Perth. Thorn made one and eleven not out. He also took one wicket for eighty-four. Hassett made 103. The match was drawn.

Thorn made his final first-class appearance against Western Australia on 9 March 1939 again in Perth. Western Australian won the toss and decided to bat making 257. Thorn bowled 20 overs taking three wickets for 68, Arthur Edwin Read caught Bill Baker for 41, the Australian test cricketer Alexander Edward Owen Barras caught Leslie Fleetwood-Smith for 54, and Rowland Leslie Mills caught Baker for three. In reply Victoria made 226, Thorn making 30 before being caught and bowled by Charlie Macgill. Frank Sides (died 25 August 1943) made 121. In their second innings Western Australia made 225. Thorn bowled 13 overs taking one wicket for 46. In reply Victoria made 78 for three. Thorn failed to bat. The match was drawn.

During his career Thorn made 48 runs his highest score being 30 against Western Australia. He bowled 1,377 balls taking 24 wickets for 644 runs, his best figures being five for 74, and he made one catch. Thorn also took part in 101 matches for Northcote in the Victoria Premier Cricket League. In 1941 he married Bertha Claire Macintosh. They weren't together long.

Frank Thorn joined the Royal Australian Air Force becoming a pilot officer. He was posted to 26 squadron and on 11 February 1942 took off from 7-Mile Drome near Port Moresby as part of a formation of three Hudsons. Thorn was flying in Lockheed Hudson A16-126 with Flight Officer G. Gibson, Sergeant A.E. Quail and Sergeant B.I. Coutie. They were detailed to attack two Japanese ships berthed in Gasmata Harbor, the *Kinryu Maru* and *Kozui Maru*. The squadron was intercepted over the target by four A5M4 Claudes of the Chitose Kōkutai that took off from Gasmata airfield. Frank's aircraft, together with Hudson A16-9, was shot down and later claimed by the Japanese pilot Satoshi Yoshino. It was seen crashing into a ridgeline and disappearing. Neither the crew nor the aircraft were recovered. Thorn is commemorated on the Rabaul Memorial, panel 35.

On 5 May 2008, sixty-six years after Frank Thorn's plane went down, it was finally discovered by accident by Mark Reichman, a missionary, and his son Jared on New Britain, Papua New Guinea. The bomber was found in several large parts with its cockpit upside down and buried in the mud. Bullet holes were found in the tail section. It is hoped that a specialist team will later return to the site and with luck recover the remains of Frank Thorn and his crew.

Frank's great nephew Russell Mark competes in shotgun events and has won two Olympic gold medals, one silver and one bronze.

Batting and fielding averages

	Mat	Inns	NO	Runs	HS	Ave	100	50	Ct	St
First-class	7	8	1	48	30	6.85	0	0	1	0

Bowling averages

	Mat	Runs	Wkts	BBI	Ave	5w	10
First-class	7	644	24	5/74	26.83	2	1

Major Anthony Owen Leo Burke
Europeans (India)
One first-class appearance
7 Gurkha Rifles
Died 17 February 1942, aged 45
Right-handed bat/Wicketkeeper

Fell holding the final bridge against the Japanese

Anthony Burke was born on 17 January 1897, the son of Peter Joseph and Mary Ellen Burke. Deciding on a career in the Army he first took a commission into the Royal Dublin Fusiliers before transferring to the 7th Gurkha Rifles and being promoted to major.

He made one first-class appearances for the Europeans (India) against the MCC at the Karachi Gymkhana Ground on 26 October 1926. The MCC won the toss and decided to bat making 377. In reply the Europeans made 151. Burke, opening for the Europeans, made seven (his only innings) before being caught by John Henry (Jack) Parsons off the bowling of Bob Wyatt. In their second innings the MCC made 139 for three. Burke stumped the MCC opener Peter Eckersley (killed 13 August 1940) off the bowling of Noel John Obelin Carbutt for 40. The match was drawn. During 1926 he also played for Quetta (in non-first-class matches) against the Parsees, The Rest, Europeans, Hindus, Muslims and Karachi.

Major Burke was killed in action on 17 February 1942 at Kyaikto, Burma, while serving with the 7th Gurkha Rifles. For his actions on this day he was mentioned in despatches. His body was never recovered or identified and he is commemorated on the Rangoon Memorial, face 67. He left a widow, Betty.

Batting and fielding averages

	Mat	Inns	NO	Runs	HS	Ave	100	50	Ct	St
First-class	1	1	0	7	7	7.00	0	0	0	1

Bowling averages

	Mat	Balls	Runs	Wkts	BBI	BBM	Ave	Econ	SR	4w	5w	10
First-class	1	-	-	-	-	-	-	-	-	-	-	-

Rangoon Memorial, Burma.

Lieutenant Colonel Gordon Calthrop Thorne DSO
Army
One first-class appearance
Royal Norfolk Regiment
2nd Battalion Cambridgeshire Regiment
Died 2/3 March 1942, aged 44
Right-handed bat

'standing on the open road in full view of the enemy block, smiling and
cracking jokes to cheer us on into battle, his helmet as usual forgotten'

Gordon Thorne was born on 3 March 1897 in Chelsea. He was the son of Frederick Gordon and Mabel. He was educated at Haileybury where he was soon in the first XI. He was also in their Rugby XV. Taking a commission into the Norfolk Regiment in 1916 and going to the Western Front he was seriously wounded and invalided home. He returned to France in 1918. Surviving the war, he was sent with his regiment to the North West Frontier of India, later in 1937 becoming commandant of the Ceylon Defense Force.

He made one first-class appearance for the Army against Oxford University on 28 May 1927 at the University Parks. Oxford won the toss and decided to field. The Army made 388, Thorne making 17 before being bowled by John Albert de Silva, Godfrey Bryan making an impressive 116. In reply Oxford made 328. Both Ronald Cecil Graham Joy and Harold Miles took five wickets. In their second innings the Army made 188, Thorne making seven before being bowled by the England test cricketer Errol Holmes. In reply, Oxford made 112 and the match was drawn.

Thorne also made six minor county matches for Norfolk, as well as playing for the Army against the Public Schools.

On leaving school Thorne joined the Army, being commissioned into the Norfolk Regiment and serving with them throughout war, being mentioned in despatches twice.

He married Pamela Meredyth and they had one son, Frederick, who was born on 18 July 1935. Colonel Thorne moved his family out of London in 1941 to keep them safe from the Blitz and they went to stay with relatives in America in 1941. After his death they remained in America. Pamela married again and died peacefully on 4 April 2001 aged 94. Frederick died in the USA on 13 August 2016.

Remaining in the army Gordon Thorne was eventually promoted to Lieutenant Colonel becoming the commanding officer of the 2nd Battalion the Cambridge Regiment. The battalion was sent to Singapore in early 1942 and reinforced the 15th Indian Brigade at Batu Pahat. The brigade held the town for ten days against continual Japanese attacks. For his leadership and determination in holding the Japanese back Lieutenant Colonel Thorne was awarded the DSO. A little over 500 members of the battalion fought their way back to Singapore where they were attacked on all sides at Braddell Road in Singapore. Running low on ammunition and with casualties mounting the battalion were ordered to surrender.

Twenty-four officers and some 760 other ranks later died in Japanese captivity. However not all the battalion were captured. Several thousand managed to escaped by ship heading for the East Indies, Australia, Ceylon and India. These ships were attacked by both Japanese planes and submarines and many sunk.

Thorne, after several adventures, together with 500 other civilian and military personnel, managed to find passage on the *Rooseboom* under Captain Marinus Cornelis Anthonie Boon, sailing from Padang to Colombo. On 1 March 1942 at 11.35 pm, *Rooseboom*, steaming west of Sumatra, was spotted and torpedoed by the Japanese submarine I-59 under the command of Lieutenant Yoshimatsu. The *Rooseboom* capsized and sank quickly, only managing to launch one lifeboat. After the *Rooseboom* had disappeared beneath the waves only eight people were left in the lifeboat and a further 135 were in the water hanging onto anything they could. Nine days later, two of the survivors were rescued by the Dutch freighter *Palopo*. Until the end of the war these were believed to be the only people to have survived the sinking, but there were others; although it is almost certain that Thorne went down with the ship. By the time the lifeboat had drifted for more than 1,000 miles, to ground on a coral reef less than 100 miles from Padang, only five of the passengers and crew were left alive and one of those drowned in the surf while trying to land. An account of the survivors' plight during their twenty-six days at sea is recounted in two books *The Boat* (1952) and *Highland Laddie* (1954) written by the only survivor from the lifeboat, Walter Gardiner Gibson, a corporal in the Argyll and Sutherland Highlanders. On the first night many of those still in the water gave up and drowned. Twenty of the men built a raft from the flotsam which they towed behind the lifeboat, but it only lasted a few days before it sank. Both men and women went mad with thirst, some drinking sea water, which sent them into hallucinations. Several more, unable to cope with the conditions, jumped over the side. A gang of five renegade soldiers positioned themselves in the bows and at night pushed the weaker survivors overboard to make the meagre rations go further. After fighting with other survivors these men were themselves thrown over the side. One white man was killed by members of the surviving Javanese crew and parts of him eaten. The Dutch captain was killed by one of his own engineers. In the end only Gibson and a Chinese girl, Doris Lin, managed to get ashore at Sipora, an island off Sumatra. They were at first looked after by local people but were later discovered by a Japanese patrol. Gibson was sent into captivity and Doris Lin shot as a spy (three Javanese seamen also managed to survive. One was drowned in the surf while trying to get ashore and the other two disappeared into the jungle and were never seen again). After the war Gibson settled in Canada, dying there on 24 March 2005, aged 90.

The late David Langton wrote this of Colonel Thorne and the position he found himself in. It fills many of the gaps in his story.

The Escape Party
The 2nd Battalion Escape Party consisted of Lt. Col. Thorne, Capt. Page, Capt. T.A.D. Ennion, Lieut. Squirrel, C.S.M. Randall, and Pts Bray, Clarke, Desborough, Powell, Pells, and Johnson. These were the only men of the Regiment detailed for this venture, since the 1st Battalion did not receive the order until too late for it to be complied with.

On leaving the Battalion this party made its way to Brigade and there joined similar parties from 5th and 6th Norfolks, afterwards proceeding to the docks. Here it was found that shipping was not available for the whole Divisional party and the greater part were returned to the Y.M.C.A. building to wait for the next night. Here Lt. Col Thorne was informed of the true nature of the 'special' mission for which he and his men had been selected and they at once asked permission to return to their unit, only to be informed that they were under orders to escape and must do their best to obey the order.

During the evening of the 14th the Y.M.C.A. building came under heavy shellfire and received several direct hits. When the 53rd Brigade party reported to the docks after dark they again found no ships and received a message to the effect that they were to attempt to find boats and make their escape unaided. The night was spent searching the docks for seaworthy craft, and with the coming of daylight this task was hampered by continual air and artillery strafing. Finally on the afternoon of 15th, the party embarked 41 strong in a ship's lifeboat and began to row in the rough direction of Sumatra.

After crossing over the Straits of Malacca and calling in at several islands for information and supplies, at one of which the lifeboat was bartered for a decrepit motor launch, the party reached Sumatra. Here they were taken in buses over to the west coast and conveyed by ship to Java. After a few days only on Java they were put aboard a small flat-bottomed river steamer and taken to Ceylon being attacked by torpedoes on the way, but escaping by reason of the vessel's light draught.

In the story of this party there is again a tragedy. While waiting in the Y.M.C.A. on the 14th, before making their escape from Singapore, Lt. Col Thorne was taken from them and ordered to join a number of senior officers who were to be evacuated first. Regretfully, Thorne said goodbye to the other Cambridgeshires and was sent off almost at once. He was never seen again. When the rest of the Battalion 'Escape Party' finally reached Ceylon, they made every endeavour to rejoin their C.O. but could find no trace of him. After extensive inquiries amongst other Officers and men who reached safety, they learned that he had arrived in Sumatra and had been embarked in a vessel which was believed to have been lost in the Indian Ocean with no survivors.

The news of the loss of Lt. Col G.C. Thorne did not reach those of his Battalion who were in captivity until long after, when one of the few letters to arrive from home gave information that he was reported missing. Even then, there was still hope that he might somehow have survived and been made prisoner somewhere in the East, but as the war drew to its close that hope died away. The best tribute that can be paid to the memory of this well loved Commander is this, that whenever, in slave camps of the East, two members of his Battalion met together they asked each other if there was news of the C.O. For those of us who served under him, he is remembered as he was that morning at Senggarang, tired, hungry, and as grimy as the rest of us, standing on the open road in full view of the enemy block, smiling and cracking jokes to cheer us on into battle, his helmet as usual forgotten.

Gordon Thorne's body was never recovered and he is commemorated on the Singapore Memorial, column 47. He is also commemorated on the Heacham War Memorial, Norfolk, as well as at Haileybury School.

His brother A.B. Thorne was killed in a flying accident on 8 May 1918.

Batting and fielding averages

	Mat	Inns	NO	Runs	HS	Ave	100	50	Ct	St
First-class	1	2	0	24	17	12.00	0	0	0	0

Bowling averages

	Mat	Balls	Runs	Wkts	BBI	BBM	Ave	Econ	SR	4w	5w	10
First-class	1	-	-	-	-	-	-	-	-	-	-	-

Flying Officer Hubert Dainton 'Trilby' Freakes
Eastern Province, The Rest
Ten first-class appearances
RAF Volunteer Reserve
Died 10 March 1942, aged 28

'The outstanding ability of HD Freakes kept on
gaining or regaining ground as Oxford battled to the last'

Hubert Freakes was born on 2 February 1914 in Durban. He was the son of Benjamin Freakes and of Blanche Eliza (née Dainton) of Durban, Natal, South Africa. He was educated at the Maritzburg College where his talent for sports was quickly appreciated. He captained both the rugby XV and the cricket XI as well as being one of the finest athletes in the college. On leaving school in 1930 aged 16 he went up to Rhodes University in Grahamstown. During this time he started to play first-class cricket for Eastern Province, making ten appearances for them between 1931 and 1934.

He made his debut for the Eastern Province against Natal in the Currie Cup on 21 December 1931 at Old Wanderers Top Back Ground, Johannesburg. Natal won the toss and decided to bat making 163. In reply Eastern Province made 190. Freakes, opening for Eastern Provence, batted throughout the innings making an impressive 122 not out. In their second innings Natal made 237. Eastern Province made a poor 48, Freakes only making three before being bowled by Harold Fawcett. The Natal bowler Richard Davies took six wickets for 21 off six overs. Despite Freakes' best efforts Natal took the match by 162 runs.

Freakes went on to play against Orange Free State (match drawn), Western Province (match drawn, despite Freakes making 59 and 111), Border (match drawn), Rhodesia (Rhodesia won by an innings and 81 runs). He then played for The Rest against Natal, Natal winning by ten wickets, and against Transvaal, making 114 in the first innings; once again his efforts were futile as Transvaal took the match by six wickets. He played his final match for The Rest against Western Province; the match was drawn. He then turned out for Eastern Province against Border, Border winning by nine wickets.

Freakes made his final first-class appearance for Eastern Province against Western Province in the Currie Cup on 10 Match 1934 at St George's Park, Port Elizabeth. Western Province won the toss and decided to field. Easter Province made 83, Freakes being run out for two. The Western Province bowler Alfred Bensimon took six wickets for 24 runs off 18 overs. In reply Western Province made 128, Colin Morietus Maritz taking five wickets for 55 off 18 overs. In their second innings Eastern Province made just 37 runs, Freakes being run out once again, for nine. Western Province won by an innings and eight runs.

During his first-class career Freakes made 660 runs including three centuries and one fifty, his highest score being 122 against Natal. He also bowled 246 balls taking five wickets for 145 runs, his best figures being two for 53. He also made four catches.

After completing his course in South Africa with distinction he won a Rhodes scholarship at Magdalen College, Oxford, in October 1936.

Freakes was also a first-rate rugby player, making three international appearances for England as a full back, against Wales at Cardiff on 15 January 1938 (England lost 8-14); against Wales again, on 21 January 1939 at Twickenham (England won 3-0); and finally against Ireland on 11 February 1939 at Twickenham (England lost 0-5).

As well as playing for the Barbarians and the Harlequins, where he picked up the nickname 'Trilby', he was selected to play in the Oxford XV against Cambridge on 8 December 1936.

The match was played in driving rain, Cambridge taking the honours six points to five. His contribution was noted in *The Times*: 'The outstanding ability of H.D. Freakes kept on gaining or regaining ground as Oxford battled to the last.'

He continued to play for Oxford the following year, gaining a second blue. The match on 7 December 1937 was the first varsity of the reign of the new King George VI, who was present at Twickenham to see it. In a tactical move Freakes moved further up the field to counter the attacking Cambridge back line. *The Times* rugby correspondent reported: '...in the capacity of a full back disguised as a centre; Freakes made his selection appear a stroke of genius.' The tactic worked, with Oxford taking the match 7-4.

For the 1938/39 season Freakes was made Oxford club captain. Playing in his third varsity match on 6 December 1938 things didn't go so well, as pointed out by *The Times* rugby correspondent: 'As the game went, Freakes may have regretted his decision to play at full back rather than centre, where last year his tackling alone was decisive.' Cambridge won the match 8-6.

With war threatening, Freakes joined the RAF Volunteer Reserve taking a commission as a pilot officer on 18 July 1939 and being promoted to flying officer on 20 July 1940. Trained as a pilot he was attached to the RAF's Ferry Command on 20 July 1941 delivering new aircraft from the factory to their operational units. So far as Ferry Command was concerned this meant from the factories in Canada and the United States to the air bases within Britain. In total Ferry Command was to transport some 9,000 desperately needed aircraft to their squadrons. Vital as it was, the work inherently entailed risk. On 10 March 1942, during a mission, a Ferry Training Unit Hudson bomber, number V8995, spun into the ground at Honeybourne airfield in Worcestershire. Its pilot, Flying Officer Hubert Freakes, and his crew were killed in the impact.

Freakes was buried in Evesham Cemetery, grave reference 1338. If passing, visit and a bring a few flowers.

Batting and fielding averages

	Mat	Inns	NO	Runs	HS	Ave	100	50	Ct	St
First-class	10	19	1	660	122*	36.66	3	1	4	0

Bowling averages

	Mat	Balls	Runs	Wkts	BBI	Ave	Econ	SR	5w	10
First-class	10	246	145	5	2/53	29.00	3.53	49.2	0	0

England v Ireland, 1939. England's last fifteen at Twickenham before World War 2, and the side which shared the Championship with Ireland and Wales: *back* Mr J. C. H. Ireland, R. S. L. Carr, R. M. Marshall, J. K. Watkins, J. T. W. Berry, H. D. Freakes, G. E. Hancock, R. H. Guest, D. E. Teden; *middle* H. F. Wheatley, J. Heaton, H. B. Toft (captain), T. F. Huskisson, R. E. Prescott; *front* G. A. Walker, P. Cooke

Major Gilbert Edgar Jose
South Australia
Two first-class appearances
Australian Army Medical Corps
AIF 10 General Hospital
Died 27 March 1942, aged 43
Right-handed bat

'and all the brothers were valiant'

Gilbert Jose was born on 1 November 1898 in Taichow, China. He was the son of the Very Reverend George Herbert Jose, who worked as a CMS missionary in China and was later Dean of Adelaide, and Clara Ellen. He was educated at St Peter's College, Adelaide, where he was captain of the XI. On leaving school he trained as a doctor, later becoming a surgeon training in Edinburgh, Scotland, and becoming MB, BS, FRCS (Edin.) and a fellow of the Royal Australian College of Surgeons. He married Mary, of Fitzroy, South Australia. He served during the later half of the First World War as a private soldier, before resuming his studies after the war.

Jose made two first-class appearances, his debut being for South Australia against Victoria at the Melbourne Cricket Ground on 1 January 1919. Victoria won the toss and made 374, the Australian test cricketer Warwick Windridge Armstrong making 162 not out. In reply South Australia made 359, Jose being run out for a duck. Percy Davies Rundell made a century. The Victoria and Australian test bowler Edgar Arthur McDonald (*Wisden* cricketer of the year 1922) taking six wickets for 111 off 20 overs. In their second innings Victoria made 252, the South Australian bowler Richard James Bruce Townsend taking five wickets for 27 off 12 overs. In reply South Australia made 159. Jose was bowled by McDonald for a duck. McDonald took six wickets during the innings for 69 off 12 overs. Victoria won by 108 runs.

Jose made his second first-class appearance for South Australia against the MCC at the Adelaide Oval on 11 March 1921. South Australia won the toss and decided to bat making 195, Jose making 16 before being caught by Jack Russell (*Wisden* cricketer of the year 1923) off the bowling of the famous Percy Fender (*Wisden* cricketer of the year 1915). Fender took seven wickets during the innings for 75 runs off 24 overs. In reply the MCC made 627. Wilfred Rhodes (*Wisden* cricketer of the year 1899) made 210, Jack Russell 210 and John William Henry Tyler Douglas (*Wisden* cricketer of the year 1915) 106. In their second innings South Australia made 369, Jose lbw Frank Woolley (*Wisden* cricketer of the year 1911) for two. Percy Rundell made 121. The MCC won by an innings and 63 runs.

Jose took a commission into the Australian Army Medical Corps on 31 October 1940 at Woodville South Australia. Rising to the rank of major, he was attached to the 10th Australian General Hospital and was taken prisoner of war when the Japanese

captured Singapore. He was kept at Changi and died there of dysentery on 27 March 1942. The record of his death notes, 'Gilbert Jose (MO Major SX11028) died at 0645 after dysentery lasting only a few days. Extreme toxaemia and delirium for about 3 days, then coma for 2. Buried in AIF Cemetery Changi, about 1½ miles from Roberts Barracks on main Singapore road. Maximum number of dysentery cases 469.'

He is buried in Kranji War Cemetery grave reference 2. A. 11.

Jose had two brothers, Wilfred Oswald who was killed in action on 2 April 1917 aged 22 as a lieutenant with the 10th Battalion Australian Infantry, and Ivan Bede, also a surgeon, who won the MC during the First World War later becoming chief surgeon at the Royal Adelaide Hospital and being knighted. His son, Tony Jose, was also a first-class cricketer playing twenty-nine first-class matches, for South Australia, Oxford University and Kent.

Batting and fielding averages

	Mat	Inns	NO	Runs	HS	Ave	100	50	Ct	St
First-class	2	4	0	18	16	4.50	0	0	0	0

Bowling averages

	Mat	Runs	Wkts	BBI	BBM	Ave	SR	4w	5w	10
First-class	2	15	0	-	-	-	-	0	0	0

Captain John Robert Shadwell
Europeans (India)
One first-class appearance
1st Battalion Wiltshire Regiment
Died 25 April 1942, aged 23

'A fine man and officer'

John Shadwell was born in 1919 in Stockbridge, Hampshire. He was the son of Frederick Charles and Elsie May of Over Wallop.

Shadwell made one first-class appearance, for the Europeans against the Indians in a Madras Presidency match played on 12 January 1941 at the Madras Cricket Club Ground, Chepauk. India won the toss and decided to bat making 209, the Indian bowler J.S. Versey-Brown taking five wickets for 47 off 22 overs. In reply the Europeans made 164. Shadwell was caught by T.D. Narayanaswami Rao off the bowling of Amritsar Govindsingh Ram Singh for one, the Indian test cricketer Commandur Rajagopalachari Rangachari taking five wickets for 41 off 19 overs. In their second innings the Indians made 168, Versey-Brown once again taking five wickets, for 64 off 24 overs. In reply the Europeans made 116, Shadwell making one before being caught and bowled by A.G. Ram Singh who took six wickets for 59 off 22 overs. The Indians won by 97 runs.

On the outbreak of war the 1st Battalion was stationed in Bangalore. Shortly afterwards they moved to Madras to take up costal defense duties. They were destined to remain in India until 1944 with many men getting posted to units elsewhere.

Captain John Robert Shadwell was taken ill and died on 25 April 1942. He is buried in Kirkee War Cemetery, Poona, on the Plateau above Bombay, grave reference 3. G. 3.

Batting and fielding averages

	Mat	Inns	NO	Runs	HS	Ave	100	50	4s	6s	Ct	St
First-class	1	2	0	2	1	1.00	0	0	0	0	0	0

Bowling averages

	Mat	Balls	Runs	Wkts	BBI	BBM	Ave	Econ	SR	4w	5w	10
First-class	1	-	-	-	-	-	-	-	-	-	-	-

Pilot Officer Ross Gerald Gregory
Australia-Victoria
Two tests, thirty-three first-class
appearances
215 Squadron Royal Australian Air Force
Died 10 June 1942, aged 26
Right-handed bat/Leg break

'one of nature's gentleman'

Ross Gregory was born on 28 February 1916 in Murchison, Victoria. He was the son of Arthur Gerald St John Gregory and Olive Annie, of Caulfield, Victoria, Australia. He was educated at the Gardenvale State School where his talent for cricket first came to notice. He was in the school XI, later captaining the side which won the premiership in 1930. By the time he was 15 he had twice been selected to play for the Victorian's schoolboys. He went up to Wesley College, Melbourne, and while there was considered a schoolboy prodigy, making his first-class debut for Victoria while still at school. The match was played against Western Australia on 15 February 1934 at the Melbourne Cricket Ground. Western Australia won the toss and decided to bat making 185. Gregory took four wickets for 50 runs off 16 overs: Francis James Alexander caught and bowled for 45, Richard John Bryant caught Edward Henry George Vernon for four, Albert James Ditchburn caught and bowled for two, and John Raymond Jones caught and bowled for seven. In reply Victoria made 438, Gregory making five before being bowled by Mervyn Inverarity. Arthur Henry Allsopp made 146. In their second innings Western Australia made 133, Gregory taking one further wicket for 23 off nine overs.

Gregory was also a gifted rower, and in the winter represented Wesley's senior Australian Rules football side. Gregory was a good student and would eventually become a qualified accountant.

He went on to play against the MCC, Queensland, New South Wales, South Australia and New Zealand in Australia. He also turned out for D.G. Bradman's XI against V.Y. Richardson's XI and K.E. Rigg's XI against S.J. McCabe's XI and D.G. Bradman's XI. On 20 November 1936 he played for an Australian XI against the MCC taking two wickets and scoring 14 runs. The match was drawn.

He made his final first-class appearance for Victoria against South Australia on 24 February 1939 in the Sheffield Shield at the Adelaide Oval. South Australia won the toss and decided to field. Victoria made 321. Gregory made 33 before being bowled by Harold Norman Jack Cotton. The Australian test cricketer Lindsay Hassett made 102. In reply South Australia made 207. Gregory bowled two overs taking no wickets for 13 runs. The match was drawn.

Gregory made his test debut a few weeks after his twenty-first birthday, being nicknamed 'Baby' because of his youth. He was selected for the fourth test during the 1936-7 Ashes series. The test was played on 29 January 1936 at the Adelaide Oval. Australia won the toss and decided to bat making 288. Gregory made 23 before being lbw off the bowling of Wally Hammond. In reply England made 330, Gregory bowling three overs for no wickets for fourteen 14 runs and Charles John Barnett making 129. In their second innings Australia made 433, Gregory making 50 before being run out. Donald Bradman made 212. Wally

Hammond took five wickets for 57 off 15 overs. In their second innings England made 243. Gregory caught George Oswald Browning 'Gubby' Allen off the bowling of Ernest McCormick. Leslie O'Brien Fleetwood-Smith took six wickets for 110 runs off 30 overs. Australia won by 148 runs.

He was selected again for the fifth test on 27 February 1937 played at the Melbourne Cricket Club. Australia won the toss and decided to bat making an impressive 604, Gregory making 80 before being caught by Hedley Verity (*Wisden* cricketer of the year 1932) off the bowling of Kenneth Farnes. Farnes took six wickets from the innings for 96 off 28 overs. Bradman made 169, McCabe 112 and Jack Badcock 118. In reply England made 239. Following on, England made 165. It was a disaster for England as Australia took the match by an innings and 200 runs. Australia also took the series 3-2.

These were to be Gregory's only two test appearances, however he continued to play for Victoria and his club side, St Kilda.

During his career played in two tests, making 153 runs his highest score being 80 against England. He also bowled 24 balls for 14 runs. He took one catch. He also made thirty-three first-class matches, making 1,874 runs, his highest score being 128 for Victoria against the MCC, his stand with Ian Somerville Lee for 262 being a fourth wicket record against an England team. He also made seventeen fifties. He bowled 3,709 balls taking 50 wickets, his best figures being five for 69. He made twenty catches.

On 18 August 1940 Gregory enlisted into the ranks of the Royal Australian Air Force, later becoming a sergeant. After his initial training, he was selected to become a navigator before embarking on the *Awatea* in June 1941 bound for England. After further training in Scotland he was posted to 99 squadron RAF where he flew in both Vickers and Wellingtons. He took part in his first operation in December 1941 in an attack on Le Havre. This was followed by several more operations over Germany and Norway. He was transferred to 215 Squadron and commissioned to pilot officer shortly before departing for India to engage the Japanese. On 10 June 1942 Gregory, together with other Boston Bomber aircraft from 215 squadron, left base in Calcutta to bomb targets in Burma. As the squadron flew across East Bengal (now Bangladesh) they were caught up in a severe storm. Witnesses on the ground stated that the aircraft was trailing smoke before it disintegrated in mid-air, scattering the aircraft and six crew over a wide area. Locals managed to retrieve the bodies of the crew, including Gregory, and bury them in a communal grave near the crash site (due to severe tropical storms the graves were later lost). Whether he had a premonition or was just trying to comfort his family if anything did happen, he wrote to his family shortly before his death, 'take a certain amount of comfort from the knowledge that I went down doing my duty.'

He is commemorated on the Singapore Memorial in Kranji War Cemetery, column 421. Fourteen days later the news of his death reached Australia. St Kilda Cricket Club's Ross Gregory Oval is named in his honour. Gregory is also commemorated on the Roll of Honour at the Shrine of Remembrance in Melbourne.

Batting and fielding averages

	Mat	Inns	NO	Runs	HS	Ave	BF	SR	100	50	4s	6s	Ct	St
Tests	2	3	0	153	80	51.00	453	33.77	0	2	7	0	1	0
First-class	33	51	2	1874	128	38.24			1	17			20	0

Bowling averages

	Mat	Inns	Balls	Runs	Wkts	BBI	BBM	Ave	Econ	SR	4w	5w	10
Tests	2	1	24	14	0	-	-	-	3.50	-	0	0	0
First-class	33			1767	50	5/69		35.34				1	0

Lieutenant Colonel Thomas Bevan
Army
One first-class match
3rd Battalion Coldstream Guards
Died 12 June 1942, aged 42
Right-handed bat

'Died fighting bravely to the end'

Thomas Bevan was born on 14 February 1900 in Crayford, Kent. He was the son of Wilfred and Ethel Marion Bevan. Bevan, a fine cricketer, was educated at Eton where he was quickly in the XI. During 1918 he played against Eton Ramblers (drawn), Charterhouse (won by an innings and 72 runs), Harrow (drawn) and Winchester (drawn).

Deciding on a career in the army he first went to Sandhurst before taking a commission into the Grenadier Guards. He continued playing cricket, turning out mainly for the Household Brigade, but also the Coldstream Guards, the MCC, and Suffolk. He also played for the Army twice, once against the Public Schools on 3 August 1927 at Lord's (drawn) and against the RAF. The latter was a first-class game.

Bevan played for the Army against the RAF on 13 June 1928 at the Oval. The RAF won the toss and decided to bat making 303. In reply the Army made 105, Bevan making six before being caught by Morton Swan Shapcott off the bowling of Richard Peter Hugh Utley. Forced to follow on, the Army made 205. Bevan made one before being caught by Reginald Fulljames off the bowling of Charles Blount. The RAF won by ten wickets.

Moving through the ranks, Bevan finally became a lieutenant colonel and commanded the 3rd Battalion the Coldstream Guards.

During all of this he also found time to meet and marry Sylvia (née Harker) of Oakham, Rutland.

Sent to the Western Desert he took part in the battle of Gazala and the Cauldron.

Between late January and May, following their withdrawal from the German front at Agedabia, the British created the 'Gazala Line'. This was made up not of a straight line of well dug-in trenches, but a series of defended 'boxes' running from Gazala on the eastern side of Jebel south into the desert. A full brigade was dug in behind belts of barbed wire, and minefields supported each box. The boxes were too widely separated to provide mutual support so the areas between them were patrolled by roving armoured units. One of these defensive positions was called the 'Knightsbridge Box'. This box was manned by the 201st Guards Brigade. German tactics against these defences involved a full-frontal assault to the north before sending their Panzers around the southern flank. The Germans put their plan into action on 26 May 1942, with a hook east and north towards Sidi Rezegh. This assault was immediately successful. By the afternoon of the 27th the German attack had shattered the 7th Armoured Division and they were in position to assault the 201st Guards Brigade in the Knightsbridge Box.

On 29 May 1942 the Kensington Box was attacked by the 15th Panzer Division who were forced to stop their advance due to lack of fuel and ammunition. The Germans started to open lanes through the British minefield, however they were engaged by artillery from Knightsbridge and the Guards. The fighting continued with the Knightsbridge Box fighting furiously and hanging on. On 11 June, Rommel pushed the 15th Panzer Division and 90th Light Afrika Division towards El Adem and by 12 June had forced the 201st Guards Brigade to withdraw from the Knightsbridge Box to the Tobruk perimeter. The following day the Knightsbridge Box was virtually surrounded and was abandoned by the Guards Brigade. Due to these defeats, 13 June became known as 'Black Saturday' to the Eighth Army. It was during this action that the much-respected Lieutenant Colonel Thomas Bevan was seriously wounded, dying of his wounds on 13 June 1942.

He is buried in Tobruk War Cemetery, grave reference 2. F 19.

Batting and fielding averages

	Mat	Inns	NO	Runs	HS	Ave	100	50	Ct	St
First-class	1	2	0	7	6	3.50	0	0	0	0

Bowling averages

	Mat	Balls	Runs	Wkts	BBI	BBM	Ave	Econ	SR	4w	5w	10
First-class	1	-	-	-	-	-	-	-	-	-	-	-

Pilot Officer Henry Filby Myles
Western Province, Rhodesia
Three first-class appearances
RAF Volunteer Reserve
Died 15 June 1942, aged 30
Right-hand bat

'Could hit a ball harder than anyone I have ever seen'

Henry Myles was born on 6 June 1911 in Cape Town. He was the son of Henry and Rebecca Myles of Rondebosch.

Myles made three first-class appearances for Western Province and Rhodesia between 1930 and 1936, his debut being for Western Province against the MCC in South Africa on 8 November 1930 at the Newlands, Cape Town. Western Province won the toss and decided to bat making 113, Myles making the top score of the innings with 35 before being stumped by George Duckworth (*Wisden* cricketer of the year 1929) off the bowling of Wally Hammond (*Wisden* cricketer of the year 1928). Maurice William Tate (*Wisden* cricketer of the year 1924) took five wickets for 18 off 12 overs. In reply the MCC made 412, Bob Wyatt (*Wisden* cricketer of the year 1930) making 138 and Hammond 100. In reply Western Province made 122, Myers making five before being bowled by Morris Leyland (*Wisden* cricketer of the year 1929). Not surprisingly, given how many cricketers of the year filled their ranks, the MCC won by and innings and 177 runs.

Myles made his second first-class appearance for Western Province against Griqualand West. The match was played on 6 December 1930 at Newlands. Western Province won the toss and decided to bat making 290. Myles made 11 before being caught by Neville Anthony

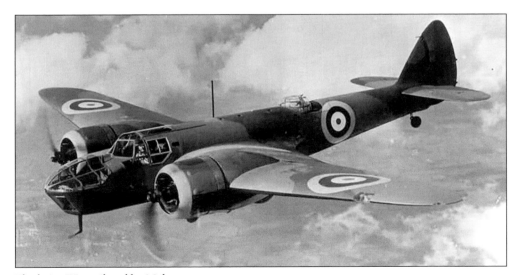

Blenheim IV, as piloted by Myles.

Quinn off the bowling of Ernest George Bock. Dave Nourse made 101 and Kenneth Charles Myburgh Hands 102. In reply Griqualand West made 148. In their second innings Western Province made 121, Myles only managing three before being bowled by Quinn. In their second innings Griqualand West made 133 all out. Western Province won by 177 runs.

Myles had to wait six years to make his final first-class appearance, this time playing for Rhodesia against the Transvaal. The match took place on 16 December 1936 at the Old Wanderers, Johannesburg. Transvaal won the toss and decided to bat making 262, John Heath Charsley taking six wickets for 92 off 29 overs. In reply Rhodesia only managed 83. Myles, opening for Rhodesia, was caught by Threlfall Werge Talbot Baines off the bowling of Neil Munro McAlpine for a duck. McAlpine took four wickets for 13 off 13 overs and Sydney Charles Parkyns five for 21 off ten overs. Forced to follow on, Rhodesia made 106. Myles made 12 before being bowled by Charles Henry Kingsley Jones. Transvaal won by an innings and 73 runs.

Myles joined the RAF Volunteer Reserve during the war being commissioned as a pilot officer and training as a pilot. Joining No. 1 (O) AFU in Scotland, he died on 15 June 1942 from multiple injuries when piloting Blenheim IV number P4858 when its engines cut out on take-off and it crashed into the ground near Trammonford Park, Wigtown. His crew was made up of Sergeant Observer John Russell and LAC Observer Ronald Stevenson Yeaman. They died with him.

Pilot Officer Henry Filby Myles is buried in Kirkinner Cemetery, grave reference 571.

Batting and fielding averages

	Mat	Inns	NO	Runs	HS	Ave	100	50	Ct	St
First-class	3	6	0	66	35	11.00	0	0	0	0

Bowling averages

	Mat	Balls	Runs	Wkts	BBI	BBM	Ave	Econ	SR	4w	5w	10
First-class	3	-	-	-	-	-	-	-	-	-	-	-

14963 Private Alastair Patrick Johnstone Monteath
Otago
Two first-class appearances
20th Battalion New Zealand Infantry
Died 27 June 1942, aged 28
Wicketkeeper

'Died holding back Rommel'

Alastair Monteath was born on 12 September 1913 in Christchurch. He was the son of James and Muriel (née Devernish Meares) of 28 Poynder Avenue, Fendalton, Christchurch.

He made two first-class appearances, both for Otago in New Zealand and both in the Plunket Shield in 1939. He made his debut against Canterbury on 23 December 1939 at Lancaster Park. Canterbury won the toss and decided to bat making 374, the New Zealand test cricketer Martin Paterson Donnelly making 104 and the Otago bowler Thomas George Frederick Lemin taking five wickets for 96 off 19 overs. In reply Otago made 249, Monteath making 12 before being caught by Harry Davis off the bowling of the New Zealand test cricketer Donald Alexander Noel McRae. Monteath, playing as wicketkeeper, also caught Francis Patrick O'Brian off Lemin's bowling. In reply Canterbury made 38. Otago didn't bat again and the match was drawn.

He made his second first-class appearance against Auckland on 30 December 1940 at Eden Park. Otago won the toss and decided to bat making 194, Monteath making one before being lbw to the bowling of the New Zealand test cricketer John Cowie. In reply Auckland made 496, the New Zealand test cricketer Verdun Scott making a century. The Otago bowler Cedric Elmes took five wickets for 133 off 45 overs. In their second innings Otago made 133, Monteath making one before being bowled again by John Cowie. Cowie took six wickets during the innings for 44 runs off 21 overs. Auckland won the match by an innings and 169 runs.

During the war Monteath enlisted as a private in the 20th New Zealand Infantry being posted to North Africa. At Mingar Qaim the division was told to hold back the advance of Rommel's Panzers. By midday on 27 June 1942 it had been surrounded by the Germans' 21st Panzer Division. The Panzers attacked the 20th Battalion's sector which was situated on the northern side of the Mingar Qaim escarpment but were beaten back. During the evening the division was ordered to break out, which they did successfully. During the action at Minqar Qaim and the subsequent breakout, the battalion suffered thirteen killed. One of these casualties was Private Alastair Patrick Johnstone Monteath.

Monteath's body was never recovered and he is commemorated on the Alamein Memorial, column 104.

Batting and fielding averages

	Mat	Inns	NO	Runs	HS	Ave	100	50	Ct	St
First-class	2	3	0	14	12	4.66	0	0	1	0

Bowling averages

	Mat	Balls	Runs	Wkts	BBI	BBM	Ave	Econ	SR	4w	5w	10
First-class	2	-	-	-	-	-	-	-	-	-	-	-

Lieutenant Colonel Francis Godfrey Bertram Arkwright DSO MC
Hampshire
Four first-class matches
12 Royal Lancers, Royal Armoured Corps
Died 1 July 1942, aged 37
Right-hand bat

'The finest bat at Eton College'

Francis Arkwright was born on 30 January 1905 in Bromley. He was the son of Bertram Harry Godfrey and Grace Emma Julie (née Hurt). He went up to Eton in 1918 where he played in the XI, turning out against the Household Brigade in 1922 (losing by three wickets), Oxford University Authentics (drawn), Scotland XI (drawn), Winchester (drawn) and Harrow (drawn). In his second appearance for Eton against Winchester Arkwright made 175 in Eton's first innings. He and E.W. Dawson, later captain of Cambridge University and Leicestershire, put on 301 for the second wicket, a record for an Eton Winchester match. The match was drawn. He headed the Eton averages with 52.44 in 1923. He also played for Lord's School against The Rest (Lord's School won by nine wickets) and Public Schools against the Army (the Army won by seven wickets).

Arkwright made four first-class appearances in the county championship, three for Hampshire and one for the Army. He made his debut for Hampshire on 11 August 1923 against Lancashire at Old Trafford. Lancashire decided to bat making 255, the England test player Alex Kennedy taking six wickets for 67 off 34 overs. In reply Hampshire made 259, Arkwright being bowled by the test cricketer Cecil Harry Parkin for 14. The England test cricketer George Brown made 104 and Frank Watson took five wickets for 57 off 29 overs. In their second innings Lancashire made 177. In their second innings Hampshire made 168, Parkin taking a further five wickets for 84 off 29 overs. The match was drawn.

He made his second first-class appearance against Yorkshire on 15 August 1923 at Headingley, again in the county championship. Yorkshire won the toss and decided to bat making 246. In reply Hampshire made 327, Arkwright making ten before being bowled by George Macaulay. In their second innings Yorkshire made 206. Hampshire didn't bat again and the match was drawn.

His third first-class appearance was against Lancashire, again in the county championship, this time played on 18 August 1923, at the County Ground, Southampton. Lancashire won the toss and decided to bat making 131. In reply Hampshire made 268, Arkwright making 11 before being bowled by his old adversary Cecil Parkin. Parkin took seven wickets for 99 off 35 overs during the innings. In their second innings Lancashire made 362, Frank Watson making 131. In their second innings Hampshire made 88, Arkwright making six before being caught by the England test cricketer George Duckworth off the bowling of William Edward Hickmott. The match was drawn.

Arkwright had to wait almost two years to make his fourth and final first-class appearance, this time a university match played for the Army against Cambridge University. The match was played at F.P. Fenner's Ground, Cambridge on 30 May 1925. The Army won the toss and decided to bat making 196, Arkwright making zero before being caught by Hamer Fraser Bagnall off the bowling of Henry John Enthoven. Godfrey Bryan made 112. Enthoven took five wickets for 51 off 19 overs. In reply Cambridge made 416, Kumar Shri Duleepsinhji making 128. Henry Raphael Kirkwood took five wickets for 100 off 27 overs. In their second innings the Army made 238, Arkwright making 23 before being bowled by Enthoven, who took six wickets for 64 off 33 overs. In their second innings Cambridge made 19, taking the game by eight wickets. Arkwright also turned out for C.F. Tufnell's XI and the Butterflies.

Deciding on a career in the Army he went up to Sandhurst where he was in the XI playing against the Royal Military Academy Woolwich, making 31 and 14 not out. He also took three wickets, Sandhurst taking the match by ten wickets. On leaving Sandhurst in March 1925 he was commissioned into the 12th Lancers. During the 1930s Arkwright was posted to the Anglo-Egyptian Sudan as a bimbashi (captain). While there he commanded No. 1 Motor Machine Gun Battery which was part of the Sudan Defence Force. During the winter-spring of 1934 he achieved his most notable feat by occupying Ain Murr, situated in the very remote Jebel Uweinat, during the Sarra Dispute with Italy. He also found time to meet and marry Joyce Nancy Evelyn of Newtownbarry, Co. Wexford.

On his return to England he was made adjutant to the 12th Lancers before going to the staff college in September 1939.

Arkwright was also a fine polo player, considered the best the regiment had produced since 1914. On the outbreak of the Second World War he was sent to France as a staff officer. In May 1940 however he was promoted to brigade major and given command of his own tank formation with the 12th Lancers, being awarded a Military Cross (*London Gazette* 18 October 1940) for his actions with this unit.

After returning to England he was sent to Libya in 1941 seeing much action before being promoted to lieutenant colonel and given command of the 4th County of London Yeomanry in May 1942. He was killed in action at Acroma in Libya on 1 July 1942.

The circumstances were explained in the regimental diary at the time:

Day 36

Ordered to move at 0700 SW to vicinity of trig Pt 97.

In the afternoon moved 4 miles North to cover South African Bde box against a threatened tank attack. Later moved South again to original position and about 1800hrs ordered 6 miles West to assist an Indian Bde box against an attack by enemy who had penetrated the minefields. The situation of the box was evidently very insecure on our arrival and the Regt was formed up on the South side of the box facing SW to meet a tank attack coming in from that direction. Guns and tanks moved forward under enemy smoke-screen.

1st RTR Stuarts arrived on our left flank and turned back an attempt to outflank us.

About 20 minutes before last light enemy guns were reported being hauled into position to attack our right flank – the move was only made possible by the failure of the box to hold the enemy attack from the NE. At this point Col Arkwright dismounted in order to discuss the situation with the Brigadier over the rear-link set in the Adjutant's tank. Whilst on the back of the Adjutant's tank he was hit and killed by an AP [Armoured Piercing Shell] shot. The command was taken over by Major Scott, who ordered a withdrawal Eastwards with the concurrence of Bde.

Leaguered about the point from which we had started, 6 miles East of the scene of the action. Col Arkwright was buried near the leaguer at map ref 887278.

For his actions on this day Arkwright was awarded a DSO (*London Gazette* 13 August 1942). His body could not be found after the war and he is commemorated on the Alamein Memorial, Column 19.

Batting and fielding averages

	Mat	Inns	NO	Runs	HS	Ave	100	50	Ct	St
First-class	4	7	0	67	23	9.57	0	0	2	0

Bowling averages

	Mat	Balls	Runs	Wkts	BBI	BBM	Ave	Econ	SR	4w	5w	10
First-class	4	-	-	-	-	-	-	-	-	-	-	-

Eton College team photograph 1922. Back Row (left to right): F.G.R. Arkwright, R.G.M. Kennerley-Rumford, W.G. Wothington (12th man), G.S. Incledon-Webber, J.E. Hurley. Middle row: E.W. Dawson, Lord Dunglass, G.K. Cox (Captain), M.R. Bridgeman, N. Llewelyn-Davies. Sitting: N.R. Barrett, W.P. Thursby.

Able Seaman David Price
Western Province
Fourteen first-class appearances
HMS *Niger* South African Naval Forces
Died 6 July 1942, aged 31
Right-handed bat/Right arm medium pace

'Went down with his ship'

HMS *Niger*.

David Price was born on 13 August 1910 in Cape Town Province, South Africa. He was the son of Harry and Mary Price, also of Cape Town.

Price made fourteen first-class appearances for Western Province between 1934 and 1939, ten of which were in the Currie Cup. He made his debut for Western Province in the Currie Cup against Griqualand West on 31 March 1934 at Newlands. Western Province won the toss and decided to bat making 438. Price, batting last, made 15 not out. Harold William Morgan made 115 and Leslie Martin Manning 123. In reply Griqualand West made 154. The South African test cricketer John Benjamin Robertson took six wickets for 22 off 13 overs. Forced to follow on, Griqualand West made 171, Price catching the opener the South African test cricketer Frank Nicholson off the bowling of Howard Hugh Watt for six. He also bowled four overs taking no wickets for ten, Gordon Blake Paull taking six wickets for 61 off 26 overs. Western Province won by an innings and 113 runs.

He went on play against Orange Free State, Transvaal, North Eastern Transvaal, Border and Natal, all in the Currie Cup. He also played against the MCC in South Africa and Australia. He made his final first-class appearance for Western Province against Transvaal on 30 December 1939 at Newlands. Transvaal won the toss and decided to bat making 383, the South African test cricketer Eric Rowan making 164. Price bowled 21 overs taking two wickets for 94, John Thorne Seccombe for one and the test cricketer Dooley Briscoe for eight. He also ran out Robert Edward Somers Vine for 39. In reply Western Province made 242, Price making five before being lbw off the bowling of South African test cricketer Athol Matthew Burchell Rowan, Norman Gordon taking five wickets for 87 off 33 overs. In their second innings Transvaal made 225, Price bowling 15 overs and taking two wickets for 65, Seccombe for 35 and James Henry Maxwell Pickerill caught George Georgeu for 44. Making a fight of it, Western Province made 354 in their second innings, Price making seven before being bowled by Rowan. Despite Andrew Ronald MacKenzie Ralph making 140, Transvaal finally took the match by 12 runs but it was a near run thing.

During his career Price made 204 runs, his highest score being 28 against North Eastern Transvaal. He bowled 3,340 taking 48 wickets for 1,785 runs. He also made nine catches. During this period he made time to meet and marry Ivy, of Salisbury, Rhodesia.

During the war Price joined the South African navy as an able seaman, finding himself serving on the cruiser *Niger*. On 14 February 1942 the *Niger* met thirteen merchant ships which constituted Convoy PQ11. The following day they sailed from Kirkwall making for Murmansk in Russia, arriving on the 22nd without loss. The convoy consisted of eight British, two Russian, one American, one Panamanian and one Honduran. It was also escorted by two destroyers, two corvettes and four ASW trawlers, supported by the *Niger*. As it approached Murmansk the convoy was joined by two Russian destroyers and five British minesweepers based at Murmansk. The return convoy QP11, which consisted of thirteen ships, sailed on 28 April 1942, escorted by the *Niger* as well as the cruiser *Edinburgh*. Later, the German submarine *U-456* attacked the convoy hitting the *Edinburgh* with two torpedoes, crippling her and forcing her to return to Murmansk. German command then sent three destroyers to attack the convoy and finish of HMS *Edinburgh*. They attacked on the afternoon of 1 May. The *Amazon* was hit twice and severely damaged. This was followed by a German torpedo salvo hitting and sinking the Soviet freighter *Tsiolkovski*. The Germans then went after the *Edinburgh*. Despite being badly damaged the *Edinburgh* still managed to hit and cripple one of the German destroyers, the *Hermann Schoemann*, later scuttled. The *Edinburgh* was hit by torpedo and eventually had to scuttle herself too. After this *Niger* joined convoy QP13, thirty-five ships. As a result of bad weather and with fog reducing visibility to 500 yards the *Niger* veered off course sailing into a minefield off Iceland. On 5 July 1942 the *Niger* hit a mine and blew up at 2240 sinking quickly. The commanding officer, 8 officers and 140 ratings went down with her.

Price's body was never recovered and he is commemorated on the Plymouth Naval Memorial, panel 74, column 2.

First-class Career Batting and Fielding

	M	I	NO	Runs	HS	Ave	100	50	Ct
Western Province	14	22	7	204	28*	13.60	0	0	9

First-class Career Bowling (1933/34-1939/40)

	Balls	Mdns	Runs	Wkts	BB	Ave	5wI	10wM	SRate	Econ
Western Province	3340	56	1785	48	5-124	37.18	1	0	69.58	3.20

Lieutenant Denis Andrew Robert Moloney
New Zealand, Canterbury, Otago, Wellington
Three tests/Sixty-four first-class appearances
20th Infantry Regiment
Died 15 July 1942, aged 31
Right-handed bat/Leg break

'Died holding back Rommel's Panzers'

D.A.R. Moloney was born on 11 August 1910 in Dunedin, New Zealand. An outstanding cricketer he went on to play for New Zealand in three tests and make sixty-four first-class appearances for Canterbury, Otago and Wellington.

Moloney made his first-class debut for Otago against Auckland in the Plunket Shield on 24 December 1929 at Eden Park. Auckland won the toss and decided to field. Otago made a disastrous start making only 67 runs, Moloney being lbw to Wensley for zero. Albert Wensley (who also played for Sussex between 1922 and 1936) took nine wickets for 36 runs off 24 overs. In reply Auckland made 356, the New Zealand test cricketer John Ernest Mills making 185. Moloney bowled 12 overs taking two wickets for 34. Sydney Albert Roberts Badeley caught John James Morrell McMullan for 28 and the New Zealand test cricketer Mal Matheson for zero. In their second innings Otago did little better making ninety-seven. Moloney making six not out. Auckland won the match by an innings and 192 runs. Moloney making seventy in the first innings and seventy-one in the second

Moloney continued to represent Otago in the Plunket Shield against Wellington, Canterbury and Auckland playing against these sides on several occasions between 1929 and 1934 playing his final game for them against Wellington on 24 December 1934 at the Basin Reserve, Wellington. Wellington winning by eight wickets. On 8 February 1935 he played for the South Island against the North Island at the Basin Reserve. South Island won by six wickets. He also took four wickets.

Joining Wellington he made his debut for them against Canterbury in the Plunket Shield once again at the Basin Reserve on 27 December 1935. Wellington won the toss and decided to bat making 196, Maloney opening the batting made twenty-three before being bowled by the New Zealand test cricketer Ian Cromb. The New Zealand test cricketer Bill Merritt taking five wickets for seventy-two off twenty-three overs. In reply Canterbury made 122. In their second innings Wellington made 112, Moloney made thirty-four before being bowled by Bill Merritt. Merritt taking five wickets for forty-nine off fourteen overs during the innings. In their second innings Canterbury made 184. The Wellington bowler Bernard Griffiths taking six wickets for fifty-five off fourteen overs. Wellington won by two runs.

Moloney went on to play for Wellington in the Plunket Shield against Otago, Auckland, Canterbury playing against the sides several times between 1935 and 1938. He also played for New Zealand against the MCC in New Zealand on 24 March 1937 at the Basin Reserve. The match was drawn. The on form Moloney was then selected to go the New Zealand Tour of the British Isles in 1937.

He made his debut for New Zealand against Surrey at the Oval on 8 May 1937. Surrey won the toss and decided to bat making 149. Moloney bowled two overs taking no wickets for nine. In reply New Zealand made 233 Moloney making nine before being caught by Edward Brooks off the bowling of the England test cricketer, Alfred Richard Gover (*Wisden* cricketer of the year 1937). Gover bowled twenty-eight overs taking six wickets for fifty-seven runs. In their second innings Surrey made 127 before the match ended. The match was drawn.

He went on to play for New Zealand against the MCC, Glamorgan, Oxford University, Cambridge University, Lancashire, Derbyshire, Worcestershire and Nottinghamshire.

Moloney was selected to play in the first test commencing on 26 June 1937 at Lord's Cricket ground St John's Wood. England won the toss and decided to bat making 424. Joseph Hardstaff making 114 and Wally Hammond 140. Moloney bowled two overs taking no wickets for nine. He also caught Joseph Hardstaff off the bowling of Albert William (Alby) Roberts of 114. In their first innings New Zealand made 295, Moloney making sixty-four before being caught and bowled by Hedley Verity (*Wisden* cricketer of the year 1932) who himself was killed in action in 1943. In their second innings England made 226 declared. In their second innings New Zealand made 175, Moloney being run out for zero. The match was eventually drawn.

After the first test Moloney went on to play against Gloucestershire, Leicestershire, Yorkshire and Scotland. Moloney was selected to play in the second test against England on 24 July 1937 at Old Trafford, Manchester. England won the toss and decided to bat making 358, Len Hutton (*Wisden* cricketer of the year 1938) made a century. In reply New Zealand made 281, Moloney, opening for New Zealand made eleven before being lbw to 'Big Jim' Smith. In their second innings England were held back to 187. Moloney also took two catches, Wally Hammond for a duck off the bowling of John Cowie and Walter Robins (*Wisden* cricketer of the year 1930) off the bowling of Cowie once again. John Cowie taking six wickets for sixty-seven off twenty-three overs during the innings. In their second innings New Zealand made 134, Moloney making twenty before being run out. Thomas Goddard (*Wisden* cricketer of the year 1938) took six wickets for 29 off 14 overs. England won by 130 runs.

After playing for New Zealand against Glamorgan and Warwickshire Moloney was selected for the third test against England, to be played at the Oval on 14 August 1937. New Zealand won the toss and decided to bat making 249, Moloney batting further down the order making 23 before being bowled by Wally Hammond. In reply England made 254, Joseph Hardstaff (*Wisden* cricketer of the year 1938) making 103. In their second innings New Zealand made 187, Moloney making 38 before being bowled by Denis Charles Scott Compton (*Wisden* cricketer of the year 1939). In their second innings England made 31 for one. The match was drawn.

Moloney went on to play against Hampshire, Kent, Sussex, and England XI, H.D.G. Leveson-Gower's XI and finally on 11 September 1937, Ireland, New Zealand taking the match by eight wickets. On the way home the New Zealand team stopped in Australia where Moloney played in all three matches, against South Australia (lost by ten wickets), Victoria (won by five wickets) and New South Wales, (lost by eight wickets). On returning to New Zealand Moloney resumed his career with Wellington, playing against Auckland (drawn). At the end of 1938 Moloney resumed playing for Otago making appearances in the Plunket Shield against Auckland, Canterbury and Wellington. He also made one more appearance for New Zealand against Sir J. Cahn's XI. The match was drawn.

Moloney made his final first-class appearance playing for Canterbury against Wellington on 1 January 1941 at Lancaster Park, Christchurch. Canterbury won the toss and decided to bat making 359, Moloney making 12 before being caught by John Lamason off the bowling of Thomas Pritchard, Pritchard taking five wickets for 87 off 22 overs. In reply Wellington made 316. In their second innings Canterbury made 233, Moloney making three before being bowled by Pritchard. In their second innings Wellington made 279, the New Zealand test cricketer Martin Donnelly making 138. Wellington won by four wickets.

Moloney also made three Hawke Cup matches playing for Manawatu against Nelson, Wairarapa and Hawke's Bay.

During his career Moloney played in three tests, making 156 runs, his highest score being 64 against England. He also bowled 12 balls for nine runs. He made three catches. During his first-class career he made 3,219 runs, his highest score being 190 against Wellington. He made two centuries and sixteen fifties. He also bowled 5,350 balls taking 95 wickets for 3,151, his best figures being five for 23 including three fine wicket hauls. He made 35 catches.

Working as an insurance clerk and living at 159 Cargill Street, Dunedin shortly after the outbreak of the Second World War, he enlisted into the 20th Battalion New Zealand Infantry being commissioned to lieutenant and posted to the Western Desert. On 14 and 15 July 1942, during the First Battle of El Alamein, the battalion became involved in the Battle of Ruweisat Ridge. The Ridge, a vital position, was held by the enemy and was in the centre of the El Alamein line, dominating the surrounding area. The 20th Battalion advanced on the position at night supported by the 18th and 19th New Zealand Battalions. At dawn it was discovered that the advance had bypassed numerous German strongpoints, leaving their front line on the ridge still intact. With the British armour, artillery and anti-tank units unable to break through to them it left the New Zealand battalions exposed on the ridge. The 15th Panzer Division counter-attacked on 15 July and, with limited means of stopping them, the infantry were quickly overrun. They were surrounded and the 20th Battalion had almost 200 men taken prisoner including Lieutenant Denis Andrew Robert Moloney, who died of wounds in German hands on 15 July 1942. He is buried in the El Alamein War Cemetery, grave reference II. E. 23.

First-class Career Batting and Fielding

	Mat	Inns	NO	Runs	HS	Ave	100	50	6s	Ct	St
Tests	3	6	0	156	64	26.00	0	1	0	3	0
First-class	64	119	7	3219	190	28.74	2	16		35	0

Bowling averages

	Mat	Inns	Balls	Runs	Wkts	BBI	BBM	Ave	Econ	SR	4w	5w	10
Tests	3	1	12	9	0	-	-	-	4.50	-	0	0	0
First-class	64		5176	3151	95	5/23		33.16	3.65	54.4		3	0

**Lieutenant Norman Henry McMillan
Auckland
One first-class appearance
4th Field Regiment New Zealand Artillery
Died 16 July 1942, aged 33
Right-handed bat**

'A fine man, a fine cricketer'

Norman McMillan was born on 2 September 1906 in Timaru, South Canterbury, New Zealand. He was the son of George and Agnes McMillan of Invercargill. He was educated at King's College (1922-4) where his talent for sports was soon recognized and he became captain of the rugby XV as well as playing for the college XI. He was also a member of College Rifles Rugby Football Club.

McMillan made one first-class appearances for Auckland against Canterbury in the Plunket Shield. The match was played on 8 January 1932 at Eden Park. Auckland won the toss and elected to bat making a very poor 56, the highest score being 17, McMillian making five before being lbw to James Thomas Burrows. In reply Canterbury made 218. McMillan bowled four overs and took no wickets for 18. He did however manage to hang on to two catches. The New Zealand test cricketer Ian Cromb bowled Henry Gifford 'Giff' Vivian, another New Zealand test cricketer, for 16 and Robert Crosbie Burns, bowled by the New Zealand test cricketer Mal Matheson for 11. Vivian took five wickets for 59 off 25 overs. In their second innings Auckland did better making 256, McMillan making seven before being caught and bowled by Bill Merritt. He also bowled one over taking no wicket for three. Merritt took eight wickets for 105 off 33 overs. In their second innings Canterbury made 98 for three taking the match by eight wickets.

McMillan married Sheilah Anne (née Wellwood) and they lived at 55 Bidwell Street, Wellington.

During the Second World War he served with the 4th Field Regiment New Zealand Artillery later being commissioned and becoming a lieutenant. He died of wounds received during the First Battle of El Alemein on 16 July 1942. He is buried in the Tel El Kebir War Memorial Cemetery, grave reference 1. N. 8. He is also commemorated on the King's College Memorial Chapel, Otahuhu, Auckland Roll of Honour, College Rifles, Rugby Union Football & Sports Club, 33 Haast Street, Remuera, Auckland.

Batting and fielding averages

	Mat	Inns	NO	Runs	HS	Ave	100	50	Ct	St
First-class	1	2	0	12	7	6.00	0	0	2	0

Bowling averages

	Mat	Balls	Runs	Wkts	BBI	BBM	Ave	Econ	SR	4w	5w	10
First-class	1	30	21	0	-	-	-	4.20	-	0	0	0

Lieutenant Colonel Howard Cyril Frederick Vella Dunbar
Europeans (India)
Three first-class appearances
40th (King's) Batt'n Royal Tank Regiment, R.A.C.
Died 23 July 1942
Aged 37
Right-handed bat

'A loss to his family, a loss to his regiment'

Howard Dunbar was born on 20 October 1904 in Poona. He was the son of Colonel B.H.V. Dunbar DSO and Helen Vella Dunbar. Returning from India, the family resided at 18 Lynette Avenue, Clapham Common.

He was educated at Ampleforth where he played for the first XI, turning out against Old Amplefordians, St Peter's York, Durham School, Scarborough, Bootham School, Yorkshire Gentlemen and West Yorkshire Regiment. Deciding on a career in the army he went up to Royal Military College Sandhurst.

He was commissioned as a 2nd lieutenant in the Royal Tank Corps on the 27 August 1924. Promoted to lieutenant on 27 August 1926 he was later posted to India.

It was while serving in India that he made his three first-class appearances. He made his debut for the Europeans against the Muslims in the final of the Lahore Tournament on 19 March 1929 at the Lawrence Gardens. The Europeans won the toss and decided to bat making 105, Dunbar making six before being caught and bowled by the Indian test cricketer Jahangir Khan. Khan took six wickets for 49 off 21 overs during the innings. In reply the Muslims made 389 declared, Ferozuddin making 140 not out and Syed Wazir Ali 153 not out. In their second innings the Europeans made 210, Dunbar making five before being caught by Fida Hussain off the bowling of the Indian test cricketer Mohammad Khan who went on to take a further four wickets for 48 off 20 overs. The Muslims won by an innings and 74 runs.

He made his second first-class appearance once again in the Lahore Tournament and once again against the Muslims. The match took place on the 26 January 1930 at the Lawrence Gardens. The Europeans won the toss and decided to bat making 84, Dunbar making 15 before being caught by Karim Baksh off the bowling of Abdus Salaam. Salaam took six wickets for 31 runs off 12 overs. In reply the Muslims made 207. Reginald Charles Keller took five wickets for 50 off 21 overs. In their second innings the Europeans made 103. Dunbar made the top score of 28 before being caught by Karim Baksh off the bowling of Mohammad Khan. Khan took eight wickets for 33 off 23 overs. The Muslims won by a convincing innings and 20 runs.

Dunbar made his third and final first-class appearance for the Punjab Governor's XI, once again against the Muslims, on 1 February 1930 at the Lawrence Gardens. The Governor's XI, batting first, made 225, Dunbar making ten before being run out. In reply the Muslims made 348, the Indian test cricketer Syed Wazir Ali making 181. In their second innings the Governor's XI made 192, George Abell (of Worcester fame) making 116. The match was eventually drawn.

On his return he was appointed assistant instructor at the Tank Driving and Maintenance School, Bovington, on 3 June 1934. In December 1934 he married Joan Helen Anderson in Marylebone. On 21 March 1936 he was promoted to captain, then to major on 27 August 1941, and later to lieutenant colonel. He served with the 40th (King's) Battalion Royal Tank Regiment and was sent out to the Western Desert to confront Rommel's Afrika Korps who had been running rings around the British.

Ampleforth Journal 28 (1922) 58 Ist XI
Photo by Kittle, Scarborough

P. J. King.   A. K. S. Roche.   R. P. H. Utley.   M. P. Davis.   C. F. Keeling.   E. A. Kelly.
P. E. Hodge.   J. B. Ainscough.   N. A. Gehlert.   H. V. Dunbar,   A. F. Pearson.

In July 1942, the Afrika Korps had been stopped at El Alamein, a few short miles from the important town of Alexandria. Despite fighting desperately, the British 8th Army, with little amour, was almost done. If they were to go on the offensive and push Rommel back, they needed reinforcement, especially tanks. The 40th Royal Tank Regiment attached to the 23rd Armoured Brigade which had arrived in July 1942 were sent into battle as soon as they arrived without waiting for the rest of the division. The Germans held the vital Ruweisat Ridge which drove a wedge into the British position. If any attack was to be successful this position must be taken. As we saw in earlier chapters the New Zealand and Indian divisions had tried and failed with heavy losses. At 8 am on 23 July, the 104 Valentine tanks of 40th and 46th RTR charged north towards the New Zealanders' positions a mile and a half away. Running into a German minefield they quickly lost over twenty tanks. Pressing on with the advance, C squadron 40th RTR leading the way, they were quickly surrounded by the tanks of the 15th and 21st Panzer Divisions. Despite being outgunned they tried to close the range and engage the German tanks. Lacking high explosive ammunition for their 2-pounder guns, it was of little use and despite their bravery within two hours both the 40th and 46th RTR battalions had been destroyed, losing ninety-three Valentine tanks out of the 104 that set out. It was during this attack that the gallant Lieutenant Colonel Howard Cyril Frederick Vella Dunbar was to lose his life.

He is commemorated in the Alexandria (Hadra) War Memorial Cemetery, grave reference 3. D. 7. He is also remembered on the Camberley Memorial.

Batting and fielding averages

	Mat	Inns	NO	Runs	HS	Ave	100	50	Ct	St
First-class	3	6	0	64	28	10.66	0	0	0	0

Bowling averages

	Mat	Balls	Runs	Wkts	BBI	BBM	Ave	Econ	SR	4w	5w	10
First-class	3	-	-	-	-	-	-	-	-	-	-	-

6856738 Corporal Wilfred John Parry
Rhodesia, Natal
Three first-class appearances
1st Battalion The King's Royal Rifle Corps
Died 23 July 1942, aged 31
Right-handed bat

El Alamein Cemetery.

'Could twist a ball better than any man I have ever seen'

Wilfred Parry was born on 17 August 1910 in Durban. He was the son of Llewellyn and Edith Mary Parry of Durban.

Parry made three first-class appearances between 1930 and 1936. He made his debut for Natal against the MCC. The match was played on 21 November 1930 in Kingsmead, Durban. Natal won the toss and decided to bat making 288, Parry making 25 before being bowled by Jack White. Maurice Tate took five wickets for 64 off 39 overs. In reply the MCC made 402. In their second innings Natal made 114 for two. The match was drawn.

He made his second first-class appearance for Natal, once again against the MCC at the City Oval, Pietermaritzburg, on 10 January 1931. Natal won the toss and decided to bat making 107. Parry made 16 before being caught by Elias Henry Hendren (*Wisden* cricketer of the year 1920) off the bowling of William Voce (*Wisden* cricketer of the year 1933). In reply the MCC made 284, Arthur Woods taking six wickets for 83 off 26 overs. In their second innings Natal made 107, Parry making five before being bowled by Bill Voce, Voce taking five wickets for 31 off 20 overs. The MCC won by an innings and 70 runs.

It was five years before Parry made his final first-class appearance, this time for Rhodesia against Australia in South Africa. The match was played on 8 February 1936 at the Raylton Club, Bulawayo. Rhodesia won the toss and decided to field. Australia made 357, Leonard Stuart Darling making 108. In reply Rhodesia made 157 for four. Parry made 47 before being bowled by Arthur Chipperfield. The match was drawn.

Parry later married Barbara, of Umtali, Rhodesia.

During the Second World War Parry served with the 1st Battalion, The King's Royal Rifle Corps. During the war the battalion was deployed to North Africa and saw action as part of the pivot group within the 7th Armoured Division at the Battle of Sidi Rezegh in November 1941 and the First Battle of El Alamein fought between 1 and 27 July 1942. Parry was killed during the First Battle of El Alamein on 23 July 1942. He is commemorated in the El Alamein Cemetery, grave reference XXV. D. 6.

Batting and fielding averages

	Mat	Inns	NO	Runs	HS	Ave	100	50	Ct	St
First-class	3	4	0	93	47	23.25	0	0	0	0

Bowling averages

	Mat	Balls	Runs	Wkts	BBI	BBM	Ave	Econ	SR	4w	5w	10
First-class	3	-	-	-	-	-	-	-	-	-	-	-

Lieutenant Clifford Mark Barker
Transvaal
One first-class appearance
1st Royal Natal Carbineers, SA Forces
Died 27 July 1942, aged 25
Right-handed bat

'One of the finest men Natal has ever produced'

Clifford Barker was born in 1917 in Pinetown, Natal. He was the son of Herbert and Evia Barker of Port Shepstone, Natal.

He made one first-class appearance for Transvaal against the Orange Free State in the Currie Cup on 21 January 1938 at the Old Wanderers, Johannesburg. Transvaal won the toss and decided to bat making 475. Barker made 13 before being lbw to K. Hayward. The two South African test cricketers, Dooley Briscoe making 175 and Denis Warburton Begbie 207. In reply Orange Free State made 334, John Cecil Newton making 112. Barker took two wickets for 83 runs off 23 overs, Edward Leonard Liddle lbw for one and Andrew Maclean Pollock lbw for zero. He also caught Murray Godfred Francis off the bowling of Norman Gordon for 99. In their second innings Transvaal made 187 for three declared. Barker failed to bat, the South African test cricketer Bruce Mitchell (*Wisden* cricketer of the year 1936) making 103. In their second innings Orange Free State made 91. Barker bowled three overs and took no wickets for four. Transvaal won by 237 runs.

During the Second World War Barker served with the 1st Royal Natal Carbineers, SA Forces, being commissioned as a lieutenant. Between 26 and 27 July 1942 the Carbineers were involved in a subsidiary action in the El Alamein defensive battles at Qattara. It was here that Lieutenant Clifford Mark Barker was killed in action on 27 July 1942.

He is buried in the El Alamein War Cemetery, grave reference IV. H. 26.

Batting and fielding averages

	Mat	Inns	NO	Runs	HS	Ave	100	50	Ct	St
First-class	1	1	0	13	13	13.00	0	0	1	0

Bowling averages

	Mat	Runs	Wkts	BBI	Ave	5w	10
First-class	1	87	2	2/83	43.50	0	0

41642 Flight Sergeant (Pilot) Allan James Edwards
Otago
One first-class appearance
129 (RAF) Squadron, Royal New Zealand Air Force
Died 18 August 1942, aged 22
Right-handed bat

'One of the few'

Allan Edwards was born on 12 April 1920 in Dunedin, Otago, New Zealand. He was the youngest of four brothers born to Lewis John and Isabella Edwards of Anderson's Bay, Dunedin.

Edwards made one first-class appearance, for Otago against Canterbury on 25 December 1940 at Lancaster Park. Otago won the toss and decided to bat making 298. Edwards made 16 before being bowled by Reginald James Westwood, Alan Thomas Burgess taking six wickets for 52 off 20 overs. In reply Canterbury made 237. In their second innings Otago made 241. Edwards was bowled for a duck, once again by Alan Burgess. In their second innings Canterbury made 306 for three, the New Zealand test cricketer Walter Hadlee making 144 and Francis Patrick O'Brien 101. Canterbury won by seven wickets.

Felixstowe New Cemetery.

Not only was Edwards a fine cricketer but also an enthusiastic rock climber. He was the first to conquer Mt Alba, near Wanaka, a difficult climb only repeated once since. In 1941 he joined the Royal New Zealand Air Force training as a pilot in Canada. On his return to England he was posted to 129 squadron (RAF). The squadron was detailed to provided bomber escort and carry out offensive sweeps over France.

While with 129 Squadron (Spitfires) he made twenty-six sorties. During a patrol, which took place on 5 June 1942, his squadron was attacked by a squadron of Focke Wulf 190s off the coast of France. Edwards' Spitfire was badly damaged in the following dogfight and he was forced to turn back home. However he didn't quite make it as his engine finally failed and he was forced to bail out, watching his Spitfire crash into the sea. He managed to inflate and get into his survival dingy. Luckily he was picked up forty-five minutes later by a Walrus seaplane and eventually returned to his squadron.

At 9.30 am on 18 August 1942, Edwards, flying Spitfire number BL 934, took off with eleven other members of his squadron as part of an offensive patrol across the English Channel. It was his third operation in three days. They spotted and attacked a Luftwaffe floatplane off the coast of Cherbourg, and then in their turn were spotted and attacked by a German fighter squadron. Edwards' fighter was hit and crashed into the sea breaking up on impact. There was no report of seeing a parachute so it was assumed he had been killed and no search and rescue mission was launched. However they were wrong. Ten days later a destroyer patrolling the Channel discovered the body of an RAF sergeant floating in a small dingy. The body was that of Flight Sergeant Allan James Edwards. He had in fact managed to bail out but there was no rescue and he died of exposure. During the Second World War 65,727 British and Dominion RAF flight crew, including 2,960 New Zealanders, were killed or reported missing.

Edwards was later buried in Felixstowe New Cemetery, grave reference block B, section K, grave 30.

Batting and fielding averages

	Mat	Inns	NO	Runs	HS	Ave	100	50	Ct	St
First-class	1	2	0	16	16	8.00	0	0	0	0

Bowling averages

	Mat	Balls	Runs	Wkts	BBI	BBM	Ave	Econ	SR	4w	5w	10
First-class	1	-	-	-	-	-	-	-	-	-	-	-

Corporal Ernest Arthur Gasson
Canterbury
Three first-class appearances
26th Battalion New Zealand Infantry
Died 7 September 1942, aged 34
Right-handed bat

'Like father, like son'

Ernest Gasson was born on 11 November 1907 in Christchurch, New Zealand. He was the son of Ernest Arthur and Vera. Gasson made three first-class appearances for Canterbury in 1937 and 1938.

He made his debut in the Plunket Shield for Canterbury against Otago on 25 December 1937 at Lancaster Park, Christchurch. Canterbury won the toss and decided to field. Otago made 172. In reply Canterbury made 213, Gasson opening for Canterbury making 14 before being bowled by the New Zealand test cricketer Jack Dunning. Dunning took six wickets for 51 off 33 overs during the innings. In their second innings Otago made 271, the Canterbury bowler Edward Mulcock taking eight wickets for 61 off 17 overs. In their second innings Canterbury made 141, Gasson making 28 before being bowled by Dunning once again. Dunning took five wickets for 47 off 14 overs. Otago took the match by 89 runs.

He made his second appearance for Canterbury against Wellington, once again in the Plunket Shield, on 31 December 1937, at the Basin Reserve. Canterbury won the toss and decided to bat making 197. Gasson made 11 before being bowled by David Stuart Wilson. In reply Wellington made 231, Mulcock taking six wickets for 53 off 24 overs. In their second innings Canterbury made 99. Gasson made one before being caught by the New Zealand test cricketer Norman Gallichan off the bowling of Thomas Leslie Pritchard. In their second innings Wellington made 66, Wellington winning by six wickets.

Gasson made his final first-class appearance again in the Plunket Shield against Auckland on the 7 January 1938 at Eden Park, Auckland. Auckland won the toss and decided to bat making a remarkable 590. The New Zealand test cricketer Paul Erskine Whitelaw made 108, Alfred John Postles 103, another New Zealand test cricketer Verdun John Scott 122, and another, Alexander Malcolm 'Mal' Matheson, 112. In reply Canterbury made 258, Gasson making 34 before being caught by Whitelaw off the bowling of Matheson. Forced to bat again, Canterbury made 139, Gasson making 12 before being caught by David Baxter Edmonds off the bowling of the New Zealand test cricketer Cecil Burke. Auckland won the match by an innings and 193 runs.

During the Second World War Gasson served as a corporal with the 26th Battalion New Zealand Infantry. He was killed in action near El Alamein on 7 September 1942. He is buried in the El Alamein Cemetery, grave reference I. F. 26.

His father Ernest Gasson (1887-1962) played six first-class games for Canterbury.

Batting and fielding averages

	Mat	Inns	NO	Runs	HS	Ave	100	50	Ct	St
First-class	3	6	0	100	34	16.66	0	0	2	0

Bowling averages

	Mat	Balls	Runs	Wkts	BBI	BBM	Ave	Econ	SR	4w	5w	10
First-class	3	-	-	-	-	-	-	-	-	-	-	-

Sydenham Cricket Club
First Grade Team
Winners of the Canterbury Cricket Championship – 1923-24

Back Row: E.L. Watt, D.J. McBeth, G. Merriman, J. McEwin, E. Cockroft, A. Winter (Scorer).
Middle Row: W. Cunningham, W. Skelton, H. King, E.A. Gasson (Captain), C. Oliver, J. Murchison, J. Young.
Front Row: J. Grenfell, G. McBeth.

SX 7031 Sergeant Edward James Ross Moyle
South Australia
Fifteen first-class appearances
AIF 2/8 Field Ambulance Australian Army Medical Corps
Died 24 October 1942, aged 29
Right-hand bat/Wicketkeeper

'Died saving others'

Ross Moyle was born on 15 October 1913 at Moonta Mines, South Africa. He was the son of William James and Cordelia Moyle.

He made fifteen first-class appearances for South Australia between 1934 and 1940, his debut being for South Australia on 3 March 1934 at the Adelaide Oval. South Australia won the toss and decided to bat. They made 287, Moyle making 45 before being caught by John Jones off the bowling of James Ditchburn. In reply Western Australia made 140, the Australian test cricketer Clarence Grimmett taking seven wickets for 57 off 19 overs. Forced to follow on, Western Australia made 93 for eight. The match was drawn.

Moyle went on to play for South Australia against New South Wales, Queensland, Victoria and the MCC, most more than once.

He made his final first-class appearance against Queensland on 6 January 1940 at Brisbane Cricket Ground, Woolloongabba. South Australia won the toss and decided to bat making 230. Moyle made 32 before being bowled by John Stackpoole. Stackpoole took six wickets for 72 off 18 overs. In reply Queensland made 133. In their second innings South Australia made 252, Moyle making six before being bowled by Patrick Leslie Dixon. In reply Queensland made 350, the Australian test cricketer William Alfred Brown making 111. Queensland took the match by two wickets.

During his career Moyle made 496 runs, his highest score being 98. He also took 19 catches.

During the Second World War Moyle served as a sergeant with the 2/8 Field Ambulance Australian Army Medical Corps. He died of wounds received during the second battle of El Alamein on 24 October 1942. He is commemorated in the El Alamein War Cemetery, grave reference A IV. D. 11.

Batting and fielding averages

	Mat	Inns	NO	Runs	HS	Ave	100	50	Ct	St
First-class	15	19	0	496	98	26.10	0	2	15	1

Bowling averages

	Mat	Balls	Runs	Wkts	BBI	BBM	Ave	Econ	SR	4w	5w	10
First-class	15	-	-	-	-	-	-	-	-	-	-	-

60434 Gunner Alfred Palmerston Cobden
Canterbury
Three first-class appearances
4th Field Regiment, New Zealand Artillery
Died 24 October 1942, aged 29
Right-handed bat/Leg break googly

'One of the first to enlist'

Alfred Cobden was born on 9 May 1913 in Christchurch, New Zealand. He was the son of Alfred Palmerston and Mabel Cobden also of Christchurch. He was educated at the Christchurch Boys' High School where he played in the school's first XI. He made three first-class appearances for Canterbury, all in the Plunket Shield.

He made his debut for Canterbury against Wellington on 27 December 1935 at the Basin Reserve, Wellington. Wellington won the toss and decided to bat making 196. Cobden caught the New Zealand test cricketer Jack Newman off the bowling of another New Zealand test cricketer Ian Cromb. The New Zealand test cricketer Bill Merritt took five wickets for 72 off 23 overs. In reply Canterbury made 122, Cobden making 23 before being bowled by Bernard Griffiths. In their second innings Wellington made 112, Merritt taking five wickets for 49 off 14 overs. In their second innings Canterbury made 184, Cobden making 16 before being lbw off the bowling of Edward Dennis Blundell, Griffiths taking six wickets for 55 off 14 overs. Wellington won the match by two runs.

He made his second first-class appearance against Auckland on 2 January 1936 at Eden Park, Auckland. Canterbury won the toss and elected to bat making 322, Cobden making 38 before being caught by the New Zealand test cricketer Paul Whitelaw off the bowling of another New Zealand test cricketer Giff Vivian. Vivian took five wickets for 98 off 56 overs. In reply Auckland made 404. In their second innings Canterbury made 349, Cobden making the (joint) top score of the innings of 79 before being caught by Glen Hall Hook off the bowling of Henry Vivian. Vivian took six wickets for 92 runs off 35 overs. In their second innings Auckland made 228, the New Zealand test cricketer Walter Mervyn Wallace making a century. The match was drawn.

Cobden made his final first-class appearance against Otago on 14 February 1936 at Lancaster Park, Christchurch. Otago won the toss and decided to bat making 173, Bill Merritt taking six wickets for 56 off 16 overs. In reply Canterbury made 174. Cobden made one before being bowled by the New Zealand test cricketer Jack Dunning. Dunning took five wickets for 50 off 25 overs. In their second innings Otago made 350, Merritt taking seven wickets for 125 off 44 overs. In their second innings Canterbury made 230, Cobden making 27 before being caught by Lankford Daniel Smith off the bowling of New Zealand test cricketer Frederick Badcock. The New Zealand test cricketer Walter Hadlee made 101. Otago won by 119 runs.

In 1940 he married Pauline, of Wellington City, and they resided at Stillman Avenue, Christchurch.

During the Second World War he enlisted as a driver into the ranks of the 2nd Regiment, New Zealand Divisional Artillery, 4th Field Regiment. On 24 October 1942, during the second battle of El Alamein, his ammunition supply truck ran over a land mine and Cobden was blown up and killed. He is commemorated at El Alamein War Cemetery, grave reference II. C. 21.

Batting and fielding averages

	Mat	Inns	NO	Runs	HS	Ave	100	50	Ct	St
First-class	3	6	0	184	79	30.66	0	1	3	0

Bowling averages

	Mat	Runs	Wkts	BBI	Ave	5w	10
First-class	3	61	2	2/40	30.50	0	0

241858 Private Conan Doyle
Orange Free State
Two first-class appearances
1st Battalion Transvaal Scottish, SA Forces
Died 24 October 1942, aged 29
Right-handed bat

El Alamein War Cemetery.

'A popular cricketer, a popular soldier'

Conan Doyle was born in 1913 in Aberdeen, Cape Province, South Africa.

He made two first-class appearances, both in the Currie Cup in February 1938. He made his debut appearance for the Orange Free State against Easter Province on 11 February 1938 at the South African Railways Club, Old Ground, Bloemfontein. Orange Free State won the toss and decided to bat making 149. Doyle made zero before being caught by Walter Noble Pearce off the bowling of James McCallum Buchanan. Buchanan took seven wickets for 66 off 11 overs. In reply Eastern Province made 94, Henry Arnold Sparks taking six wickets for 35 off 14 overs. In their second innings Orange Free State made 235, Doyle making 29 before being bowled by Buchanan who took a further four wickets for 81 off 23 overs. In reply Eastern Province made 105. Orange Free State won by 185 runs.

He made his second and final first-class appearance for the Orange Free State against North Eastern Transvaal. The match was played on 26 February 1938 again at the Railways Club. North Eastern Transvaal won the toss and elected to bat making 71. Dudley Alexander Sparks took six wickets for 21 off 12 overs. In reply Orange Free State didn't do much better making 94. Doyle made seven before being bowled by the South African test cricketer Lennox Brown. Brown took six wickets for 55 off 18 overs. In their second innings North Eastern Transvaal made 414. Raymond Walker Currer made 150 and Robert Hicks 121. In their second innings Orange Free State only managed 46. Doyle was bowled by William Henderson for five. Henderson took seven wickets for four in nine overs devastating the Orange Free State batting and also making a hat-trick, Conan Doyle, Dirk Johannes Pretorius and Henry Sparks. He also took five wickets with six balls, Doyle, Pretorius, Henry Sparks, Dudley Sparks and Benjamin Herholdt.

During the Second World War Doyle served with the Transvaal Scottish, SA Forces. Becoming part of the Eighth Army he took part in the Second Battle of El Alamein being part of the force that halted the German assault on Egypt. Private Conan Doyle was killed in action on 24 October 1942. He is commemorated in the El Alamein War Cemetery, grave reference III. D. 2.

Batting and fielding averages

	Mat	Inns	NO	Runs	HS	Ave	100	50	Ct	St
First-class	2	4	0	41	29	10.25	0	0	0	0

Bowling averages

	Mat	Balls	Runs	Wkts	BBI	BBM	Ave	Econ	SR	4w	5w	10
First-class	2	-	-	-	-	-	-	-	-	-	-	-

Lieutenant Freeman Frederick Thomas Barnardo
Cambridge University, Middlesex
Two first-class appearances
Queens Bays (2nd Dragoon Guards) Royal Armoured Corps
Died 25 October 1942, aged 24
Right-handed bat

'great-nephew of Thomas Barnardo who began
the famous children's charity'

Freeman (Freddie) Barnardo was born on 16 May 1918 in Bombay, son of Dr Frederick Barnardo. The Barnardos returned to England where Freeman's father worked in Harley Street. He was educated at a prep school at Broadstairs before going to Eton, where he was in the XI playing against Charterhouse, Winchester, Harrow, R.C. Matthews' Canada XI, Hampstead, Haileybury and Marlborough. On leaving Eton he went up to Magdalen Cambridge where he read history, completing his course in 1939. Freddie was also a member of the Eton Ramblers, Old Etonians, and an enthusiastic member of the Butterflies Club.

He made two first-class appearances, both in 1939. He made his debut for Middlesex against Cambridge University at F.P. Fenner's on 13 May 1939. Middlesex won the toss and decided to bat making 398. Barnardo made zero being bowled by Patrick Dickinson, Dickinson taking five wickets for 95 off 27 overs. The England test player John David Benbow (Jack) Robertson (*Wisden* cricketer of the year 1948) made 106. In reply Cambridge made 244, John Ross Thomson making 133. The match was eventually drawn.

He made his second first-class appearance for Cambridge University against Yorkshire on 24 May 1939, once again played at F.P. Fenner's. Cambridge won the toss and elected to bat making 84, Barnardo making zero before being bowled by Cyril Turner. In reply Yorkshire made 350 for two, declared, the England test cricketer Len Hutton (*Wisden* cricketer of the year 1938) making 102 and another England test cricketer Norman Yardley 140 (*Wisden* cricketer of the year 1948). In their second innings Cambridge made 369, Barnardo making 75 before being lbw to Len Hutton, Ellis Pembroke Robinson taking five wickets for 80 off 19 overs. In their second innings Yorkshire made 104 for one. Yorkshire took the match by nine wickets.

After leaving school he first went up to Sandhurst before taking a commission into the 2nd Dragoon Guards. Army life seemed to suit him and he wrote home to his mother from Risborough barracks on 17 December 1939:

one way and another it isn't too bad … We undoubtedly lead a pretty hard life, getting up at six and going right through till five without really a moment to take it easy. However we begin with the aid of such things as PT three times a week to get inured and I was amazed at my fitness yesterday when after a ten mile route march in the morning I played rugger in the front row of the scrum and earned some praise for being always up with the ball and did not feel at all exhausted at the end of it and in fact had dinner and went to a dance hall in Folkestone not getting to bed till 12 and did not feel any the worse today. I very much doubt if I could have done that in my fittest days at Eton, certainly not since.

Despite this, he seems to have wanted to change careers and apply for the colonial administrative service or Sudan Political Service. To this end he asked the then headmaster of Eton College, C.A. Elliott, for a reference. Elliott wrote,

> *He bore an excellent character throughout. He was not a scholar but he was a good and intelligent worker and always tried his hardest. In the last two years he specialised in modern languages. He was a first rate athlete. For two years he was in the school cricket XI; in his second year he was vice-captain. He was also in the school rugby XV and he was a good Fives player and the best squash player in the school. He was in the Eton Society (Pop) for a considerable time and he was an efficient section commander in the OTC. For his last year he was captain of his house and captain of games in his house and his Housemaster has told me that he was one of the best captains of his House that he has had. I know from my own knowledge of him that he was an excellent influence both in the School and in his house and that he exerted considerable authority without making a display of it. He was always admirably behaved.*

Not everyone was as keen on his desire for a career in the colonies, as this letter, written in December 1939, from Arnold Churchill, Freeman's prep school headmaster, shows:

> *I may seem grossly impertinent but are you quite sure you would like the Sudan? All your life you have lived in a 'herd'. London, your home, schools, varsity, endless games and large family and you would choose one of the loneliest lives imaginable. So you think you would really really like natives? … with never another white man to talk to for months on end … so I beg of you to think very hard. I have seen so little of you for years and years that it may seem absurd for me even to beg of you to ponder deeply. But I have seen so many young people cajoled tempted and weedled into wrong jobs with the inevitable wasted lives … there is no job I would have loved more than the Sudan but then I do not mind being alone a bit. And I love those simple child-like natives. Just put this in the fire and think no more of it. Any hope of ever seeing you? AC.*

Serving with his regiment in the Western Desert, he was killed during the second battle of El Alamein on 25 October 1942. He was killed together with his crew when a German 88-millimetre gun destroyed his and five other tanks.

To add to Dr Barnardo's grief, his wife, Freddie's mother, died a few weeks after her beloved son. The family received many letters of condolence, one of the most poignant being from a family friend, R.D. Brewis, a chartered accountant of Cannon Street, London, whose son, a good friend and school mate of Freddie's, had also been killed in North Africa in July 1942. He wrote:

> *I shall never forget Freddie's gallant and graceful innings at Lord's which so largely contributed to his side's victory. These and many other proud and tender memories will I hope be of some consolation in your profound grief. The expression time is a healer is I fear a misstatement. The passage of time of itself will never heal the sense of loneliness or help to fill the gap in your life but from my own experience existence becomes more tolerable if one can evolve or cling to the faith that our sons have found peace and serenity. If in addition one can resolve not to disturb that peace by grieving too much then I believe that as time passes the sorrow will lessen; but never the void.*

Lieutenant Roddison Douglas Brewis (King's Scholar Eton College) 2nd King's Royal Rifle Corps is commemorated on the Alamein Memorial, Column 65. Freddie Barnardo is buried in the El Alamein War Cemetery grave reference coll. XVII. H. 16.

Batting and fielding averages

	Mat	Inns	NO	Runs	HS	Ave	100	50	Ct	St
First-class	2	3	0	75	75	25.00	0	1	0	0

Bowling averages

	Mat	Balls	Runs	Wkts	BBI	BBM	Ave	Econ	SR	4w	5w	10
First-class	2	-	-	-	-	-	-	-	-	-	-	-

Squadron Leader Claude Thesiger Ashton
Cambridge University, Essex, Free Foresters, England
127 first-class appearances
256 Squadron RAF (Auxiliary Air Force)
Died 31 October 1942, aged 41
Right-handed bat/Right arm medium

'To the boys of East London he was already a hero,
modest, unselfish, and amazingly generous'

Claude Ashton was born on 19 February 1901 in Calcutta. He was the youngest of the six sons born to Hubert Shorruck Ashton and Victoria (née Inglis). His mother was the daughter of Sir John Eardley Wilmot Inglis, who commanded the British Forces at the Siege of Lucknow during the Indian Mutiny. He was educated at Lindisfarne Prep School, Blackheath (which later became Abberley Hall, moving to Worcestershire), then going on to Winchester (three of his brothers were already attending). A good all round sportsman he was soon in the Winchester XI playing against Harrow, Eton, Marlborough, Charterhouse, Bradfield, New College Oxford, Free Foresters and H.S. Altham's XI. He also captained the side in his final year. He also captained the football, rackets and fives teams. On leaving Winchester he went up to Trinity Cambridge where he represented the university at hockey, cricket and football (triple blue) as well as captaining the England soccer team in their 0-0 draw against Ireland on 24 October 1925. He also won his blue for cricket.

Ashton made a total of 127 first-class appearances between 1921 and 1938 for Cambridge University, Essex, Free Foresters and an England XI. He made his debut at a university match on 11 May 1921 for Cambridge University against Lancashire at F.P. Fenner's. Cambridge won the toss and decided to field. Lancashire made 185. Ashton managed to hang on to a catch from the England test cricketer George Tyldesley (*Wisden* cricketer of the year 1920) off the bowling of Robert Gordon Evans for 34. In reply Cambridge made 205. Ashton made 27 before being bowled by the England test cricketer Harry Dean. Dean took six wickets for 67 off 23 overs. In their second innings Lancashire made 174, Ashton taking one wicket for 14 off three overs, George Owen Shelmerdine caught by the England test cricketer Arthur Percy Frank Chapman (*Wisden* cricketer of the year 1919) for 54. In their second innings Cambridge made 155 for five wickets. Ashton failed to bat. Cambridge won the match by five wickets.

He went on to play against Somerset, Yorkshire, Australia in the British Isles, Warwickshire, Free Foresters, Surrey, MCC, H.D.G. Leveson-Gower's XI and Oxford University.

During the long university holidays Ashton found himself playing for Essex, making his debut for them on 13 July 1921 at the Nevill Ground, Tunbridge Wells, in the county championship against Kent. Essex won the toss and decided to bat making 163. Ashton made zero before being caught by Geoffrey Norman Foster off the bowling of George Collins. Collins took five wickets for 37 off 12 overs. In reply Kent made 346, Lionel Paget Hedges (*Wisden* cricketer of the year 1919) making 116. Ashton bowled five overs for 16 and took no wickets, but he caught George Collins off the bowling of the test cricketer Jack

Russell. In their second innings and fighting back hard Essex made 343, Ashton making 12 before being caught and bowled by William John Fairservice. In their second innings Kent made 161 for two and won the match.

Returning to Cambridge University he continued to play for them during 1922 making twelve more appearances in university matches before returning to Essex and making eleven appearances for them during 1922.

Ashton played for Cambridge University until leaving in 1923. He continued to play for Essex (with one appearance for the Free Foresters) making his final first-class appearance against Australia on 4 June 1938 at Southchurch Park, Southend-on-Sea. Australia won the toss and decided to bat making 145. In reply Essex made 114, Ashton making eight before being caught and bowled by the Australian test cricketer Frank Ward. Ward took seven wickets for 51 off 23 overs. In their second innings Australia made 153, Stanley Nichols taking six wickets for 25 off 18 overs. In their second innings Essex made a poor 87, the Australian test cricketer Leslie O'Brian (Chuck) Fleetwood-Smith taking five wickets for 28 off 11 overs. Australia won by 97 runs.

During his career Ashton made 4,723 runs including four centuries and twenty-six fifties, his highest score being 118 against Surrey. He bowled 7,718 balls taking 139 wickets for 4,299 runs, his best figures being seven for 51. He took five wickets in an innings five times and ten wickets in an innings once. He also made 113 catches.

After graduating he qualified as a chartered accountant, getting a job with Price Waterhouse & Co before taking a job as a stockbroker. He was also chairman of the London Federation of Boys' and Girls' Clubs. In 1929 he married Isabel Norman-Butler and they had three children.

In 1938 he was commissioned in No. 909 (County of Essex) Squadron of the Auxiliary Air Force, promoted to flying officer that same year, flight lieutenant in 1939, and then squadron leader in 1941. In 1942 he qualified as a radio observer before being posted to No. 256 Squadron RAF, a night fighter unit flying Bristol Beaufighters. On 31 October 1942, while carrying out mock attacks on Wellington bombers in Beaufighter X7845, his aircraft collided with Wellington BK234. Both aircraft crashed at Perfeddgoed Farm near Bangor, both crews being killed. Ashton died with another celebrated Wykehamist, Squadron Leader Roger Winlaw (died 31 August 1942), who was piloting the plane.

He was buried in Fryerning Cemetery, section B, grave 145. *The Times* reported his burial: 'members of his squadron were bearers, and a RAF chaplain took part in the service.' A memorial service was held the following Tuesday at St Michael's, Cornhill, attended by representatives from Hoare's, the MCC, Essex and Surrey County Cricket Clubs and Winchester College.

On his death, the Warden of the Ashton Playing Fields at Woodford Bridge, Essex, wrote in *The Times*:

To the general public... Claude T. Ashton was chiefly known for his prowess at games, but there was another side to his character, which should be mentioned –

his work for and interest in providing the best facilities for organized recreation for those least able to afford them. Before the war he acted as the first chairman of the joint committee of the London Federation of Boys' and Girls' Clubs, who had recently acquired a lease of the old Essex County Cricket Ground, Leyton. Here was established, largely through his guidance, a youth centre for both indoor and outdoor recreation, under the best conditions – a forerunner of the Board of Education Service of Youth work. He was also chairman of the South-West Essex Fitness Council, whose work was just beginning to bear fruit when war came. The largest private open space outside London, fifty acres in extent, known as the Ashton Playing Fields and Cultural Centre, at Woodford Bridge, Essex, will, for generations to come, be associated with his name, as a centre where young people from the congested areas of east and central London can play games under the best conditions. To the boys of East London he was already a hero, modest, unselfish, and amazingly generous.

The fields still bear his name to this day.

Batting and fielding averages

	Mat	Inns	NO	Runs	HS	Ave	100	50	Ct	St
First-class	127	204	15	4723	118	24.98	4	26	113	0

Bowling averages

	Mat	Balls	Runs	Wkts	BBI	Ave	Econ	SR	5w	10
First-class	127	7718	4299	139	7/51	30.92	3.34	55.5	5	1

Squadron Leader Roger de Winton Kelsall Winlaw
Cambridge University, Surrey
Fifty-two first-class appearances
256 Squadron RAF Volunteer Reserve
Died 31 October 1942
Aged 30
Right-handed bat

'A classicist, he was known at school for being a
hard-working scholar and a first-rate athlete'

Roger Winlaw was born on 28 March 1912 in Morden, Surrey. He was the eldest son of the Reverend George and Minnie Winlaw. At Winchester he was in Mr Altham's House and was known for being a hard-working classics scholar, but it is for his supporting prowess that he will be remembered. One of the very best fives players ever at Winchester, he won Watneys and Thorntons three times, and in the open public schools fives competition he was twice the winner in the singles and once in the doubles. He was also in the cricket XI playing against Charterhouse, Harrow, Eton, Marlborough and Butterflies, as well as representing The Rest against Lord's Schools. He captained the XI in his last two years.

Winning a sizarship, he went up to St John's College Cambridge in 1931. Playing soccer as a freshman for the university XI, he scored the winning goal against Oxford in 1931, captaining the side in 1933. He also represented Cambridge at fives from 1932 to 1934, but where he really excelled was cricket, getting his blue, representing the university for three years, and captaining the side in 1934.

He made his debut for Cambridge in a university match against Yorkshire on 11 May 1932 at F.P. Fenner's Ground. Cambridge won the toss and elected to bat making 68, Winlaw making five before being caught by the England test cricketer Arthur Mitchell off the bowling of another England test cricketer Hedley Verity (*Wisden* cricketer of the year 1932). Arthur Rhodes took six wickets for 19 off 15 overs. In reply Yorkshire made 195. The Cambridge bowler Rodney Rought-Rought took six wickets for 53 off 25 overs. The weather closed in and the match was drawn.

Playing throughout 1933, he also appeared against Essex, Middlesex, Nottinghamshire, Surrey, H.D.G. Leveson-Gower's XI, MCC, Oxford, Sussex, West Indies in England, Northamptonshire, Lancashire and the Free Foresters. He played against many of the sides more than once.

For the rest of 1933 while on holiday from Cambridge he played for Surrey. He made his debut for them in the county championship on 9 August 1933 at the Central Recreation Ground, Hastings, against Sussex. Sussex won the toss and decided to bat making 441, the England test cricketer James Horace Parks making 163. The Surrey and England test cricketer Percy Fender (*Wisden* cricketer of the year 1915) took six wickets for 105 off 41 overs. In their first innings Surrey made 214, Winlaw making 25 before being bowled by the England test cricketer James Langridge (*Wisden* cricketer of the year 1932). Following on, Surrey made 36 for two. Winlaw failed to bat. The match was drawn.

For the rest of 1933 Winlaw made a further six county championship appearances, against Northamptonshire, Essex, Middlesex (twice), Yorkshire and Leicestershire. Returning to Cambridge, he made eleven appearances for them in 1934 against Yorkshire, Australia in the British Isles, Glamorgan, Essex, Free Foresters, Sussex, Surrey, Worcestershire, MCC and Oxford. For the rest of 1934 he continued to play for Surrey in the county championship and in 1935 he turned out for the MCC against Yorkshire, and in 1936 for the MCC against Kent and Yorkshire.

He made his final first-class appearance for an England XI against New Zealand on 1 September 1937 at the Cheriton Road Sports Ground, Folkestone. England won the toss and decided to bat making 464, Roger Kimpton making 23 before being bowled by Alby Roberts, and Bryan Valentine making 102. In reply New Zealand made 431. Winlaw caught D.A.R. Moloney off the bowling of William John Edrich for 140, John Lambert (Jack) Kerr also made a century, making 112. In their second innings England made 186, Winlaw making 25 before being bowled by Jack Dunning. In their second innings New Zealand made 182 for two. The match was drawn.

Winlaw also made thirty-four minor county championship matches for Bedfordshire. He made 2,708 first-class runs, making seven centuries and eleven fifties, his highest score being 161 against Essex.

After taking a second class in history, he became a master at Harrow and in 1936 married Marsali Mary Seymour Seal, a schoolmistress, and they had a daughter and a son.

In 1936 he joined the RAFVR, as an officer with the air training section of the OTC at Harrow. In 1940 he served as a flight lieutenant in the Air Ministry, in charge of the ATC in schools, later being promoted to squadron leader. Training as a pilot, he was posted to 256 Squadron, a night fighter unit flying Bristol Beaufighters.

On 31 October 1942, flying with another first-class cricketer and former Wykehamist Claude Ashton (died 31 October 1942), he took off in Beaufighter X7845 from Woodvale for an exercise over North Wales. Winlaw was at the controls and Ashton was his navigator and radar operator. While they were carrying out mock attacks on Wellington bombers, their aircraft collided with Wellington BK234 and both aircraft crashed at Perfeddgoed Farm, near Bangor, with the loss of both crews. Winlaw was cremated, and his ashes were scattered over the sea. He is commemorated in panel 3 at the Anfield Crematorium, Liverpool, and on the War Memorial at All Saints' Church, Houghton Conquest, Bedfordshire.

Batting and fielding averages

	Mat	Inns	NO	Runs	HS	Ave	100	Ct	St
First-class	52	89	13	2708	161*	35.63	7	17	0

Bowling averages

	Mat	Balls	Runs	Wkts	BBI	BBM	Ave	Econ	SR	4w	5w	10
First-class	52	41	31	0	-	-	-	4.53	-	0	0	0

Commander Robert Hearfield Stephenson DSO
Royal Navy
Three first-class appearances
Royal Navy (HMS *Cromer*)
Died 9 November 1942, aged 36
Right-hand bat

'Went down with his ship like the Officer and Gentleman he was'

Robert Stephenson was born on 3 June 1906 in Brough, Yorkshire, the son of William Hugh and Ethel Stephenson. On leaving school Stephenson decided on a career in the Royal Navy and was commissioned as an acting sub-lieutenant on 15 September 1926, promoted to sub-lieutenant on 30 May 1927, lieutenant on 16 May 1929, lieutenant commander on 16 May 1937 and finally commander on 30 June 1941.

He made three first-class appearances for the Royal Navy between 1927 and 1928. He made his debut for them on 10 August 1927 against the Royal Air Force at the Kennington Oval. The Royal Navy won the toss and decided to bat making 347. Stephenson made 75 before being caught by Ernest Augustus Fawcus off the bowling of Reginald Fulljames. Cyril Cooke took five wickets for 82 of 29 overs. In reply the Royal Air Force made 321. Stephenson caught Charles Blount (died 23 October 1940) off the bowling of Reginald Brooks for 35 and Cecil George Wigglesworth off the bowling of Sidney Boucher for 19. Fawcus made 115. Brooks took eight wickets for 90 off 32 overs. In their second innings the Royal Navy made 81. Stephenson failed to score and was caught by Gerald Livock off the bowling of Cooke. In reply the RAF made 108 for four. The RAF won by six wickets.

His second first-class match was against the Army on 20 June 1928 at Lord's. The Army won the toss and decided to bat making 589 for five declared. Edward Williams made 228. In reply the Royal Navy made 298. Stephenson made two before being bowled by Harold Philip Miles. Frederick Georg Arnold took six wickets for 41. Forced to follow on, the Royal Navy made 332. Stephenson made four before being bowled by Miles for a second time. In their second innings the Army made 44 for no wicket. The Army won by ten wickets.

His third and final first-class game was against the RAF on 25 August 1928 at the Oval. The Royal Navy won the toss and decided to bat making 296. Stephenson made ten before being bowled by Richard Utley. Thomas Halsey made 102 not out. Cyril Cooke took seven wickets for 76 off 27 overs. In reply the RAF made 285. In their second innings the Royal Navy made 146. Stephenson made 31 before being caught by Ernest Fawcus. Reginald Fulljames took five wickets for 36. In reply the RAF made 158. Stephenson caught Fulljames off the bowling of Sidney Boucher for one. The RAF won by three wickets.

Stephenson played a total of fourteen matches for the Royal Navy.

Commander Stephenson was later awarded the DSO for his actions while serving on the Bangor-class minesweeper HMS *Cromer* (named after the seaside town in Norfolk) at Diego Suarez (*London Gazette* 25 August 1942) during the Battle of Madagascar. The battle was fought on 5 May 1942 to capture Vichy French controlled Madagascar. It began with Operation Ironclad which involved the seizure of the port of Diego Suarez situated at the northern tip of the island.

Commander Stephenson was killed when his ship hit a mine on 9 November 1942 off Marsa Matruh, Egypt. HMS *Cromer* was sailing from Alexandria with two other minesweepers of the 14 Minesweeping Flotilla, HMS *Cromarty* and HMS *Boston*. Their orders were to clear a route for a coastal convoy heading for Bardia. The *Cromer* detonated a magnetic mine from Italian barrage 'MM', laid in the area on 7 August 1942 by the Italian destroyers *Antonio Pigafetta* and *Giovanni da Verazzano*.

HMS *Cromer* was the first ship to be mentioned in the internationally popular broadcast *An American in England*.

Stephenson's body was never recovered and he is commemorated on the Plymouth Naval Memorial, panel 101, column 1.

Batting and fielding averages

	Mat	Inns	NO	Runs	HS	Ave	100	50	Ct	St
First-class	3	6	0	122	75	20.33	0	1	3	0

Bowling averages

	Mat	Balls	Runs	Wkts	BBI	BBM	Ave	Econ	SR	4w	5w	10
First-class	3	-	-	-	-	-	-	-	-	-	-	-

Captain Roger Henry Charles Human
Berkshire, Cambridge University, Oxfordshire,
Worcestershire
Fifty-nine first-class appearances
6th Battalion Ox and Bucks Light Infantry
Died 21 November 1942, aged 33
Right-handed bat/Right arm medium

'A sad end to a very popular master'

Roger Human was born on 11 May 1909 in Gosforth, Newcastle upon Tyne. He was the son of Arnold Henry and Emily Margaret Human. Educated at Repton, he was in the first XI, playing against Harvard College, Shrewsbury, Uppingham and Malvern. He also appeared at Lord's playing for The Rest against Lord's Schools, for the Public Schools against the Army, and for the Young Amateurs (captain) against the Young Professionals. He captained Repton in 1928, when he averaged 37.27. At the age of 17 he also began playing minor county cricket, representing Berkshire and playing for them on thirty-nine occasions.

On leaving Repton he went up to Cambridge winning his blue in soccer and cricket. Human made fifty-nine first-class appearances between 1930 and 1939, mostly for Cambridge University and Worcestershire. He made his first-class debut for Cambridge against Leicestershire in a university match on 21 May 1930 at F.P. Fenner's. Leicestershire won the toss and decided to bat making 229. In reply Cambridge made 245, Human making nine before being caught by Harold Riley off the bowling of Horace Charles Snary. The match was drawn.

Human went on to play nineteen times for Cambridge during the 1930-31 season, playing against the Australians in the British Isles, Free Foresters, Sussex, Surrey, MCC, Oxford, Yorkshire, Middlesex, Nottinghamshire, Leicestershire and H.D.G. Leveson-Gower's XI.

Joining Worcestershire, he made his debut for them against Cambridge in a university match on 27 June 1934 at the County Ground, Worcestershire. Worcestershire won the toss and decided to bat making 217, Human making the highest score of the innings with 75 before being lbw by Frank King. King took six wickets for 64 off 20 overs. In reply Cambridge made 116, Percy Frederick (Peter) Jackson taking five wickets for 31 off 14 overs. In their second innings Worcestershire made 251, Human making the (joint) highest score of the innings with 45 before being caught by his brother John off the bowling of King. The Indian test cricketer Jahangir Khan took five wickets for 90 off 41 overs. In their second innings Cambridge made 353, John Human making 146 not out (passing his thousand runs in first-class cricket). Cambridge won by three wickets.

Between 1934 and 1939 Human played thirty-nine times for Worcestershire, making his final first-class appearance for Worcestershire against Kent in the county championship on 16 August 1939 at the County Ground, Worcestershire. Worcestershire won the toss and decided to field, which as it turned out was a bit of a mistake. Kent made 492, the England test cricketer Leslie Ames making 201 and another England test cricketer Bryan Valentine 113. The Worcestershire and England bowler Reginald Thomas David Perks took five wickets for 75 off 19 overs. In reply Worcestershire made 142. Human made 15 before being bowled by the England test cricketer Douglas Wright (*Wisden* cricketer of the year 1940). Wright took seven wickets for 46 off 16 overs. Forced to follow on, Worcestershire made 241, Human making nine before being caught by William 'Hopper' Levett off the bowling of Claude Lewis. Douglas Wright took a further six wickets for 77 runs off 16 overs. Kent won the match.

Human was chosen for the 1939–40 tour of India but the tour never took place and Human lost out owing to the outbreak of the Second World War.

During his career Human made 2,236 runs including fourteen fifties, his highest score being 81. He also bowled 3,903 balls taking 51 wickets for 1,947 runs, his best figures being four for 42. He also made 34 catches. He also played for the MCC, and the Players against the Gentlemen.

On leaving Cambridge, Human became a master at Bromsgrove, playing his cricket during the school holidays. He married Rosalind M. Gepp in 1933 and they had two children.

During the war Human served with the Ox and Bucks Light Infantry becoming a captain. He died while serving in India on 21 November 1942. He is buried in Madras War Cemetery, grave reference 1. F. 18. He's also commemorated on the Bromsgrove School Second World War Memorial.

Batting and fielding averages

	Mat	Inns	NO	Runs	HS	Ave	100	50	Ct	St
First-class	59	95	4	2236	81	24.57	0	14	34	0

Bowling averages

	Mat	Balls	Runs	Wkts	BBI	Ave	Econ	SR	5w	10
First-class	59	3903	1947	51	4/42	38.17	2.99	76.5	0	0

Lieutenant Arthur Chudleigh Beaumont Langton
South Africa and Transvaal
Fifteen tests, fifty-two first-class appearances.
23 Squadron South African Air Force
Died 27 November 1942, aged 30
Right-handed bat/Right arm fast-medium

'one of South Africa's most prominent players'

Arthur (Chud) Langton was born on 2 March 1912 in Pietermaritzburg, the son of Arthur H. and Alice E. M. Langton of Isipingo Beach, Natal. He was educated at King Edward VII High School Johannesburg. Langton was one of South Africa's most prominent players. He played in fifteen tests and made fifty-two first-class appearances.

He made his debut first-class appearance for Transvaal against Griqualand in the Currie Cup on 21 December 1931 at the Old Wanderers, Johannesburg. Griqualand West won the toss and decided to bat making 186, Eiulf Nupen taking nine wickets for 48 off 23 overs. In reply Transvaal made 323. Langton made eight before being bowled by James Patrick McNally who took five wickets for 69 off 23 overs. Fred Susskind made 119. In their second innings Griqualand West made 219, Nupen taking a further seven wickets for 88 off 30 overs. In their second innings Transvaal made 86 for two. Transvaal won by eight wickets.

Langton went on to play against Natal, Western Province and Orange Free State, all in the Currie Cup.

In 1935 he was selected to play for South Africa in their tour of England, playing against Leicestershire, Cambridge University, Surrey, Oxford University, MCC, Middlesex, Derbyshire, Lancashire and Glamorgan.

As a result of his consistent form he was selected to play in the first test against England played at Trent Bridge on 15 June 1935. Langton failed to score and took one wicket, the England opener Herbert Sutcliffe (*Wisden* cricketer of the year 1920.). The match was drawn.

Selected to play in the second test, he was to be part of a historic victory for South Africa. The match was played on 29 July 1935 at Lord's. South Africa won the toss and decided to bat making 228, Langton making four before being caught by Errol Holmes (*Wisden* cricketer of the year 1936) off the bowling of Wally Hammond (*Wisden* cricketer of the year 1928). In reply England made 198, Xen Balaskas taking five wickets for 49 off 32 overs and Langton taking two wickets for 58 off 21 overs. Stanley Nichols (*Wisden* cricketer of the year 1934) caught Jock Cameron (*Wisden* cricketer of the year 1936) for ten and bowled Hedley Verity lbw for 17. In their second innings South Africa made 278. Langton made 44 before being caught and bowled by Wally Hammond. The star performer however had to be Bruce Mitchell (*Wisden* cricketer of the year 1936) who made 164 not out and batted throughout the innings. In their second innings England made 151, Langton taking four wickets for 31 off 11 overs: Herbert Sutcliffe lbw for 38. Wally Hammond caught Jock Cameron (*Wisden* cricketer of the year 1936) for 27, Leslie Ames (*Wisden* cricketer of the year 1929) for eight and Errol Holmes (*Wisden* cricketer of the year 1936) for eight. He also caught Verity off the bowling of Balaskas for eight. South Africa took the match, the first time South Africa had defeated England in their home county.

Langton was selected for the third test, taking four wickets. The match was drawn.

In the fourth test Langton took two wickets and in the fifth test he made 75 runs in the first innings, failing to bat in the second. He also took two wickets. The match was drawn.

In 1935-36 he was selected to play in all five tests against Australia. Australia took the first test by nine wickets, the second test was drawn, Australia won the third by an innings and 78 runs, they lost the fourth by an innings and 184 runs, and they lost the fifth by an innings and six.

Langton continued to play for Transvaal, making appearances against Natal, Western Provinces and Griqualand West.

He was selected to play for South Africa against the MCC in South Africa during their 1938-39 tour. The first test was played at the Old Wanderers on 24 December 1938. The match was drawn. The second test was played at Newlands, Cape Town, on 31 December 1939. Again the match was drawn. The third was played at Kingsmead, Durban, on 21 January 1939, England winning by an innings and 13 runs. The fourth was played at the Old Wanderers on 18 February 1939, the match was drawn. The fifth was played at Kingsmead on 3 March 1939. The match was drawn. This was the final test match Langton played in.

Langton made his final first-class appearance for Transvaal against Western Province at Newlands on 1 January 1942. Western Province won the toss and decided to bat making 237, Langton taking two wickets for 41 off 17 overs. Kenneth Gerard Fismer caught Lawrence Stanley Dacey for 54 and Alexander Bernard John Reid caught Charles George Bromham for 16. In reply Transvaal made 251, Langton making 50 before being caught by the South African test cricketer John Erskine Cheetham off the bowling of Reginald Lofthouse. In their second innings Western Province made 236, Sidney Kiel making 128 not out batting through the innings. Langton took two more wickets for 66 off 16 overs, Tobias Mostert Henry van der Spuy lbw for seven and Cheetham for a duck. He also caught Fismer off the bowling of Frank Belmont Warne for four. In their second innings Transvaal made 166, Langton making 39 before being bowled by Reginald Lofthouse. The match was drawn.

During his career Langton played in fifteen tests making 298 runs including two fifties, his highest score being 73 against England. He also bowled 4,199 balls, taking 40 wickets for 1,827 runs, his best figures being five for 58 including one five-wicket haul. He made eight catches. He also made 1,218 first-class runs including seven fifties, his highest score being 73. He also bowled 11,317 balls, taking 193 wickets for 4,969 runs, his best figures being six for 53. He also made nine five-wicket hauls and two ten-wicket hauls. He made 41 catches.

During the Second World War Langton served with the South African Air Force as a pilot, being posted to 23 Squadron. He was killed on 27 November 1942 in a flying accident in Maiduguri, Nigeria, while delivering a Lockheed B-34 Ventura II number 6096.

He is commemorated in the Maiduguri Cemetery, European section, grave 2.

Batting and fielding averages

	Mat	Inns	NO	Runs	HS	Ave	100	50	6s	Ct	St
Tests	15	23	4	298	73*	15.68	0	2	4	8	0
First-class	52	74	13	1218	73*	19.96	0	7		41	0

Bowling averages

	Mat	Inns	Balls	Runs	Wkts	BBI	BBM	Ave	Econ	SR	4w	5w	10
Tests	15	23	4199	1827	40	5/58	6/89	45.67	2.61	104.9	4	1	0
First-class	52		11317	4969	193	6/53		25.74	2.63	58.6		9	2

Flying Officer Charles William Walker
South Australia
109 first-class appearances
50 Squadron Royal Australian Air Force
Died 18 December 1942, aged 33
Right-handed bat/Wicketkeeper

'Fell serving over Germany with the RAF'

Charles Walker (Chilla) was born on 19 February 1909 in Brompton, Adelaide, South Australia. He was the son of Edward and Myrtle May Walker. He began his cricketing career for the local Coglin Street Mission Cricket Club before making his Adelaide Grade cricket debut for West Torrens Cricket Club, later moving to Prospect Cricket Club. He went on to make 109 first-class appearances between 1 March 1929 and 25 December 1940.

He made his debut first-class appearance for South Australia against New South Wales in the Sheffield Shield on 1 March 1929 at Sydney Cricket Ground. New South Wales won the toss and elected to bat making 326. Playing as wicketkeeper, Walker caught two and stumped two: Australian test cricketer Archibald Jackson bowled John Drake Scott for six, Don Bradman bowled by the Australian test cricketer Clarence Grimmett (*Wisden* cricketer of the year 1931) for 35, he stumped Frank Slater Jordan off the bowling of Grimmett for 65, and John Edward Halford Hooker bowled Grimmett for 62. In reply South Australia made 280. Walker made 26 before being bowled by Norman O'Neil Morris. Gordon William Harris, opening for South Australia, made 107. In their second innings New South Wales made 399. Walker stumped three, caught one, and ran out one. He stumped the Australian test cricketer Alan George Fairfax bowled Grimmett for 41, Archibald Jackson for 38, and Halford Hooker bowled Grimmett for six. He caught Don Bradman bowled Thomas Andrew Carlton for 175 and ran out William Henry Warwick Lampe for 17. In their second innings South Australia made 385, Walker making three before being caught by Jackson off the bowling of Fairfax. New South Wales took the match by 60 runs.

He went on to play against the MCC in Australia, J. Ryder's XI against W.M. Woodfull's XI, Queensland, Victoria and Tasmania.

He represented an Australian XI against Western Australia, being chosen to go on the tour of the British Isles between 21 March 1930 and 27 August 1930. On returning to Australia he continued to play for South Australia, and went on tour to the British Isles again in 1938.

He made his final first-class appearance for South Australia against Victoria on 25 December 1940 at the Adelaide Oval. South Australia won the toss and decided to bat making 191. Walker made 40, the second highest score of the innings before being caught by Everard Audley 'Bill' Baker off the bowling of the Australian test cricketer Ian William Geddes Johnson. He reply Victoria made 172. Walker caught Desmond Hugh Fothergill off the bowling of Philip Lovett Ridings for 18 and Ian Johnson off the bowling of Harold Cotton for 29. He also stumped the Australian test cricketer Morris William Sievers off the bowling of Frank Ward for 14. In their second innings South Australia made 421. Walker made four before being caught by George Stanley Meikle off the bowling of the Australian test cricketer Douglas Thomas Ring. The Australian test cricketer Jack Badcock made 172. In their second innings Victoria made 265. Walker stumped Gordon Erle Tamblyn off the bowling of Grimmett for ten. He also ran out Ring for 24.

Unfortunately for Walker, a succession of finger injuries hampered his career and he missed the 1934 England tour. Chosen for the 1938 Ashes tour of England, he again suffered a succession of injuries and did not play in a single test.

During his career Walker made 1,754 runs including two fifties, his highest score being 71. He also made 171 catches and 149 stumpings.

He married Daphne Lucy of Brompton, South Australia.

Walker enlisted in the Royal Australian Air Force on 3 February 1941 becoming a flying officer, assigned to 14 Operational Training Unit, flying Lancaster bombers with 50 Squadron RAF. Walker was killed when he was shot down over Soltau, Germany, on 18 December 1942. His body was never recovered and he is commemorated on the Runnymede memorial, Panel 111.

The South Australian Cricket Association now presents the Charlie Walker Trophy to the best wicketkeeper in Adelaide Grade cricket. Walker's nephew Greg Quinn won the award seven times.

Batting and fielding averages

	Mat	Inns	NO	Runs	HS	Ave	100	50	Ct	St
First-class	109	152	35	1754	71	14.99	0	2	171	149

Captain Peter Henry Bairnsfather Cloete
Western Province
Nine first-class matches
Duke of Edinburgh's Own Rifles, SA Forces attached 1st SA
Division HQ staff
Died 19 December 1942, aged 25
Right-handed bat/Right arm slow

A pleasure to play against

Peter Cloete was born on 5 March 1917 in Cape Town, the son of Hugh and Nicolette Bairnsfather of Wyberg. He was educated at the Western Province preparatory school and the Diocesan College (1927–1935). He owned the Alphen, Constantia, a first-class hotel which is still there today.

Cloete made nine first-class appearances for Western Province between December 1936 and March 1940, six in the Currie Cup. He made his debut for Western Province against Griqualand West on 26 December 1936 in the Currie Cup played at Newlands. Western Province won the toss and decided to bat making 460, Cloete making four before being bowled by Alexander Dunn. The South African test player Pieter Gerhard Vintcent van der Bijl made 195. In reply Griqualand West made 222. Cloete bowled 22 overs taking four wickets for 58: Thomas Henry Boggan for 11, Lisle Ernest McNamara for 27, Patrick Gallagher stumped Abraham Glantz for one, and Charles William Millar also stumped Glantz for zero. Forced to follow on, Griqualand West made 241. Cloete bowled 33 overs taking three further wickets for 75: the South African test cricketer Frank Nicholson for zero, Arthur Schulze caught Andrew Ralph for 56, and Millar for five. In their second innings Western Province made five for no wicket, taking the game by ten wickets.

He next played against Transvaal on 1 January 1937 in the Currie Cup, again at Newlands. He failed to take a wicket or make a run (only batting in Western Province's first innings). The match was drawn.

His third match was against the Orange Free State once again in the Currie Cup, on 20 February 1937 at Newlands. He failed to make any runs but did take eight wickets, five in Orange Free State's second innings. Western Province won by an innings and 99 runs.

He next turned out against Natal, again in the Currie Cup, on 6 March 1937 at Kingsmead, Durban. He made 13 and took four wickets. Natal won by an innings and 80.

Border was next, played on 13 March 1937 at Jan Smuts Ground, East London, in the Currie Cup. Cloete made five and took five wickets. Western Province won by an innings and 106 runs.

His final match in the Currie Cup came on 18 March 1937 against Eastern Province at St George's Park, Port Elizabeth. Cloete failed to bat or take a wicket.

It was another three years before Cloete made his next first-class appearance, playing against Natal on 2 March 1940 at Kingsmead. Cloete made 20 runs and failed to take a wicket.

He made his penultimate first-class appearance against Border on 8 March 1940 at Jan Smuts Ground, East London. He took five wickets and made no runs in his only innings. Western Province won by six wickets.

Cloete made his final first-class appearance against Eastern Province on 13 March 1940 at St George's Park. Easter Province won the toss and decided to field. Western Province made 187, Cloete making 29 before being caught by Robert Summer Gouldie off the bowling of Steytler Abbott Thwaits. John Meyer Leibbrandt took five wickets for 55. In reply Easter Province made 195. Cloete bowled ten overs but failed to take a wicket. In their second innings Western Province made 318. Cloete made three before being caught by Leibbrandt off the bowling of Arthur Heder Coy, John Cheetham making 108 not out and Sidney Kiel 120. In reply Eastern Province made 38 for one. Cloete bowled one over and failed to take a wicket for three. The match was drawn.

During his first-class career Cloete made 74 runs, his highest score being 29 against Easter Province. He bowled 1,832 balls taking 29 wickets for 969 runs, his best figures being five for 112. He also took seven catches.

During the war Cloete served as a captain with the Duke of Edinburgh's Own Rifles, SA Forces, becoming attached to 1st SA Division HQ staff. He was killed on 19 December 1942 when the plane in which he was a passenger, a Lockheed Lodestar, crashed into Kavirondo Gulf, Lake Victoria, shortly after leaving Kisumu Airport. It appeared that the undercarriage could not be raised after take-off because of an electrical fault in the undercarriage safety lock circuit. The aircraft was returning to South Africa from Cairo.

He is buried in the Thaba Tshwane (Old No. 1) Military Cemetery, grave reference L. 7.

Batting and fielding averages

	Mat	Inns	NO	Runs	HS	Ave	100	50	Ct	St
First-class	9	11	1	74	29	7.40	0	0	7	0

Bowling averages

	Mat	Runs	Wkts	BBI	Ave	5w	10
First-class	9	969	29	5/112	33.41	1	0

Officers of the Dukes shortly after the victorious Battle of Alamein in 1942. They are (back row, l. to r.) Lt. S. Bucher, Lt. T. G. Stone, Lt. G. E. Crighton, Lt. J. Fitzgerald, Lt. J. R. Bruckman and Lt. L. M. R. Grant; (middle row) Lt. G. W. Howarth, Capt. R. C. B. Riches, Capt. A. V. Bird (MO), Capt. G. A. H. Halverson (Chaplain), Lt. V. E. Dickson, Cpt. P. V. G. van der Byl, Capt. S. Weinstein (Chaplain), Lt. G. E. Pettit, Lt. J. A. Morrison, Lt. E. H. Wedgewood, Capt. E. H. Martin and Capt. P. Bairnsfather-Cloete; (seated) Capt. E. R. P. Davies, Capt. E. B. Edmeades, Capt. E. Hare, Capt. P. J. O'Sullivan, Maj. L. Lees, Lt-Col. S. B. Gwillam, Maj. A. Georgeu, Capt. G. B. Sharpe, Capt. A. D. F. Sales, Capt. D. A. H. Wells and Capt. J. G. Haswell; (in foreground) Lt. R. Fellows and Lt. I. Foster.

1943

66435 Gunner Ronald Clarence Crook
Wellington
Nine first-class matches
New Zealand Artillery, 6th Field Regiment
Died 17 January 1943, aged 35
Right-handed bat/Right arm fast

Loved his country as much as his cricket

Ronald Crook was born on 28 January 1907 in Wellington, New Zealand. He was the son of Bert and Florrie Crook.

He made nine first-class appearances for Wellington between December 1930 and February 1934, eight of which were in the Plunket Shield. He made his debut for Wellington against Otago in the Plunket Shield on 25 December 1930 at the Basin Reserve. Wellington won the toss and decided to bat making 189. Crook made 32 not out. In reply Otago made 161. Crook bowled 17 overs taking four wickets for 43: the New Zealand test cricketer D.A.R. Moloney and Otago opener caught Alex Newman for five, Reginald William Henry Cherry (the other Otago opener) caught Kenneth James for 44, Arthur Galland caught Alex Newman for six, and Cedric Elmes for 17. In their second innings Wellington made 369. Crook made 22 before being bowled by Thomas Lemin. The New Zealand test cricketer Herbert Mendelson McGirr made 141. In reply Otago made 195. Crook bowled 22 overs taking a further three wickets for 62: Victor George Cavanagh caught McGirr for 14, Cherry caught James for 48, and William Hawksworth caught James for one. Wellington won by 202 runs.

His next match was against Canterbury on 1 January 1931 at Lancaster Park. Crook took three wickets and made 17 runs. Canterbury won by 139.

His next match was played against Auckland on 23 January 1931 at Eden Park. Crook made 16 runs and took one wicket. Auckland won by 167 runs.

On 25 December 1931 he played against Auckland, again at the Basin Reserve. Crook took two wickets and made 34 runs. Wellington won by six wickets.

His next match was played against Canterbury on 1 January 1932 at the Basin Reserve. Crook took no wickets and made 19 runs. The match was drawn.

On 19 February 1932 Crook turned out against Otago at Carisbrook, Dunedin. Crook failed to take a wicket and made no runs. Wellington won by two wickets.

Against Auckland on 23 December 1933 at the Basin Reserve, Crook made 33 runs and took no wickets. Auckland won by 178.

He made his penultimate first-class match against Otago on 16 February 1934 at Carisbrook. It was also his final Plunket Shield match. Crook took two wickets and made 41 runs. Otago won by 199.

Crook made his final first-class match against Canterbury on 23 February 1934 at Lancaster Park. Wellington won the toss and decided to bat making 305. Crook made seven before being bowled by Leslie Ernest Riley. The New Zealand test cricketer Eric William Thomas Tindill made 102. In reply Canterbury made 349, Percy Frederick Allen making 103. Crook bowled five overs and failed to take a wicket for 24. In their second innings Wellington made 196, Crook making 24 runs before being caught, bowled by Riley once again. Riley bowled twenty-six overs taking five wickets for fifty-seven. In reply Canterbury made 158 for two, taking the match by eight wickets.

During his career Crook made 253 runs, his highest score being 32. He also bowled 983 balls taking 15 wickets for 464 runs, his best figures being four for 43. He also made ten catches.

During the war Crook served as a gunner with the New Zealand Artillery, 6th Field Regiment. He died on 17 January 1943 and is buried in the Tripoli War Cemetery, collective grave 12. B. 4-8.

Batting and fielding averages

	Mat	Inns	NO	Runs	HS	Ave	100	50	Ct	St
First-class	9	17	2	253	32	16.86	0	0	10	0

Bowling averages

	Mat	Balls	Runs	Wkts	BBI	Ave	Econ	SR	5w	10
First-class	9	983	464	15	4/43	30.93	2.83	65.5	0	0

Captain Sydney George Fairbairn MC
MCC
Eight first-class appearances
Grenadier Guards
Died 19 January 1943, aged 51
Right-handed bat

Wounded in the first war only to die in the second

Sydney Fairbairn was born on 13 October 1892 in Cape Town. He was the son of the well-known Victorian rower Steve Fairbairn, who rowed in the Boat Race 1882, 83, 86 and 87, and was an early proponent of the slide seat.

Fairbairn made eight first-class appearances all for the MCC during their 1913 tour of the West Indies, his debut being on 30 January 1913 against Barbados at the Kensington Oval, Bridgetown. The MCC won the toss and decided to bat making 306. Fairbairn made 31 before being caught by Robert Challenor off the bowling of the West Indies test player George Challenor. Edward Humphreys made 106. In reply Barbados made 520 declared. Fairbairn caught Chester Allan Browne off the bowling of Sydney Gordon Smith for 64. George Challenor made 118 and Will O'Brian Gibbs made 129 not out. In their second innings the MCC made 185. Fairbairn made eight before being caught by Percy Hamilton Tarilton off the bowling of Walter Sydney Herbert Fields. Fields took five wickets for 58. Barbados won by an innings and 29 runs.

He made his second first-class appearance on 3 February 1913 once again against Barbados at the Kensington Oval. Fairbairn made zero in both innings. He also bowled nine overs taking no wickets for 58. Barbados won by an innings and ten runs.

He played his third match against the West Indies on 6 February 1913 once again at the Kensington Oval. Fairbairn made 17 and zero not out. The MCC won by seven wickets.

His fourth match was against Trinidad at the Queen's Park Oval, Port of Spain on 17 February 1913. Fairbairn made zero and 31. He also bowled nine overs taking two wickets for 31. The match was drawn.

His next match was against the West Indies at the Queens Park Oval. On 20 February 1913. Fairbairn made 31 and 17. He also bowled eight overs taking no wickets for 42. The West Indies won by an innings and six runs.

He next turned out against British Guiana on 1 March 1913 at the Bourda ground, Georgetown. Fairbairn made zero in both innings. He bowled ten overs taking two wickets for 26 in the first innings but no wickets in the second. The MCC won by 66 runs. This match was followed by his third against the West Indies on 6 March 1913. He made 44 in his only innings. He bowled eleven overs taking one wicket for 61 in the first innings and three wickets for 55 off sixteen overs in the second. The MCC won by ten wickets.

He made his final first-class appearance against British Guiana on 11 March 1913 at Bourda, Georgetown. British Guiana won the toss and decided to bat making 188. Fairbairn bowled 12 overs taking two wickets for 23, Jules Elwin Chabrol caught Arthur William FitzRoy Somerset for 21 and Edwin Richard Denys Moulder also caught Somerset for 30. In reply the MCC made 396. Fairbairn made 62 not out. In their second innings British Guiana made 123. Fairbairn bowled 12 overs taking two further wickets for 28, Moulder clean bowled for 13 and Simon Denzil Hinds caught Edward Humphreys for zero. Fairbairn also caught Paul Francis Ouckram off the bowling of Humphreys for nine. Humphreys took five wickets for 36 off 13 overs. The MCC won by an innings and 85 runs. He also made seven minor county appearances for Buckinghamshire between July 1913 and July 1914.

Fairbairn was commissioned into the Royal Buckingham Hussars and served with them during the Gallipoli campaign being seriously wounded during their attack on Chocolate Hill. On recovery in 1916 he joined the Grenadier Guards serving with them for the rest of the war. He was awarded the MC in 1919. His citation read:

10 December 1919 Lt Sydney George Fairbairn of the Grenadier Guards (Special Reserve) and attached to the 3rd Battalion is awarded the Military Cross for conspicuous gallantry and devotion to duty at Preux au Sart of 4th November 1918. He worked his platoon through the village, driving the enemy out of several positions, and capturing their machine guns and eighteen prisoners. The skill and speed with which he accomplished his task enabled the troops on his flanks to consolidate at dusk in a sound defensive position.

For a short time during the war Fairbairn was married to the writer, heiress and political activist Nancy Cunard. Their marriage lasted less than two years however and they separated in 1919. She died in 1965 in Paris. In 1926 Fairbairn married Angela Fane who survived him.

During the Second World War he rejoined the Grenadier Guards, dying on active service in London on 19 January 1943.

He was buried in the south east corner at St Nicholas Churchyard, Steveton, Hampshire.

Batting and fielding averages

	Mat	Inns	NO	Runs	HS	Ave	100	50	Ct	St
First-class	8	14	2	241	62*	20.08	0	1	3	0

Bowling averages

	Mat	Runs	Wkts	BBI	Ave	5w	10
First-class	8	373	12	3/55	31.08	0	0

Major Ronald Anderson Gerrard DSO
Somerset
Three first-class matches
7 Field Squadron Royal Engineers
Died 22 January 1943, aged 31
Right-handed bat

'The Bravest of the Brave'

Ronald Gerrard was born on 26 January (some records have the 18th) 1912 in Hong Kong. He was the son of William George, who was serving as assistant commissioner of police, and Elizabeth Ann Gerrard. On his father's death Ronald was sent home to England aged 15 to be educated at the Taunton School. His ability as an athlete was soon recognized and he played most sports including tennis, water polo, fives, rifle shooting and soccer. He was also in the first XV and first XI. An opening batsman, he headed the Taunton batting averages on three occasions, his best innings being 123. As if this wasn't enough he won the public schools weight-putting at Stamford Bridge in 1929 and 1930. Upon leaving school he became articled to a Bath firm of civil engineers.

Gerrard made three first-class appearances for Somerset, all in July 1935 in the county championship. He made his debut appearance against Worcestershire at Tipton Road, Dudley, on 6 July 1935. Worcestershire won the toss and decided to bat making 225. In reply Somerset made 197, Gerrard making 15 before being stumped by Bernard William Quaife off the bowling of the England test cricketer Richard Howorth. Howorth took five wickets for 60 during the innings. In their second innings Worcestershire made 273. In reply Somerset managed only 128, Gerrard knocking up 18 (second highest score of the innings) before being bowled by Peter Jackson. Jackson took a remarkable nine wickets during the innings for 45 runs. Worcester took the match by 173 runs.

He made his second first-class appearance against Glamorgan at Ynysangharad Park, Pontypridd, on 13 July 1935. Glamorgan won the toss and decided to bat making 119, the Somerset and West Indies bowler John Cameron taking five wickets for 50. In reply Somerset made 199. Gerrard made zero, bowled by John Mercer (*Wisden* cricketer of the year 1927). Mercer took six wickets during the innings for 72 runs. In their second innings Glamorgan made 225, the England test cricketer Jack White taking five wickets for 73. In their second innings Somerset made 146. Gerrard failed to bat. Somerset won the match by seven wickets.

Gerrard made his third and final first-class appearance against Worcestershire once again. It was played on 17 July 1935 at Rowdens Road, Wells. Worcestershire won the toss and decided to bat making 314, George Abell making 131. The England test cricketer Arthur Wellard took seven wickets for 74. In reply Somerset made a poor 56. Gerrard made three before being bowled by Percy Jackson. The England test cricketer Reginald Perks took seven wickets for 21. Forced to follow on, Somerset made 153, Gerrard being run out for zero. Worcestershire took the match by an innings and 105 runs.

Gerrard was also an outstanding Rugby player, turning out for both Bath and Somerset as a centre three-quarter and captaining both sides. He made a total of 157 appearances.

He made his debut appearance for Somerset on 11 October 1930 at the tender age of 17 retaining his place in the County XV until the outbreak of war in 1939, by which time he had made forty-five appearances for Somerset, twenty as captain. He also made fourteen international appearances for England, including their two successful Home Nations campaigns in 1932 and 1934, the latter a Triple Crown. He took part in eight victories, five losses, and one draw. He also turned out a couple of times for the Barbarians. He played his final game on 7 April 1942.

In 1937 he married Miss Mollie Taylor, a local architect who went on to become the first lady president of Bath Rugby Club.

Having been commissioned into the Territorial Army, he was called up at the beginning of the war, rising to the rank of major and serving with the 7 Field Squadron Royal Engineers. Sent to North Africa he was decorated with the DSO (*London Gazette* 31-12-42) for clearing a minefield while under heavy fire. His action in hazardous conditions contributed to the Allied advance in the North African campaign. His citation read: 'Major Gerrard showed the greatest courage and determination in his leadership which was an inspiration to all who saw it. The successful piercing of the enemy fields in this sector was largely due to his personal efforts and example.'

Three months later, on 22 January 1943, Major Gerrard was killed in action near Tobruk.

He is buried in the Tripoli War Cemetery, grave reference 8. E. 3.

Batting and fielding averages

	Mat	Inns	NO	Runs	HS	Ave	100	50	Ct	St
First-class	3	5	0	36	18	7.20	0	0	1	0

Bowling averages

	Mat	Balls	Runs	Wkts	BBI	BBM	Ave	Econ	SR	4w	5w	10
First-class	3	-	-	-	-	-	-	-	-	-	-	-

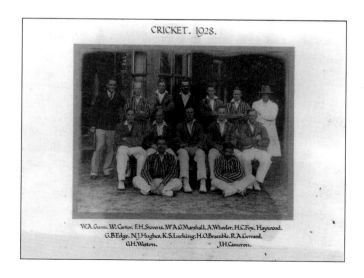

CRICKET. 1928.

W.A.Gunn. W.Carter. E.H.Stevens. W.A.G.Marshall. A.Wheeler. H.C.Fox. Haywood.
G.B.Edge. N.J.Hughes. K.S.Lucking. H.O.Bramble. R.A.Gerrard.
G.H.Weston.   J.H.Cameron.

Lieutenant Colonel Lancelot Townley Grove
Army/Combined Services
Four first-class matches
Royal Engineers
Died 9 February 1943, aged 37

'A very decent man, on and off the field'

Lancelot Grove was born in Satra, India, on 22 August 1905, the son of Colonel Percy Lynes and Lorina Harriette Grove of Tenterden, Kent. He was educated at Charterhouse where he was soon in the first XI. Deciding on career in the army he attended the Royal Military Academy Woolwich. While there he twice turned out against the Royal Military College Sandhurst, being on the losing side on both occasions. On leaving Woolwich he was commissioned into the Royal Engineers. He represented the Engineers against the MCC, the Royal Artillery, and R.C. Mattews' Canada XI. He made thirteen appearances for the Army between 1936 and 1939, four of which were first-class matches.

He made his debut first-class appearance for the Army against Oxford University on 22 May 1937 at the University Parks. The Army won the toss and decided to bat making 251, Grove scoring 96, just missing out on his century, being caught by Robin Evelyn Whetherly (died 27 November 1943) off the bowling of Richard West. West took five wickets for 74 during the innings. In reply Oxford made 137, John Stephenson taking six wickets for 54. In their second innings the Army made 115, Grove being caught by Barrington Julian Warren Hill off the bowling of Peter Michael William Whitehouse (died 19 November 1943) for a duck. William Murray-Wood took six wickets for 29. In their second innings Oxford made 230, taking the match by six wickets.

He made his second first-class appearance for the Army against Cambridge University on 29 June 1937 at F.P. Fenner's. The Army won the toss and decided to bat making 265, Gove making 70 before being caught by Wilfred Ernest Granville Payton off the bowling of Duncan Carmichael. In reply Cambridge made 395, Robert Hunt making 117. In their second innings the Army made 146, Grove being bowled by William White for 16. In their second innings Cambridge made 18 winning the match by ten wickets.

He played his next first-class match for the Combined Services against New Zealand in the British Isles on 18 August 1937 at the United Services Ground, Portsmouth. Combined Services won the toss and decided to bat making 180. Opening for the Combined Services, Grove was bowled for one by John Cowie. Richard Borgnis made 101. In reply New Zealand made 189. Grove caught Thomas Lowry off the bowling of Borgnis for 22. In their second innings Combined Services made 148, Grove making 43 before being caught by Jack Kerr off the bowling of Norman Gallichan (the highest score of the innings). In their second innings New Zealand made 140 for one, taking the match by nine wickets.

Grove made his final first-class appearance for the Army against Cambridge University on 28 May 1938 at F.P. Fenner's. Cambridge won the toss and decided to bat making 169. Grove bowled three overs taking one wicket for 11, John Philip Blake (died 3 June 1944) lbw for 70. John Stephenson took five wickets for 56. In reply the Army made 387. Grove made his highest first-class score of 106 before being bowled by Norman Yardley. Charles

Packe (killed 1 July 1944) made 176. In their second innings Cambridge made 79 for one. The match was drawn.

Grove also made three minor county championship matches for Kent Second XI against Norfolk and the Middlesex Second XI, twice. He also represented Band of Brothers against Queen's Own Royal West Kent Regiment and a Lord's XI against the Public Schools.

He married Joan Blanche of Camberley, Surrey.

Grove became a lieutenant colonel before he was killed in an accidental plane crash at Gander, Newfoundland, on 9 February 1943. He is buried in the Gander War Cemetery, plot 4, row 8, grave 28.

Batting and fielding averages

	Mat	Inns	NO	Runs	HS	Ave	100	50	Ct	St
First-class	4	7	0	332	106	47.42	1	2	1	0

Bowling averages

	Mat	Balls	Runs	Wkts	BBI	Ave	Econ	SR	5w	10
First-class	4	42	22	1	1/11	22.00	3.14	42.0	0	0

Grove can be seen on the first row of adults, fourth from the right wearing a white jacket.

Flight Lieutenant Frederick Gerald Hudson Chalk DFC
Oxford University, Kent, Gentlemen, MCC, England XI, Sir
P.F. Warner's XI, Gentlemen of England
156 first-class matches
Honourable Artillery Company/124 Squadron RAF
Died 17 February 1943, aged 32
Right-handed bat

'batted and fielded so brilliantly that he became
an attractive figure whenever he played'

Gerald Chalk was born on 7 September 1910 in Sydenham. Son of Arthur and Edith Blanche Clarissa Chalk of Cooden Beach, East Sussex. He was educated at Uppingham where he was quickly in the first XI. He played against Haileybury, Repton, Rugby and Shrewsbury, as well as representing W.D. Johnson's XI against Oakham. In 1928 he headed his school averages with 44.

Leaving Uppingham he went up to Brasenose Oxford, winning his cricket blue as a freshman in 1931. Chalk went on to make an impressive 156 first-class appearances. He made his first-class debut for Oxford University against Kent on 9 May 1931 at the University Parks. Oxford won the toss and decided to bat making 297. Chalk made 31 before being bowled by the England test cricketer Alfred Percy 'Tich' Freeman (*Wisden* cricketer of the year 1923). Freeman took eight wickets for 99 during the innings. The Oxford opener Brian William Hone made 105. In reply Kent made 486. Although three players, Ashdown, Woolley and Todd, got into the nineties, no-one managed a century. In their second innings Oxford made 280, Chalk making 59, the highest score of the innings, before being lbw to Freeman. Once again Freeman was deadly, taking five more wickets during the innings and reaching 2,450 wickets taken in first-class matches. In their second innings Kent made 92 without losing a wicket. Chalk bowled four overs for 19 runs and failed to take a wicket. Kent won by ten wickets.

Chalk continued to play for Oxford University until 1934, captaining the side in the same year. He made his final appearance for Oxford against Cambridge on 9 July 1934 at Lord's. Oxford won the toss and decided to bat making 415. Chalk made a brilliant 108 before being bowled by Jack Davies, who also took five wickets for 43 during the innings. The England test cricketer David Townsend made 193. In reply Cambridge made 400, Anthony William Allen making 115. In their second innings Oxford made 182, Chalk making 12 before being caught by Allen off the bowling of James Grimshaw. In their second innings Cambridge made 94 for two. The match was drawn.

Chalk began playing for Kent in 1933. He made his debut for them against Surrey on 15 July 1933 while on holiday from Oxford at the Rectory Field, Blackheath. Kent won the toss and decided to bat making 251, the England test cricketer Alfred Gover taking six wickets for 82. In reply Surrey made 261, the England test cricketer Jack Berry Hobbs (*Wisden* cricketer of the year 1909 and 1926) making 101. Freeman took six wickets for 110. In their second innings Kent made 377, Chalk who opened for them only making one before being bowled by Frederick Charles Gamble. Leslie Ames made 137 and Leslie John Todd 121. In their second innings Surrey made 152, Freeman once again proving deadly and taking a further five wickets. Kent won by 215 runs.

Chalk went on to play for Kent ninety-three times between July 1933 and August 1939. He made his final first-class appearance for Kent against Lancashire on 26 August 1939 at Crabble Athletic Ground, Dover, in the county championship. Lancashire won the toss and decided to bat making 262, Norman Walter Harding taking five wickets for 54. In reply Kent made 182, Chalk making eight before being bowled by the England test cricketer Richard Pollard. The England test cricketer Leonard Litton Wilkinson took five wickets for 54. In their second innings Lancashire made 301. In their second innings Kent made 382, Chalk making a solid 94 before being bowled by Wilkinson. Arthur Edward Fagg made 138. Kent won by five wickets. It was a good end to a distinguished career.

Chalk also made five minor counties championship matches for Kent Second XI. During his career Chalk made 6,732 runs with eleven centuries and thirty-one fifties, his highest score being 198 against Sussex. He also bowled 605 balls taking seven wickets for 409 runs. He made 62 catches.

He married Rosemary, daughter of G.N. Foster, of the Worcestershire family, who also played for Kent.

At the beginning of the war Chalk enlisted into the ranks of the Honourable Artillery Company as a gunner. Later he took a commission as a pilot officer (*London Gazette* 28 June 1940) in the RAF. After training he joined Bomber Command in February 1941 as a rear gunner with 218 Squadron. During a raid on Hanover his Wellington was attacked by a German fighter, probably a Messerschmitt ME 110. As a result of Chalk's accurate fire the fighter was driven off and probably shot down, last seen plunging towards the ground on fire. For his actions he was awarded the DFC. His citation read,

> One night in June, 1941, this officer was the rear gunner of an aircraft which took part in an attack on Hanover. On the return journey, whilst over the Amsterdam area, the aircraft was attacked by a Messerschmitt which pressed home two attacks from close range. Chalk fired two steady bursts which were observed to enter the enemy aircraft causing it to break away with flames coming from the starboard side. By his cool and accurate fire, Pilot Officer Chalk undoubtedly saved his aircraft and probably destroyed the attacker. Since February, 1941, this officer has participated in 20 operational missions and has shown high courage and devotion to duty throughout.

He was promoted to flying officer (*LG* 28 August 1941) and after training joined 124 Squadron as a Spitfire pilot. He was shot down on 17 February 1943 while flying Spitfire VI BR 585 during a dogfight over the St Omer area. No one saw his plane crash but his death was assumed to have happened on that date.

Mr G. de L. Hough, the Kent secretary later wrote,

> Gerry Chalk will be greatly missed by his many cricket friends – especially in Kent. Apart from his ability as a batsman and fielder, he was an excellent captain in the field. The way in which he nursed the bowling in 1939 was outstanding. He nearly always managed to keep one bowler fresh for use at a pinch, and I think it is fair to say that our rise in the Championship from twelfth in 1938 to fifth was largely due to this, and his example in, and placing of, the field.

Neither his aircraft nor his body were discovered and he was commemorated on the Runnymede Memorial to the missing. However in 1989 a positive identification of his remains was made and Chalk was finally interred in Terlincthun British Cemetery, grave reference, plot 14, row F, grave 12, on 30 June 1989.

Batting and fielding averages

	Mat	Inns	NO	Runs	HS	Ave	100	50	Ct	St
First-class	156	259	20	6732	198	28.16	11	31	62	0

Bowling averages

	Mat	Balls	Runs	Wkts	BBI	Ave	Econ	SR	5w	10
First-class	156	605	409	7	2/22	58.42	4.05	86.4	0	0

Wing Commander (pilot) Geoffrey Phelps Longfield
Royal Air Force
Two first-class appearances
105 Squadron RAF Volunteer Reserve
Died 26 February 1943, aged 33
Right-hand bat/Right arm bowler

Bravest of the brave, died in an accident over the target

Geoffrey Longfield was born on 4 December 1909 at High Halstow, Kent. He was the son of the Reverend Thomas William Longfield of High Halstow Rectory, Rochester, Kent. He was educated at the Aldenham School in Elstree, London where he played in the first XI. On leaving he took a commission with the RAF.

Longfield made two first-class appearances, his debut being for the RAF against the Army at the Oval on 4 July 1931. The RAF won the toss and decided to bat making 192. Longfield made one before being caught by Francis Hugonin of the bowling of Bernard Howlett (killed in action 29 November 1943). Adrian Clements Gore (*Wisden* cricketer of the year 1919) took five wickets for 51. In reply the Army made 416. Longfield bowled 16 overs taking two wickets for 51, Alexander Wilkinson caught Reginald Fulljames for 74 and Gore caught Brian Edmund Baker for 13. In their second innings the RAF made 187. Longfield made two before being caught by Montagu Burrows off the bowling of Bernard Howlett. Ernest Dynes took five wickets for 31 of 11 overs. The Army won by an innings and 37 runs.

He made his second first-class appearance just under a year later once again against the Army at the Oval on 29 June 1932. The Army won the toss and decided to bat making 490. Longfield bowled 19 overs and failed to take a wicket for 87. Reginald Eustace Hamilton Hudson made 217 and Cyril Hamilton (killed in action 10 February 1941) 105. Roy Scoggins took five wickets for 112. In reply the RAF made 159. Longfield made seven before being caught by Arthur Wellesley Tyler off the bowling of John Walford. Forced to follow on, the RAF made 201. Longfield made 26 before being caught by John Stephenson off the bowling of Arnold Minnis. The Army won by an innings and 130 runs.

Longfield also made two Second XI appearances for Kent in August 1928. He also made five further non-first-class appearances for the RAF against the Frogs, Royal Navy and the Army. He married Margaret Joan of Shorne, Kent.

Promoted to wing commander he was given command of 105 Squadron, a fighter Mosquito squadron. On 26 February 1943 he took off from RAF Marham in Norfolk in a Mosquito FB Mk IV DZ 365 for an attack on Rennes in France. The official report takes us from there:

op.Rennes. Collided with DZ413 and crashed in target area. T/o at 16:45 hrs. Seven aircraft successfully bombed target from heights varying from 50 to 800 feet. Clouds of smoke and debris seen in target area, which was severely damaged. One aircraft unable to bomb on first run up, circled and bombed from 800'. Smoke seen from distance of 20 miles, visibility being very good. One aircraft abandoned task over target, owing to leading aircraft's bombs exploding just as aircraft was in run up to target. W/Cdr

Longfield led the formation, and owing to a navigational error, turned sharply, causing a collision with the second aircraft, piloted by F/O Kimmel. The W/Cdr's aircraft was seen to crash out of control, and F/O Kimmel's aircraft was seen to be losing height with a glycol leak, apparently under control.

Longfield is buried in Rennes Eastern Communal Cemetery, grave reference section 18, plot 1, row C, grave 6.

His brother Thomas made eighty-two first-class appearances, mostly for Cambridge and Kent. He died in 1981.

Batting and fielding averages

	Mat	Inns	NO	Runs	HS	Ave	100	50	Ct	St
First-class	2	4	0	36	26	9.00	0	0	0	0

Bowling averages

	Mat	Balls	Runs	Wkts	BBI	Ave	Econ	SR	5w	10
First-class	2	210	138	2	2/51	69.00	3.94	105.0	0	0

Longfield is seated on the floor with legs crossed on the left.

Flying Officer Stuart Patrick King
Victoria
Twelve first-class matches
20 Squadron Royal Australian Air Force
Died 28 February 1943, aged 36
Right-handed bat/Wicketkeeper

'Australian hero on and off the field of play'

Stuart King was born on 22 April 1906 in Ararat, Victoria. He was the son of David James and Emily King of Victoria. A well-known all round Australian sportsman, King played twelve first-class matches for Victoria between 1926 and 1933, seven in the Sheffield Shield.

He made his debut for Victoria against Queensland on 17 December 1926 in the Sheffield Shield at the Melbourne Cricket Ground. Queensland won the toss and decided to bat making 147. King managed to catch William Rowe off the bowling of the Australian test cricketer Donald Dearness Blackie for 23. In reply Victoria made an impressive 533. King made 50 before being bowled by the Australian test cricketer Ronald Keven Oxenham. The Australian test cricketer William Harold Ponsford (*Wisden* cricketer of the year 1935) made 151 and the Australian test cricketer Hunter Scott Thomas Laurie Hendry made 140. In their second innings Queensland made 217. Victoria won by an innings and 169 runs.

King went on to play against New South Wales (won by an innings and 656 runs), South Australia (won by 571 runs), Queensland (lost by 234 runs), Tasmania (won by five wickets), Tasmania (twice, matches drawn), South Australia (lost by three wickets), New South Wales (drawn) and South Australia (Victoria won by 73 runs).

King made his final first-class appearance for Victoria against Tasmania on 14 March 1933 at the Richmond Cricket Ground, Melbourne. Tasmania won the toss and decided to bat making 90. King made two catches, Arthur Owen Burrows bowled by the Australian test cricketer Chuck Fleetwood-Smith for 15, and Gerald Thomas Henry James bowled Fleetwood-Smith for 13. Fleetwood-Smith took nine wickets for 36 during the innings. In reply Victoria made 229, King making 32 before being caught by Burrows off the bowling of James Michael Walsh. In reply Tasmania made 162, Fleetwood-Smith taking a further five wickets for 49. King bowled five overs taking one wicket for 33. Walsh stumped Stanley Oldfield Quin for zero. In their second innings Victoria made 34 for four. Victoria won by six wickets.

During his career King made 417 runs including three fifties, his highest score being 73 against Tasmania. He also bowled 126 balls taking two wickets for 98 runs. He made five stumping's and ten catches as a wicketkeeper.

As well as cricket King played Australian Rules football for Victoria League Club, Saint Kilda. Playing mostly as a defender he made forty-three appearances during three seasons between 1931 and 1933, scoring fourteen goals. He was also made captain and coach. King later studied to become a solicitor, practising in Ararat. He married Kathleen, of Glen Iris, Victoria, and they had two children, Diana and Gerald.

On 30 March 1942 King enlisted into the Royal Australian Air Force and was posted to 20 Squadron as an intelligence officer and reached the rank of flying officer. In August 1942 he wrote a moving letter to his wife:

> It's Saturday evening and I'm going to the pictures tonight. Bud Costello and some other equally exciting feature, but there is nothing much for a man in love with his wife to do . . . Lots of love darling, to you and the little ones

He was reported missing on 28 February 1943 after flying in a Catalina A24-25 from 11 Squadron and is presumed to have crashed into the sea on that date. The Catalina was on anti-submarine patrol off Cairns to protect a convoy. A garbled message was received at around 11 pm which contained the words 'force land', then nothing. An RAAF guard reported that he had seen an aircraft circling Fitzroy Island. The aircraft rounded Cape Grafton and disappeared in a north-easterly direction. A three-day search was mounted for the crew but found nothing. It was assumed that the Catalina had crashed into the sea north-east of Green Island. The crew consisted of Captain, 140 Wing Commander John (Jack) William Daniell, 2nd Pilot, 250281 Squadron Leader Eric Hamilton Barkley, Navigator, 406672 Flying Officer Lewis (Lou) Melvin Dunham, 1st Engineer, 408861 Sergeant Norman Notley Moore, 2nd Engineer, 2437 Corporal John Corbett Stain (No. 20 Squadron), 1st W/T Operator, 402703 Sergeant Allen Richard Eather, 2nd W/T Operator, 415378 Sergeant Alexander Eric John Elsbury, Rigger, 5778 Sergeant John Daniel O'Grady, Armourer 13970 Corporal Douglas Giffen Shaw Russell, Supernumerary, 22692 Sergeant Keith Arnold Watson and Supernumerary, 255266 Flying Officer Stuart Patrick King (Intelligence Officer No. 20 Squadron).

King's daughter Diana later recalled getting the telegram giving her family the awful news: 'I was wearing a yellow and brown spotted dress. Gerald and I were outside playing in the garden and a telegram boy came to the front gate and gave us the telegram. We ran inside to mum and said "Look what we've got". Mum came to the front door with my grandmother, and she opened the telegram and simply collapsed. I remember the doctor came.'

His son Gerald later recalled, 'When I was a youngster, I used to think he just got lost and one day that there would be a knock at the door and he'd be back. I was young, [but] reality soon set in.'

His wife never fully recovered from his loss and never remarried.

King is commemorated on the Port Moresby Memorial in Papua New Guinea, panel 9.

This wasn't quite the end of the story. The wreck of King's plane was discovered by a recreational diver from Cairns, near the Frankland Islands, about forty kilometres north-east of Innisfail in 2013.

Batting and fielding averages

	Mat	Inns	NO	Runs	HS	Ave	100	50	Ct	St
First-class	12	17	2	417	73	27.80	0	3	10	5

Bowling averages

	Mat	Runs	Wkts	BBI	Ave	5w	10
First-class	12	98	2	1/16	49.00	0	0

1487094 Gunner Norman Henry Bowell
Hampshire/Northamptonshire
Three first-class matches
HQ 35 Light Anti-Aircraft Regiment Royal Artillery
Died 5 March 1943, aged 39
Right-handed bat/Right arm slow

'Son of a famous father, who suffered as a PoW under the Japanese'

Norman Bowell was born on 2 February 1904 in Oxford. He was the son of Alex Bowell (1880-1957) who played 475 matches for Hampshire between 1902 and 1927 scoring over 18,000 runs.

Norman made three first-class appearances, two for Hampshire and one for Northamptonshire, in 1924/5, his debut being in the county championship for Hampshire against Northamptonshire on 11 June 1924 at the County Ground, Northampton. Northamptonshire won the toss and elected to bat. After only two overs had been bowled and one run scored the match was abandoned as a draw due to the weather.

He made his second first-class appearance against Nottinghamshire at Trent Bridge on 14 June 1924. Nottinghamshire won the toss and decided to bat making 273. Bowell bowled seven overs and took no wickets for 32. In reply Hampshire made 217, Bowell making two before being lbw to the England test cricketer Samuel James Staples (*Wisden* cricketer of the year 1929) for two. In their second innings Nottinghamshire made 307. The England test cricketer William Wilfred Whysall (*Wisden* cricketer of the year 1925) batted throughout the innings and made 150 not out. Bowell bowled three overs taking no wickets for 27. Nottinghamshire won by 124 runs.

Bowell made his final first-class appearance for Northamptonshire against Dublin University at the Country Ground, Northampton on 18 July 1925. Dublin won the toss and decided to bat making 197. Philip Wright took five wickets for 45. Bowell bowled four overs taking no wickets for 16. In reply Northamptonshire made 396, Bowell making 48 before being bowled by Acheson William Blake Kelly. In their second innings Dublin made 143. Northamptonshire won by an innings and 56 runs.

Bowell also made three minor county matches for Oxfordshire all against Monmouthshire all in 1927.

During the war Bowell enlisted into the ranks of the Royal Artillery as a gunner. Serving in the Far East he was captured by the Japanese during the fall of Singapore and imprisoned in Changi. He was one of the casualties during the infamous Kokopo and Ballalae massacres. At the end of 1942 Bowell, together with 517 other PoWs, was shipped to a camp on Ballalae Island in the Solomons to build an airstrip for the Japanese. They were very badly treated by their captors. Kicked, beaten, punched, thrashed and clubbed on a daily

Norman's father, Alex Bowell.

basis they were soon in a terrible state. This combined with dysentery, malaria and beriberi, took hundreds of lives including that of Norman Bowell who succumbed to his ill treatment on 5 March 1943. Not a single one of the 518 soldiers who had been shipped to the island survived the war. It was later discovered that, as the allies closed in, those prisoners who had survived the awful conditions and allied bombings were rounded up and either shot, bayonetted or decapitated by sword. In December 1945, an Australian War Graves unit exhumed 436 bodies from one mass grave and reinterred the remains in the Bomama War Cemetery at Port Moresby. A total of 188 war crimes trials were held at Rabaul after the war. The courts sentenced 93 Japanese war criminals to death, 78 were hanged and 15 were shot by firing squad.

Norman Bowell's remains were never identified and he is commemorated on the Singapore Memorial Column 13.

Batting and fielding averages

	Mat	Inns	NO	Runs	HS	Ave	100	50	Ct	St
First-class	3	3	0	56	48	18.66	0	0	0	0

Bowling averages

	Mat	Balls	Runs	Wkts	BBI	BBM	Ave	Econ	SR	4w	5w	10
First-class	3	84	72	0	-	-	-	5.14	-	0	0	0

Lieutenant Peter Henry Blagg
Oxford University
Ten first-class matches
1st Battalion Royal Welsh Fusiliers
Died 18 March 1943, aged 24
Right-handed bat/Wicketkeeper

'showed valor which has rarely been surpassed'

Peter Blagg was born on 11 September 1918 in Basford, Nottinghamshire. He was the son of Thomas Noel Blagg and Dorothy née Willis. He was educated at Shrewsbury where his sporting abilities were quickly recognized and he was selected to play in the first XI playing between 1935 and 1937. He made appearances against Malvern, Rossall, Repton, Uppingham and Repton. He also represented the Young Amateurs against the Young Professionals. On leaving Shrewsbury he went up to Oriel College Oxford. In 1939 he gained his blue for cricket, replaced the regular Oxford wicketkeeper Manning Clark (1915-91), and played for Oxford on ten occasions.

Blagg made his first-class debut for Oxford University against Derbyshire on 10 May 1939, at the University Parks. Derbyshire won the toss and decided to bat making 210. In reply Oxford made 72. Blagg was bowled by the England test cricketer William Henry Copson (*Wisden* player of the year 1937) for zero. Copson took five wickets for 12 during the innings. In their second innings Derbyshire made 72. Blagg caught two and stumped one, the England test cricketer Denis Smith bowled Stewart Pether for 36, Albert Ennion Groucott Rhodes bowled by Pether for two, and stumped Copson bowled Pether for zero. Pether took five wickets during the innings for seven runs. Oxford made 47 during their second innings, Blagg making one before being bowled by Copson. Copson took five wickets for nine and Alfred Pope took five wickets for 30.

He went on to play against Lancashire, West Indies in England, Free Foresters, Leicestershire, Somerset, Surrey, Sussex and the MCC. In the match against the MCC Blagg stumped three off the leg spin of Algernon Marsham, including the legendary Denis Compton.

Blagg made his final first-class appearance for Oxford against the old enemy Cambridge. The match was played at Lord's on 1 July 1939. Oxford won the toss and decided to bat making 313. Blagg was zero not out. Alan Shirreff took five wickets for 64. Cambridge made 157. Blagg caught Jack Webster off the bowling of David Henry Macindoe for four. In their second innings Oxford made 273 for two. In their second innings Cambridge made 384, Patrick Dickinson making a century. Gwynn Evans took five wickets for 127. Oxford won by 45 runs.

During his career Blagg made 67 runs, his highest score being 28 against Somerset. He also took 17 catches and made 12 stumpings. He also received his blue for football in 1939.

During the war he was commissioned into the 1st Battalion Royal Welsh Fusiliers, later becoming a lieutenant. He was killed in action during the Battle of Donbaik (in Burma) on 18 March 1943 while attacking at Japanese strongpoint. The action failed in its objective and the Royal Welsh Fusiliers lost 162 casualties, but they won two DSOs and two MMs. After the war, Field Marshal Slim said of the Royal Welsh Fusiliers that 'they showed valor which has rarely been surpassed,' in a battle which he admitted should never have been fought.

Blagg's body was never discovered or identified and he is commemorated on the Rangoon Memorial, face nine.

Batting and fielding averages

	Mat	Inns	NO	Runs	HS	Ave	100	50	Ct	St
First-class	10	13	5	67	28*	8.37	0	0	17	12

Bowling averages

	Mat	Balls	Runs	Wkts	BBI	BBM	Ave	Econ	SR	4w	5w	10
First-class	10	-	-	-	-	-	-	-	-	-	-	-

Captain Geoffrey Everingham Fletcher
Oxford, Somerset
Five first-class matches
1st Battalion Rifle Brigade
Died 27 March 1943, aged 23
Right-handed bat

'We will never know what great heights he might have reached'

Geoffrey Fletcher was born on 20 July 1919 in Charterhouse, Godalming, Surrey. He was the son of Major Philip Cawthorne MC and Edith Maud Fletcher of Hinton Charterhouse, Somerset. He was educated at Marlborough where he was a good enough cricketer to be selected for the first XI. He played against Harrow, Wellington, Winchester, Cheltenham College, Rugby and Eton. He also played Lord's School against The Rest and for the Public Schools against the Army. *Wisden* said that he was 'one of the best school cricketers of the year'.

On leaving Marlborough, Fletcher went up to New College Oxford as a scholar. During the 1939 season he was among a large number of freshmen at Oxford identified by *Wisden* as 'particularly promising'. He played both cricket and hockey for his university. He made his debut for Oxford University against Derbyshire on 10 May 1939 at the University Parks. Derbyshire won the toss and decided to bat making 210. Fletcher made two catches, the England test cricketer Denis Smith (*Wisden* cricketer of the year 1936) off the bowling of Gwynn Evans for 15, and the England test cricketer Leslie Fletcher Townsend (*Wisden* cricketer of the year 1934) off the bowling of David Henry Macindoe for 11. In reply Oxford made 72. Fletcher made 13 before being caught by Albert Edward Alderman off the bowling of the England test cricketer George Henry Pope. Copson took five wickets for 12. In their second innings Derbyshire made 72, Stewart Pether taking five wickets for seven. In their second innings Oxford made 47, Fletcher making three before being bowled by Alfred Pope (George's older brother). Alfred took five wickets for 30. Copson took five wickets for nine.

He made his second appearance for Oxford against Lancashire on 17 May 1939 at the University Parks. Oxford won the toss and decided to bat making 117, Fletcher making ten before being caught by Albert Nutter off the bowling of the England test player Richard Pollard for ten. Richard Pollard took five wickets for 39. In their first innings Lancashire made 200. In their second innings Oxford made 227. Fletcher made 65 which *Wisden* described as 'faultless' before being caught by Richard Pollard off the bowling of the England test cricketer Len Hopwood. The match was drawn.

Fletcher next played for Oxford University against the West Indies in England on 24 May 1939, at the University Parks. The West Indies won the toss and elected to bat making 480. Three of their batsmen made centuries, Herbert Peter Bayley 104, John Cameron 106 not out, and Ernest Albert Vivian Williams 126 not out. Fletcher bowled one over and took no wickets for 15. In reply Oxford made 232. Fletcher made 12 before being bowled by John Cameron. Forced to follow on, Oxford made 243. Fletcher made 14 before being bowled by Williams. The West Indies won by an innings and five runs.

Fletcher made his final first-class appearance for Oxford University against Somerset on 17 June 1939 at the Recreation Ground, Bath. Somerset won the toss and decided to bat making 226, David Russell Hayward taking six wickets for 79. In reply Oxford made 120, Fletcher making 14 before being caught by the England test cricketer Harold Gimblett (*Wisden* cricketer of the year 1953) off the bowling of the England test cricketer Arthur Wellard (*Wisden* cricketer of the year 1936). Wellard took seven wickets for 57 during the innings. In their second innings Somerset made 257. In reply Oxford made 144. Fletcher was stumped by Walter Luckes of the bowling of Herbert Buse for a duck. William Andrews took five wickets for 43. Somerset won by 219.

Fletcher made his final first-class appearance for Somerset against Northamptonshire in the county championship on 29 July 1939 at the County Ground, Northamptonshire. Somerset won the toss and decided to bat making 157. Fletcher, batting in the middle order, made 19 not out. Bill Merritt took five wickets for 42. In reply Northamptonshire made 246, their opener Eric Dixon making 123. The England test cricketer Arthur Wellard took seven wickets for 91. In their second innings Somerset made 290, Fletcher making 15 before being caught by Robert Nelson off the bowling of Christopher William Stuart Lubbock. In their second innings Northamptonshire made 110, Fletcher catching John Edward Timms off the bowling of Arthur Wellard for ten. Wellard took five wickets off the innings for 41. The match was eventually drawn.

Following the outbreak of the Second World War on 23 March 1940, Fletcher took a commission as a second lieutenant in the Rifle Brigade. He was posted to North Africa to serve with the Eight Army. He was killed in action on 27 March 1943 during an assault on the Mareth Line in the Matmata Hills, Tunisia, during Operation Pugilist.

He is buried in the Sfax War Cemetery, grave reference XI. VI. E. 14. and is also commemorated on the Godalming War Memorial 1939-43.

Batting and fielding averages

	Mat	Inns	NO	Runs	HS	Ave	100	50	Ct	St
First-class	5	10	1	165	65	18.33	0	1	4	0

Bowling averages

	Mat	Balls	Runs	Wkts	BBI	BBM	Ave	Econ	SR	4w	5w	10
First-class	5	8	15	0	-	-	-	11.25	-	0	0	0

Paul Ewart Francis Cressall
British Guiana
Four first-class appearances
Civilian judge
Died 8 April 1943, aged 50
Right-hand bat

A high court judge and victim of the Japanese

Paul (Frank) Cressall was born in Bromley, Kent, on 2 May 1893, the son of Paul and Katherine Mary Elizabeth Cressall of 35 Charleville Mansions, West Kensington. He was educated at Cranleigh where he played in the first XI, captaining the side in his final year.

On leaving school he settled in British Guiana. While there he made four first-class appearances for British Guiana, making his debut for them on 12 January 1912 against Trinidad at the Kensington Oval, Bridgetown. British Guiana won the toss and decided to field. Trinidad made 249. Cressall took no wickets but caught Lebrun Samuel Constantine off the bowling of Frederick Henri Abraham for 37. In their first innings British Guiana made 97. Cressall made 15 before being caught by the West Indian test cricketer Joseph Small off the bowling of Andre Cipriani. Forced to follow on, British Guiana made 116. Cressall made two before being bowled by Joseph Cephas Rogers. Rogers took seven wickets during the innings for 25 off 14 overs. Trinidad won by an innings and 36 runs.

His next match was against the MCC on 1 March 1913 at Bourda, George Town. Cressall was run out for zero in the first innings and not out four in the second. The MCC won by 66 runs.

His third appearance came on 11 March 1913, again against the MCC at the Bourda. Cressall made ten before being caught by Sydney Smith off the bowling of Arthur Plantagenet Francis Cecil Somerset. In his second innings Cressall made eight before being caught by Edward Humphreys off the bowling of Sydney Smith. Cressall also bowled five overs taking one wicket for 14: Mordaunt Henry Caspers Doll for 50. The MCC won by an innings and 85 runs.

During the First World War Cressall was commissioned into the British West Indies Regiment, rising to the rank of captain and serving in both Africa and Palestine and winning an MC in 1918 (*London Gazette* 27 July 1918).

On returning to British Guiana he made one final first-class appearance, against Trinidad on 23 September 1922 once again at the Bourda. British Guiana won the toss and decided to field. Trinidad made 107. In reply British Guiana made 133, Cressall making 23 before being bowled by Joseph Small. The Trinidad bowler Victor Pascall took five wickets for 36. In their second innings Trinidad made 190. In reply British Guiana made 135. Cressall made six before being caught by George Alric Dewhurst off the bowling of Pascall. Pascall took six wickets for 26. Trinidad won by 29 runs.

Cressall was called to the Bar at Gray's Inn in 1923, and appointed a stipendiary magistrate in British Guiana the following year. After seven years' service in that position he was posted to Jerusalem as chief magistrate and became president of the British courts in Palestine in 1936. Due to the death of the previous puisne judge Roger Lindsell in 1941, Cressall was offered the job and took it, travelling to Hong Kong to take up the position.

He arrived in Hong Kong in April 1941. Unable to escape the Japanese invasion Cressall was captured and interned. He was held prisoner at the Stanley Internment Camp. He died aged 50 of paralysis on 8 April 1943. The paralysis started in his legs and then moved to the rest of his body including his lungs. The disease was diagnosed as spreading paralysis of the spinal cord.

Shortly before the war he had been appointed chairman of the public enquiry relating to corruption in the Public Works and the Air Raid Precautions (ARP) departments. This was a major scandal at the time. Although it was known he had all the relevant papers with him when he was captured, they were never seen again and the case was dropped after the war.

During his internment Paul Cressall wrote a collection of verse, which is now held in the Hong Kong Public Records Office.

His wife Olga died in 1955. They had three children, Harry, Joan and Peter.

Batting and fielding averages

	Mat	Inns	NO	Runs	HS	Ave	100	50	Ct	St
First-class	4	8	1	68	23	9.71	0	0	1	0

Bowling averages

	Mat	Runs	Wkts	BBI	Ave	5w	10
First-class	4	30	1	1/14	30.00	0	0

Cressall can be seen in the middle row, second from the right.

174

323478 Sergeant Charles Thomas Worsfold Mayo
Somerset
Six first-class matches
Royal Armoured Corps/North Somerset Yeomanry
Died 10 April 1943, aged 40
Right-handed bat

'Despite going to Eton, insisted in staying with the ranks'

Charles Mayo was born on 5 February 1903 in Victoria, British Columbia. He was the son of Henry Herbert Worsfold and Florence Bartlett Mayo. At Eton his natural talent for cricket was quickly recognized and he was selected to play in the XI. Between 1919 and 1920 he appeared in matches against, Oxford University Authentics, Eton Ramblers, Free Foresters, MCC, Harrow, Liverpool and Winchester. He played in a number of matches with Gubby Allen (Sir George Oswald Browning Allen 1902-89) who went on to captain England in eleven test matches.

Mayo went on to make six first-class appearances for Somerset in May-July 1928, all in the county championship. He made his first-class debut for Somerset against Nottinghamshire at Trent Bridge on 12 May. Nottinghamshire won the toss and decided to bat making 333. Mayo caught Willis Walker off the bowling of William Territt Greswell for 39. The England test player Jack White took six wickets for 90. In reply Somerset made 159, Mayo making 35 before being run out. Forced to follow on, Somerset made 260, Mayo making the highest score of the innings with 60. Sam Staples took six wickets for 85. In their second innings Nottinghamshire made 87 for three. Nottinghamshire won by seven wickets.

He made his next appearance against Warwickshire at Edgbaston on 16 May. Mayo made 48 in his only innings. The match was drawn.

He next turned out against Derbyshire at Queens Park, Chesterfield on 19 May. The weather closed in and Mayo failed to bat. The match was drawn.

Mayo next appeared against Kent on 26 May at the Country Ground, Taunton. Mayo made 16 and 13. Kent won by 84.

Mayo played against Gloucestershire next at the Fry's Ground, Bristol on 30 May. He made zero and five. Gloucestershire won by ten wickets.

He made his final first-class appearance against Derbyshire at the County Ground, Taunton on 25 July. Somerset won the toss and decided to bat making 213. Mayo made 14 before being caught by the England test player Thomas Stanley Worthington (*Wisden* cricketer of the year 1937) off the bowling of Garnet Morley Lee. Cecil Charles Coles Case made 98 not out, running out of partners before he could make his century. Charles Kerrison Hill Hill-Wood took five wickets for 76. In reply Derbyshire made 302. Mayo caught Worthington off the bowling of the England test cricketer Jack White for four. In their second innings Somerset made 178. Mayo batting number three made two before being bowled by Hill-Wood. In their second innings Derbyshire made 90 for five. Mayo caught Lee off the bowling of White for seven. Derbyshire won by four wickets.

Unusually for a man who went to Eton College, Mayo enlisted into the ranks, first the North Somerset Yeomanry, then transferring to the Royal Armoured Corps. He was promoted to sergeant before being killed in action on 10 April 1943.

He is buried in Alexandria (Hadra) War Memorial Cemetery, grave reference 4. J. 8.

Batting and fielding averages

	Mat	Inns	NO	Runs	HS	Ave	100	50	Ct	St
First-class	6	9	0	193	60	21.44	0	1	3	0

Bowling averages

	Mat	Balls	Runs	Wkts	BBI	BBM	Ave	Econ	SR	4w	5w	10
First-class	6	-	-	-	-	-	-	-	-	-	-	-

**Flying Officer John Hamilton Bryan Barnes
(Flying instructor)
Ireland
One first-class appearance
RAF Volunteer Reserve
Died 22 April 1943, aged 26
Right-handed bat/Right arm fast**

'And now 'tis man who dares assault the sky'

John Barnes was born on 14 November 1916 in Armagh, the son of Robert and Martha Barnes. He was educated at the Royal School, Armagh before being employed by the local gas company.

He made one first-class appearance, for Ireland against New Zealand on 11 December 1937 at the Observatory Lane, Rathmines, Dublin. Ireland won the toss and decided to bat making 79. Barnes made zero before being bowled by Norman Gallichan. In reply New Zealand made 64. Barnes bowled six overs taking no wickets for seven. James Chrysostom Boucher took seven wickets for 13. In their second innings Ireland made 30. Barnes was run out for one. John Cowie took six wickets for three during the innings. During their second innings New Zealand made 46 for two. New Zealand won by eight wickets.

In 1938 Barnes joined the RAF rising to the rank of flying officer. During the war he served as a flying instructor and was killed in a flying accident on 22 April 1943 at Kneesall in Nottinghamshire. His body was returned to Ireland and is now in the Armagh (St Marks) Church of Ireland Churchyard, new ground, row 4, grave 5. He left a widow, Kathleen.

Batting and fielding averages

	Mat	Inns	NO	Runs	HS	Ave	100	50	4s	6s	Ct	St
First-class	1	2	0	0	0	0.00	0	0	0	0	0	0

Bowling averages

	Mat	Runs	Wkts	BBI	BBM	Ave	SR	4w	5w	10
First-class	1	7	0	-	-	-	-	0	0	0

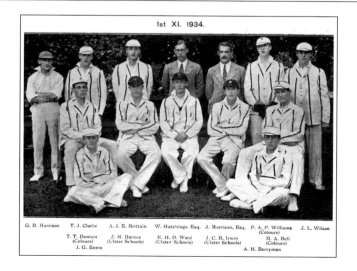

1st XI. 1934.

G. B. Harrison   T. J. Clarke   A. J. E. Brittain   W. Hutchings, Esq.   J. Morrison, Esq.   P. A. P. Williams   J. L. Wilson
(Colours)

T. T. Dawson   J. H. Barnes   E. H. D. Ward   J. C. B. Irwin   M. A. Bell
(Colours)   (Ulster Schools)   (Ulster Schools)   (Ulster Schools)   (Colours)

J. G. Ennis   A. H. Berryman

**Lieutenant Colonel Leigh Arbuthnot Alexander
Europeans (India)
Five first-class matches
2nd King Edward VII's Own Gurkha Rifles (The Sirmoor
Rifles) Commanding 3rd Battlion
Died 28 April 1943, aged 45**

'Led his men with the greatest bravery to the very end'

Leigh Alexander was born on 4 July 1898 in Umzinto, a town around 70 kilometres from Durban in the Kwazulu/Natal province of South Africa. He was the son of Major William Alexander and Ethel Rubina Arbuthnot of Etchingham, Sussex. He was educated at Glenalmond College in Scotland. Deciding on a career in the army Leigh was commissioned into the Indian Army on 27 October 1917, aged 19. He was posted to the Officers' Cadet College in Quetta before being gazetted 2nd lieutenant in the 2/5 Royal Gurkha Rifles and posted to Abbottabad. During the First World War Alexander served with the 2/5 Royal Gurkha Rifle Frontier Force on the Northwest Frontier.

Alexander made three first-class appearances (some records have him playing five but I can only find records for three). He made his debut first-class appearance for the Europeans against the Hindus on 2 March 1923 during the Lahore Tournament at the Lawrence Gardens. The Europeans won the toss and decided to bat making 218, Alexander making 15 before being bowled by Brij Lall. In reply the Hindus made 51, Roy Kilner taking six wickets for 16. In their second innings the Europeans made 237, Alexander making 20 before being bowled by Bawi Ram. In their second innings the Hindus made 98. Alexander bowled seven overs taking two wickets for 14, Brij Lall and Basheshar Nath Khanna. The Europeans won by 306 runs.

He made his second first-class appearance for the Europeans against the Muslims in the final of the Lahore Tournament on 5 March 1923 at the Lawrence Gardens. The Europeans won the toss and elected bat making 227. Alexander was run out for 13. In reply the Muslims made 80, Frederick Roland Studdert Shaw taking seven wickets for 30. In their second innings the Europeans made 112, Alexander making 14 before being bowled by the Indian test cricketer Syed Wazir Ali. Iftikharuddin took five wickets for 48. In their second innings the Muslims made 90, Shaw taking seven wickets for 53. The Europeans won the match by 169 runs.

Alexander had to wait three years before making his third and final first-class appearance, playing once again for the Europeans this time against the MCC in India and Ceylon on 3 November 1926 at the Pindi Club Ground, Rawalpindi. The Europeans won the toss and decided to field. The MCC made 43, the England test cricketer Andrew Sandham making 150. Alexander bowled ten overs taking one wicket for 36, Jack Parsons stumped John James Crofts Cocks for 45. Cyril Bourchier Barlow took five wickets for 93. In reply the Europeans made 145, Alexander making one before being bowled by Ewart Astill (*Wisden* cricketer of the year 1933). In their second innings the MCC made 185. Alexander bowled four overs taking no wickets for 15. He did however catch Guy Fife Earle off the bowling of Barlow for 27. In their second innings the Europeans made 85 for one. The match was drawn.

He was promoted captain in 1922, major in 1935, and then lieutenant colonel, taking command of the 3rd battalion 2nd King Edward VII's Own Gurkha Rifles, marrying Nancy Alexander (née Paisley) along the way.

He trained for an operation named Longcloth, which involved long-range penetration behind enemy lines. Some of the conditions were later outlined:

> News from this Battalion is very scarce. They live in the backwoods and are immersed in the toughest possible training. A route march of 200 miles is a fairly normal occurrence for them. They have no comforts, no homes, no paper and probably no time for writing letters…
>
> During the recent rains they were overtaken by serious floods and the battalion lost a good deal of its property. This occurred at night and I understand the battalion had to take shelter in the nearby trees. Some of the men did useful rescue work.

During Operation Longcloth, Alexander took command of the Southern Group. This was made up of two Gurkha columns, and group headquarters. Wingate intended to use these columns as a decoy to the main Chindit operation taking place with the Northern group who were detailed to attack targets along the Mandalay-Myitkhina railway. Alexander's column used the main trails, marching openly towards their target, the railway station at Kyaikthin. Supplies were dropped from the air and everything was done to advertise their presence. The tactic worked and Japanese attention was focused on the Southern units while the Northern units went unmolested. What neither of the Southern columns realized however was that the Japanese had set an ambush for them. To make the situation worse both columns had lost radio contact. Lieutenant Ian MacHorton later recalled events:

> We shuffled to a halt as the guides probed forward. There came the sound of just one bang up front, then an inferno of noise engulfed the world around me. There came the high-pitched staccato scream of a machine gun, then overwhelmingly many others joined in, the crash and ping of rifle bullets, the banging of grenades as the battle reached a fearful crescendo. Men and mules were lying, twisted and contorted, twitching and writhing, others were still erect, stark in the moonlight, heaving and jerking in the midst of this chaos. Then a sinister scuffling noise made by men of all kinds in close combat. The close combat of bayonet and kukri, the fanatical, personal slaughter with blood-dripping cold steel.

MacHorton also later recalled how Alexander dealt with the situation with compassion and understanding, but looked worn out and exhausted. Despite this Colonel Alexander managed to extract the majority of his headquarters staff from the chaos and devastation at Kyaikthin. By 10 April the group had reached the banks of the fast flowing Shweli River. At this point Colonel Alexander reluctantly agreed to change course and head directly west for India. It was during this period that the party, now numbering some 480 men, began to show signs of fatigue. Things went from bad to worse as the Japanese once again managed to ambush the column. This time a mortar bomb seriously wounded Alexander, wounds from which he later died.

After the war Alexander's body was recovered and buried in the Taukkyan War Cemetery, joint grave reference 19. G. 1-2.

First-class Career Batting and Fielding averages

	M	I	NO	Runs	HS	Ave	100	50	Ct
Europeans	3	6	1	79	20	15.80	0	0	1

First-class Career Bowling

	Balls	Mdns	Runs	Wkts	BB	Ave	5wI	10wM	SRate	Econ
Europeans	126	3	65	3	2-14	21.66	0	0	42.00	3.09

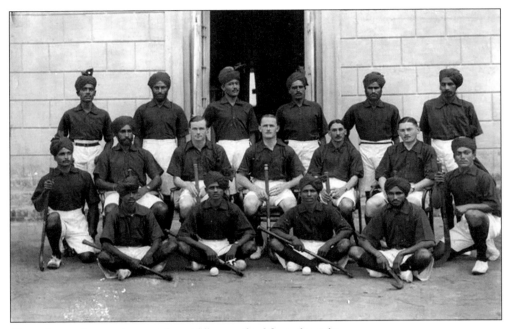

Alexander can be seen here on the middle row, third from the right.

Flight Lieutenant Dudley Tabor Everett
Western Australia
One first-class match
Royal Australian Air Force
Died 3 May 1943, aged 31
Right-handed bat

'A natural pilot lost in a sad accident'

Dudley Everett was born on 9 March 1912 in Perth, Western Australia. He was the son of Robert Tabor and Effie Selina Everett. He was educated at the independent Anglian Hale School in Wembley Downs, Perth. While there he played football and cricket for the first XIs. He also played cricket for North Perth (now Joondalup). On leaving school he qualified and practiced as an accountant.

Everett made one first-class appearance for Western Australia against MCC in Australia and New Zealand. The match took place on 31 October 1935 at the Western Australia Cricket Association Ground, Perth. The MCC won the toss and elected to bat making 344. In reply Western Australia made 232, Everett making a duck before being bowled by Arthur Douglas Baxter, the England test cricketer James Morton Sims taking seven wickets for 95 runs. In their second innings the MCC made 266. In reply Western Australia made 23 for one. Everett failed to bat. The match was drawn.

Everett was not only a first-class cricketer but also a talented hockey player. Playing centre-half or inside-right, he represented Perth, Old Haleians and Western Australia. A keen flyer, he qualified as a pilot in January 1935.

During the Second World War he joined the Royal Australian Air Force. He was stationed at RAAF Pearce, Perth, before becoming an instructor at the Central Flying School, Camden Aerodrome and the Elementary Training School at RAAF Narrandera, New South Wales. While stationed at Narrandera he was lucky to escape with his life when a Tiger Moth being flown by a trainee crashed into the hut in which he was working. The pilot of the Tiger Mouth was killed and Everett broke his leg. The incident was later reported:

W.A. FLIER HURT IN AIR FATALITY
Sydney, Today Dudley F. Everett, of W.A., was injured in an R.A.A.F. plane fatality. When a Tiger Moth training plane crashed near Narrandera today, Sgt. Pilot A. L. B. Smith (24), of Darling Point, Sydney, was killed and three other members of the R.A.A.F, Flying Officer Dudley T. Everett, of W.A., Leading Aircraftsman Lyall N. Ross, of Baldwin, Vic, and Sgt Pilot D. J. Bourke were injured. Everett received a compound fracture of the ankle.

Transferring to the RAF in Great Britain as part of the Empire Training Scheme, he was sent to Canada for pilot training serving with the Royal Canadian Air Force at Trenton South Ontario. Everett arrived in San Francisco on 12 April 1943. He would hardly have had time to see much of any Canadian training establishments and was only at Trenton for a few days before being killed while on a solo training flight in a Harvard II aircraft on 3 May 1943 crashing outside Ameliasburgh.

He was later buried in the Trenton (St George's) Cemetery, grave reference lot 1, plot 203, grave 3.

Batting and fielding averages

	Mat	Inns	NO	Runs	HS	Ave	100	50	4s	6s	Ct	St
First-class	1	1	0	0	0	0.00	0	0	0	0	0	0

Bowling averages

	Mat	Balls	Runs	Wkts	BBI	BBM	Ave	Econ	SR	4w	5w	10
First-class	1	-	-	-	-	-	-	-	-	-	-	-

Flying Officer Kenneth Lovett Ridings
South Australia
Nineteen first-class matches
10 Squadron RAVR
Died 17 May 1943, aged 23
Right-handed bat/Leg break googly

All the brothers played cricket for their state

Kenneth Ridings was born on 7 February 1920 at Malvern, Adelaide, South Australia. He was one of four brothers (all of whom played cricket for their state) born to Rowland Bradshaw and Olive Elizabeth Jane Ridings of Brooklyn Park, South Australia.

Kenneth Ridings, like his four brothers, played for West Torrens Cricket Club. He made nineteen first-class appearances between December 1938 and February 1941, twelve of them in the Sheffield Shield.

He made his debut first-class appearance in the Sheffield Shield for South Australia against New South Wales on 16 December 1938 at the Adelaide Oval. South Australia won the toss and decided to bat making 600 runs. Opening the batting Ridings made 31 before being bowled by the Australian test cricketer Bill O'Reilly. Donald George Bradman (later knighted, *Wisden* cricketer of the year 1931 and *Wisden* cricketer of the century 2000) made 143, followed by another Australian test cricketer Jack Badcock who made 271 not out. In reply New South Wales made 390. The Australian test cricketer Sidney George Barnes making 117 and another Australian test cricketer Arthur Chipperfield making 154. The Australian test cricketer Clarence Grimmett took seven wickets for 116. Following on, New South Wales made 155. South Australia won by an innings and 55 runs.

He made his second appearance against Queensland on 24 December 1938, again in the Sheffield Shield and again at the Adelaide Oval. Ridings made seven in his only innings. Don Bradman knocked up 225. South Australia took the match by an innings and 20 runs. He next played against Victoria on 30 December 1938 in the Sheffield Shield at Melbourne Cricket Ground. Riding made 27 and 18 not out. Bradman made 107 passing 21,000 runs in first-class cricket. The match was drawn.

His next match was against Queensland, played at the Brisbane Cricket Ground in the Sheffield Shield. Ridings made 122 and 10 not out. He also took two wickets in the first innings and four in the second. Bradman made186. South Australia won by ten wickets.

His next match was against New South Wales in the Sheffield Shield on 14 January 1939 at the Sydney Cricket Ground. Ridings made 28 in his only innings. Bradman made 135. The match was drawn.

His next Sheffield Shield match was against Victoria at the Adelaide Oval. Ridings made 14 in his only innings and took one wicket. The match was drawn.

It was another nine months before Ridings would play his next first-class match. Once again it was against Victoria in the Sheffield Shield at the Adelaide Oval, played on 17 November 1939. Ridings made six and one. South Australia won by three wickets.

His next game was played against New South Wales at the Adelaide Oval on 15 December 1939. Ridings made 29 and 20. Bradman made 251 not out in the first innings and 90 not out in the second. South Australia won by seven wickets.

His next match was against Queensland at the Adelaide Oval in the Sheffield Shield on 22 December 1939. Ridings made 151 in his only innings. Bradman made 138. South Australia won by an innings and 222 runs.

Ridings went on to play in three more Sheffield Shield matches, against Victoria (Ridings made 56 and 29, Bradman made 267. Match drawn), Queensland (Ridings 35 and one, Queensland won by two wickets), and New South Wales (Ridings made three and one, New South Wales won by 237 runs). It was Ridings' last appearance in a Sheffield Shield match.

Ridings' next match was for a Don Bradman XI against S.J. McCabe's XI. The match was played on 1 January 1941 at the Melbourne Cricket Ground. McCabe's XI won the toss and decided to bat making 449. Jack Badcock made 105 and Sid Barnes 137. Ridings made 50 before being lbw to John Albert Ellis. Forced to follow on, Bradman's XI made 141, Ridings making five before being caught by the Australian test player Donald Tallon off the bowling of another Australian test player Keith Ross Miller (cricketer of the year 1954). McCabe's XI took the match by an innings and 103 runs.

Ridings made his final first-class appearance against New South Wales at the Adelaide Oval on 21 February 1941. South Australia won the toss and decided to bat making 132. Ridings made 11 before being bowled by Cecil George Pepper. The Australian test player Bill O'Reilly (*Wisden* cricketer of the year 1935) took five wickets for 28. In their first innings New South Wales made 512. Sid Barnes made 103 and Colin Leslie McCool 100. In their second innings South Australia made 335, Ridings making 62. McCool took five wickets for 65. New South Wales won by an innings and 45 runs.

During his career Ridings made 919 runs including two centuries and four fifties, his highest score being 151 against Queensland. He also bowled 320 balls taking seven wickets for 182, his best figures being four for 62. He made six catches.

During the war Ridings was commissioned into the Royal Australian Air Force, training as a pilot and becoming a flying officer. He later joined 10 Squadron flying the Short S.25 Sunderland with Coastal Command. Ridings was shot down and killed together with his eleven-man crew on 17 May 1943 while flying Short Sunderland Mark III W4004/Z on an anti-submarine patrol in the Bay of Biscay, probably by a long-range German fighter. No trace of the crew or the plane was ever discovered.

He is commemorated on the Runnymede memorial, panel 189.

Batting and fielding averages

	Mat	Inns	NO	Runs	HS	Ave	100	50	Ct	St
First-class	19	31	3	919	151	32.82	2	4	6	0

Bowling averages

	Mat	Runs	Wkts	BBI	Ave	5w	10
First-class	19	182	7	4/26	26.00	0	0

Lieutenant Richard James Evans
Border
Ten first-class matches
South Africa Air Force
Died 29 May 1943, aged 28
Right-handed bat/Leg break googly

'Died training his pupils'

Richard Evans was born on 11 October 1914 in East London, Cape Province, South Africa. He was the son of Professor Edward J. and Edith C. Evans. He later married Merlen, of Cambridge, East London.

The Alamein Memorial.

Evans made ten first-class appearances for Border between 1934 and 1940, five in the Currie Cup. He made his debut for Border on 21 December 1934 against Transvaal in the Currie Cup at the Jan Smuts Ground, East London. Border won the toss and decided to bat making 202.

Evans made 11 before being bowled by Anthony Hubert Gyngell. In reply Transvaal made 371, the South African test cricketer Dooley Briscoe making 140. Evans bowled four overs, taking no wickets for 38. In reply Border made 154, Evans being lbw to Frank Arthur Walsh for zero, the South African cricketer Bruce Mitchell taking five wickets for 61. Transvaal won by an innings and 15 runs.

Evans made his second appearance for Border on 11 January 1936 against the Australians at the Jan Smuts Ground. Evans made four and ten. He also bowled 18 overs taking two wickets for 77. The Australians won by an innings and 14 runs.

He next appeared against Western Province on 27 December 1937 at Newlands, Cape Town, in the Currie Cup. Evans bowled 18 overs taking five wickets for 72 in the first innings. He bowled 17 overs in the second innings, taking four further wickets for 92 runs. He also made 24 and zero. Border won by seven wickets.

He next turned out for Border against Eastern Province on 1 January 1938 at the St George's Park, Port Elizabeth, again in the Currie Cup. Evans bowled 15 overs taking four wickets for 50 in the first innings. He bowled nine overs during the second innings taking six wickets for 40. He also made 22 in his only innings. Border won by one run.

Evans next played against Natal on 12 January 1938 at the Jan Smuts Ground in the Currie Cup. He made 20 and 10 and failed to take a wicket in either over. Natal won by six wickets.

Evans played his next game in the Currie Cup on the 12 March 1938 against the Orange Free State at the Jan Smuts Ground. Evans made one and three. He bowled seven overs in the first innings taking five wickets for 27. He bowled five overs in the second innings taking two further wickets for 28. Border won by 33 runs.

His next match was against the Transvaal on 19 March 1938 at the Jan Smuts Ground in the Currie Cup. He bowled eight overs in the first innings taking two wickets for 29. In the second innings he bowled 16 overs taking eight wickets for 64. He also scored one and zero. Transvaal won by 158 runs. Evans next turned out against the MCC on 13 January 1939, again at the Jan Smuts Ground. Evans scored 11 and an impressive 88. He bowled 15 overs during the first innings taking one wicket for 103. He bowled four overs in the second innings taking no wickets. The MCC won by nine wickets.

A year later on 9 February 1940 he was brought in to play against Eastern Province at the Jan Smuts Ground. He made 23 in his only innings. He bowled 11 overs taking two wickets for 42 during the first innings, and in the second innings bowled 12 overs taking four wickets for 52. Border won by an innings and 15 runs.

He made his final first-class appearance against Western Province on 8 March 1940 at the Jan Smuts Ground. Border won the toss and decided to bat making 189. Evans made one before being lbw to Johan Gerhard Brussell Brinkhaus. Brinkhaus took seven wickets for 60. In reply Western Province made 206. Evans bowled 18 overs taking three wickets for 68, George Edwin Crighton stumped George Gray Locke Mandy for 28, Leslie Manning bowled for 29, and George Georgeu stumped Mandy for 19. In their second innings Border made 162. Evans made five before being caught by Abraham Glantz off the bowling of the South African test cricketer Jack Bruce Plimsoll. In their second innings Western Province made 146 for four. Evans bowled eight talking one wicket for 29, Crighton caught Harold Vivian Loraine Whitfield for eight. He also caught Manning off the bowling of the South Africa test bowler Martin Andrew Hanley for zero. Western Province won by six wickets.

During his career Evans made 234 runs, his highest score being 88 against the MCC. He also bowled 1,543 balls, taking 49 wickets for 906 runs. He also made seven catches.

During the Second World War Evans joined the South African Air Force. He was killed on 29 May 1943 serving with the 66 Air School in Cape Town when the Avro Anson (1130) he was piloting ran out of fuel and crashed into the sea. His remains were not recovered and he is commemorated on the Alamein Memorial, column 277. Air Pupils Reginald John Felton and Laurence Francis Comyns were also killed when the Anson crashed.

Batting and fielding averages

	Mat	Inns	NO	Runs	HS	Ave	100	50	Ct	St
First-class	10	18	0	234	88	13.00	0	1	7	0

Bowling averages

	Mat	Runs	Wkts	BBI	Ave	5w	10
First-class	10	906	49	8/64	18.48	4	2

Captain James Bruce-Jones
Scotland
Two first-class appearances
8th Battalion Argyll and Sutherland Highlanders
Died 29 May 1943, aged 32
Right-hand bat

A true son of Scotland

James Bruce-Jones was born on 19 August 1910 at Larbert, Stirlingshire. He was the first son of Captain Tomas Bruce-Jones OBE and of Edith (née Nicoll). He was educated at Charterhouse and then became a director of the family timber and foundry business, 'James Jones, timber merchants'. During this time he was commissioned into the Territorial Army becoming a second lieutenant in the 8th Battalion Argyll & Sutherland Highlanders.

He made two first-class appearances, both for Scotland. James made his debut for Scotland against Ireland on 20 June 1936 at Raeburn Place, Edinburgh. Scotland won the toss and decided to bat making 292. Jones, opening for Scotland, made nine before being caught by Francis James Anthony Reddy off the bowling of Charles William Billingsley. Bed Ross Tod made 143 not out. In reply Ireland made 64. In their second innings Scotland made 155, James making 35, the highest score of the innings before being bowled by Edward Ingram. In their second innings Ireland made 169. Scotland won by 214 (James played alongside his brother James Forbes Jones who made ten first-class appearances for Scotland).

He made his second appearance for Scotland against Ireland on 19 June 1937 at Ormeau, Belfast. Ireland won the toss and decided to bat making 227. In reply Scotland made 163. Jones made zero before being bowled by James Boucher. In their second innings Ireland made 146. Alexander Paris took six wickets for 35 off 16 overs. In their second innings Scotland made 147. Bruce-Jones made 47, the highest score of the innings, before being bowled by Boucher. Boucher took six wickets during the innings for 42. Ireland won by 63 runs.

James Bruce-Jones died of wounds in Tunisia on 29 April 1943. He is buried in Oued Zarga War Cemetery, grave 1.D.22.

One of his two brothers, Reid Bruce-Jones, was killed in July 1943 in Sicily.

Batting and fielding averages

	Mat	Inns	NO	Runs	HS	Ave	100	50	Ct	St
First-class	2	4	0	91	47	22.75	0	0	0	0

Bowling averages

	Mat	Balls	Runs	Wkts	BBI	BBM	Ave	Econ	SR	4w	5w	10
First-class	2	-	-	-	-	-	-	-	-	-	-	-

Second Lieutenant Alastair Keyon Campbell
Hampshire
Seven first-class appearances
Royal Artillery
Died 16 June 1943, aged 53
Right-handed bat

At the going down of the sun

Alastair Campbell was born on 25 May 1890 in South Stoneham, Hampshire. He made seven first-class appearances, all in the County Championship between August 1908 and July 1909. He made his debut against Northamptonshire on 13 August 1908 at the County Ground Northampton. Hampshire won the toss and decided to bat making 291. Campbell made four before being bowled by William Wells. In reply Northamptonshire made 196. John Alfred Newman took six wickets for 45 off 24 overs. In their second innings Hampshire made 211. Campbell made 20 before being caught by William Wells off the bowling of William East. In their second innings Northamptonshire made 192. Hampshire won by 115.

Royal Artillery emblem.

His next appearance was against Gloucestershire on 17 August 1908 at the College Ground, Cheltenham. Campbell made four in his only innings. Hampshire won by nine wickets.

He next appeared against Derbyshire on 21 June 1909 at the Miners Welfare Ground, Blackwell. Campbell made three in his only innings. The match was drawn.

His fourth match was against Middlesex, played on 24 June 1909 at the United Services Ground, Portsmouth. Campbell made five, again in his only innings. The match was drawn.

He played against Leicestershire next at Aylestone Road, Leicester, on the 28 June 1909. He made 21 in his only innings before being caught by Samuel Coe off the bowling of Ewart Astill. Astill took seven wickets for 34 off 25 overs. Hampshire won by seven wickets.

Campbell made his sixth first-class appearance against Warwickshire on 1 July 1909 at Arlington Avenue, Leamington Spa. Campbell made eight before being caught by Alfred Charles Stirrup Glover off the bowling of Sydney Santall in his first innings and seven in his second before being caught and bowled by the England test cricketer William George Quaife (*Wisden* cricketer of the year 1902). Hampshire won by 55 runs.

He made his final first-class appearance against Northamptonshire on 5 July 1909 at the County Ground, Northamptonshire. Hampshire won the toss and decided to bat making 271. Campbell made 18 before being bowled by the England Test cricketer George Joseph Thompson (*Wisden* cricketer of the year 1906). The Hampshire opener and England test player Charles Philip Mead (*Wisden* cricketer of the year 1912) made 114. In reply Northamptonshire made 271, the Northamptonshire opener George Alfred Turner Viala making 129. In their second innings Hampshire made 113. Campbell made one before being bowled by Thompson once again. Thomson took seven wickets for 53 off 18 overs. In their second innings Northamptonshire made 114, John Newman taking six wickets for 49. Northamptonshire won by one wicket.

Campbell died in hospital on 16 June 1943 at Cosham in Hampshire as a result of a serious illness. He was cremated at the Southampton Crematorium and is commemorated on panel 2.

Batting and fielding averages

	Mat	Inns	NO	Runs	HS	Ave	100	50	Ct	St
First-class	7	10	0	91	21	9.10	0	0	1	0

Bowling averages

	Mat	Balls	Runs	Wkts	BBI	BBM	Ave	Econ	SR	4w	5w	10
First-class	7	-	-	-	-	-	-	-	-	-	-	-

Lieutenant Eric Peter Hamilton
City of Transvaal, Transvaal
Two first-class appearances
21 Squadron South African Air Force
Died 15 July 1943, aged 30

'Died before his promise could be fulfilled'

Eric Hamilton was born on 5 May 1913 in Johannesburg. He was the son of Frederick J. and Myrtle R. Hamilton.

Hamilton made two first-class appearances, one in 1936, one in 1937. He made his debut first-class appearance for the City of Johannesburg against The Rest on 5 October 1936 at the Old Wanderers. The City of Johannesburg won the toss and elected to bat making 188. Hamilton made one before being bowled by the South African test cricketer Eric Quail Davies. The South African test cricketer Eric Rowan (*Wisden* cricketer of the year 1952) made 102. In reply The Rest made 299. The South African test cricketer Dudley Nourse (*Wisden* cricketer of the year 1948) making 149. In their second innings the City of Johannesburg made 358, Hamilton making 31 before being caught by George Georgeu off the bowling of the South African test cricketer Xen Balaskas. The South African test player Bruce Mitchell (*Wisden* cricketer of the year 1936) made 116 and the South African test cricketer Dooley Briscoe made 100 not out. In their second innings The Rest made 117. The match was drawn.

Hamilton made his second first-class appearance for the Transvaal against the Orange Free State in the Currie Cup on 29 January 1937 at the Ramblers Cricket Ground, Bloemfontein. Transvaal won the toss and decided to field. Orange Free State only managed 37, the South

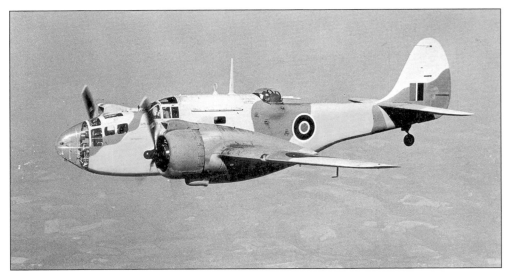

Martin Baltimore Mk III, as flown by Hamilton.

African test cricketer Eiulf Nupen taking six wickets for 21. In reply Transvaal made 328. Hamilton made 33 before being lbw of the bowling of Henry Sparks. The South African test player Kenneth George Viljoen made 118 not out. In their second innings the Orange Free State did slightly better making 115. Transvaal took the match by an innings and 176 runs.

During the war Hamilton trained as a pilot, joining 21 Squadron South African Air Force and rising to the rank of lieutenant. In July 1943 the squadron took its Baltimores to Malta from where it supported the Allied invasion of Sicily. This was quickly followed by a move to Italy, where the squadron operated as a daytime tactical bomber squadron, attacking German positions, bases and communications. It was during one of these raids over Sicily on the 15 July 1943 that Hamilton, together with this two-man crew, was shot down and killed while flying Martin Baltimore Mk III #AG930. His crew consisted of Flight Sergeant Dudley Phelan and Lieutenant Charles Frank Hodgkinson. Both of these men are commemorated on the Alamein Memorial.

Hamilton is buried in the Syracuse War Cemetery, Sicily, grave reference VII. H. 10. He was married.

Batting and fielding averages

	Mat	Inns	NO	Runs	HS	Ave	100	50	Ct	St
First-class	2	3	0	65	33	21.66	0	0	0	0

Bowling averages

	Mat	Balls	Runs	Wkts	BBI	BBM	Ave	Econ	SR	4w	5w	10
First-class	2	-	-	-	-	-	-	-	-	-	-	-

Flight Lieutenant (Pilot Officer) Edward George Titley
Cambridge University
Two first-class matches
609 Squadron RAF
Died 17 July 1943, aged 31
Right-handed bat/Wicketkeeper

'One of the Few'

Edward Titley was born on 7 August 1911 in Carlton, Nottingham. He was the son of Edward Addison and Harriett Reynolds Titley. At Uppingham he kept wicket for the first XI. At Pembroke College Cambridge he appeared in both the freshman's and senior's matches.

Titley made two first-class appearances, both in June 1932 for Cambridge. He made his debut for Cambridge University against Sussex at F.P. Fenner's on 1 June. Cambridge won the toss and decided to bat making 72. Titley, batting last, made zero before being bowled by the England test player James Parks (*Wisden* cricketer of the year 1938). In reply Sussex made 283, Thomas Edwin Reed Cook making 141 (Cook also played football for Brighton and Hove Albion, Bristol Rovers and England). In their second innings Cambridge made 151. Titley made one before being lbw off the bowling of Albert Wensley. Wensley took six wickets for 56. Sussex won by an innings and 60 runs.

Titley's final first-class appearance for Cambridge University came against India in the British Isles on 8 June, again at F.P. Fenner's. Cambridge won the toss and decided to bat making 92. Titley, batting last, made zero before being caught by Jahangir Khan off the bowling of Ladhabhai Nakum Amar Singh. Amar Singh took five wickets for 30 during the innings. In reply India made 308. Keeping wicket, Titley made two catches, Naoomal Jaoomal Makhija of the bowling of the England test cricketer Kenneth Farnes (*Wisden* cricketer of the year 1939) for zero (Farnes died flying for the RAF on 20 October 1941), and Natwarsinhji Bhavsinhji off the bowling of Rodney Rought-Rought for zero. Rought-Rought took five wickets for 71 during the innings. In their second innings Cambridge made 274. Titley made three before being bowled by Phiroze Edulji Palia. Alan Ratcliffe made 112 not out. Amar Singh took six wickets for 70. In their second innings India made 59. India won by nine wickets.

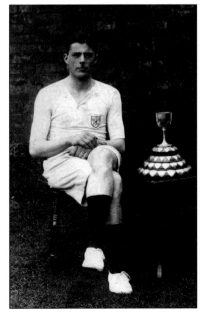

Titley also played for the Free Foresters and was captain of the Eton fives team. He married Dorothy Lancaster of Northam, Devon.

He left Cambridge in 1933, going into the City and becoming a Lloyds underwriter.

In 1938 Titley joined the RAF Volunteer Reserve as an airman and trainee pilot. He was called up on

1 September 1939. After completing his training he became a pilot with 609 Squadron on 20 October 1940 at Middle Wallop under Squadron Leader Robinson. He helped with the evacuation of Dunkirk. During a scramble take-off at Middle Wallop he apparently suffered a minor blackout and, leaving formation, almost collided with the Spitfire of John Bisdee DFC (Battle of Britain six victories). After landing safely Pilot Officer Titley was examined and it was discovered he had a problem with his inner ear and was declared unfit for any further high-altitude flying. As a result he was posted instead to Training Command.

He later became a squadron leader, losing his life on 17 July 1943 in a flying accident at Ryefield, County Armagh, flying Beaufort JM514 when at 1510 hrs his plane was seen to spin into the ground and burst into flames. Sergeant James Waclaw Hoba of the Royal Canadian Air Force was killed in the same crash.

Titley is buried in St Margaret's Churchyard in Northam, section A, grave 4.

Titley's grave in St Margaret's Churchyard, Northam.

Batting and fielding averages

	Mat	Inns	NO	Runs	HS	Ave	100	50	Ct	St
First-class	2	4	0	4	3	1.00	0	0	2	0

Bowling averages

	Mat	Balls	Runs	Wkts	BBI	BBM	Ave	Econ	SR	4w	5w	10
First-class	2	-	-	-	-	-	-	-	-	-	-	-

Captain Robert Alexander
Ireland
One first-class match
2nd Battalion Royal Inniskilling Fusiliers
Died 19 July 1943, aged 32
Right-handed bat/Right arm fast medium

'Played both First Class Cricket and International Rugby for Ireland'

Robert Alexander was born on 24 September 1910 in Belfast, Ireland. Although better known as an international rugby player he made one first-class cricket appearance for Ireland against Scotland at Glenpark, Greenock, on 18 June 1932. Ireland won the toss and elected to bat making 242. Alexander, batting last, made seven before being bowled by Arthur Baxter. Baxter took five wickets during the innings for 75. In reply Scotland made 325. Alexander bowled 19 overs and took no wickets for 38. In their second innings Ireland made 318. Alexander, batting last again, was bowled by Baxter again, this time for 22. Trevor George Brooke McVeagh made 109. Baxter took a further four wickets for 102. In their second innings Scotland made 177. Alexander bowled three overs taking no wickets for 17. Ireland won by 58 runs.

As a rugby player he turned out for Royal Belfast Academical Institution, Queen's University, North of Ireland Football Club, Police Union, British Lions and the Barbarians. Between 1936 and 1939 Alexander made eleven appearances for Ireland. He made his debut for Ireland against England at Lansdowne Road on 8 February 1936, Ireland taking the match 6-3 (they had been 0-3 down at half time). In 1936 he went on to compete against Scotland (22 February, won 10-4), Wales (14 March, lost 0-3), and England (13 February, lost 8-9). During the 1937 season he played against Scotland (27 February, won 11-4) and Wales (3 April, won 5-3). During the 1938 season he played against England (12 February, lost 14-36) and Scotland (26 February, lost 14-23). During the 1939 season he played against England (11 February, won 5-0), Scotland (25 February, won 12-3) and Wales (11 March, lost 0-7). Alexander scored one try against Scotland in 1937. He also played three times for the British Lions against South Africa in 1938: 6 August, Johannesburg, lost 12-26; 3 September, Port Elizabeth, lost 3-19; and Cape Town, 10 September, won 21-16. He scored one try against South Africa during the Cape Town match. One of the founders of the Special Air Service and most highly decorated soldiers of the Second World War, the legendary Paddy Mayne, was also on the South Africa tour.

Alexander was a member of the Royal Ulster Constabulary before the war and at the outbreak of war he took a commission into the Royal Inniskilling Fusiliers. Still keen on playing in 1942 while on home leave he captained Ireland in a friendly game against the British Army. It was to be his last game for his country.

Rising to the rank of captain, Alexander was killed in action near Catania, Sicily, on 19 July 1943 while leading his troops in an attack on the Simento River. A fellow officer, David Cole, who saw Alexander shortly before he was killed, said, 'Bob passed me on the way. I wished him luck. He paused for a second and whispered to me with a smile, "It's suicide", and then went on.'

He is buried at the Catania War Cemetery, Sicily, grave reference III. F. 1.

Batting and fielding averages

	Mat	Inns	NO	Runs	HS	Ave	100	50	Ct	St
First-class	1	2	0	29	22	14.50	0	0	0	0

Bowling averages

	Mat	Balls	Runs	Wkts	BBI	BBM	Ave	Econ	SR	4w	5w	10
First-class	1	126	55	0	-	-	-	2.61	-	0	0	0

The Ireland squad that lost to England in 1938. Alexander is in the middle row on the far right.

Pilot Officer Frank Bevan Kerr
Otago
Eight first-class matches
Pilot Royal New Zealand Air Force
Died 24 July 1943, aged 26
Right-handed bat

'Murdered by the Japanese'

Frank Kerr was born on 28 October 1916 in Perth, Western Australia. He was the son of H. Douglas and Gwendoline Lisle Kerr. Although he was born in Australia he played most of his cricket in New Zealand. Kerr made eight first-class appearances, all for Otago between 1935 and 1937, all but one in the Plunket Shield.

Kerr was only 18 when he made his first-class debut for Otago against Canterbury at Carisbrook, Dunedin, on 22 February 1935 in the Plunket Shield. Otago won the toss and decided to bat. They made 248. Kerr made two before being lbw to Stanley Andrews. The New Zealand test player Frederick Badcock made 136. Maurice Graham took five wickets for 76. In reply Canterbury made 141. The New Zealand test cricketer George Ritchie Dickinson took five wickets for 26. In their second innings Otago made 241. Kerr was ten not out. In reply Canterbury made 151 for five. The match was drawn.

Kerr made his next appearance against Auckland on 24 December 1935 at Eden Park, Auckland, once again in the Plunket Shield. Kerr made 44 not out and 11. Auckland won by 292 runs.

His third appearance was against the MCC in Australia and New Zealand. It was played on 31 December 1935 at Carisbrook. Kerr made four and 44. The MCC won by an innings and 115 runs.

His next appearance was against Wellington on 24 January 1936, again at Carisbrook and again in the Plunket Shield. Kerr made 27 and zero. Wellington won by 80 runs.

Canterbury was next in the Plunket Shield on 14 February 1936 at Lancaster Park. Kerr made 23 and zero. Otago won by 119 runs.

His next Plunket Shield match was against Wellington on the 25 December 1936 at the Basin Reserve. Kerr made zero and two. The match was drawn.

On the 31 December 1937, Kerr made his penultimate first-class appearance in the Plunket Shield, against Auckland. He made nine and three, William Carson knocking up a remarkable 290. Auckland won by an innings and 175 runs.

Kerr made his final first-class appearance against Canterbury on 19 February 1937 at Carisbrook. Otago won the toss and decided to bat making 124. Kerr made zero before being bowled by Walter Oliver Mapplebeck. Mapplebeck took six wickets for 43. In reply Canterbury made 243, Francis O'Brien making 113. In their second innings Otago made 451. Kerr made 14 before being stumped by Charles Keith Quentin Jackman off the bowling of Thomas Murray Sharp, Kenneth Frank McNeill Uttley making 145. Otago won by 66 runs.

During the war Kerr trained as a pilot with the Royal New Zealand Air Force. He was killed on 24 July 1943 in the Solomon Islands while co-piloting a Lockheed Hudson between

Bougainville and New Georgia. The Hudson NZ2021 was detailed to carry out a patrol between New Georgia and Bougainville. During the patrol the Hudson was attacked by eight Japanese Zeros. The Hudson's passenger was Lieutenant Colonel C.N.F. Bengough who was the CO of the BSIPDF (British Solomon Islands Protectorate Defence Force) and the resident commissioner. He was killed in the initial attack. The rear gunner Sergeant Trevor Ganley was hit in the hip, hand, arm and leg but survived. Despite the attack the Hudson flew on for a further forty miles, being continually attacked by the Zeros. Eventually the aircraft's engines caught fire and they were obliged to ditch into the sea two miles west of Baga Island (Baanga or Mbava) off the west coast of Vella Lavella. All five members of the crew managed to escape although three were wounded. The Zeros then strafed the survivors for more than ten minutes, killing everyone but Gantley. Gantley, despite being wounded, swam four miles to a deserted island where he discovered a damaged US life raft. With only 'D' rations, some coconuts and chocolate he survived on the island for nine days. Repairing the raft he managed to paddle to Vella Lavella, which was in the hands of the Japanese. By great good luck he was found and hidden by local resistance fighters who tended his wounds. A month later he was picked up by an American PT boat and returned to his squadron. For his actions on that day he was awarded the Distinguished Flying Medal (DFM).

The crew that day were made up of:
Pilot, Flight Lieutenant William George Clifford Allison
Co-pilot, Pilot officer Frank Bevan Kerr, 424473
Navigator, Sergeant Ronald Graham Douglas, 413041
Gunner, Sergeant James Henry Johnstone, 412916
Tail gunner, Sergeant Trevor Ganley

Kerr was survived by his wife Flora Margaret Mary of Cashmere, Christchurch. He is commemorated on the Bourail Memorial, panel 5.

Batting and fielding averages

	Mat	Inns	NO	Runs	HS	Ave	100	50	Ct	St
First-class	8	16	2	193	44*	13.78	0	0	0	0

Bowling averages

	Mat	Balls	Runs	Wkts	BBI	BBM	Ave	Econ	SR	4w	5w	10
First-class	8	-	-	-	-	-	-	-	-	-	-	-

Captain Hedley Verity
England, Yorkshire, MCC, Players, H.D.G. Leveson-Gowers XI
Forty tests/378 first-class matches
1st Battalion Yorkshire Regiment (Green Howards)
Died 31 July 1943
Right-hand bat/Slow left arm orthodox

He dismissed Don Bradman eight times in Tests, more than any other bowler. He took fourteen wickets in one day in the 1934 Lord's Test, a feat so famous it was mentioned over fifty years later in an episode of the TV series Hercule Poirot.

Hedley Verity was born on 18 May 1905 in Headingley, Leeds. He was the eldest child of Hedley and Edith Verity. Hedley Senior worked in the coal industry and was a committed Christian. Verity had two sisters, Grace and Edith. He was educated at Yeadon and Guiseley School playing cricket for the school XI as a left arm medium-paced bowler able to bowl both outswingers and inswingers. He left school at 14 to assist his father in his coal business at Guiseley. During this time he played club cricket for Rawdon's seconds, later playing for the first XI and being described as 'one of the most promising cricketers in the Leeds district'. He was spotted by Yorkshire scouts George Hirst and Bobby Peel and given a trial but was not picked up. Later he went on to play for Horsforth Park where his form secured him a second trial for Yorkshire. He played several matches for the Yorkshire Colts before signing professionally for the Accrington Cricket Club in the Lancashire League in September 1926. He was only there a season before moving to Middleton in the Central Lancashire Cricket League. In 1929 he changed his style to spin, drawing attention from several clubs. By the end of the season he had taken 100 wickets for Middleton and topped the Central Lancashire League bowling averages. Although offered contracts by other clubs on higher salaries he stuck with Middleton. Middleton allowed Verity to play for Yorkshire during 1930 season and later released him from his contract. With the retirement of Wilfred Rhodes, Yorkshire were desperate for a new spin bowler and Verity was considered the best of all those that tried. He went on to make 378 first-class appearances for Yorkshire and several other clubs, and made forty appearances for England.

On 7 March 1929 Verity married Kathleen Alice Metcalfe, a bookbinder. The two had known each other since childhood. They had two sons, Wilfred, named after the Yorkshire spin bowler Wilfred Rhodes, and George Douglas, named after George Hirst and Douglas Jardine.

Verity made his first-class debut for Yorkshire against Sussex on 21 May 1930 at Fartown, Huddersfield. Yorkshire won the toss and decided to bat making 322. Verity made 11 before being bowled by James Langridge. In reply Sussex made 321. Verity bowled 23 overs taking two wickets for 66, England test cricketer Maurice Tate caught Arthur Mitchell for 43, and Reginald Allen Hollingdale bowled for seven. In reply Yorkshire made 212, Verity making 13 before being bowled lbw by James Parks. In their second innings Sussex made 157 for five. The match was drawn.

Verity made his debut first-class appearance in the County Championship on 31 May 1930 for Yorkshire against Leicestershire at the Circle, Hull. Leicestershire won the toss and decided to bat making 113. Verity bowled 32 overs taking four wickets for 45, Alan Shipman the Leicestershire opener caught Emmott Robinson for 19, George Berry the other Leicestershire opener lbw for 32, Charles Alfred Richard Coleman bowled for 12, and Thomas Edgar Sidwell bowled for 13. In reply Yorkshire made 319, Verity making zero not out. Arthur Mitchell made 136 not out. In their second innings Leicestershire made a poor 43, Verity taking a further four wickets, George Berry bowled for 11, Ewart Astill lbw for one, Coleman bowled for four, Haydon Smith stumped by Arthur Wood for zero. He also caught Harold Riley off the bowling of George Macaulay (died 13 December 1940) for zero. Yorkshire won by an innings and 163 runs.

Verity went on to play against a variety of sides between 1930 and 1931 improving all the time eventually coming to the attention of the England test selectors. He was selected to play in the second test against New Zealand on 29 July 1931 at the Kennington Oval. England won the toss and decided to bat making 416, Herbert Sutcliffe making 117, Kumar Shri Duleepsinhji 109, and Wally Hammond 100 (not out). England declared after losing just three wickets and so Verity failed to bat. In reply New Zealand made 193. Verity bowled 22 overs taking two wickets for 52, Ian Cromb caught Hammond for eight, and Bill Merritt also caught Hammond for eight. Gubby Allen took five wickets for 14. Forced to follow on, New Zealand made 197. Verity bowled 12 overs taking two wickets for 33, Kenneth James caught Ian Alexander Ross Peebles (*Wisden* cricketer of the year 1931) for ten, and Cyril Francis Walter Allcott caught Allen for one. England won by an innings and 26 runs.

From 1932 to 1939 Verity played in many test matches and was *Wisden* cricketer of the year 1932.

He made his final test appearance against the West Indies in the British Isles. The first test was played on 24 June 1939 at Lord's. The West Indies won the toss and decided to bat making 277. George Alphonso Headley (*Wisden* cricketer of the year 1934) made 106. Verity bowled 16 overs failing to take a wicket for 34. William Copson took five wickets for 85. In reply England made 404 declared, large thanks to Len Hutton's 196 and Denis Compton's 120. Verity failed to bat. In their second innings the West Indies made 225, Headley making 107. Verity bowled 14 overs taking two wickets for 20, Kenneth Hunnell Weekes caught Arthur Wood for 16, and Learie Nicholas Constantine (*Wisden* cricketer of the year 1940) caught Hammond for 17. In their second innings England made 100 for two, taking the match by eight wickets.

Verity made his final first-class appearance for Yorkshire against Sussex on 30 August 1939 at the County Ground, Hove. Sussex won the toss and decided to bat making 387, George Cox making 198. Verity bowled 18 overs taking two wickets for 108, Albert John Holmes for 11 and the England test cricketer Billy Griffith caught Thomas Smailes for 17. In reply Yorkshire made 392. Len Hutton made 103 and Norman Yardley 108. Verity made seven not out. In their second innings Sussex made a poor 33. This was largely thanks to Verity who bowled six overs and took a remarkable seven wickets for nine, James Parks lbw for seven, Henry William Parks caught Len Hutton for nine, George Cox caught Arthur Wood for nine, Langridge caught Arthur Mitchell for zero, Hugh Bartlett for three, Holmes for four and Billy Griffith for one. An exceptional final first-class over. In their second innings Yorkshire made 30 for one. Yorkshire won by nine wickets.

PLAYER'S CIGARETTES

H. VERITY

Verity made 40 test appearances making 699 runs including three fifties his highest score being 66 against India. He bowled 11,173 balls taking 144 wickets for 3,510 including five five-wicket hauls and two ten-wicket hauls. He also made 30 catches. During his first-class career he made 5,603 runs including one century and thirteen fifties. His highest score was 101 against Jamaica. He also bowled 82,595 balls taking 1,956 wickets for 29,145. He made 164 five-wicket hauls and 54 ten-wicket hauls. He made 269 catches. He also made 12 minor county appearances and 24 Lancashire League appearances. Not only did he play for England and Yorkshire but also for the MCC, Players, H.D.G. Leveson-Gower's XI, and The Rest.

In January 1940 Verity took a commission as a second lieutenant into the Green Howards, 1st Battalion Yorkshire Regiment. After training he served in various training centres and was used, due to his fame no doubt, in recruiting. He also played in several cricket matches. He was posted to Ranchi in India in 1942 but after catching dysentery was returned home. Later he was posted to Persia and then in March 1943 was sent with his battalion to Kibrit air base in Egypt followed by Qatana in Syria. While here the battalion prepared for the invasion of Sicily.

After initial success in Sicily the Germans put up stiff resistance on the plains of Catania. To help break through the German lines the Green Howards made a night attack on 19 July 1942. Verity, by now a captain and commanding B Company, led his men forward, but in the confusion his company came under heavy fire and were surrounded. During the fighting Verity was hit in the chest and seriously wounded. It was not possible to carry him and he was left behind as the Howards pulled back. His last order was, 'Keep going.' Captured by the Germans he was taken to a hospital and underwent an operation. After this he was transferred to the Italian hospital at Caserta. His condition worsened and he underwent a second operation. Despite this the gallant Verity died on 31 July 1942 and was buried with full military honours. His remains were later removed to the Caserta War Cemetery, grave reference VI. E. 15.

News of his death came on 1 September, exactly four years after he had played his last match for Yorkshire. Several Yorkshire players later visited the grave, and in 1954 members of the MCC team under Len Hutton's captaincy, including Hutton, journalists and former Yorkshire player Abe Waddington paid tribute at Verity's grave while en route to Australia.

There is so much more you could write about Hedley but alas I am limited by space.

Batting and fielding averages

	Mat	Inns	NO	Runs	HS	Ave	100	50	6s	Ct	St
Tests	40	44	12	669	66*	20.90	0	3	0	30	0
First-class	378	416	106	5603	101	18.07	1	13		269	0

Bowling averages

	Mat	Inns	Balls	Runs	Wkts	BBI	BBM	Ave	Econ	SR	4w	5w	10
Tests	40	73	11173	3510	144	8/43	15/104	24.37	1.88	77.5	9	5	2
First-class	378		84219	29145	1956	10/10		14.90	2.07	43.0		164	54

Major Kenneth Bertram Scott MC
Oxford University, Free Foresters, Sussex
Fourteen first-class matches
6th Battalion Queen's Own West Kent Regiment
Died 9 August 1943, aged 27
Right-handed bat/Right arm medium pace

'The greatest loss his battalion ever suffered'

Kenneth Scott was born on 17 August 1915 in Dechmont, West Lothian. He was the fifth and youngest son of the Honourable Osmund Scott and Mary Cecilia. He went to the Grange, Crowborough, before going to Winchester and joining Culver's Close House. A fine cricketer he played in the Winchester XI against Charterhouse, Marlborough, Harrow and Eton. At Trinity Oxford he read history.

Scott made fourteen first-class appearances, nine for Oxford and five for Sussex. He made his debut for Oxford against Gloucestershire on 8 May 1935 at the University Parks. Gloucestershire won the toss and decided to bat making 460, Charles Christian Ralph Dacre making 108. Scott bowled 23 overs taking one wicket for 68, Lionel Montague Cranfield lbw for three. In reply Oxford made 386. Scott, batting last, made seven not out. Roger Kimpton made 160. In their second innings Gloucestershire made 240 for seven. Scott bowled eight overs and failed to take a wicket for 34. In their second innings Oxford made 126. Scott failed to bat. The match was drawn.

He made his next appearance for Oxford against Lancashire at the University Parks on 11 May 1935. Scott made zero and five. He took one wicket during the first innings. The England test cricketer and Lancashire opener Cyril Washbrook (*Wisden* cricketer of the year 1947 later awarded the CBE) made a fine 228. Lancashire won by an innings and 30 runs.

He next turned out against Yorkshire at the University Parks on 22 May 1935. Scott made zero and two not out. He bowled six overs in the first innings taking no wickets for zero. Yorkshire won by an innings and 59.

His next match was against Derbyshire on 9 May 1936 at the University Parks. Scott made three and zero. He bowled 16 overs in the first innings failing to take a wicket, but he managed to catch the England test cricketer Stanley Worthington (*Wisden* cricketer of the year 1937) off the bowling of Tristan Ballance (died 4 December 1943) for 174. Derbyshire won by an innings and 130 runs.

On 20 May 1936 Scott turned out again against Lancashire at the University Parks. He made nine not out in his first innings and failed to bat in the second. The match was drawn.

He played for the Free Foresters next against Oxford University on 29 May 1937 at the University Parks. Scott made 29 and 56. He took one wicket in the first innings. Oxford won by ten wickets, despite Scott's best efforts.

Scott made his debut for Sussex against Oxford University on 26 June 1937 at the County Ground, Hove. Sussex won the toss and decided to bat making 341. Scott made 11 before being bowled by Randle Darwall-Smith. Darwall-Smith took six wickets for 104 during the innings. In reply Oxford made 225. Scott bowled three overs taking two wickets for 13: Kimpton caught John Kent Nye for 95, and Darwall-Smith for four. Alfred George Tuppin took five wickets for 54. In their second innings Sussex made 230. Scott made two before being caught by Ballance off the bowling of Darwall-Smith. Darwall-Smith took six wickets for 79. In their second innings Oxford made 347. Norman Mitchell-Innes made 109. Scott bowled 20 overs taking two wickets for 55, Mitchell-Innes for 109 and Michael Richard Barton lbw for five. Oxford won by three wickets.

Scott next played for Oxford University against the MCC at the Lord's on 30 June 1937. Scott made 11 and 41. He bowled three overs taking no wickets for seven. He also managed to catch the South African test cricketer Harold Owen-Smith (*Wisden* cricketer of the year 1930) off the bowling of Ballance for 16. The England test cricketer Dennis Compton (*Wisden* cricketer of the year 1939, CBE 1958) made 116. The South African test player Harold Owen Smith (*Wisden* cricketer of the year 1930) made 168. The MCC won by 226.

His final university match came against the old enemy Cambridge. The match was played at Lord's on 5 July 1937. Cambridge won the toss and elected to bat making 253. The England test cricketer Norman Yardley (*Wisden* cricketer of the year 1948) made 101. In their first innings Oxford made 267. Scott made ten before being caught by the England test cricketer Paul Gibb off the bowling of the West Indian test cricketer John Cameron. John Grover made 121. In their second innings Cambridge made 173. In their second innings Oxford made 160 for three. Oxford took the match by seven wickets.

Joining Sussex, he made his second appearance for them, this time in the county championship on 7 August 1937 at the Central Recreation Ground, Hastings. Scott made 41 in his only innings. He also took two wickets in the first innings for 76 and two wickets in the second innings for 43. Sussex won by ten wickets.

He turned out next against Warwickshire at the County Ground, Hove on 11 August 1937. Scott made 22 and seven. Scott bowled six overs failing to take a wicket. Sussex won by 164.

Gloucestershire came next at the College Ground, Cheltenham on 14 August 1937. Scott failed to bat and bowled four overs taking no wickets for eight. The match was drawn.

He made his penultimate appearance against Derbyshire at the County Ground, Derby on 18 August 1937. He made five and ten. He bowled eighteen overs in the first innings taking one wicket for sixty-four. Derbyshire won by nine wickets.

Scott made his final first-class appearance for Sussex against Somerset at the Saffrons, Eastbourne on 21 August 1937. Somerset won the toss and decided to bat making 411, Rollo John Oliver Meyer making 125 and John Cameron making 113. Scott bowled eight overs taking no wickets for 21. In reply Sussex made 401, Scott making three before being bowled by Horace Leslie Hazell. James Parks made 112. In their second innings Somerset made 188. Scott bowled two overs taking no wickets for 11, but managed to catch William Andrews off the bowling of James Parks for 36. In their second innings Sussex made nine. Scott made zero before being caught by Walter Luckes off the bowling of the England test cricketer Arthur Wellard. The match was drawn.

Scott was a fine golfer. He not only became captain of the university team but also played for England against Scotland and Wales, only narrowly missing selection for the Walker Cup team.

In 1937 he married Miss Denise Clark of Tadworth, Surrey, and they had one son.

During the Second World War he took a commission into the 6th Battalion Queen's Own Royal West Kent Regiment. He was posted to Tunisia where the battalion distinguished itself by holding the crossroads at Djebel Abiod for four days against a German armoured column. After being halted in their advance at Green Hill on 30th November, where the 6th Battalion lost 11 officers and 150 other ranks, they were heavily engaged at Djebel bou Diss. Due to Scott's brave actions during the battle he was decorated with the Military Cross. The recommendation for the award read,

On 13.4.43 Captain Scott was in command of 'D' Company in the attack on Bou Diss. When halfway to the objective, his Company came under heavy machine-gun and mortar fire. Captain Scott immediately rushed to the front of his Company and despite heavy enemy fire led his Company to the top of the hill. When on the objective, the Company again came under heavy fire from field guns and mortars. Captain Scott, again with great coolness and skill, reorganized what remained of his Company and due to his efforts an enemy counterattack which came in the following morning was repulsed. Throughout the operation his coolness and courage was an inspiration to all those serving with him.

The following September he was mentioned in despatches for his outstanding services in Tunisia.

After the Tunisian campaign Scott's battalion took part in the invasion of Sicily. Their advance along the east coast was blocked by heavy fighting at a place called Centuripe. After two days they managed to take the town and press on to capture and hold Monte Rivoglia. It was here on 9 August 1943 while commanding 'D' company that the brave Major Scott was killed by a shell. It was said that he was the battalion's greatest loss.

He is buried in Catania War Cemetery, Sicily, grave reference, IV. J. 15.

Batting and fielding averages

	Mat	Inns	NO	Runs	HS	Ave	100	50	Ct	St
First-class	14	22	4	274	56	15.22	0	1	3	0

Bowling averages

	Mat	Balls	Runs	Wkts	BBI	Ave	Econ	SR	5w	10
First-class	14	1248	715	12	2/13	59.58	3.43	104.0	0	0

Flying Officer Harry Lascelles Carr
Glamorgan/H.D.G. Leveson Gower's XI
Three first-class appearances
RAF Volunteer Reserve
Died 18 August 1943, aged 35
Right-handed bat/Wicketkeeper

A fine wicketkeeper and man

Harry Carr was born on 8 October 1907 in Lambeth, one of twins born to the *News of the World* editor (for more than fifty years) Sir Emsley Carr and Jenny Lascelles. Together with his twin brother Walter he was educated at Clifton College, Bristol. Their skill at cricket was quickly recognized and he was selected for the first XI. Harry also played in the first XV. On leaving Clifton he went up to Trinity Hall, Cambridge, where he gained a blue in billiards and golf but not cricket. After graduating he worked as a journalist with his father at the *News of the World*. He also served as High Sheriff of Glamorgan in 1940.

Harry Carr made three first-class appearances. He made his debut for H.D.G. Leveson-Gower's XI in a university match against Oxford at the Saffrons, Eastbourne. Oxford won the toss and decided to bat making an impressive 483, the England test cricketer Iftikhar Ali Khan the Nawab of Pataudi (*Wisden* cricketer of the year 1932) making 138. Carr, playing as wicketkeeper, made three catches, William O'Brien Lindsay bowled by the England test cricketer Frederick Somerset Gough Calthorpe for 25, the South African test cricketer Alan Melville (*Wisden* Cricketer of the year 1948) bowled George Christopher Newman for 87, and the South African test cricketer Harold Owen-Smith bowled Clement Herbert Gibson (*Wisden* cricketer of the year 1918) for 29. In their first innings Leveson-Gower's XI made 217, Carr making 15 before being bowled by Melville. Melville took five wickets during the innings for 27. In their second innings Oxford made 202 for six declared. Carr stumped the Oxford opener Brian Hone off the bowling of Harold James Palmer for 51. He also stumped the Nawab of Pataudi off the bowling of Palmer for 68. In their second innings Leveson-Gower's XI made 320, Carr making 33 before being lbw Melville. Oxford University won by 148 runs.

He made his second first-class appearance once again for Leveson-Gower's XI this time against Cambridge University at the Saffrons, Eastbourne on 1 July 1931. Leveson-Gower's XI won the toss and decided to bat making 229. Carr was caught by Denys Robert Wilcox off the bowling of Roger Human (killed in 1942) for a duck. In reply Cambridge made 503 for four declared. Carr, playing as wicketkeeper, caught Donald Morris Parry off the bowling of Denijs Morkel for 34. George Kemp-Welch (died 18 June 1944) made 126, Wilcox made 114 not out, and the England test cricketer Frederick Richard Brown (*Wisden* cricketer of the year 1933) made 100 not out. In their second innings Leveson-Gower's XI made 224. Carr made zero before being caught by Aubrey Howard Fabian off the bowling of Brown once again. Brown took five wickets for 58 off 18 overs during the innings. Cambridge won by an inning and 50 runs.

Carr made his final first-class appearance on 30 June 1934 for Glamorgan against Cambridge University at Cardiff Arms Park. Cambridge won the toss and decided to bat making 389, Roger Winlaw (died 31 October 1942) making 108. In reply Glamorgan made 390. Carr was stumped by the England test cricketer Billy Griffith off the bowling of John Human. Human took seven wickets during the innings for 119 runs. Richard George Duckfield made 115. In their second innings Cambridge made 265 for two. Grahame Parker made 100 and Winlaw 109. The match was drawn.

A CAMBRIDGE GOLFING BLUE MARRIED: MR. HARRY LASCELLES CARR AND MISS EILEEN BRACEWELL SMITH.

Carr later married Eileen Mary of Walton-on-the-Hill.

During the war he was commissioned into the RAFVR working with the intelligence branch for two and a half years before being taken seriously ill. He died on 18 August 1943 in a nursing home in Marylebone following an operation. He is buried in Walton-on-the-Hill (St Peters) Churchyard.

His twin brother Walter died in 1944.

Batting and fielding averages

	Mat	Inns	NO	Runs	HS	Ave	100	50	Ct	St
First-class	3	5	0	54	33	10.80	0	0	4	2

Bowling averages

	Mat	Balls	Runs	Wkts	BBI	BBM	Ave	Econ	SR	4w	5w	10
First-class	3	-	-	-	-	-	-	-	-	-	-	-

Wing Commander Rowland Gascoigne Musson
Combined Services
One first-class appearance
172 Squadron Royal Air Force
Died 24 August 1943, aged 31
Right-hand bat

Held world records for flying

Rowland Musson was born on 7 February 1912 in Clitheroe, Lancashire. He was the son of Alfred and Alice Maude Musson (née Slater). He was educated at Tonbridge where he played in the first XI for three seasons against Sherborne, Clifton and Lancing.

Musson made one first-class appearance for the Combined Services against the visiting New Zealanders on 18 August 1937 at the United Services Ground, Portsmouth. Combined Services won the toss and decided to bat making 180. Musson made 24 before being caught and bowled by Bill Carson (died of wounds 8 October 1944). Richard Borgnis made 101. In reply New Zealand made 189. In their second innings Combined Services made 148. Musson was unable to bat due to an injury. John Cowie took five wickets for 36 off 13 overs. In their second innings New Zealand made 140 for one. New Zealand won by nine wickets.

Musson also made fifty-one appearances in Lancashire League Matches and four appearances in Lancashire League Worsley Cup. While serving in Egypt he played for Egypt and the Gezira Sporting Club.

Returning to England he played for the RAF against the Royal Navy, the Army, Sussex, RAF South, Lancashire and Gloucestershire.

He was commissioned into the RAF as a pilot in 1933, serving for several years in Egypt. He became a well-known navigation specialist and for just half an hour held the world long distance flight record, navigating a Vickers Wellesley of the RAF Long Distance Flight non-stop for over 6,000 miles from Ismailia to Australia in 1937 until his tanks ran dry. A second Wellesley of the flight, piloted by Squadron Leader Dick Kellett and guided by another pilot navigation specialist, Flight Lieutenant 'Nick' R.T. Gething, was able to reach Darwin before their fuel ran out and took the record.

During the Second World War, Musson was given command of 172 Squadron, Coastal Command, based at Chivenor, North Devon. He was killed on 24 August 1943 while flying a Wellington bomber MP624 when he inexplicably flew into telegraph wires in low cloud on the cliffs above Clovelly a few minutes after taking off at night to attack U-Boats in the Atlantic. Musson was killed together with the five-man crew. The court of enquiry never conclusively established if the crash was caused by pilot error or a systems failure.

He is buried at Heanton Punchardon (St Augustine) Churchyard, grave reference row P, grave 13.

His older brothers Alfred and Francis Mutton were also first-class cricketers.

Batting and fielding averages

	Mat	Inns	NO	Runs	HS	Ave	100	50	Ct	St
First-class	1	1	0	24	24	24.00	0	0	0	0

Bowling averages

	Mat	Balls	Runs	Wkts	BBI	BBM	Ave	Econ	SR	4w	5w	10
First-class	1	-	-	-	-	-	-	-	-	-	-	-

Tonbridge School 1st XI 1929

Willcocks R.J.M., Orton C.T., Peal C.A., Tilling T.H., Sherwell W.Y., Leach G.M.; Davies J.G.W., Crawford T.A. (Captain); Musson R.G.; Blakelock R.C.B.   Richardson D.G.

QX 15400 Lance Sergeant Francis William Sides
Queensland and Victoria
Twenty-six first-class matches
2/3 Independent Company (2/3 Commando Unit) Australian
Infantry
Died 25 August 1943, aged 29
Left-handed bat

A rare breed of man, a rare breed of soldier

Francis (Frank) Sides was born on 15 December 1913 in Mackay, Queensland. He was the son of John Alfred Leahy and Florence Ellen Sides of Julatten. A farmer by profession, Sides was a natural cricketer who went on to play twenty-six first-class matches for Queensland and Victoria.

He made his debut first-class appearance for Queensland against South Australia in the Sheffield Shield on 31 October 1930 at the Exhibition Ground, Brisbane. He was 17 years old, making him the youngest player ever to turn out for Queensland. Queensland won the toss and decided to bat making 289. Sides made three before being caught by Charles Sydney Deverson off the bowling of Tom Carlton. Malcolm Biggs made 108. In reply South Australia made 72. The Australian test player Hugh Motley Thurlow took five wickets for 25. Following on, South Australia managed 304. In their second innings Queensland made 88 for three. Queensland won by seven wickets.

Sides made twelve appearances for Queensland, eleven in the Sheffield Shield between 31 October 1930 and 15 February 1935. He made his final first-class appearance for Queensland against New South Wales in the Sheffield Shield on 15 February 1935 at Brisbane Cricket Ground. New South Wales won the toss and decided to bat making 233. Edward Gilbert took six wickets for 64. In reply Queensland made 261. Sides made 68 before being lbw off the bowling of Edward Clive Stewart White. In their second innings New South Wales made 337. Alexander Edward Marks made 107. In reply Queensland made 281. Sides made 32 before being bowled by Hugh Cecil Chilvers. Chilvers took six wickets during the innings for 124. New South Wales won by 28 runs.

Moving to Victoria he made his first-class appearance for them on 17 November 1937 at the Melbourne Cricket Ground against Western Australia. Western Australia won the toss and decided to field. Victoria made 316. Sides made three before being caught by Oswald Ifould Lovelock off the bowling of Gordon Eyres. The Australian test cricketer Leo Patrick Joseph O'Brien made 102. The Australian test player Ernest Harvey Bromley 114. George Alan Gardiner took five wickets for 21. In reply Western Australia made 194. In their second innings Victoria made 142 for one. Sides failed to bat. In reply Western Australia made 139, Maxwell William Rayson taking five wickets for 56. Victoria won by 125.

Sides made fourteen appearances for Victoria between 17 November 1937 and 9 March 1939, eleven in the Sheffield Shield. He made his final first-class appearance for Victoria against Western Australia on 9 March 1939 at the Western Australia Cricket Association Ground, Perth. Western Australia won the toss and decided to bat making 257. In reply Victoria made 226, Sides making a fine 121, his highest score in first-class cricket, before being bowled by Charles William Terry Macgill. Gordon Eyres took five wickets for 47. In their second innings Western Australia made 225 declared. In reply Victoria made 78 for three. Sides made 13 not out. The match was drawn. For Sides, getting his first first-class century was a fitting end to a fine career.

During his career Sides made 1,308 runs with one century and nine fifties. He also made seven catches and made one stumping.

He enlisted into the ranks on 26 March 1941, later becoming a lance sergeant. He joined Australian Infantry (2/3 Commando unit) fighting as a commando. Formed in October 1941 as the 2/3rd Independent Company, it undertook training at the Guerrilla Warfare Camp at Foster, Victoria. After six months training, the unit, under the command of Major George Warfe, was sent to New Guinea in February 1943. They landed at Port Moresby and from there were shipped to Wau, participating in the Australian pursuit of the Japanese towards Mubo and later assisting the 3rd Division's campaign around Salamaua. Their main task was to launch a guerrilla campaign against the Japanese to harass and pursue them wherever they were located.

The 2/3rd patrolled deep into Japanese held territory, setting ambushes and gathering intelligence. The most notable of these actions came in May 1943 when in an outstanding action the unit captured a place called Ambush Knoll. This was an important position as it controlled Bobdubi Ridge and hence threatened the Japanese supply lines to Mubo and Salamaua. As a result the Japanese made several counter-attacks in force to try to retake the Knoll. Despite the Japanese best efforts and with only fifty-two men the 2/3rd managed to hold the Knoll. They suffered heavy casualties, one of whom alas was Lance Sergeant Sides. He was killed on 25 August 1943 at Kunai Spur, Salamaua, New Guinea. The 2/3rd were credited with killing around a thousand Japanese soldiers. Their losses were 65 killed, 119 wounded and 226 evacuated sick.

Francis William Sides is buried in the Lae War Cemetery, grave reference Q. A. 3.

Batting and fielding averages

	Mat	Inns	NO	Runs	HS	Ave	100	50	Ct	St
First-class	26	46	4	1308	121	31.14	1	9	7	1

Bowling averages

	Mat	Balls	Runs	Wkts	BBI	BBM	Ave	Econ	SR	4w	5w	10
First-class	26	-	-	-	-	-	-	-	-	-	-	-

**Group Captain Francis (Frank) Samuel Hodder
RAF
One first-class match
106 Squadron RAF
Died 6 September 1943, aged 37
Right-handed bat/Right arm (unknown)**

Died trying to experience what his men experienced

Francis Hodder was born on 11 February 1906 at Ringabella House, Carrigaline, Co Cork, the second son of Samuel and Maud Hodder. He was educated at Forest Hill House School. A fine sportsman he played cricket for the school's first XI. In one match he made a century and then took all ten wickets. On leaving school he initially joined the Midland Bank. However the life didn't suit him and on 18 July 1925 he was commissioned into the RAF as a pilot officer on probation. He became a pilot officer on 30 September 1939 and a flying officer on 30 September 1940. He also married Evelyn Margaret Bowden-Smith of Brockenhurst, Hampshire, in 1940 and they had two sons.

Hodder made one first-class appearance for the RAF against the Army on 4 July 1931 at the Oval, Kennington. The RAF won the toss and elected to bat making 192. Hodder, batting last, made one not out. The wartime hero Douglas Bader also played in the match in his one and only first-class appearance making 65, the best score of the innings. Adrian Gore took five wickets for 51. In reply the Army made 416. Hodder bowled 28 overs taking one wicket for 69, William Murray Leggatt lbw for 28. He also caught Leoline Williams off the bowling of Douglas MacFadyen for 103. In their second innings the RAF made 187. Hodder, again batting last, made ten not out. Bader only managed one before being caught by Edward Williams off the bowling of Ernest Dynes. Dynes took five wickets during the innings for 31. The army won by an innings and 37 runs.

Hodder went on to play for the RAF on five more occasions between 15 July 1931 and 17 July 1939, against the Civil Service (won by 66 runs), the Royal Navy (lost by five wickets), the Army (lost by 146 runs), the Royal Navy (lost by 40 runs), and finally the Royal Navy once again (drawn).

As well as cricket Hodder was a fine rugby player. He played in the first XV at school, an RAF XV in nine inter-service matches, represented the Combined Services, and played county rugby for Kent. He played for London Irish for ten seasons, and took part in a trial for Ireland.

He served in Iraq and Aden and passed a specialist course in engineering. On 1 February 1937 he was promoted to squadron leader and on I March 1940 to wing commander. He was stationed in France at the outbreak of the war and was mentioned in despatches for his outstanding work with the advanced air striking force during the Germans' advance through France.

Returning home, he was given engineering duties, first with Messrs Rootes and then with the Handley-Page Aircraft Company. He was promoted group captain on 1 March 1942. In July 1943 he was given command of RAF Syerston, a bomber command station near Newark in Nottinghamshire. Wanting to experience what the men he led experienced on an almost nightly basis, he hitched a ride with a Lancaster bomber DV 182 of 106 Squadron on the night of 5/6 September 1943 during an operation to Mannheim. The Lancaster was shot down by a night fighter whose opening burst of fire killed the pilot and mortally wounded the flight engineer. A fire then broke out, after which there was no further communication from the Lancaster. There was only one survivor.

The crew consisted of:

Pilot Officer (pilot) A.A. Robertson
Flying Officer (air gunner) R.R. Shadbolt DFC
Sergeant (flight engineer) J. Cunliffe
Pilot Officer (navigator) F.S. Green (Canadian)
Pilot Officer (wireless operator/air gunner) A.E. Taylor (American)
Sergeant (air gunner) F.W. Tysall

One member of the crew survived, Flying Officer G. Willat. He was captured by the Germans and interned in camp L3, PoW number 2393. Later he wrote the book *Bombs and Barbed Wire*.

Frank Hodder, together with his crew, is buried in Rheinberg War Cemetery, coll grave 18. A. 3-7.

Batting and fielding averages

	Mat	Inns	NO	Runs	HS	Ave	100	50	Ct	St
First-class	1	2	2	11	10*	-	0	0	1	0

Bowling averages

	Mat	Balls	Runs	Wkts	BBI	Ave	Econ	SR	5w	10
First-class	1	168	69	1	1/69	69.00	2.46	168.0	0	0

Officers of the three flying boat's which are leaving Plymouth on an exploratory flight to Basra. Group comprises Group-Capt. R. E. Saul, Sq.-Ldr. E. F. Waring, Flt.-Lieut. F. S. Hodder, Flt.-Lieut. K. F. T. Pickles, Flg.-Off. C. H. Brandon, Flg.-Off. A. N. Combe, Pilot-Off. Rump, and Pilot-Off. Wheeler.—"Western Morning News" Photo

Lieutenant David James Falshaw Watson
Oxford University
Two first-class matches
Royal Naval Volunteer Reserve
HMS *Saker*
Died 3 October 1943, aged 25
Right-handed bat

Was only spectating when he was asked to make his debut first-class appearance

David Watson was born on 18 November 1919 in St Pancras, London. He was the son of Mr and Mrs G. L. Watson, of South Kensington. He was educated at Sedbergh School where he played in the first XI against Rossall School on three occasions in 1935-7. He also played for a C.F. Tufnell's XI against a Lord's XI in August 1934, making 18 and 40 not out. The match was drawn.

On leaving school Watson went up to Brasenose College, Oxford. While there he made two first-class appearances, both in June 1939.

He made his debut for the Minor Counties against Oxford University on 7 June at the University Parks. Oxford won the toss and decided to bat making 281, Walter Stuart Surridge (*Wisden* cricketer of the year 1953) taking five wickets for 41. In reply Minor Counties made 236. Watson made 33 before being caught by Richard Michael England off the bowling of Michael Humphrey Farebrother. In their second innings Oxford made 256. In their second innings Minor Counties made 304, Watson making 35 before being lbw to Farebrother. Alan Herring Parnaby made 101. Minor Counties won by four wickets. An interesting event took place during this match involving Watson. Having bowled nine overs for Minor Counties during Oxford's first-innings, Francis Wilkinson was injured and unable to continue. David Watson had been watching the match from the stands when he was asked to play and replace the unlucky Wilkinson. Surprisingly Oxford and the umpires agreed and Watson took the field helping the Minor Counties to take the match. It was the last instance of this happening for more than sixty years.

He made his second and final first-class appearance for Oxford University against Leicestershire on 14 June 1939 at the University Parks. Oxford won the toss and elected to bat making 147. Watson made seven before being bowled by Victor Edward Jackson. James Sperry took five wickets for 65. In reply Leicestershire made 237, Gwynn Evans taking six wickets for 80. In their second innings Oxford made 90. Watson made eight not out. The match was drawn.

Watson married Veronica Josephine Rodgers in Chelsea on 22 June 1942.

During the Second World War Watson was commissioned into the Royal Naval Volunteer Reserve becoming a sub-lieutenant. Joining the Fleet Air Arm he was posted to HMS *Saker* in the United States to train as a pilot. It was while he was undergoing pilot training on 3 October 1943 with an F4U Corsair that his plane was involved in a mid-air collision with fellow Fleet Air Arm pilot and fighter ace Alfred Jack Sewell DSC, a thirteen-kill fighter ace, close to the Maine town of New Gloucester. Both pilots were killed in the collision.

Watson was buried in the Portsmouth Naval Shipyard Cemetery, lot 137.

Batting and fielding averages

	Mat	Inns	NO	Runs	HS	Ave	100	50	Ct	St
First-class	2	4	1	83	35	27.66	0	0	0	0

Bowling averages

	Mat	Balls	Runs	Wkts	BBI	BBM	Ave	Econ	SR	4w	5w	10
First-class	2	-	-	-	-	-	-	-	-	-	-	-

Captain James Edward Mayne Alexander
Bengal
Two first-class matches
Indian Engineers
Died 23 October 1943, aged 27
Left-handed bat/Left arm fast medium

A fine mind and excellent sportsman

James Alexander was born on 3 September 1916 at Tonbridge, Kent. He was the son of Edward Murray Mayne and Florence Eleanor Wilson Alexander.

Alexander played in two first-class matches, both for Bengal in 1937 and 1938, both in the Ranji Trophy. He made his debut for Bengal against Nawanagar on 6 February 1937 at the Gymkhana Ground Bombay in the Ranji Trophy final. Nawanagar won the toss and decided to bat making 424, the Indian test cricketer Mulvantrai Himmatlal Mankad (*Wisden* cricketer of the year 1947, Indian cricketer of the year 1946/47) making 185. Alexander bowled 11 overs taking no wickets for 51. He also caught Mulvantrai Mankad off

Calcutta (Bhowanipore) Cemetery.

the bowling of Kamal Bhattacharya for 185. In reply Bengal made 315. Alexander made two not out. In their second innings Nawanagar made 383. Alexander bowled four overs taking no wicket for 19. In their second innings Bengal made 236. Alexander made five before being stumped by Abdul Aziz Durani off the bowling of Albert Wensley, Alfred Graham Skinner making 125. Nawanagar won by 256 runs.

He made his second first-class appearance for Bengal against Central India on 29 January 1938 in the Ranji Trophy (East Zone) at Eden Gardens, Calcutta. Bengal won the toss and decided to bat making 110. Alexander was bowled by the Indian test cricketer Vijay Samuel Hazare (Indian cricketer of the year 1946/47, *Wisden* India Hall of Fame 2015) for one. In reply Central India made 154. Alexander bowled 12 overs taking three wickets for 40: Syed Ishtiaq Ali bowled for zero, Kamal Vinayak Bhandarkar lbw for seventeen and Sardar Mohammad Khan bowled for zero. In their second innings Bengal made 217. Alexander made six before being caught by the Indian test cricketer Vijay Hazare off the bowling of another Indian test cricketer Syed Mushtaq Ali (Indian cricketer of the year 1949/50). Vijay Hazare took five wickets for 89. In their second innings Central India made 145. Alexander bowled 18 overs taking four wickets for 32: the Indian test player Cottari Kanakaiya Nayudu (*Wisden* cricketer of the year 1933, Indian cricketer of the year 1950/51) caught Charles Edwin Inder for one, Syed Mushtaq Ali for four, P Tata Rao bowled for zero, and Sambu Singh caught Paul Ian van der Gucht for zero. Bengal won by 28 runs.

During the Second World War, Alexander served with the Indian Engineers. He died in Calcutta on 23 October 1943 and was buried in the Calcutta (Bhowanipore) Cemetery, grave reference plot O, row C, grave 4. He left a widow, Diana.

Batting and fielding averages

	Mat	Inns	NO	Runs	HS	Ave	100	50	Ct	St
First-class	2	4	1	13	6	4.33	0	0	1	0

Bowling averages

	Mat	Runs	Wkts	BBI	Ave	5w	10
First-class	2	142	7	4/32	20.28	0	0

Pilot Officer John Alan Jeffreys
Western Australia
Four first-class appearances
61 Squadron Royal Australian Air Force (RAAF)
Died 3 November 1943, aged 30
Right-hand bat

Bomber Command Memorial, London.

Alan Jeffreys was born on 17 April 1913 in Fremantle, Western Australia. He was the son of John Alfred and Amelia Jeffreys. He made four first-class appearances, all for Western Australia between November 1937and February 1940.

He made his debut for them on 17 November 1937 against Victoria at the Melbourne Cricket Ground. Western Australia won the toss and decided to field. Victoria made 316. The Australian test cricketers Leo O'Brien and Ernest Bromley made 102 and 114. George Gardiner took five wickets for 21 off nine overs. In reply Western Australia made 194. Jeffreys, opening for Western Australia, made ten before being bowled by the Australian test cricketer Hans Irvine Ebeling. In their second innings Victoria made 142 for one declared. In their second innings Western Australia made 139. Jeffreys made 14 before being caught by John Gladstone Stanes off the bowling of Ebeling. Maxwell Rayson took five wickets for 56 off 15 overs. Victoria won by 125 runs.

His next appearance was against South Australia on 3 December 1937 at the Adelaide Oval. Jeffreys made two and 27. South Australia won by ten wickets.

His next appearance was against an Australian XI on 18 March 1938 at the Western Australia Cricket Association Ground, Perth. Western Australia won the toss and decided to bat making 192. Jeffreys opening for Western Australia made 12 before being lbw to William O'Reilly (*Wisden* cricketer of the year 1935). The Australian XI made 391. Jeffreys caught Lindsay Hassett (*Wisden* Cricketer of the year 1949) off the bowling of Anthony George Zimbulis. Donald Bradman and Stanley McCabe made centuries. In their second innings Western Australia made 73. Jeffreys was bowled by Frank Ward for 14. O'Reilly took five wickets for twelve off nine overs. The Australian XI won by an innings and 126 runs.

His final first-class appearance came against South Australia on 10 February 1940 at the Western Australia Cricket Association Ground. South Australia won the toss and decided to bat making 248. Jeffreys caught Vincent Roy Gibson off the bowling of Zimbulis for 35 and John Michael Kierse off the bowling of Arthur David Watt for 23. In reply Western Australia made 275. Jeffreys made a solid 36 before being caught by Thomas Elliott Klose off the bowling of Frank Ward. Ward took six wickets for 105 off 26 overs. In their second innings South Australia made 306 for three declared, Bradman making 209 not out. In their second innings Western Australia made 121 for three. Jeffreys made eight before being caught by Bradman off the bowling of Kierse. The match was drawn.

He later represented the Royal Australian Air Force but none of his matches were first-class games.

During the Second World War Jeffreys served with the Royal Australian Air Force going on to serve with 61 Squadron RAAF. Flying from RAF Skellingthrope, Lincolnshire, in

Lancaster 1 NG179 to raid the Trondheim U-Boat pens he was seriously wounded, dying from his wounds on 3 November 1943 in Shipham, Somerset.

He is commemorated in the Cambridge City Cemetery, grave reference 14322. He left a widow, Florence Isobel, of Perth, Western Australia.

Batting and fielding averages

	Mat	Inns	NO	Runs	HS	Ave	100	50	Ct	St
First-class	4	8	0	123	36	15.37	0	0	3	0

Bowling averages

	Mat	Balls	Runs	Wkts	BBI	BBM	Ave	Econ	SR	4w	5w	10
First-class	4	-	-	-	-	-	-	-	-	-	-	-

Jeffrey's can be seen on the back row, fifth from left.

Lieutenant Peter Michael William Whitehouse
Kent, Oxford University
Twenty-four first-class matches
13 Frontier Force Rifles (6th Royal Battalion)
Died 19 November 1943, aged 26
Right-handed bat/Right arm medium

The mainstay of any cricketing side

Peter Whitehouse was born on 27 April 1917 in Birchington, Kent. He was the son of Henry Charles and Marjorie Winifred Whitehouse of Nether Wallop, Hampshire. He was educated at Marlborough where he was in the first XI playing on fourteen occasions against Harrow, Wellington, Winchester, Cheltenham College and Rugby, also turning out for Lord's School against The Rest. On leaving Marlborough he went up to New College, Oxford. While there he was selected to play for Oxford University going on to play twenty-four first-class matches for Oxford and Kent.

He made his debut for Oxford University on 10 June 1936 against the Minor Counties at the University Parks. Minor Counties won the toss and decided to bat making 251. Whitehouse bowled nine overs taking two wickets for 40, Frederick Cecil de Saram caught Michael Matthews (died 29 May 1941) for six, and Horace Cedric Lee bowled for 61. In reply Oxford made 288. Whitehouse knocked up a solid 50 not out. William Alfred Smith took five wickets for 95. In their second innings Minor Counties made 294. Whitehouse bowled seven overs taking two wickets for 28, Lee caught and bowled for 45 and Edward Montague Nash bowled for zero. In their second innings Oxford made 23 for no wicket, Whitehouse failed to bat. The match was drawn.

During the 1936 season Whitehouse played in one further match, against Leicestershire. He took two wickets and made 91 not out in his only innings. The match was drawn.

During the 1937 season he played for Oxford against Yorkshire (Yorkshire won by 160 runs), Army (Oxford won by six wickets), and Free Foresters (Oxford won by ten wickets).

In the same season, on 19 June, Whitehouse made his debut first-class appearance for Kent in the county championship playing against Somerset at the Recreation Ground, Bath. Somerset won the toss and decided to bat making 344. Whitehouse bowled 23 overs taking two wickets for 60. Walter Luckes made 121. In reply Kent made 116, Whitehouse making eight before being bowled by the England test player Arthur Wellard (*Wisden* cricketer of the year 1936). William Andrews took six wickets for 62. In their second innings Somerset made 264 declared. Whitehouse bowled 14 overs taking three wickets for 49, Herbert Dickinson Burrough caught Ronald Thurston Bryan for 133, Andrews caught William Henry Ashdown for four, and Wellard caught Ashdown for eight. In their second innings Kent made 73. Whitehouse made 12 before being caught by Luckes off the bowling of Horace Hazell. Somerset won by 419 runs.

Whitehouse played for Kent on two more occasions during the 1937 season, against Gloucestershire (lost by an innings and 31 runs), and Middlesex (lost by an innings and 37 runs).

Returning to Oxford University for the 1938 season he played against Minor Counties (won 230 runs), Leicestershire (drawn), Glamorgan (drawn), Middlesex (won by two wickets), Free Foresters (lost by five wickets), Lancashire (lost by seven wickets), MCC (won by nine wickets), Sussex (won 112 runs), Army (drawn), Surrey (drawn) and finally Cambridge University (drawn). Returning to Kent he played in five county championship matches during the 1938 season: against Surrey (lost by six wickets), Glamorgan (won by seven wickets), Middlesex (won by 265 runs) and Lancashire (won by 125 runs).

Whitehouse made his final first-class appearance for Kent against Sussex in the county championship on 6 August 1938 at the Central Recreation Ground, Hastings. Sussex won the toss and decided to bat making 447. Whitehouse bowled 16 overs taking no wickets for 40. Hugh Bartlett made 114. In reply Kent made 115. Whitehouse made 25 before being caught by John Nye off the bowling of the England test player James Parks (*Wisden* cricketer of the year 1938). James Langridge took five wickets for 28. Following on, Kent made 317. Whitehouse made 30 before being bowled by Langridge, who took six wickets for 91 during the innings. Sussex won by an innings and 15 runs.

Whitehouse also made ten minor county appearances between 1935 and 1937 for Berkshire and Kent's second XI.

During his career Whitehouse made 927 runs including seven fifties, his highest score being 91 for Oxford University against Leicestershire. He also bowled, taking 43 wickets for 2,755, his best figures being five for 33.

Whitehouse took a commission into the Indian Army serving with the 13 Frontier Force Rifles (6th Royal Battalion). During the war he took part in the actions in Iraq, Syria and Iran including pushing back Vichy French troops and capturing the Mosul to Aleppo railway. In 1942, as part of the 18 Brigade, he fought against Rommel in North Africa giving valuable support to the 8th Army but taking heavy casualties. In September 1943 they landed at Taranto to take part in the Italian campaign. Moving up the Adriatic front on the eastern part of the country they took part in the actions around the River Sangro. It was here that Lieutenant Whitehouse was killed by a shell on 19 November 1943. He is buried in the Sangro River War Cemetery, grave reference V. B. 40.

Batting and fielding averages

	Mat	Inns	NO	Runs	HS	Ave	100	50	Ct	St
First-class	24	39	7	927	91*	28.96	0	7	4	0

Bowling averages

	Mat	Balls	Runs	Wkts	BBI	Ave	Econ	SR	5w	10
First-class	24	2815	1267	43	5/33	29.46	2.70	65.4	1	0

Major Robin Evelyn Whetherly MC
Oxford University
Eleven first-class matches
Royal Armoured Corps
1st King's Dragoon Guards
Died 27 November 1943, aged 27
Right-handed bat/Wicketkeeper

A real James Bond

Robin Whetherly was born on 23 July 1916 in Westminster. He was the son of Lieutenant Colonel William Stobart Whetherly DSO, a veteran of the Boer and First World Wars, and Marjorie Isobel. He was educated at Harrow where he was in the XI and kept wicket in his final year. On leaving Harrow he went up to Magdalen College, Oxford and read history.

He made eleven first-class appearances, all for Oxford University between 1937 and 1938. He made his debut against Gloucestershire between 1 and 4 May 1937 at the University Parks. Gloucestershire won the toss and decided to bat making 224. He didn't bowl but managed to take three catches, Richard Haynes off the bowling of Tristan Ballance for 24, the test cricketer Reginald Sinfield off the bowling of Randle Darwall-Smith for 53, and Thomas Goddard again off the bowling of Darwell-Smith for two. In reply Oxford made 384, Whetherly making 22 before being caught by Thomas Neale off the bowling of Sinfield. The Oxford opener Michael Barton made 192. In their second innings Gloucestershire made 190. Whetherly took one wicket, stumping Sinfield off the bowling of Ballance for two. It only left Oxford 32 to get, which they knocked up quickly to win the match by eight wickets.

Whetherly went on to play for Oxford University against Yorkshire, Lancashire, Middlesex, New Zealand, the Army, Free Foresters, MCC, and the Australians.

He made his final first-class appearance for a combined Oxford and Cambridge side against Jamaica between the 10 and 13 August 1938 at Sabina Park, Kingston, during the Oxford and Cambridge Universities tour of Jamaica between July and August 1938. Oxford and Cambridge won the toss and decided to bat making 355. Whetherly made six before being lbw off the bowling of Hophnie Hobah Hines Johnson. In reply Jamaica made 227. In their second innings Oxford and Cambridge collapsed to 99 all out, Whetherly being caught and bowled by Leslie Hylton for seven. In their second innings Jamaica made 204. Whetherly catching the Jamaican opener Kenneth Weekes off the bowling of John Cameron after he had made 106. The match was drawn.

During his career Whetherly made 146 runs, his highest score being 63 against the MCC. He also took 22 catches and made five stumpings.

He also occasionally turned out for the Harrow Wanderers and the Gentlemen of Worcestershire. Interestingly he travelled with the Gentlemen of Worcestershire on their tour of Nazi Germany in 1937. Given that Hitler thought cricket was decadent and un-German it was surprising that it happened at all. However thanks to the enthusiasm of the cricket-loving Felix Menzel, Hitler was persuaded to let the tour go ahead. Whetherly played in two of the three matches, the first played at the Berliner Sport-Verein ground on 6 August 1937 which the Gentlemen won by 101 runs, Whetherly making one in the first innings, 57 in his second, and taking three catches. He failed to play in the second match which took place on 7 August at the Tip-Platz. He played in the third, at the famous Olympic Stadium, Berlin, between 10 and 11 August 1937. The Gentlemen took the match by 249 runs, Whetherly making ten in his first innings and three in his second. He also made two catches.

It is almost certain that Whetherly, who spoke fluent German, was sent on the tour as an English spy. Although, as we have seen, he was a fine cricketer, he had nothing to do with either Worcestershire or the Gentlemen's cricket club. He also travelled to Germany on his own and not with the team.

On leaving university he worked for some time in a travel agent's before deciding to make a career in the army and taking a commission into the 1st King's Dragoon Guards at the beginning of the Second World War. Posted to Libya in April 1941 he was to see plenty of action and after his regiment was attacked by the German Africa Korps his quick and brave actions not only saved the lives of many of his men but saved many more from becoming prisoners. He was awarded the MC.

Remaining with his regiment in 1943 he was eventually posted to the Special Operations Executive. After training he was dropped behind enemy lines in Yugoslavia to train and work with the partisans, serving under the legendary Fitzroy Maclean (who Ian Fleming probably used as a model for 007 and was one of only two men to be raised from private to brigadier, the other being Enoch Powell). Whetherly was killed on 27 November 1943 by strafing aircraft while inspecting a captured Dornier with fellow SOE officer Captain Donald Knight who was also killed.

He is buried in Belgrade War Cemetery, grave reference 3. C. 8. He is buried beside Donald Knight, grave reference 3. C. 9.

Batting and fielding averages

	Mat	Inns	NO	Runs	HS	Ave	100	50	Ct	St
First-class	11	16	4	146	63	12.16	0	1	20	6

Bowling averages

	Mat	Balls	Runs	Wkts	BBI	BBM	Ave	Econ	SR	4w	5w	10
First-class	11	-	-	-	-	-	-	-	-	-	-	-

Brigadier Bernard Howlett DSO & bar
Europeans (India), Kent, Bombay, MCC
Forty-two first-class matches
Queen's Own Royal West Kent Regiment
36th Infantry Brigade, late 6th Battalion
Died 29 November 1943, aged 44
Right-hand bat/Right arm fast

A commanding officer killed leading his men

Bernard Howlett, better known as 'Swifty', was born on 18 December 1898 in Stoke Newington. He was the son of the Reverend Thomas Edwin (1853-1904) and Gertrude Howlett. He was educated at St Edmund's School, Canterbury. He entered the Junior School September 1908 (Foundationer) East House where he became house captain. He played football, cricket and hockey for his school as well as being a sergeant in OTC. In December 1916 he went up to the Royal Military College Sandhurst where he turned out for the cricket XI. He was commissioned into the Queens Own Royal West Kent Regiment becoming a second lieutenant on 24 April 1918. Sent to France with his regiment he took part in the last few months of the First World War, being promoted to lieutenant on 24 October 1919.

Howlett made forty-two first-class appearances, mainly for Kent, but he also turned out for the Europeans in India, the Army, Bombay and the MCC. He made his debut for Kent against Worcestershire between 31 May and 1 June 1922 at the Bat and Ball Ground, Gravesend. Kent won the toss and decided to bat making 498, Howlett making one not out. The England test cricketer Harold Hardinge made 166 and James Seymore 114. In reply Worcestershire made 101, Howlett bowling four overs and taking no wickets for 17. The Kent bowler Alfred Freeman took six wickets during the innings. Following on, Worcestershire made a further 161. Howlett bowled nine overs for 28, this time with more success, taking the wickets of the two Worcestershire openers, Frederick Bowley for four and

Frederick Pearson caught Seymore for 11. He also caught John MacLean off the bowling off Frank Woolley for 22 (Woolley took five wickets in the innings). Kent won the match by an innings and 236 runs. Howlett went on to play against Lancashire, Essex, Gloucestershire and Northamptonshire.

Posted to India he began to turn out for the Europeans (India) making his debut for them in the Bombay Quadrangular Tournament against the Muslims at the Gymkhana Ground between 20 November and 2 December 1925. The Muslims won the toss and decided to bat making 252. Howlett bowled 24 overs taking one wicket for 95 runs; he bowled S Ghulam

Rasool for 19. He also caught Syed Wazir Ali for five and Ghulam Mohammad for seven, both off the bowling of Norton Hughes-Hallett. Hughes-Hallett took eight wickets in the innings. In reply the Europeans made 450, Howlett making 33 before being caught and bowled by S Ghulam Rasool. Francis Travers made 121 not out. In their second innings the Muslims made 267. Howlett bowled 25 overs taking one wicket for 77, that of the Muslim opener ME Sheikh, caught Alexander Hosie for 12. Hughes-Hallett took a further five wickets in the innings. In their second innings the Europeans only needed to make 70 to win, which they did, by eight wickets.

Howlett also represented the Europeans against the Parsees, the Indians and the Hindus. He made his final first-class match against the Indians between 14 and 15 January 1928 at the Madras Cricket Club Ground in a Madras Presidency Match. The match was drawn.

On returning to England Howlett resumed his first-class career with Kent, his first match being against Oxford University between the 9 and 11 May 1928 at the University Parks. Kent won the toss and decided to bat making 499, Howlett making 14 before being caught by Colin Melville off the bowling of Robert McIntosh. Harold Hardinge made 152, Peter Cazalet 150 and Frank Woolley 100 during the same innings. In reply Oxford made 216. Howlett bowled three overs taking three wickets for 68, Colin Melville for one, Anthony Tew caught Geoffrey Legge (died 21 November 1940) for a duck, and Charles Hill-Wood caught Leslie Ames for one. Following on, Oxford made 346, Herbert Garland-Wells making 128. Howlett bowled 16 overs taking two wickets for 40, Aidan Crawley caught Leslie Ames for 28, and Thomas Welch caught Ames for 21.

He went on to play many other county matches. Briefly returning to India in 1929 he put in one appearance for the Europeans against India at the Madras Cricket Club Ground, the Europeans wining by eight wickets.

Howlett made his final first-class appearance for the Army against the RAF at the Oval between the 4 and 6 July 1931. The RAF won the toss and decided to bat making 192. Howlett bowled 19 overs taking three wickets for 80 runs, Geoffrey Longfield caught Francis Hugonin for one, Albert Holmes caught William Leggatt for 13, and Cyril Adams caught Adrian Gore for four. In reply the Army made 416, Howlett making two not out. In their second innings the RAF made 187. Howlett bowled 12 overs taking two wickets for 46, Edmund Hudleston lbw, and Geoffrey Longfield caught Montagu Burrows for two. The Army won by an innings and 37 runs.

As well as his first-class appearances Howlett made four minor counties championship matches for Kent's second XI in 1923.

During his first-class career Howlett made 319 runs including one fifty, his highest score being 58. He also bowled 6,443 balls for 3,156 runs and took 108 wickets, his best figures being six for 35. He also made 23 catches.

On 2 April 1929 he married Helena Beatrice Joan Whitby in Bangalore. They had one daughter.

He was promoted to captain on 18 February 1930, major on 1 August 1938, lieutenant colonel on 7 October, and brigadier on 17 December 1942. Between 1939 and 1940 he was a brigade major with the 132nd Infantry Brigade, BEF, and was given command of the 6th Battalion Queen's Own Royal West Kent Regiment. Between December 1942 and November 1943 he commanded the 36th Infantry Brigade in North Africa before being given temporary command of the 139th Brigade also in Africa. Shortly after this he returned to the 36th Brigade, commanding them in North Africa, Sicily and Italy. He was mentioned in despatches in 1940 (*London Gazette* 20 December 1940), won the DSO in Tunisia (*LG* 15 June 1943), and a bar for his DSO in Sicily (*LG* 18 November 1943).

Bernard Howlett was killed in action at Santa Maria Imbaro, just north of the Sangro River in Italy, on 29 November 1943. He was mentioned in despatches once again, this time posthumously (*LG* 24 August 1944). Howlett is buried at the Sangro River War Cemetery, plot II, row E, grave 25.

Batting and fielding averages

	Mat	Inns	NO	Runs	HS	Ave	100	50	Ct	St
First-class	42	55	21	319	58	9.38	0	1	23	0

Bowling averages

	Mat	Runs	Wkts	BBI	Ave	5w	10
First-class	42	3156	108	6/35	29.22	3	0

Major Tristan George Lance Ballance MC
Oxford University
Twenty-three first-class appearances
16th Battalion Durham Light Infantry
Died 4 December 1943, aged 27
Right-handed bat/Slow left arm orthodox

Won the first Military Cross for the 16th Battalion
Durham Light Infantry of the Second World War

Tristan Ballance was born on 21 April 1916 in Norwich. He was the son of Sir Hamilton Ashley Ballance KBE CB MS FRCS and Lady Ballance of Redgrave, Suffolk. He had one brother Ivor and a sister Rosemary. He was educated at Uppingham where he was soon in the cricket XI. He bowled slow left arm and during the 1932 season took 76 wickets for less than ten runs apiece. During the 1933 season he took a further 54 wickets for just over ten runs each, his school winning ten of their eleven matches. He played for Uppingham against Haileybury, Repton, Rugby, Shrewsbury and Oundle. He also played for The Rest against Lord's School and for the Public Schools against the Army. He also represented Norfolk against the West Indies (during their 1933 tour).

At Brasenose College, Oxford, he took part in the Freshmen's match, taking six wickets for 41.

Ballance made twenty-three first-class appearances, all for Oxford University between 1935 and 1937. He made his debut for Oxford against Worcestershire between 4 and 7 May 1935 at the University Parks. Worcestershire won the toss and decided to bat making 191. Ballance bowled two overs for 25, taking one wicket, caught Michael Barton for ten. In reply Oxford made 439, Ballance making nine not out. During their second innings Worcestershire made 235. Ballance bowled 31 overs for 74 taking three wickets, Bernard Quaife caught Norman Mitchell-Innes for 62, Sidney Martin caught Barton for ten, and Roger Human stumped Roger Kimpton for 29. Oxford took the match by an innings and 13 runs.

Ballance went on to play against Gloucestershire, South Africa, the Minor Counties, Free Foresters, H.D.G. Leveson-Gowers XI, Sussex, Surrey, MCC, Cambridge University, Derbyshire, Leicestershire, Yorkshire and New Zealand.

He made his final first-class appearance against the old enemy Cambridge at Lord's between 5 and 7 July 1937. Cambridge won the toss and decided to bat making 253. Ballance bowled nine overs and took no wickets for 29. In reply Oxford made 267, Ballance not out for nine and John Grove making 121. In their second innings Cambridge made 173. Ballance bowled 23 overs for 43 and took a further two wickets, Peter Studd caught Mitchell-Innes for twelve, and Bharat Khanna for one. Ballance made 160 in their second innings, Oxford winning the match by seven wickets.

Ballance also made fifty minor county appearances for Norfolk. During his first-class career Ballance made 190 runs with one fifty, his highest score being 63 against Leicestershire. He also bowled 4,238 balls for 1,875 runs taking 61 wickets, his best figures being five for 30.

During the war, Ballance was commissioned into the 16th Battalion Durham Light Infantry rising to the rank of captain temporary major. He was recommended for the MC for his actions during the aftermath of the Battle of Sedjenane in North Africa in mid-March 1943:

> This officer was very strongly recommended for an immediate award of the Military Cross for an independent action fought at Sedjenane. He commanded a composite force of some 20 men and occupied a native village at about 1900 hours on 3 March 43 on the left flank of the 6 Lincs. By his leadership and example he was able to keep his men firing and the enemy in check until all his ammunition had been exhausted. This action undoubtedly contributed to a great degree in enabling Sedjenane to be held until 1530 hrs the following day.
>
> Shortly afterwards this officer assumed command of a Rifle Coy, which he was ordered to move to the MINE at 1257, from where he was ordered to find out whether there was any enemy in the GERMAN mine, some three miles away to the N.E. Finding it to be unoccupied, he went immediately to Bde and asked permission to hold it in greater strength owing to its obvious tactical importance. This was confirmed by the Bde Comd and he thereupon moved his Coy forward and held the position until relieved by the 6 R West Kents. By his quick appreciation he was able to secure the base from which 138 Bde launched its attack as part of the general offensive of 46 Div.
>
> It should also be pointed out that when he arrived at the Mine (1257) the enemy were on the saddle to the NE, transecting the Beja–Djebel Abiod road. Unless offensive action had been taken immediately the situation might have become serious.
>
> *Recommended by A/Lt Col J C Preston, Comd 16th Bn The Durham Light Infy.*

It was the Durham Light Infantry's first Military Cross of the Second World War (*London Gazette* 23 September 1943).

Ballance was killed in action three months later on 8 December 1943. The regimental history details the action in which Ballance was killed:

> December was notable mainly for the attack on Camino-Massif in which the Battalion took part. For this operation of breaking the enemy's Winter Line, 139 Bde was given the task of entering the Calabritto Basin and protecting the left flank, whilst 56 Division moved to the mountain and attacked the Massif proper. This role was successfully carried out by 2/5th Leicesters and the Foresters and B Coy 16th DLI. Whilst fighting on the Western heights was still in progress, the remainder of the Battalion was used to attack the Cocuruzzo Spur, which formed the Western side the Calabritto Basin. This attack which was made from the high ground on the enemy's left flank completed the task of finally opening the Basin.

He was buried in the Minturno War Cemetery in Italy, grave reference, II. E, 21.

He was the fourth member of the 1937 Oxford XI to be killed in the war.

His brother, Lieutenant Ivor Hamilton Ballance, RNVR, HMS *Trinidad*, was killed on 29 March 42 while on Artic Convoys.

Batting and fielding averages

	Mat	Inns	NO	Runs	HS	Ave	100	50	Ct	St
First-class	23	32	12	190	63	9.50	0	1	18	0

Bowling averages

	Mat	Runs	Wkts	BBI	Ave	5w	10
First-class	23	1875	51	5/30	36.76	2	0

Lieutenant Glen George Baker
Queensland
Twenty-nine first-class matches
Australian Army Ordnance Corps, AIF 4 Ordnance Depot
Died 15 December 1943, aged 28
Right-handed bat/Right arm medium

A Fine Australian

Glen Baker (some sources have his middle name as William) was born on 9 August 1915 in Townsville, Queensland, the son of Mark Baker. Baker made twenty-nine first-class appearances between 1936 and 1941, all for Queensland and the majority in the Sheffield Shield.

Baker made his debut for Queensland against the MCC (MCC in Australia and New Zealand) between 27 November and 1 December 1936 at Brisbane Cricket Ground. The MCC won the toss and decided to bat. They made 215 all out, Baker catching Charles Barnett off the bowling of Patrick Dixon for 20 and helping in the running out of Laurence Fishlock for six. In reply Queensland made 243, Baker making five before being caught and bowled by the famous Yorkshire and England test player Hedley Verity (killed 31 July 1943). In their second innings the MCC made 528, Arthur Fagg making 112 and Charles Barnett 259. By way of revenge for taking his wicket in the first innings Baker caught Verity off the bowling of Gordon Amos for eight. In their second innings Queensland made 227, Baker making their top score of 63 before being lbw off the bowling Kenneth Farnes. The match was eventually drawn.

Baker made his debut in the Sheffield Shield against Victoria between 18 and 21 December 1936 at Melbourne Cricket Ground. Victoria won the toss and decided to field. It was a good decision as they skittled Queensland out for 49, Baker being out lbw off the bowling of Leslie Fleetwood-Smith for a duck (Fleetwood-Smith took seven wickets during the innings). Victoria made 309 in return, Leonard Darling the Australian test cricketer making 111. In their second innings Queensland didn't do much better, making 175. Baker was out once again lbw off the bowling of William Pearson for 18. This time Fleetwood-Smith took eight wickets during the innings. Victoria won by an innings and 85 runs.

Barker went on to play against South Australia, New South Wales and Victoria several times. He made his final first-class game against New South Wales between 28 November and 1 December 1941 at the Brisbane Cricket Ground. Queensland won the toss and decided to bat making 334, Baker making 40 before being lbw off the bowling of William O'Reilly. In reply New South Wales made 310, Baker catching Stan McCabe off the bowling of Albert McGinn for eight. In their second innings Queensland made 249, Baker being bowled by Raymond Lindwall for four. In their second innings New South Wales made 254, Baker bowling George Powell lbw for zero. Queensland took the match by 19 runs.

During his twenty-nine appearances Baker made 1,531 runs including one century and eleven fifties with a high score of 157 against New South Wales. He also bowled 1,021 balls for 558 runs taking 13 wickets, with his best figures being three for 17. He also made 19 catches.

He married Mavis Jean of New Farm before being commissioned into the Australian Army Ordnance Corps attached to the Australian 4 Advanced Ordnance Depot on the 13 February 1943, rising to the rank of lieutenant. He died from illness on 15 December 1943 while serving in Papua New Guinea. He is buried in Port Moresby (Bomana) War Cemetery, grave reference B6. D. 1.

Batting and fielding averages

	Mat	Inns	NO	Runs	HS	Ave	100	50	Ct	St
First-class	29	52	3	1531	157	31.24	1	11	19	0

Bowling averages

	Mat	Runs	Wkts	BBI	Ave	5w	10
First-class	29	558	13	3/17	42.92	0	0

Baker sitting far right.

Lieutenant Colonel Kenneth Wilkinson
Cambridge University
One first-class appearance
East Yorkshire Regiment
Commanding 1st Battalion Royal Fusiliers (City of London Regiment)
Died 15 December 1943, aged 36
Right arm fast medium

Died commanding the regiment he loved

Kenneth Wilkinson was born on 11 January 1908 in Newbold, Derbyshire, the son of Walter John and Mary Ethel Wilkinson.

He made one first-class appearance, for Cambridge University against the Army on 1 June 1927 at F.P. Fenner's. The Army won the toss and decided to bat making 262. Wilkinson bowled 13 overs taking no wickets for 85. The England test Cricketer Maurice James Carrick Allom took nine wickets for 55 of 29 overs. In reply Cambridge made 301 for seven declared. Wilkinson failed to bat as a result. Norman Gordon Wykes made 145 not out, batting throughout the innings. Philip Havelock Davies took five wickets for 70. In their second innings the Army made 150. Allom took a further five wickets for 47 off 16 overs. In their second innings Cambridge made 112 for two. Wilkinson failed to bat for a second time. Cambridge won by eight wickets.

Originally serving with the East Yorkshire Regiment he was transferred to command the 1st Battalion Royal Fusiliers (City of London Regiment). He was killed while serving with them on 15 December 1943 at Caldari, near Naples. He is buried in the Sangro River War Cemetery, grave reference XI. E. 29.

He left a widow, Rosemary Farrer, of Hollingbourne, Kent.

Batting and fielding averages

	Mat	Inns	NO	Runs	HS	Ave	BF	SR	100	50	4s	6s	Ct	St
First-class	1	-	-	-	-	-	-	-	-	-	-	-	0	0

Bowling averages

	Mat	Balls	Runs	Wkts	BBI	BBM	Ave	Econ	SR	4w	5w	10
First-class	1	120	99	0	-	-	-	4.95	-	0	0	0

48118 Corporal George Logan Talbot
Canterbury
One first-class match
20th New Zealand Armoured Corps
Died 15 December 1943, aged 36
Right-handed bat/Right arm medium

Died in his tank leading the attack

George Talbot was born on 2 April 1907 in Christchurch. He was the son of Horace Norman and Elizabeth Stevenson Talbot.

His talent for cricket was quickly recognized and he played for a number of local sides. He made one first-class appearance for Canterbury in the Plunket Shield. The match took place against Otago between 28 February and 1 March 1930 at Lancaster Park, Christchurch. Otago won the toss and decided to bat making 172. Talbot caught the Otago opener Walter Wilson Strang off the bowling of his cousin Ronald Talbot (who made 51 first-class appearances) for 32. He then bowled Alexander Gale, caught Neil Dorreen for three, followed by Thomas Lemin clean bowled for one. In reply Canterbury made 523 declared, with John Powell making 164 and Dorreen 105 not out. Otago made 124 in their second innings, Talbot bowling John Dunning, caught James Burrows for four. Canterbury won by an innings and 227 runs.

During the war Talbot served as a corporal with the 20th New Zealand Armoured Corps. He was killed on 15 December 1943 in the battle for Orsogna. Orsogna was strategically important to the allied advance through Italy and had to be taken. However the Germans had turned it into a stronghold, making the task difficult. Several attempts to take the town were repulsed with heavy casualties. It was during one of these attacks that Talbot's tank was destroyed by a well-positioned German 88-millimetre gun. He is buried in the Sangro River War Cemetery, grave reference IX. D. 14.

Batting and fielding averages

	Mat	Inns	NO	Runs	HS	Ave	BF	SR	100	50	4s	6s	Ct	St
First-class	1	-	-	-	-	-	-	-	-	-	-	-	1	0

Bowling averages

	Mat	Runs	Wkts	BBI	Ave	5w	10
First-class	1	28	3	2/24	9.33	0	0

1944

Flight Lieutenant William Jack Pershke
Oxford University
Eight first-class matches
RAF Volunteer Reserve 105 OTU
Died 21 January 1944, aged 25
Right-handed bat/Right arm fast medium

The most natural of Cricketers

William Pershke was born on 8 August 1918 in Richmond-upon-Thames. He was educated at Uppingham where his talent for cricket was recognized and he was soon playing in the XI. He made appearances against Haileybury, Repton, Shrewsbury, Rugby, and Oundle. He headed the Uppingham averages with 36.38 and took and impressive 31 wickets. At Brasenose College he continued with his cricket, making eight first-class appearances for Oxford University during the 1938 season.

He made his debut against Glamorgan on 25-27 May 1938 at the University Parks. Glamorgan won the toss and decided to bat making 159. Pershke bowled 22 overs for 46 runs and took an impressive six wickets: David Emrys Davies caught William Murray-Wood for four, Thomas Brierley caught Richard Luyt for 16, William Morgan caught David Macindoe for 15, William Jones caught Luyt for a duck, David Davies bowled for six, and finally the England test cricketer John Clay caught by Luyt for 14. In reply Oxford made 188, Pershke making two before being stumped by Brierley off the bowling of Davies. In their second innings Glamorgan made 214, Pershke bowling 21 overs for 60 and taking the wickets of the two Glamorgan openers, Arnold Herbert Dyson for 22 and Davies for one, both caught by Macindoe. Oxford made 15 for no wicket in their second innings. The match was eventually drawn. A good start for the young fast bowler.

In his next match, against Middlesex, he took a further five wickets. Against the Free Foresters, two wickets. Against the MCC he failed to take a wicket. Against Sussex two more. Against the Army he took six wickets in an innings. Against Surrey, two.

He made his final first-class match for Oxford against the old rivals Cambridge between 2 and 5 July 1938 at Lord's. Oxford won the toss and elected to bat making 317, Pershke making one not out. In reply Cambridge made 425. Pershke bowled 24 overs for 54 taking three wickets, John Thompson bowled for 79, John Langley caught Douglas Young for 15, and Peter Studd caught Peter Whitehouse (died 19 November 1943) for zero. Oxford made 126 in their second innings. The match was eventually drawn.

During his first-class career Pershke made 57 runs, his highest score being 17. He bowled 1,494 balls for 752 runs and took 28 wickets, his best figures being six for 46. He took five catches. He also turned out for the Young Amateurs against the Young Professionals (losing by nine wickets); he played against Rajputana during their tour of England in 1938 taking five wickets (match drawn); for the Harlequins against Harrow in 1939 (match drawn); and for Sussex against the RAF in 1940 taking six wickets for 25 in the one day match – Sussex won by 15 runs, largely thanks to Pershke who was bowling against the likes of the England test player Leslie Ames whom he bowled for 19 (caught Stobart).

During the war Pershke served with the RAF Volunteer Reserve becoming a pilot and flying with No. 105 Operational Training Unit. The unit was formed to retain crews for Transport Command. It mostly used Wellingtons with reduced crews. He was killed while flying Wellington IC DV695 on 21 January 1944 on a navigational exercise. His body wasn't recovered and he is commemorated on the Runnymede Memorial, panel 203.

Batting and fielding averages

	Mat	Inns	NO	Runs	HS	Ave	100	50	Ct	St
First-class	8	10	5	57	17*	11.40	0	0	5	0

Bowling averages

	Mat	Balls	Runs	Wkts	BBI	Ave	Econ	SR	5w	10
First-class	8	1494	752	28	6/46	26.85	3.02	53.3	3	0

Surgeon Lieutenant Alastair Simpson Bell McNeil
Scotland
One first-class match
Royal Naval Volunteer Reserve
Died 26 January 1944, aged 28
Slow left arm orthodox

Last seen ignoring his own safety in an attempt
to save the lives of other people

Alastair McNeil was born on 28 June 1915 in Edinburgh. He was the son of David Bell and Isabella McNeil of 7 Marchmont Street. Educated at George Watson's College he captained both the Rugby XV and Cricket XI in 1933. In his final year at school he played in the Public Schools Rugby International. Joining the Watsonian XV, he became a prominent forward and received his Scottish cap during the home internationals on 23 February 1935 in the game against Ireland in Dublin, taking the honours 12-5.

Deciding on a career in medicine he attended the University of Edinburgh, qualifying MB ChB (Bachelor of Medicine, Bachelor of Surgery) in 1938. He was appointed a house surgeon at Worthing Hospital and later medical officer at the Royal National Hospital, Ventnor.

McNeil made one first-class appearance, playing for Scotland against Yorkshire. The match was played on 11-12 August 1937 at St George's Road, Harrogate. Yorkshire won the toss and decided to bat. Yorkshire made 291 all out. In reply Scotland made 104, McNeil making five before being caught by the test cricketer Thomas Smailes off the bowling of Herbert Hargreaves. Forced to follow on, Scotland made 143, McNeil being run out for 23. Yorkshire won by an innings and 44 runs. McNeil made two further appearances for Scotland both against Sir J. Cahn's XI neither being first-class matches. Both matches were drawn. He also turned out for the East of Scotland against the West of Scotland. West of Scotland won by seven wickets.

McNeil joined the RNVR in April 1940 becoming a surgeon lieutenant. He took part in landings at Madagascar, in North Africa and Sicily and at Salerno and Anzio. He was killed on 26 January 1944 during the Anzio landings while serving on board the HM LST-422 Class Tank Landing Ship. The ship left Naples as part of a convoy of thirteen other LSTs carrying troops and supplies to Anzio, mainly trucks, Jeeps, M3 halftracks, ammunition and gasoline. While waiting in an unloading queue at Anzio docks a force 8 gale blew up creating twenty-foot waves. Lieutenant Commander Broadhurst later wrote about the sinking of the 422:

At about 5.20 hours, the gale blew the L.S.T.-422 onto a German laid underwater mine, the explosion of which blew a 50ft hole in her bottom and starboard side and caused the fuel oil supply to ignite. This in turn ignited the gasoline tanks of the vehicles on the tank deck. With the whole upper deck a sheet of flame the order was given to 'abandon ship'.

It was noted in the ship's log that the weather was deteriorating all the time the ships were in convoy. The wind veered from southerly to westerly Force 8 (gale). If the ships were allowed to fall just one point from the wind they would not steer. LST 11 and 65 (in a different convoy) collided and several other incidents were narrowly averted.

Casualties of the LST-422 were 454 US soldiers and 29 British sailors killed. The minesweepers USS *Pilot* and USS *Strive*, together with other small craft, rescued between 150 and 171. At 2.30 pm the LST-422 broke in two and went under.

His commander late wrote of McNeil that he was last seen 'ignoring his own safety in an attempt to save the lives of other people'.

His body was never recovered and he is commemorated on the Chatham Naval Memorial, panel 79.3.

Batting and fielding averages

	Mat	Inns	NO	Runs	HS	Ave	100	50	Ct	St
First-class	1	2	0	28	23	14.00	0	0	0	0

Bowling averages

	Mat	Balls	Runs	Wkts	BBI	BBM	Ave	Econ	SR	4w	5w	10
First-class	1	-	-	-	-	-	-	-	-	-	-	-

D A Thom   W G S Johnston   W A Burnet   G S Cottington   A S B M'Neil   K W Marshall
R M Grieve   W R Logan   J Beattie   R W Shaw (Captain)   J A Waters   R C S Dick   L B Lambie
K C Fyfe   H Lind

441603 Signalman David Wyatt Monaghan
South Island Army
One first-class match
New Zealand Corps of Signals
Died 27 January 1944, aged 21

A New Zealander through and through

David Monaghan was born in 1923 in New Zealand, the third son of five children born to Archdeacon Harold Monaghan of Timaru and Rangitikei, who had also been a first-class cricketer playing for Wellington and Canterbury, and his wife Jessie Marion (née Butler).

Monaghan made one first-class appearance for the South Island Army against the North Island Army, between 19 and 22 February 1943 at the Basin Reserve, Wellington. South Island Army won the toss and decided to bat making 140, Monaghan making ten before being caught by Matthew O'Brian off the bowling of John Lamason. In reply the North Island Army made 100. In their second innings South Island Army made 191, Monaghan making nine before being caught by William Norris off the bowling of Thomas Pritchard. In reply North Island Army made 190. South Island Army took the match by 31 runs.

During the war he served with the New Zealand Corps of Signals. He was killed on 27 January 1944 in Caserta, Italy. He is buried in the Caserta War Cemetery, VI, C, 14.

Batting and fielding averages

	Mat	Inns	NO	Runs	HS	Ave	100	50	Ct	St
First-class	1	2	0	19	10	9.50	0	0	0	0

Bowling averages

	Mat	Balls	Runs	Wkts	BBI	BBM	Ave	Econ	SR	4w	5w	10
First-class	1	-	-	-	-	-	-	-	-	-	-	-

Captain Joseph Maurice Francis Connaughton
Middlesex, Oxford University
Two first-class matches
Royal Artillery
attached 301 Field Regiment East African Artillery
Died 12 February 1944, aged 25
Right-handed bat/Leg break

Died in one of the greatest sea disasters of the Second World War

Joseph Connaughton was born on 15 August 1918 in Paddington, London. He was the son of Squadron Leader Patrick Francis and Sarah Connaughton of Oxford. He was educated at the Oratory School, Woodcote, near Reading, where he played in the first XI against Beaumont College (on three occasions). He went up to Brasenose College Oxford and made two first-class appearances, both university matches, both in 1939.

He made his debut for Middlesex against Oxford University between 6 and 9 May 1939 at the University Parks. Oxford won the toss and decided to bat. They made 195. Connaughton took three wickets, Christopher Lubbock caught Ian Peebles (English test cricketer) for seven, Stewart Pether caught Jack Robertson (English test cricketer) for zero, and David Hayward caught Alexander Thompson for three. Middlesex made 334 in their first innings, Connaughton scoring 16 not out. In their second innings Oxford University made 223. Middlesex made 85 in their second innings, winning the match by seven wickets (Connaughton didn't bat).

Connaughton made his second and final first-class appearance for Oxford University against Minor Counties, playing between 7 and 9 June 1939 at University Parks. Oxford won the toss and decided to bat making 281, Connaughton making six before being bowled by Walter Surridge (who took five wickets in the innings). In reply Minor Counties made 236. Connaughton bowled eight overs for 28 and took no wickets, however he did catch Alan Parnaby off the bowling of David Macindoe for 29. In their second innings Oxford made 256, Connaughton making zero before being bowled by Walter Surridge. In their second innings Minor Counties made 304, Parnaby making 101. Connaughton bowled six overs for 18 and took no wickets. Minor Counties took the match by four wickets.

During the war Connaughton served with the Royal Artillery and was attached to the 301 Field Regiment East African Artillery, rising to the rank of captain. On 5 February 1944, the SS *Khedive Ismail* left Mombasa heading for Colombo as part of convoy KR8. She had on board 1,324 passengers. Among their number there were 996 members of the East African Artillery's 301st Field Regiment, 271 Royal Navy personnel, 19 WRNS, 53 nursing sisters, their matron, and nine members of the First Aid Nursing Yeomanry. At approximately 2.30 pm on Saturday, 12 February 1944, the ship was attacked by the Japanese submarine *I-27* who fired four torpedoes at her, two of which struck. The *Khedive Ismail* was so badly damaged that she sank in three minutes, giving few people time to get off the ship. Two P-class destroyers attacked the submarine steaming through many of the survivors (very much like the book *The Cruel Sea* by Nicholas Monsarrat). The destroyers then dropped depth charges, the explosions from which killed more survivors. Finally, after a battle which lasted over two and a half hours, the *I-27* was sunk with all hands. Of the 1,511 people aboard *Khedive Ismail*, 208 men and 6 women survived. Captain Connaughton was not one of them.

The sinking of the *Khedive Ismail* was the third largest loss of life from Allied shipping in the Second World War and the largest loss of servicewomen in the history of the Commonwealth Nations. It wasn't until forty years later that the Admiralty papers were finally released. Serious issues over the sinking of the *Khedive Ismail* had been raised. The failure to zigzag, the lack of air cover, and the decision of the two escorting destroyers to attack the *I-27* through the survivors.

Joseph Connaughton's body was never recovered and he is commemorated on the East African Memorial, column 1.

The writer, aviator and explorer, Kenneth Cecil Gandar-Dower also went down with the ship.

Batting and fielding averages

	Mat	Inns	NO	Runs	HS	Ave	100	50	Ct	St
First-class	2	3	1	22	16*	11.00	0	0	1	0

Bowling averages

	Mat	Balls	Runs	Wkts	BBI	Ave	Econ	SR	5w	10
First-class	2	243	85	3	3/19	28.33	2.09	81.0	0	0

Private Denys March Witherington
Cambridge University
Four first-class matches
1st Battalion, The Loyal North Lancashire Regiment
Died 16 February 1944, aged 24
Right-handed bat/Wicketkeeper

'And all the brothers were valiant'

Denys Witherington was born on 25 July 1921 at Hendon, Sunderland, one of three sons born to Arthur Simpson and Catherine Witherington. Attending the Leys school in 1933 at the age of 13 he went into West House. A good all-round sportsman he was in their first XI from 1935 to 1938, playing against Felsted several times and the Eastern Canadian Schools, captaining the side for several terms.

He represented The Rest against Lord's School at Lord's on 1-2 August 1938. He made 31 in his only innings and failed to take a wicket. The match was drawn.

On leaving school he went up to Cambridge where in 1939 he narrowly missed his blue. During the Freshman's match he scored 20 and 38, and while keeping wicket stumped three and caught two, playing an important part in his side's victory by 161 runs.

While at the university he made four first-class appearances. He made his debut for Cambridge University against Nottinghamshire at F.P. Fenner's Ground between 10 and 12 May 1939. Cambridge won the toss and decided to bat. Cambridge made 239, Witherington making 18 before being caught and bowled by the England test cricketer Bill Voce. In reply Nottinghamshire made 418, Voce making 104. During the Nottinghamshire innings Witherington caught Charles Harris off the bowling of Patrick Dickinson for 67 and the England test player Joseph Hardstaff off the bowling of Derek Gillespie for nine. In their second innings Cambridge made 221 with Witherington making a respectable 27 before being bowled by George Gunn. Nottingham only had to knock up 46 to win the match by ten wickets.

Witherington's next match was against Yorkshire two weeks later on 25-26 May again at F.P. Fenner's. Yorkshire won by nine wickets, Witherington making 24 runs in the first innings (he failed to bat in the second) and taking no wickets. Len Hutton made 102 and Norman Yardley 140.

Cambridge next played against Leicestershire at F.P. Fenner's between 3 and 6 June 1939. Leicestershire made 410 in their first innings with Norman Foster Armstrong making 131 and Francis Prentice 163 not out. Witherington stumped Norman Armstrong off the bowling of John Mann for 131 before catching William Henry Flamson off the bowling of Patrick Dickinson for a duck. In their first innings Cambridge made 531 with Francis Mann making 128, John Thompson 130 and Arthur Brodhurst 111. Witherington made 17. In their second innings Leicestershire made 187, Witherington catching Francis Prentice off the bowling of Jack Webster for 65. The match was eventually drawn.

Witherington made his final first-class appearance against the Army at F.P. Fenner's between 7 and 9 June 1939. Cambridge won the toss and decided to bat making 411, Witherington making 51 not out, his highest first-class score. In reply the Army made 537,

George Grimston making 104 and Charles Packe 145 (Packe was killed in Normandy in 1944). Witherington also caught John William Steel off the bowling of Arthur Brodhurst for six. In their second innings Cambridge made 149, Witherington failing to bat. The match was drawn.

During his short first-class career Witherington played seven innings making 147 runs with a high score of 51, his average being 29.4. He made five catches and one stumping.

He also played in the Durham Senior League, doing well both with the bat and behind the wicket as keeper. In his last match for Sunderland against Whitburn he knocked up an impressive 159 not out.

During the war Witherington served as a private with the Loyal North Lancashire regiment. Given his public school and Cambridge background this was a little unusual. After basic training he was sent first to North Africa and then Sicily. He was killed in action during the Battle of Anzio on 16 February 1944. He is buried in the Anzio War Cemetery, grave number II. S. 4.

His brother John had been killed on 16 September 1941while serving as a sergeant pilot with 56 Squadron RAF. While guiding his seriously damaged Wellington bomber back from a mission over Germany he ordered his crew to bail out, remaining at the controls to give them the best chance of getting out safely. His self-sacrifice allowed all but one of his crew to escape unscathed before the Wellington crashed. He was 20 years old.

Denys's obituary appeared later in the Leys school magazine:

DENYS MARCH WITHERINGTON
West House,
1933-1938,
Killed in action, February, 1944

Most Leysians of his generation will remember Denys Witherington primarily as a cricketer. He had a natural flair for all games, but it was at cricket that he really excelled. His promise was tremendous; he looked a great batsman in embryo. When he was keeping wicket, his was the art which conceals art; a graceful, unspectacular efficiency. His talents took him to the verge of the Cambridge side in his first year and many people believed that, had he set any store by success, there were few triumphs beyond his reach.

But no schoolboy athlete was ever freer than Denys from the loss of proportion which success at games often brings. To him a game was a game, and its purpose was enjoyment. His modesty was unaffected; he never had to pose because he was completely unspoilt. No-one has ever been more generally and thoroughly liked, in School and House, than he, but few people knew of the serious and sensitive nature which he kept well out of sight in an apparently happy-go-lucky and casual personality. He did not speak easily or to many people of his genuine love of beauty in nature and literature.

Army life can never have been very congenial to him, but he accepted his lot without grumbling. After prolonged and varied training in this country, he saw service in Africa and in Sicily, and he was killed in action after a short period on the Italian front. His friends will feel, as they read this, that something rare and vital has been taken out of life, and they will know the inadequacy of words. It is just over two years since John Witherington was killed in operations in the R.A.F. We offer our deep sympathy to his family.

He is buried at Sunderland (Ryhope Road) Cemetery, grave number 16.

Batting and fielding averages

	Mat	Inns	NO	Runs	HS	Ave	100	50	Ct	St
First-class	4	7	2	147	52*	29.40	0	1	5	1

Bowling averages

	Mat	Balls	Runs	Wkts	BBI	BBM	Ave	Econ	SR	4w	5w	10
First-class	4	-	-	-	-	-	-	-	-	-	-	-

Captain David Arthur Sydney Day
Europeans (India)
One first-class match
1st Battalion Wiltshire Regiment
Died 22 February 1944, aged 27

Refused to fall back, made his final stand

David Day was born in 1916 in Greenwich. He was the son of Arthur Perceval and Ada Christine Day of Reigate. He was educated at Tonbridge where he played in the XI against Lancing, Sherborne, Dulwich and Clifton School.

Day made one first-class appearance for the Europeans against India in a Madras Presidency Match played 12-14 January 1941 at the Madras Cricket Club Ground. India won the toss and decided to bat making 209 in their first innings. The Europeans made 164 with Day making three before being stumped by M.O. Srinivasan off the bowling of C.R. Rangachari. In their second innings India made 168, Day running out B.S.R. Bhadradri for 54. In their second innings the Europeans made 116, Day being bowled for a duck again by Rangachari. The Indians won by 97 runs.

Day also made three second XI matches for Kent, against Surrey, Wiltshire and Norfolk in June-August 1935. During this time he also found time to meet and marry his wife Valerie.

Day was commissioned into the 1st Battalion Wiltshire Regiment during the Second World War rising to the rank of captain. At the beginning of the war his battalion was stationed in India on policing duties, but by 1943, during the reorganization of the Burma front, it became responsible for guarding lines of communication and support for the Arakan offensive, the first tentative Allied offensive into Burma following the Japanese conquest of the country in 1942. Due to a lack of readiness the offensive was repulsed. In October 1943, together with the 26th Indian Division, the 1st Wiltshires took part in the Battle of the Admin Box. The battle was fought on the southern front during the Burma campaign between 5 and 23 February 1944. It was during this action that on 22 February Captain Day was killed.

He is buried in Taukkyan War Cemetery, grave reference 3. G. 11.

Batting and fielding averages

	Mat	Inns	NO	Runs	HS	Ave	100	50	4s	6s	Ct	St
First-class	1	2	0	3	3	1.50	0	0	0	0	0	0

Bowling averages

	Mat	Runs	Wkts	BBI	BBM	Ave	SR	4w	5w	10
First-class	1	4	0	-	-	-	-	0	0	0

1944

First Eleven.
·1933·

W. L. Popple. C. C. La Fontaine. D. C. B. Ball. A. C. Sutcliffe. T. A. La Fontaine. E. C. Cobb.
D. A. S. Day. R. F. Harding. R. W. W. Morrison. W. A. Brooks. A. H. Leach.

245

Surgeon Lieutenant Foster (Peter) Moverley McRae
Somerset
Twenty-five first-class matches
HMS *Mahratta* Royal Naval Volunteer Reserve
Died 25 February 1944, aged 28
Right-handed bat

'There's not enough room for us all'

Foster (better known as Peter) Moverley McRae was born on 12 February 1916 in Buenos Aires. He was the son of Sydney Spencer Redgrave and Sophie Moverley McRae, although it appears that at some point he was adopted by the Reverend Percy and Mrs P. Shattock of St Mary's Cottage, Kingston, Taunton, Somerset. He was educated at Christ's Hospital School and, deciding on a career in medicine, trained at St Mary's Hospital qualifying MRCS LRCP in 1941.

He made twenty-five first-class appearances between 1926 and 1939 all for Somerset. McRae made his debut against Worcestershire in the county championship between 22 and 25 August 1936 at Chester Road, Kidderminster. Somerset won the toss and decided to bat. Somerset made 401, the England test cricketer Norman Mitchell-Innes making 182. McRae made four before being lbw by another England test cricketer, Richard Howorth. In reply Worcestershire made 315. In their second innings Somerset were all out for 110, McRae making eight before being bowled by the England test cricketer Reginald Perks. Worcester only made 100 in their second innings, Somerset winning by 97 runs. McRae went on to play many matches against English counties, as well as the West Indies.

McRae made his final first-class appearance again in the county championship against Northamptonshire on 30 August 1939 at the County Ground, Taunton. Northamptonshire won the toss and decided to bat. They made 138 all out. In reply Somerset made 380, McRae making 50 before being lbw to John Timms. In their second innings Northamptonshire only managed 150, Somerset winning by an innings and 92 runs.

During his first-class career he played 45 innings and made 972 runs, including one century and four fifties, his highest score being 107 against Hampshire (1 July 1939). He also made nine catches. As well as making first-class appearances he also played for Christ's Hospital, United Hospitals, Lord's XI, Sir P.F. Warner's XI and his own side F.M. McRae's XI.

He was also a fine rugby player, trying out for England. However persistent injuries curtailed what might have been an international career.

During the war he served as a surgeon lieutenant with the RNVR. He was killed while serving on the M-class destroyer HMS *Mahratta* in the Barentz Sea on 25 February 1944 when it was torpedoed by the German U-Boat *U-990*. At around 20.55, while escorting the stern sector of the convoy JW 57 280 miles from the North Cape, it was hit by a torpedo fired from U-990. The damage was catastrophic. The destroyer exploded and sank within a few minutes. Despite valiant rescue attempts by HMS *Impulsive* and HMS *Wanderer*, only sixteen survivors were recovered. Life expectancy in those freezing waters must have been measured in minutes. The commander, 10 officers and 209 ratings lost their lives. In *1941–*

1945 The Arctic Lookout Noel Simon wrote about Dr Peter McRae's actions after the ship had gone down:

I talked to a group of *Mahratta* ratings – none of the officers had survived – who told me of the heroism of their doctor. Having managed to climb onto one of the few Carley floats to have come through the sinking, he set about hauling the others aboard. The float soon became overcrowded.

Remarking almost casually, 'There's not enough room for us all,' the doctor slipped over the side into the sea and was never seen again.

The straightforward manner in which the survivors recounted this event, and the admiration and affection with which they spoke of their doctor – whose name (oddly enough) none of them knew – made a deep impression upon me.

Not until months later, and then quite by chance, did I discover that *Mahratta's* doctor was none other than Peter McRae, a contemporary of mine at school. As a boy he had been one of the most delightful and gifted of people. A good all-rounder, successful in all he undertook, yet completely unassuming. I remember him as an exceptionally fine rugger player – certainly the most outstanding fly-half in the school during my time there. Several years after the war, a proposal was made that his self-sacrifice should be recognised by a suitable award but, sadly, the Admiralty did not concur.

McRae is commemorated on the Portsmouth Naval Memorial, panel 93, column 1. He is also commemorated on the Kingston St Mary War Memorial in Somerset.

U-990 didn't survive the war. It was sunk on 25 May 1944 in the Norwegian Sea after being depth-charged by an RAF Liberator of 59 Squadron. Twenty of her crew were killed and thirty-three survived.

Batting and fielding averages

	Mat	Inns	NO	Runs	HS	Ave	100	50	Ct	St
First-class	25	45	5	972	107	24.30	1	4	9	0

Bowling averages

	Mat	Balls	Runs	Wkts	BBI	BBM	Ave	Econ	SR	4w	5w	10
First-class	25	-	-	-	-	-	-	-	-	-	-	-

Flying Officer Alan Louden Pearsall
Tasmania
Seven first-class matches
16 Squadron Royal Australian Air Force
Died 8 March 1944, aged 28
Right-handed bat/Right arm medium

A finer sportsman you will never discover

Alan Pearsall was born on 24 May 1915 in Hobart, Tasmania. He was the son of Benjamin James and Olive Pearsall. After leaving school Pearsall worked as a farmer, a clerk and a salesman in Hobart. A talented all-round sportsman he played his club cricket for Kingborough, leading them to the premiership and scoring a century in the final. The local paper *The Mercury* said of him that Pearsall was 'able to adapt himself to any sort of game, [and] on many occasions he turned what looked like certain defeat into victory.'

Pearsall made seven first-class appearances all for Tasmania between 1934 and 1938. He made his debut against Australia between 10 and 13 March 1934 at the North Tasmania Cricket Association Ground, Launceston. Tasmania won the toss and decided to bat. Bowling eight balls per over, Tasmania made 345 all out. Pearsall made a single run before being stumped by William Oldfield off the bowling of Leslie Fleetwood-Smith, who took five wickets during the innings. Australia made 537 with William Woodfull making 126 and Stan McCabe 119. Pearsall bowled 12 overs for 82 runs taking one wicket, that of the Australian opener William Brown for 96. In the second innings Tasmania made 214, Pearsall only making a single run before being stumped by Benjamin Barnett off the bowling of Clarence Grimmett. The match was eventually drawn.

Pearsall went on to play against Victoria five times and South Australia. He made his final first-class appearance against Victoria between on 30-31 December 1938 at the Tasmanian Cricket Association Ground, Hobart. Tasmania won the toss and decided to bat. They made 315, Pearsall making 42 before being bowled by Robert Dempster. In reply Victoria made 491, Hector Herbert Oakley 162 and Percy James Beames 169. Pearsall bowled 14 overs for 94, taking two wickets, Harcourt Dowsley caught Julian Murfett for 64, and the Australian test cricketer Keith Miller for three. In their second innings Tasmania made 196, Pearsall making 27 before being run out. Victoria made 23 in their second innings taking the game by ten wickets.

Pearsall also made seven (not first-class) appearances for the South against the North. During his first-class career he made 300 runs with a high score of 56 against Victoria. He bowled 472 balls for 345 runs, and took six wickets, his best figures being two for 64. He also made two catches.

Pearsall was also a fine footballer, playing full back for his local team, Leroy. He also made appearances for South Melbourne Football Club in the Victorian Football League.

On 15 March 1941 Alan Pearsall married his girlfriend Dorothy. The following January Dorothy gave birth to their daughter Kaye.

In July 1941 Pearsall joined the Australian Air Force and began pilot training. In August 1942 he was posted overseas as part of the Empire Air Training Scheme, one of 16,000 Australians who trained as aircrew.

While in Britain he represented Australia in the RAAF cricket team during the 1943 season. His highest batting score was 97 and his best bowling figures were 7/13 including a hat-trick.

In July 1943 Pearsall joined 16 Squadron RAF, a high-altitude photo-reconnaissance squadron that flew Spitfires and P-51 Mustangs. On 2 June 1943 the squadron had become part of the Strategic Reconnaissance Wing of the 2nd Tactical Air Force as a high-altitude photo-reconnaissance unit with Spitfire PR Mk XIs. In the build-up to D-Day, No. 16 supplied photographs instrumental to the planning of the landings. On 8 March 1944 Pearsall was flying a mission out of his RAF base at Hartford Bridge, Hampshire, to photograph various areas of north-east Calais in Spitfire Mk XI, PA863. On his return back to base flying over the English Channel, he radioed that he was experiencing engine trouble. It has never been clear whether or not this was a result of enemy action. Flying at around 2,000 feet his engine finally failed and he was instructed to bail out. Although a rescue mission was launched at once, strong gales and rough seas made their mission difficult and they failed to find him. Forty-eight hours later the search was called off. He was listed as missing and later as killed.

Pearsall's body was never recovered and his name is commemorated on the Air Forces Memorial at Runnymede, panel 257.

Lieutenant Tom Pearsall, Alan's brother, served with the 2/29th Battalion AIF and was taken prisoner by the Japanese while fighting in Malaya and Singapore in 1942, one of 22,000 Australians who became a prisoner of the Japanese in 1942. Unlike Alan he survived the war, returning home to Tasmania in 1945.

Batting and fielding averages

	Mat	Inns	NO	Runs	HS	Ave	100	50	Ct	St
First-class	7	13	0	300	56	23.07	0	1	2	0

Bowling averages

	Mat	Runs	Wkts	BBI	Ave	5w	10
First-class	7	345	6	2/64	57.50	0	0

Squadron Leader (pilot) Edward (Jimmy) Henry Moss DFC
Oxford University/H.D.G. Leveson-Gower's XI
Five first-class appearances
61 Squadron RAF Volunteer Reserve
Died 31 March 1944, aged 32
Right-handed bat

his whole love of humanity, and humble thankfulness to God

Edward Henry Moss (better known as Jimmy) was born on 25 May 1911 in Godden Green, Seal, Kent. He was the son of William Henry and Rose Winifred Moss of Sevenoaks. He was educated at Hawtreys and Malvern College, playing in the cricket XI for four years (captain in his last two) against Cheltenham, Repton, Shrewsbury, Wolverhampton and the Free Foresters. He was also in the rackets pair. On leaving Malvern he went up to Trinity Oxford.

He made four first-class appearances for Oxford University between 31 May 1933 and 26 May 1934 and one appearance for H.D.G. Leveson-Gower's XI in 1934.

He made his debut for Oxford in a university match on 31 May 1933 against Leicestershire at the University Parks. Oxford won the toss and elected to bat making 297. Moss made 15 before being lbw to Haydon Smith. Smith took five wickets for 84 off 31 overs. David Townsend made 118, Gerald Chalk (killed in action 17 February 1943) made 104. In reply Leicestershire made 306. Norman Armstrong made 130. In their second innings Oxford made 204. Moss made zero before being clean bowled by Alan Wilfred Shipman. In their second innings Leicestershire made 160. The match was eventually drawn.

His next appearance came against Worcestershire on 5 May 1934 at the University Parks. He made 50 and 30, the match was drawn.

This was followed by a match against the mighty Yorkshire on 9 May 1934 again at the University Parks. Moss made nine and 28. He also caught the England player Morris Leyland off the bowling of John Dyson for 100. The match was drawn.

His final match for Oxford came against the Free Foresters on 26 May 1934 at the University Parks. Moss scored one and 37; the match was drawn.

He made his final first-class appearance against Oxford playing for H.D.G. Leveson-Gower's XI. The match took place on 4 July 1934 at Park Lane, Reigate. Oxford won the toss and decided to bat making 399. Frederick 'Derrick' de Saram made 208. Arthur Baxter took five wickets for 105 off 29 overs. Moss managed to hang on to a catch from John Wemyss Seamer off the bowling of Baxter for ten. In reply Leveson-Gower's XI made 341. Moss, opening, made 12 before being lbw to Kenneth Leslie Tattersall Jackson. In their second innings Oxford made 215. Baxter once again took five wickets, this time for 77 off 20 overs. In their second innings Leveson-Gower's made 185. Opening for them, Moss made 24 before being caught by David Townsend off the bowling of John Dyson. Alexander Singleton took six wickets for 44 off 19 overs. Oxford won by 88 runs. He also played golf for the university for four years and was captain in his last two years.

On leaving Oxford with a degree in history, Moss became a master at Radley College in 1936. He was there until the war broke out in 1939 when he took a commission into the Wiltshire Regiment. He was promoted to captain in 1940 and was evacuated from the beeches at Dunkirk.

He transferred to the RAF in 1941 training as a pilot. He became an instructor before becoming operational with 61 Squadron flying Lancasters. Detailed to attack Nuremburg he was shot down and killed near Rimbach north west of Fulda during his twentieth operation shortly before midnight on 31 March 1944. He was flying Lancaster 'P-Peter', the German night fighter Hauptmann Fritz Rudusch of 6/NJG6 flying a BF-110 claiming his first victory. Moss's entire crew were also killed. It was one of the worst nights of the war for the RAF, losing 106 bombers and 545 men. Shortly before he died he was awarded the DFC (*London Gazette* 24 March 1944). His citation read,

This officer has completed very many sorties and on five occasions has attacked Berlin. On one of these sorties when returning from the German capital, his aircraft was hit by anti-aircraft fire. The front and mid-upper turrets were damaged, the flaps and the tail trim were rendered unserviceable and a tyre on one of the landing wheels was punctured but Squadron Leader Moss brought his aircraft safely back to an airfield and effected a safe landing. This officer has displayed great leadership, skill and courage, setting a fine example to all.

Part of his obituary from Radley College perhaps best sums up the man:

Many who heard him talk of Bomber Command will remember how moving was his enthusiasm for his service, his admiration of his brother airmen from all parts of the Empire and America, his warm appreciation of the ground crews that served him – in fact his whole love of humanity, and humble thankfulness to God.

He is buried in Hanover War Cemetery, grave reference 8. J. 6.

Batting and fielding averages

	Mat	Inns	NO	Runs	HS	Ave	100	50	Ct	St
First-class	5	10	0	206	50	20.60	0	1	2	0

Bowling averages

	Mat	Balls	Runs	Wkts	BBI	BBM	Ave	Econ	SR	4w	5w	10
First-class	5	-	-	-	-	-	-	-	-	-	-	-

Flying Officer David Merry
Trinidad and Tobago
Two first-class matches
RAF Volunteer Reserve
Died 4 May 1944, aged 21
Right-handed bat

Lost his life saving others

David Merry was born in 1923 in Tobago. He was the son of the Venerable Francis Lee and Mary Graham Merry of Port of Spain, Trinidad. He was educated at Queen's Royal College in Trinidad and Tobago. A natural sportsman he played cricket and football for the college.

Merry made two first-class appearances, both in February 1941 and both for Trinidad against Barbados. His first match took place on the Queen's Park Oval, Port of Spain, between 1 and 5 February 1941. Trinidad won the toss and decided to bat. Merry opened the batting with Victor Stollmeyer and made 47 before being caught and bowled by Michael Clarke. Trinidad went on to make 332. In reply Barbados made 337 with Merry catching Ernest Williams off the bowling of Rupert Tang Choon for two. Barbados' top scorer was Michael Clarke who made 153. In the second innings Merry made 80 before being lbw to Herman Griffith. Trinidad went on to make 191. Barbados made 89 in their second innings and the match was drawn.

Merry made his second first-class appearance a week later between 8 and 12 February 1941 again at the Queens Park Oval. Barbados won the toss and decided to bat making 301, their opening bat George Carew making a century. In their first innings Trinidad made 452, Merry making only four before being lbw off the bowling of James Sealy. In their second innings Barbados made 332, Roger George Blackman making 140. In their second innings Trinidad made 182, Victor Stollmeyer making 86 and Jeffrey Stollmeyer 94. Merry made four not out. Trinidad won by nine wickets.

Merry also represented North Trinidad against South Trinidad on two occasions (neither first-class matches) scoring 114 on his second appearance. He also represented the West Indies on one occasion against a Lancashire XI at East Road, Longsight, Lancashire, on 7 June 1942; Merry made nine in his only innings (it was a one day match).

During the war Merry was commissioned into the RAFVR. While training at Penhold, Alberta, Canada, at 2335 on 4 May 1944, he crashed while piloting an Oxford X6734 (a twin-engine aircraft used at the time for training British Commonwealth aircrews in navigation, radio-operating, bombing and gunnery) when doing a night-flying trial. The plane burnt out amongst the trees two miles south of Penhold. Although Merry was killed his brave and selfless actions saved the lives of his crew. Ordering his pupils to parachute to safety he held the plane steady so his crew could jump. He was 21 years of age.

His brother Cyril (1911-64) played test cricket for the West Indies and first-class cricket for Trinidad.

David Merry is buried in Red Deer Cemetery, Alberta, grave reference lot 7, block F.

Batting and fielding averages

	Mat	Inns	NO	Runs	HS	Ave	100	50	Ct	St
First-class	2	4	1	135	80	45.00	0	1	1	0

Bowling averages

	Mat	Balls	Runs	Wkts	BBI	BBM	Ave	Econ	SR	4w	5w	10
First-class	2	-	-	-	-	-	-	-	-	-	-	-

Lieutenant Colonel George Geoffrey James Fenton
Viceroy's XI
One first-class match
85 Mountain Regiment Royal Artillery
Died 26 May 1944, aged 34

Died as a commanding officer

George Fenton was born on 2 July 1909 in Derby, England.

He made one first-class appearance for the Viceroy's XI against Roshanara Club on 6-8 February 1933 played at the Roshanara Club Ground, Delhi. The Viceroy's XI won the toss and decided to bat making 264, Fenton making 11 not out. The Roshanara Club made 140. In the second innings Fenton made 41 not out, the Viceroy's team making 276. Roshanara's second innings score was 185, the Viceroy's XI winning by 215 runs.

In 1944 he was given command of the 85th Mountain Battery, Royal Artillery. He was killed in action on 26 May 1944 during the Italian campaign close to the Sangro River. He is buried in the Sangro River War Cemetery, grave reference XV. D. 24. He is also commemorated on the Milverton War Memorial, which stands just inside the west gate of St Michael and All Angels church, St Michael's Hill, Milverton. Somerset.

Batting and fielding averages

	Mat	Inns	NO	Runs	HS	Ave	100	50	Ct	St
First-class	1	2	2	52	41*	-	0	0	0	0

Bowling averages

	Mat	Balls	Runs	Wkts	BBI	BBM	Ave	Econ	SR	4w	5w	10
First-class	1	-	-	-	-	-	-	-	-	-	-	-

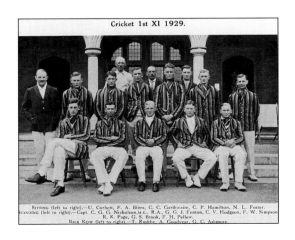

Cricket 1st XI 1929.

SITTING (left to right).—U. Corbett, F. A. Bibra, C. C. Garthwaite, C. P. Hamilton, N. L. Foster.
STANDING (left to right).—Capt. C. G. G. Nicholson, M.C., R.A., G. G. J. Fenton, C. V. Hodgson, F. W. Simpson
R. K. Page, G. S. Brook, F. H. Pellew.
BACK ROW (left to right).—T. Rushby, A. Goodyear, G. C. Ashmore.

Air Sergeant Cyril Matthew Francois
South Africa, Griqualand West, J.M.M. Commaille's XI
Five tests, thirty-three first-class appearances
South African Air Force
Died 26 May 1944, aged 46
Right-hand bat/right arm fast medium

Hard hitting batsman unlucky not to be picked for the 1924 tour of England

Cyril Francois was born in Lewisham on 20 June 1897, the son of Leo and Florence E. Francois. At some point his family moved to South Africa and it was here that Francois blossomed as a cricketer.

He made his first-class debut for Griqualand West against Transvaal in the Currie Cup on 16 December 1920 at the Old Wanderers, Johannesburg. Transvaal won the toss and elected to bat making a decent 457. The South African test player Waldemar Frederick Eric Marx made 240. Francois bowled 29 overs taking three wickets for 118: Stanley de la Courtte Snooke for 50, Alfred Henry Cecil Cooper for one, and Thomas Alfred Ward for one – all three were South African test players. In reply Griqualand West made 141. Francois made eight before being caught by the South African test player Fred Susskind off the bowling of William Dick Duff. Forced to follow on, Griqualand West made 221. Francois made 23 before being stumped by Ward off the bowling of the South African Test player Alfred Ewart Hall. Transvaal won by an innings and 95.

He went on to play against Border, Orange Free State, Western Province and Natal, most several times.

He played against the MCC during their tour of South Africa on 2 December 1922 at the Athletic Club Ground, Kimberley. Griqualand West won the toss and decided to bat making 198. Francois made zero before being bowled by the legendary Percy Fender. In reply the MCC made 353. Francois bowled 27 overs taking seven wickets for 114: Andrew Sandham (*Wisden* criceter of the year 1923) caught and bowled for 68, Frank Woolley (*Wisden* criceter of the year 1911) hit his own wicket for 83, Arthur William Carr (*Wisden* cricketer of the year 1923) bowled for 17, Francis Mann lbw for 15, Percy Fender for 20, Greville Stevens (*Wisden* cricketer of the year 1918) for 11, and finally Arthur Edward Robert Gilligan (*Wisden* cricketer of the year 1924) for four – quite a haul of English celebrity cricketers. In their second innings Griqualand West made 196. Francois made 15 before being caught by Vallance Jupp (*Wisden* cricketer of the year 1928) off the bowling of Stevens. In reply the MCC made 42 for two. Francois bowled seven overs taking one wicket for 14, the MCC opener Alex Kennedy (*Wisden* cricketer of the year 1933) for 13. The MCC won by eight wickets.

Almost certainly because of this remarkable bowling performance Francois was selected to play in all five tests against England (MCC). The first test was played against England on 23 December 1922 at the Old Wanderers, Johannesburg. South Africa won the toss and decided to bat making 148. Francois made 19 before being caught by Percy Fender off the bowling of Valance Jupp. In reply England made 182. Francois bowled ten overs taking three wickets for 23: Frank Woolley lbw for 26, Arthur Carr bowled for 27, and Greville Stevens bowled for 11. He also caught Francis Mann off the bowling of Eeiulf Peter Nupen for four. Jimmy Blanckenberg took six wickets for 76 runs off 22 overs. In their second innings South Africa made 420. Francois made nine before being caught by Mann off the bowling of Jupp. Herbert Wilfred Taylor made 176. In their second innings England made 218. Francois bowled 29 overs taking one wicket for 52, Woolley caught Buster Nupen for 27. Nupen took five wickets during the innings for 53 off 30 overs. South Africa won by 168 runs.

The second test was played at Newlands, Cape Town, on 1 January 1923. South Africa won the toss and elected to bat making 113. Francois made 28 before being run out. In reply the England made 183. Francois bowled four overs and took no wickets for 13. In their second innings South Africa made 242. Francois made 19 before being caught and bowled by George Macaulay (*Wisden* cricketer of the year 1924, died 13 December 1940). In their second innings England made 173. Francois bowled three overs taking no wickets for four. England won by one wicket.

The third test was played on 18 January 1923 at Kingsmead, Durban. England won the toss and decided to bat making 428. Charles Mead made 181. Francois bowled 30 overs taking no wickets for 55. In their first innings South Africa made 368. Francois made a career best of 72 before being caught by Jupp off the bowling of Kennedy. In their second innings England made 11 for one. The match was drawn.

The fourth test was played at the Old Wanderers on 9 February 1923. England won the toss and decided to bat making 244. Francois had another disappointing spell, bowling ten overs and taking no wickets for 13. In reply South Africa made 295. Francois made a decent 41. In their second innings England made 376, Woolley making 115 not out. Francois bowled nine overs taking no wickets for 17. In their second innings South Africa made 247 for four, Herbert Taylor making 101. The match was once again drawn.

The fifth and final test was played on 16 February 1923 at King's Mead, Durban. England won the toss and decided to bat making 281, the England opener Charles Albert George (Jack) Russell making 140. Francois bowled 11 overs and took one wicket for 23, Charles Mead lbw for 66. In reply South Africa made 179. Francois made a useful 43. In their second innings England made 241, Russell making 111. Francois bowled eight overs and took one wicket for 15, Andrew Sandham clean bowled for 40. He also caught Russell off the bowling of Blanckenberg for 66. In their second innings South Africa made 234. Francois made 18 and Taylor made 102, but England won by 109 runs taking the series two one.

It was the last test Francois was to take part in, although many thought him unlucky not to be selected for the 1924 tour of England. He did however play against the MCC on one further occasion on the 19 November 1927 making 54 and 11 and failing to take a wicket. The MMC beat Griqualand West by an innings and 75 runs.

Returning to Griqualand West he played against Natal, Transvaal, Western Province, Border, OFS, S.B. Joel's XI and made one appearance for J.M.M. Commaille's XI against N.V. Lindsay's XI taking four wickets and making 80 runs.

He played his final first-class match against the Orange Free State on 2 January 1928 at the Ramblers Ground, Bloemfontein. Griqualand West won the toss and decided to bat making 243. Francois just missed his century making 97 before being caught by Campbell Munro off the bowling of Alan Newton. In reply OFS made 292. Francois bowled 16 overs taking one wicket for 42, Munro lbw for seven (sweet revenge). In their second innings Griqualand West made 259. Francois made 54 before being bowled by Cecil William Travers. In their second innings OFS made 211 for three. Murray Godfred Francis making 115 not out. The Orange Free State won by seven wickets.

During his career Cyril Francois played in five test matches making 252 runs with a high score of 72 against England. He bowled 684 balls and took six wickets for 225 runs, his best figures being three for 23. He also made five catches. He played in thirty-three first-class games making 1,232 runs including six fifties, his highest score being 97. He also bowled 5,888 balls taking 101 wickets for 2,873 runs, his best figures being seven for 114. He also took 24 catches.

During the Second World War he served as an air sergeant with the South African Air Force. He was killed in a car accident near Pretoria on 26 May 1944. He is commemorated in the Thaba Tshwane (New) Military Cemetery, grave reference 291.

He left a widow, Constance, of Kimberley.

Batting and fielding averages

	Mat	Inns	NO	Runs	HS	Ave	100	50	6s	Ct	St
Tests	5	9	1	252	72	31.50	0	1	0	5	0
First-class	33	58	4	1232	97	22.81	0	6		24	0

Bowling averages

	Mat	Inns	Balls	Runs	Wkts	BBI	BBM	Ave	Econ	SR	4w	5w	10
Tests	5	9	684	225	6	3/23	4/75	37.50	1.97	114.0	0	0	0
First-class	33		5888	2873	101	7/114		28.44	2.92	58.2		3	0

Major Aubrey Davies Hodges
MCC
One first-class appearance
Nigeria Field Ambulance
Died 27 May 1944, aged 32
Right-handed bat

'His research into the habits and life-history of the tsetse fly did much to solve the problem of dealing with the fly and the control of sleeping sickness in early days.'

Aubrey Hodges was born on 3 February 1912 in Kampala, Uganda. He was the son of H. B. Hodges, a surgeon, of Watton, in Hertfordshire. He was educated at Epsom College, was a member of the rugby XV, and played in the first XI against the City of London School, Saint John's School Leatherhead, Brighton College, Merchant Taylors, Whitgift Grammar school, Christ's Hospital, King's College School, Wimbledon and Old Epsomians.

Following in his father's footsteps Hodges decided on medicine as a career. He completed his medical training at the London Hospital, graduating MB in 1890, and after serving a period of medical residencies was appointed Resident Medical Officer at the South-East Fever Hospital at New Cross. In 1898 he was appointed Medical Officer in Uganda. From 1908 until 1918 he was Principal Medical Officer for the Uganda Protectorate specialising in the investigation of sleeping sickness (trypanosomiasis).

During the First World War he was appointed lieutenant colonel of the East Africa Expeditionary Force, commanding the Uganda Medical Service. His work on the life history and bionomics of the tsetse fly was important and in many ways paved the way towards the eradication and understanding of sleeping sickness. His diaries are in the library of the London School of Hygiene and Tropical Medicine and well worth a read, outlining interestingly life at the time. He also wrote that in 1899 he played cricket for Uganda against East Africa and noted with delight hat he took six wickets during the match.

Hodges made one first-class appearance for the MCC against Ireland on 1 August 1936 at the Observatory Lane, Rathmines, Co Dublin. Ireland won the toss and decided to bat making 296. In reply the MCC made 124. Hodges made 34 (the highest score of the innings) before being caught by Francis Reddy off the bowling of James Boucher. In their second innings Ireland made 228, James MacDonald making 108 not out. In their second innings the MCC made 115, Hodges opening for them making ten before being caught by MacDonald off the bowling of Boucher. Boucher took five wickets for 26 off 13 overs during the innings. Ireland won by 285 runs.

Hodges served with the Nigeria Field Ambulance in 1939 and was a company commander throughout the East Africa campaign. As a result of his failing health he resigned his commission in 1943, returning to his civilian job. He died on 27 May 1944 at Minna, Nigeria, from an illness contracted while serving in Nigeria.

Captain B.B. Waddy RAMC later wrote movingly of his friend:

> A great number of people will have heard of Aubrey Hodges' death with shock and regret. He was not only a good all-round athlete, with the usual long roll of acquaintances but he had the gift of attracting people into lasting friendships, as I have had good opportunity of observing. Travelling round Nigeria the mention of his name was a universal passport and though he had spent only a few months in England since 1937, he is not forgotten here.
>
> He was at King's College Hospital, 1933-36, captaining the Cricket and Rugby sides, and also playing lawn tennis, squash and (rugger permitting) hockey for the Hospital. After qualifying and taking D.T.M. and H. he went out to Nigeria in 1937, playing hockey and cricket for that colony. He joined the Nigeria Field Ambulance in 1939, and was a Company Commander throughout the East Africa campaign, after which, in 1943, he returned to his civil job.
>
> Those who knew Aubrey will not forget the fun which he got out of life, and was shared by any company in which he happened to be.
>
> *King's College Hospital Gazette, Summer 1944.*

Batting and fielding averages

	Mat	Inns	NO	Runs	HS	Ave	100	50	Ct	St
First-class	1	2	0	44	34	22.00	0	0	0	0

Bowling averages

	Mat	Balls	Runs	Wkts	BBI	BBM	Ave	Econ	SR	4w	5w	10
First-class	1	-	-	-	-	-	-	-	-	-	-	-

Hodges sitting second from the left.

Captain Stanley William Emile Behrend
Bengal, Europeans (India)
Sixteen first-class matches
4th Battalion 15th Punjab Regiment
Died 30 May 1944, aged 35
Right-handed bat/Right arm fast medium.

Helped change the course of the Japanese campaign

Stanley Behrend was born on 15 November 1908 in Kidderpoor, Bengal, the son of Ernest Stanley and Fanny Eliza Behrend. He was educated at Felsted between 1924 and 1927 where he was in the first XI. The school's most successful bowler, he made centuries for the school and his house. A good all-round athlete, he was also in the XV where his size and power made him a dangerous three-quarter, the hockey XI, and he also boxed for the school. He later married Marjorie Irene Nina of Streatham.

Returning to India, Behrend made sixteen first-class appearances between 1929 and 1941. He made these in two Indian cricket competitions, the Bombay Quadrangular Tournament, an influential tournament held in Bombay from 1912 to 1936, also known at various times as the Presidency Match, the Bombay Triangular, and the Bombay Pentangular, and the Ranji Trophy. This competition was launched as 'The Cricket Championship of India' in July 1934, with the first fixtures taking place in1934-35. The trophy was donated by Maharaja Bhupinder Singh of Patiala. The first match of the competition was held on 4 November 1934 between Madras and Mysore at Chepauk.

Behrend made his first-class debut for the Europeans against the Parsees at the Gymkhana Ground in the Bombay Quadrangular Tournament played between 3 and 5 December 1929. The Europeans won the toss and decided to bat making 141, Behrend making 36 not out (the highest score of the first innings). The Parsees went on to make 186. Behrend bowled 17 overs taking two wickets for 43. He took the wickets of the two Parsees openers, Framroze Edulji Kapadia lbw for 49, followed by Framroze Kaikobad Nariman clean bowled for two. He also managed to catch Bomanji Khurshedji Kalapesi off the bowling of Rolo Mayer for one. In the second innings the Europeans made 314, Behrend making 14 before being caught off the bowling of Nariman Marshall. The star of the innings was Alexander Hosie, not out for 104. In their second innings the Parsees made 168 with Behrend bowling 15 overs for 32 runs, taking one further wicket, that of the Indian test cricketer Phiroze Palia lbw for one. Although the match was drawn the Parsees took the match based on their first innings score.

He made his debut in the Ranji Trophy for Bengal against Central India at Eden Gardens, Calcutta, 18-20 January 1936. Bengal won the toss and decided to bat. Behrend made 38 before being bowled by Cottari Nayudu, Bengal going on to make 283. In reply Central India made 200 with Behrend bowling 10.4 overs for 29 runs and taking three wickets: the Indian test cricketer Syed Ali lbw for eighteen, Vijay Hazare for two, and SR Kalewar for two. In Bengal's second innings Behrend made nine before being bowled by Nayudu. In Central India's second innings they made 195, Behrend bowling six overs for 26, taking the wickets of both of the openers for Central India, Syed Ali lbw for 29 and Madhavsinh

Jagdale 38. The match was drawn, Bengal taking the honours based on their first innings score.

Behrend made his final first-class appearance between 16 and 18 December 1941 for the Europeans against the Parsees in the Bombay Pentangular Tournament, played at the Brabourne Stadium. The Parsees won the toss and decided to bat making an impressive 532, with Mermadi Mistry making 152, Rustomji Modi 144 and Jehangir Khot 103. Behrend bowled 14 overs for 60 runs taking no wickets. The Europeans were skittled out for 117. Behrend made zero before being bowled by Phiroze Palia. Following on, the Europeans did little better, making 153 all out, Behrend making zero, bowled by Minocher Mobed. The Parsees won by an innings and 262 runs.

During his first-class career Behrend made 669 runs, scoring one century and two fifties, his highest score being 107 against United Provinces. He also bowled 1,956 balls taking fifty wickets for 1,076 runs, his best figures being 5/29. He also made ten catches.

During the war Behrend was commissioned into the Indian Army, serving with the 4th Battalion 15th Punjab Regiment rising to the rank of captain. He died on 30 May 1944 of wounds received while leading a gallant action against the Japanese on the Imphal front. The Battle of Imphal took place in the region around the city of Imphal, the capital of the state of Manipur in northeast India between March and July 1944. The Japanese plan was to destroy the Allied armies at Imphal and invade India. However, thanks to determined resistance, the Japanese forces were driven back into Burma with very heavy losses. The battle was the turning point of the Burma campaign and the biggest defeat inflicted on the Japanese army to that date and as important as a Stalingrad as the beginning of the end for the Japanese. Now the allied armies knew they could be defeated.

Captain Stanley Behrend is buried in Kohima War Cemetery, grave reference 6. B. 3.

Batting and fielding averages

	Mat	Inns	NO	Runs	HS	Ave	100	50	Ct	St
First-class	16	27	1	669	107	25.73	1	2	10	0

Bowling averages

	Mat	Runs	Wkts	BBI	Ave	5w	10
First-class	16	1076	50	5/29	21.52	2	0

Captain John Philip Blake MC
Cambridge University and Hampshire
Twenty-nine first-class matches
Royal Marines, No. 43 Commando
Died 3 June 1944, aged 26
Right-handed bat

Outstanding man gone too soon

John Blake was born on 17 November 1917 in Portsmouth. He was the son of Philip, a local dentist, and Marjorie Flora, of Havant. He had two sisters, and a brother who also played first-class cricket. He went first to Emsworth House School and then as a scholar to Aldenham where he became head of house and the school. A fine athlete from an early age, he played in the first XI captaining the side as well as getting his school colours for fives and hockey. Going up to St John's College, Cambridge, he studied mathematics and represented the university in the cricket XI. In September 1939 he became a maths teacher at Sherborne and a tutor in Westcott House. However he only managed one term before being called up, becoming a naval instructor at Greenwich.

Blake made twenty-nine first-class appearances, his debut being for Hampshire between 19 and 22 June 1937 against Sussex in the county championship at the Manor Sports Ground, Worthing. Sussex won the toss and decided to bat. They made 288 all out. In Hampshire's first innings Blake made two before being lbw to James Parks. In their second innings Sussex declared after scoring 308. Blake did little better, scoring seven before being caught by John George Langridge off the bowling of (his brother) James Langridge. Hampshire made 136, Sussex taking the honours by 153 runs.

It was almost a year before he made his second first-class appearance, this time for Cambridge University against the Army, although he had turned out for Hampshire in several second XI matches between times. The match took place 28-31 May 1938 at F.P. Fenner's. Cambridge won the toss and elected to bat. Blake made the highest score of the first innings with 70, Cambridge making a total of 169. The Army went on to make 387, with Lancelot Grove making 106 and Charles Packe (killed 1 July 1944) 176. The match was eventually drawn.

As with so many others Blake played for his university in term time and for his county during the holidays, playing many matches in 1938/9. He made his final first-class appearance for Hampshire against Kent in the county championship on 5-8 August 1939 at the St Lawrence Ground, Canterbury. Kent won the toss and decided to bat making 161 all out. Blake was lbw to Claude Lewis for zero. Hampshire went on to make 135, Lewis taking six wickets. In their second innings Kent managed a poor 83. Blake failed to bat during Hampshire's second innings, in which they made 111 to win by seven wickets.

Blake made 1,095 runs during his first-class career including seven fifties, his highest score being 88 against the MCC, and he took eighteen catches. He also played for the University Wanderers Hockey Club and the Hawks Club, and won his blue for hockey.

Talking a commission into the Royal Marines during the war, eventually rising to the rank of captain, he took part in the abortive Dakar expedition known as Operation Menace.

This was an attempt in September 1940 to capture the strategic port of Dakar in French West Africa (now Senegal). The plan was to overthrow the pro-German Vichy French government and replace it by one headed by Charles de Gaulle, but it failed badly with troops lost and ships damaged.

On Blake's return his battalion went through arduous training at the famous commando school at Achnacarry in Scotland. Together with 450 other officers and men he became part of 43 Royal Marine Commando. He was posted to North Africa in late 1943. In early 1944 the commando landed at Anzio in Italy and with 9 Army Commando given the task of capturing three peaks with bare, rocky, precipitous slopes to extend the bridgehead over the River Garigliano. After a long and exhausting night climb under mortar and machine gun fire Captain John Blake's D Troop seized Monte Ornito (2,400ft). For this fine achievement and his personal courage and leadership he was awarded the Military Cross. The citation read:

> Temporary Lieutenant (A/Captain) John Philip BLAKE, Royal Marines. For outstanding gallantry and leadership shown while serving with the 43rd Royal Marine Commando in the attack which led to the capture of Mt Ornito, Italy on 3rd February 1944. On reaching the top of the Mount, through heavy machine gun fire, without hesitation and heedless of the danger from grenades, he led the forward section of his Troop in a bayonet charge on the enemy position and captured 20 prisoners. Later in the day during a strong enemy counter attack, this gallant officer moved from position to position encouraging his men and directing their fire.
> MC-LG 27 June 1944

43 Commando was withdrawn to the island of Vis in the Adriatic. The Germans commenced an offensive against Tito's partisans in Bosnia and to help distract them Tito asked for an operation on the Dalmatian coast. To this end the island of Brač was attacked. The German garrison on Brač was over a thousand strong with several strongpoints each sited on top of a hill south of the village of Nerežišća. A joint British/partisan attack against these strongpoints was planned but due to confusion following the D-Day landings, 43 Commando went into the attack unsupported. Blake led his troop through a minefield onto the objective but was killed when the Germans counter-attacked on 3 June 1944.

Blake was the only casualty out of the twelve members of Sherborne School teaching staff who fought in the Second World War.

He is buried in Belgrade War Cemetery, grave reference 9. E. 7. He is also commemorated on a lectern at St Faith's Church, Havant.

The following obituary appeared in *The Shirburnian*, March 1945:

Captain John Philip Blake, M.C. (Royal Marines).

John Blake came to Sherborne as a teacher of Mathematics in 1939. He was present at the Dakar incident and remained in the tropics for a large part of 1940-41 before being transferred to the Mediterranean. In July 1943, he joined the 43rd R.M. Commando and commanded a troop of 70 men. He went to Italy in January 1944, was awarded the Military Cross 'for his outstanding gallantry and leadership shown while serving with the 43rd R.M. Commando in the attack on Mt. Ornito on 3rd February'; was present at the Anzio landing, and later crossed over to the Dalmatian Islands. He returned to Italy and on 13th June was reported missing as the result of leading an attack on a German strong point. His death was confirmed at the beginning of August.

Few will ever know the tremendous loss the School has sustained. It is hard to realise that such a splendid personality will not return to give us of his best, as it was his impatient desire to be able to do.

The essence of John Blake's character was naturalness and simplicity. His successes at school and university were more than enough to turn his head, but he never showed the slightest sign of conceit nor any desire to find his friends chiefly from among the athletically successful. He was Head of his Preparatory School at Emsworth and captain of all games; Head of the School and of Mead's House at Aldenham, where he was also captain of cricket and a school colour for fives and hockey. At Cambridge he won his Blue for cricket, was a member of the University Wanderers Hockey Club and of the Hawks Club, and was captain of Cricket and Hockey at St John's. But no one would ever learn these things from his own lips. Amongst his own interests cricket stood out pre-eminently. All his letters to me contained some reference to it, no matter what time of year it might be. Sound and stylish bat though he was, it was his fielding which most impressed and gave such pleasure to all who saw him play. Whether he was playing for Cambridge or Hampshire or in some club match or on the village green, it was equally keen and polished, a perfect expression of himself. He had a most retentive brain and great powers of concentration.

But the most outstanding features of his life were his deep devotion to his family and to his faith and the enormous enjoyment he got out of life and friendship. He made friends wherever he went, for he entered whole-heartedly into the joys and sorrows of others in a natural way. All his officers stressed that he was a born leader of men and that all his men were so proud of him and so fond of him and talked of his outstanding personality. Perhaps the words of his Commanding Officer to his parents sum him up as well as words can: 'John's loss to you is irreparable, as it is to the Corps and to the nation – an officer of his quality is quite irreplaceable.'

R.S. Thompson (Housemaster of Westcott House 1936-52)

His brother David Eustace (1925-2015) played for Hampshire and the MCC.

Batting and fielding averages

	Mat	Inns	NO	Runs	HS	Ave	100	50	Ct	St
First-class	29	51	3	1095	88	22.81	0	7	18	0

Bowling averages

	Mat	Balls	Runs	Wkts	BBI	BBM	Ave	Econ	SR	4w	5w	10
First-class	29	-	-	-	-	-	-	-	-	-	-	-

Lieutenant Colonel Arthur Denis Bradford Cocks
Army
Two first-class appearances
1st Assault Brigade Royal Engineers, 5th Assault Regiment
Died 6 June 1944, aged 39
Right-handed bat

First British officer to be killed on D-Day

Arthur Cocks was born on 29 July 1904 at Dharmsala, Bengal, India. He was the son of George Arthur Cocks CBE CIE and Annie Violet. He was educated at Bedford School where he played in the first XI.

Deciding on a career in the army he went up to the Royal Military Academy Woolwich later playing for them against Sandhurst. Sandhurst won by ten wickets.

On finishing his training he was commissioned into the Royal Engineers as a second lieutenant on 28 January 1925, promoted to lieutenant on the 28 January 1927 and then captain on 28 January 1936. During his time with the engineers he played against the MCC, Royal Artillery and I Zingari. Cocks made two first-class appearances for the Army, both in 1927.

He made his debut against Oxford University on 28 May at the University Parks. Oxford won the toss and decided to field. The Army made 388, Godfrey Bryan making 116. In reply Oxford made 328. Cocks caught John Vincent D'Alessio Rowley off the bowling of Harold Miles for one. Ronald Joy took five wickets for 70 off 29 overs. In their second innings the Army made 188 for six declared. Cocks failed to bat. In reply Oxford made 112 for two. The match was drawn.

Cocks made his second and final first-class appearance for the Army against Cambridge University on 1 June 1927 at F.P. Fenner's. The Army won the toss and decided to bat making 262. Cocks made four before being bowled by the England test cricketer Maurice Allom. Allom took nine wickets for 55 off 29 overs during the innings. In reply Cambridge made 301. Cocks bowled 17 overs taking no wickets for 33. He did however catch Ralph Cobbold for 13 and Ian Rutherford Mann for 26, both off the bowling of Philip Havelock Davis. The Cambridge opener Norman Wykes made 145. In their second innings the Army made 150, Allom taking a further five wickets for 47 off 16 overs. In reply Cambridge made 112 for two, and won by eight wickets.

In 1932 Cocks married Majorie Du Caurroy Chads and later served in India. He became a staff captain in December 1937, was promoted to major in January 1942, and later to lieutenant colonel. Cocks was killed when landing on Sword Beach with the 5th Assault Regiment Royal Engineers on D-Day, 6 June 1944, being the first British officer to be killed on that fateful day. The 5th were a specialist unit equipped with so-called 'Hobart's Funnies', intended to clear the beaches and make exits onto the first inland road. An account of Lieutenant Cocks's death was later reported by Lieutenant Lambton Burn who was serving with the RNVR and was aboard the landing craft LCT-947:

Shells are bursting all round. They are not friendly shorts from bombardment warships, but vicious stabs from an enemy who has held his fire until the final two hundred yards. He is shooting well, shooting often. Mortar shells whine and burst with sickening inevitability. An L.C.T. to port goes up in flames.

There is a sudden jerk as our bows hit the beach. Down goes the ramp, with Sub-Lieutenant Monty Glengarry, R.N.Z.N.V.R. and his party working like madmen at the bows.

There is a roar of acceleration and Donald Robertson in Stornoway [the first Crab which managed to disembark] is away like a relay runner.

Cocks is pictured here on the far left. This picture was taken shortly before his death.

Dunbar [the second Crab] moves forward. Colonel Cocks leans from his turret [he had elected to command from the Plough] and motions the other tank-commanders to follow. But enemy fire is now concentrated on us. There are bursts on both sides and then snap two direct hits on our bows followed by a third snap like a whip cracking over the tank hold.

The First Lieutenant is flung sideways against a bulkhead and lies stunned. Dunbar stops in her tracks slews sideways blocks the door. Another and greater explosion as the bangalore shafts of Barbarian [the Log Carpet AVRE with Captain Fairie in command] explode with a flash of red.

Colonel Cocks is killed as he stands, and there is a scream from within his tank. Cold with anger, Tom Fairie moves Barbarian forward tries to edge Dunbar to the ramp but fails. He vaults from his turret and is joined by other tank-men who strain furiously to bring chain and tackle to bear.

Lieutenant Colonel Cocks's body was returned to England and is buried in St Peters Churchyard, Frimley, Surrey, grave reference 239. He is also commemorated on the Camberley War Memorial and in Portsmouth Cathedral.

Batting and fielding averages

	Mat	Inns	NO	Runs	HS	Ave	100	50	Ct	St
First-class	2	3	1	30	26*	15.00	0	0	3	0

Bowling averages

	Mat	Balls	Runs	Wkts	BBI	BBM	Ave	Econ	SR	4w	5w	10
First-class	2	306	113	0	-	-	-	2.21	-	0	0	0

415828 Flight Sergeant William Alexander Roach
Western Australia
Three first-class appearances
455 Squadron Royal Australian Air Force
Died 8 June 1944, aged 29
Left-handed bat

A true son of Australia

William Roach was born on 12 December 1914 in South Fremantle, Western Australia. He was the son of William Henry and May Barrie Roach.

Roach made three first-class appearances, all for Western Australia between February and March 1934. He made his debut against Victoria on 27 February 1934 at the Melbourne Cricket Ground. Victoria won the toss and elected to bat making 243. In reply Western Australia made 423 for seven declared. Roach made 17 before being caught and bowled by Hugh Joseph Plant. Their opener, Francis Joseph Bryant, made 115 and his brother Richard John Bryant made 103. In their second innings Victoria made 130, hanging on to make a draw.

Roach's second match was against South Australia, played on 3 March 1934 at the Adelaide Oval. South Australia won the toss and decided to bat making 287. In reply Western Australia made 140. Roach made zero before being stumped by Charles Walker (died 18 December 1942) off the bowling of the Australian test bowler Clarence Grimmett (*Wisden* cricketer of the year 1931). Grimmett took seven wickets for 57 off 19 overs. Forced to follow on, Western Australia made 93 for five. Roach made 14 not out. The match was drawn.

Roach made his third and final first-class appearance against an Australian XI on 23 March 1934 at the Western Australian Cricket Association Ground, Perth. Western Australia won the toss and decided to bat making 305. Roach made zero before being clean bowled by Grimmett. Grimmett took five wickets for 90 off 28 overs during the innings. The Australian XI made 274 for five. Roach caught Bill Ponsford (*Wisden* cricketer of the year 1935) off the bowling of Stanley George Francis for 39. The weather closed in and the match was declared a draw.

Roach also represented Western Australia against Newcastle, the Royal Australian Air Force against the Royal Air Force, The Rest, and an England XI, all in 1944.

During the Second World War Roach served as a flight sergeant with 455 Squadron Royal Australian Air Force flying Bristol Beaufighters on attacks on German shipping. During these operations the Australians faced heavy naval anti-aircraft fire as well as enemy fighters. Often attacking targets in narrow Norwegian fiords, they suffered heavy casualties. It was during one of these operations that Roach was shot down and killed. His body was never recovered and he is commemorated on the Runnymede Memorial, panel 261.

He left a widow, Mignon Elizabeth, of South Perth, Western Australia.

Batting and fielding averages

	Mat	Inns	NO	Runs	HS	Ave	100	50	Ct	St
First-class	3	4	1	31	17	10.33	0	0	1	0

Bowling averages

	Mat	Balls	Runs	Wkts	BBI	BBM	Ave	Econ	SR	4w	5w	10
First-class	3	-	-	-	-	-	-	-	-	-	-	-

Major Peter Marriott Raleigh Scott MC & Bar
Oxford University
Five first-class matches
Royal Armoured Corps
4th County of London Yeomanry (Sharpshooters)
13 June 1944, aged 32
Left-handed bat/left arm fast

The bravest of tank commanders, finally killed by the
German tank ace Michael Wittmann

Peter Scott was born on 1 February 1912 in Paddington. He was the second son of Thomas Gilbert and Violet Anne Scott (née Marriott). He was educated at Winchester between 1925 and 1930 being in D house and went up to Magdalen College Oxford where he read law. While at Oxford he made five first-class appearances all for the University.

He made his debut against Leicestershire between 11 and 13 May 1932 at the University Parks, Oxford. Leicestershire won the toss and decided to bat. Scott bowled 11 overs for 22 and took two wickets, English test cricketer William Astil caught Peter Oldfield for seven, followed by William Hurd for zero. Leicestershire went on to make 314. Scott made zero in his first innings being caught by William Marlo off the bowling of Haydon Smith (who took seven wickets during the innings). Oxford made 194. Scott bowled ten overs during the second innings for 21 and took no wickets. Leicestershire made 115 in their second innings before the weather closed in and the match was drawn.

Scott went on to play for Oxford University against Lancashire, the South Americans (in the British Isles) and Essex. He made his final first-class appearance against Worcestershire between 13 and 16 May 1933 at the University Parks. Worcestershire won the toss and decided to bat. They made 467 all out. In Oxford's first innings Scott made one before being lbw off the bowling of George Brook. Oxford made 383 helped by a fine 133 by David Townsend. In their second inn innings Worcestershire made 139 before declaring. Scott bowled eight overs for 19 and failed to take a wicket. He didn't bat in the second innings, Oxford making 92. The match was drawn.

During his career Scott also turned out for T. Gilbert Scott's XI and the MCC. In total he made 114 runs, his highest score being 37, and made one catch. He also bowled 678 balls for 321 runs and took five wickets, his best figures being two for 22. His brother Robert (1909-57) made eighty first-class appearances, mostly for Oxford University and Sussex. His grandfather Charles Marriott also played for Oxford, as did his three great uncles, George, Charles and John Marriott. In 1938 Scott married Katherine Smith.

During the war Scott served with the 4th County of London Yeomanry. In early 1941 he was sent to the Middle East and took part in several actions in the Western Desert during 1942, especially during fierce fighting around the 'boxes' of the British defensive lines near Maabus er Rigel. On 14 June 1942 he was wounded when the tank he was commanding was hit and caught fire. The crew managed to escape. The following year as a result of his actions on 23 February 1943 he was decorated with the MC and took over the command of

C company. The regiment's war diary records, 'February 23rd 1943: Remained in the same position all day, halfway between Medenine and Mareth about three miles north of the road. Withdrew the squadron forming the roadblock in the morning. Captain PMR Scott assumed command of 'C' Squadron when it was heard that Captain IB Aird had caught pneumonia. Practically no change in the positions of the enemy...'

Scott was promoted to major and in April 1943 took part in the action at Wadi Akarit in Tunisia. His actions that day were later recalled by Lieutenant C.W. Pearce of C Squadron:

There seemed to be hundreds of wounded or dead Highlanders everywhere... The Highland brigadier wanted more tanks across the wadi. Major Peter Scott agreed to send two Sherman troops plus the two Grants with Tony Jarvis to control. Our chaps got through the minefield and pushed out a bit the other side. Shelling was heavy all the time, especially on the minefield gap. The brigadier wanted more tank support. Peter Scott led, then my troop, followed by the others. The Shermans went forward; I went right and Mike Ritchie left. Suddenly all six Shermans blew up; direct hits. A few people got out but they were mostly killed. The order came to pull back, but too late... There was an absolute shambles, Italians and Highlanders all together. Firing was coming from all directions, including from behind... Six Messerschmitt 109s came down this wadi and really let us have it.

(Lieutenant C.W. Pearce, 'C' Squadron 4CLY)

Scott was awarded a bar to his MC for this actions on this day. Together with his battalion he was one of the first to enter Tunisia after pursuing the Germans across the desert.

Scott landed in Salerno in October 1943, taking part in the crossing of the River Volturno. In December, Scott and his battalion were returned to England to prepare for the invasion of France. On 7 June 1944, the day after D-Day, he landed at Gold Beach and on 13 June the 7th Armoured Division, of which 4th City of London Yeomanry were part, was ordered to take Villers-Bocage. While carrying out their orders they were ambushed by II Kompanie 101st SS Heavy Panzer Battalion, equipped with Tiger tanks and led by the tank ace Michael Wittmann. Wittmann started by destroying tanks at the front and rear of the British column, preventing the others from moving, and then drove through the British lines shooting anything he could see. Scott, who was in charge of A Squadron by this time, was killed during this action when a shell burst overhead killing him instantly. Wittmann was killed a few weeks later on 8 August 1944.

Besides winning an MC and bar Scott was also mentioned in despatches several times. The brave Major Scott is buried in Bayeux War Cemetery, grave reference II. B. 9.

Batting and fielding averages

	Mat	Inns	NO	Runs	HS	Ave	100	50	Ct	St
First-class	5	8	1	114	37	16.28	0	0	1	0

Bowling averages

	Mat	Balls	Runs	Wkts	BBI	Ave	Econ	SR	5w	10
First-class	5	678	321	5	2/22	64.20	2.84	135.6	0	0

Lieutenant Harold William Dods
Minor Counties, Sir T.E.W. Brinckman's XI
Three first-class matches
Scots Guards
Died 18 June 1944, aged 35
Left-handed bat

Died in the Guards Chapel in the worst V1 attack of the war

Harold Dods was born on 25 March 1909 in Gosberton, Lincolnshire. He was the son of Harold (who had played minor counties cricket for Lincolnshire) and Florence Dods of Donington. He was educated at Tonbridge where he was in the first XI. For a while he even had his own team, H. Dods' XI, who played several matches against Oakham School. He also turned out for the MCC.

He made three first-class appearances, two for the minor counties both against Oxford University and one for Sir T.E.W. Brinckman's XI against Argentina. He made his debut against Oxford at the University Parks on 10-12 June 1936. Minor Counties won the toss and decided to bat making 251. Dods made nine before being caught by Norman Mitchell-Innes off the bowling of Richard West. Oxford replied with 288 all out. Dods made 22 in his second innings before being caught once again by Mitchell-Innes off the bowling of West. The Minor Counties made 294 in their second innings and Oxford only made 23 before the weather closed in and the match was drawn.

Dods had to wait almost two years for his second first-class appearance, this time playing for Sir T.E.W. Brinckman's XI during their 1937/8 tour of Argentina. They played eleven matches, five of them against Argentina. Although Dods played in seven of the matches only one was a first-class match, the one played against Argentina at the Belgrano Athletic Club, Buenos Aires, between 15 and 17 January 1938. Brickman's XI won the toss and decided to bat. Dods excelled, hitting 104 before being caught by Cyril Ayling off the bowling of Kenneth Bush. Brickman's XI made 417. Argentina did poorly in their second innings making only 164 and were forced to bat again. This time they did a lot better making 384 all out. Brinckman's XI made 91 in their second innings and the match was drawn. He later played for Brinckman's XI during their tour of South America making seven appearances but none were first-class matches.

Five months later Dods made his third and final first-class match, this time for the Minor Counties against Oxford University between 11 and 13 May 1938 at the University Parks. Oxford won the toss and decided to bat making 217. In reply the Minor Counties made 175 with Dods making 30 before being bowled by Edward Scott. In their second innings Oxford made 319 with Edward Eagar making 147 and Eric Dixon 92, before declaring. The Minor Counties made 131 with Dods run out for seven. Oxford won by 230 runs.

Dods also made ninety-five Minor Counties appearances mostly for Lincolnshire between 1927 and 1939. During this time he also found time to meet and marry Marigold Bird JP of Sleaford.

During the Second World War he was commissioned into the Scots Guards becoming a lieutenant. He wasn't killed in action but in the V1 rocket attack on the Guards Chapel,

The Coming Storm

Wellington Barracks, at 11.20am, Sunday, 18 June 1944, not far from Buckingham Palace. The chapel was almost totally destroyed. It had been full at the time with Sunday worshippers and 121 people were killed and 141 injured. It was the worst V1 attack of the war.

Dods is buried in Donington Cemetery, grave 380. Worth a visit and a few flowers.

Batting and fielding averages

	Mat	Inns	NO	Runs	HS	Ave	100	Ct	St
First-class	3	5	0	172	104	34.40	1	0	0

Bowling averages

	Mat	Balls	Runs	Wkts	BBI	BBM	Ave	Econ	SR	4w	5w	10
First-class	3	-	-	-	-	-	-	-	-	-	-	-

272

Captain George Durant Kemp-Welch
Warwickshire-Cambridge University-LH Tennyson's XI-MCC
114 first-class matches
Grenadier Guards
18 June 1944, aged 37
Right-handed bat/Fast medium.

Killed in the Guards Chapel in the Worst VI attack of the war

George Kemp-Welch was born on 4 August 1907 in Chelsea. He was son of Brian Kemp-Welch, managing director of the Schweppes company (his grandfather had been chairman and managing director) and Verena Georgina. He had a twin brother, Peter, and a sister Elizabeth who in her day became quite famous writing a column in the *Tatler* magazine called *Jennifer's Diary*.

George was educated at Charterhouse where he was in the first XI playing against Harrow, Winchester, Wellington, Westminster and Harvard, before going up to Sidney Sussex Cambridge where he took his blue for both cricket and football (in which he played centre forward). No less a publication than *The Times* said of him, 'a first-rate constructive player in mid-field, but also knows how to score plenty of goals'. He went on to captain both teams.

Kemp-Welch made 114 first-class appearances, fifty-four of them in the county championship. He made his debut for Warwickshire at the tender age of 19 at Lord's between 18 and 20 May 1927. Middlesex won the toss and decided to bat making 490. Kemp-Welch bowled three overs for 18 and failed to take a wicket. The England test cricketer Elias Hendren made 156. Warwickshire went on to make 237, Kemp-Welch making 23 before being stumped by Gerald Livock off the bowling of another England test cricketer Nigel Haig (who took five wickets during the innings). Warwickshire followed on, making 507 before declaring, their openers Norman Kilner and the England test player Ernest Smith making 299 between them (167 and 132). They were assisted by Alfred Croom who made 75. Warwickshire declared so Kemp-Welch failed to bat and the match was eventually drawn.

While still playing for Warwickshire he was selected to play for L.H. Tennyson's XI during their tour of Jamaica in February 1928. He played in three of the five games all against Jamaica all played at Sabina Park, Kingston and Melbourne Park, Kingston. Tennyson's XI lost the first two matches convincingly, the first by 218 runs the second by an innings and 98 runs before drawing their final match.

Going up to Cambridge he was quickly selected for the university XI, playing his first match against Nottinghamshire at F.P. Fenner's between 15 and 17 May 1929. Nottinghamshire won the toss and decided to bat making 396 in their first innings, Kemp-Welch taking two catches, Arthur Staples off the bowling of Edward Blundell for 94, and the England test player Arthur Carr again off the bowling of Blundell for 82. Kemp-Welch made five in his first innings before being caught by Ben Lilley off the bowling of Bill Voce. Cambridge made 278. During their second innings Nottinghamshire made 274, Kemp-Welch making another catch taking the wicket of Arthur Staples off the bowling once again of Blundell for 16. Kemp-Welch made 14 not out in his second innings. The match was drawn.

He continued turning out for Warwickshire during the Cambridge holidays. He also turned out for the Gentlemen against the Players and The Rest (against the MCC South African Touring Team).

He was again selected to represent Tennyson's tour of Jamaica in 1932, playing in three of the five matches, all against Jamaica. In the first game the Jamaican sixth-wicket pair of George Headley and Clarence Passailaigue put on an unbeaten 487 which remains a sixth-wicket record to this day. Kemp-Welch did his best to pull it back, scoring 105 in the Tennyson XI's reply, but to no avail and the game was lost by an innings. In the second match Kemp-Welch made 186, his highest ever first-class score, but once again the match was lost. Jamaica won all three matches.

He also turned out for the MCC and H.D.G. Leveson-Gower's XI, and made his final first-class match for the Free Foresters against Cambridge played at F.P. Fenner's between 13 and 16 June 1936. Cambridge won the toss and decided to bat making 228 all out. The Free Foresters made 335, Kemp-Welch making 20 before being bowled by Duncan Carmichael (who took six wickets during the innings). Cambridge made 132 in their second innings but due to bad weather the match was drawn.

During his first-class career Kemp Welch made 4,170 runs, his highest score being 186. His best county score was against Glamorgan in 1934: captaining Warwickshire he made an unbeaten 123. He made six centuries and took fifty catches, and bowled 1,716 balls taking 41 wickets, his best figures being 4/41.

On 24 February 1934 he married Mrs Diana Munro at the Kensington Registry Office. The wedding, considering it was a high society event, was hardly recorded, which is unusual. There were several reasons for this: the bride was the daughter of Stanley Baldwin, she was twelve years older than Kemp-Welch, and she was a divorcee. Although the couple were married for ten years they had no children and due to George's untimely death Diana outlived her husband by thirty-eight years. In 1932 he was appointed to the 'West End board' of the Scottish Union and National Insurance Company before, in 1936, taking a seat on the board of Schweppes, the family business.

During the war Kemp-Welch served with the Grenadier Guards becoming a captain. Like Harold Dods, he was killed on 18 June 1944 when the Guards Chapel was hit by a V1 flying bomb.

He is buried in the south-east corner of the churchyard of St Peter's, Astley, Worcestershire, 2nd extension. Worth a visit while your passing and a few flowers.

Batting and fielding averages

	Mat	Inns	NO	Runs	HS	Ave	100	Ct	St
First-class	114	182	14	4170	186	24.82	6	50	0

Bowling averages

	Mat	Runs	Wkts	BBI	Ave	5w	10
First-class	114	1716	41	4/41	41.85	0	0

14548443 Private John William Lee
Middlesex, Somerset, Players
243 first-class matches
208 Corps Pioneer Corps
20 June 1944, aged 42
Right-hand bat/Leg break

Landed on D-Day only to die in a tragic accident

John (Jack) Lee was born on 1 February 1902 in Marylebone.

He made 243 first-class appearances, 230 in the county championships between 1923 and 1936, mostly for Somerset but once for Middlesex.

He made his debut for Middlesex against Somerset on 27-29 June 1923 at the County Ground, Taunton. Middlesex won by eight wickets, Lee failing to score or take a wicket, though his brother the test cricketer Henry Lee, opening for Middlesex, made 16.

Unable to keep his place in the Middlesex team he moved to Somerset and began playing for the first team in 1925. He made his debut for them against Cambridge University at the Recreation Ground, Bath, between 24 and 26 June 1925. Somerset made a total of 437 runs but still lost the match by 112. Lee again made no runs but took the wicket of Noel Sherwell caught Peter Johnson for 41.

His debut against Cambridge was a university match and his only first-class match for another two seasons. This was because he hadn't been born in Somerset, nor did he have the residential qualifications to play in county matches. To keep his hand in he began to play club cricket for Lansdown Cricket Club, Bath. Interestingly, two years after Jack moved to Somerset, his brother Frank, who went on to make 331 first-class appearances, joined him at the club and also had to wait two years before he could play county cricket for them.

Jack made his first county appearance for Somerset at Old Trafford against Lancashire on 11 and 12 May 1927. Somerset won the toss and decided to bat. Opening for Somerset Jack made 22 before being bowled by the test cricketer Richard Tyldesley (*Wisden* cricketer of the year 1925). Somerset were all out for a rather poor 92. During Lancashire's first innings Lee bowled nine overs for 39 taking one wicket, Frank Watson caught by Willaim Greswell for zero. During his second innings Lee made four before being bowled by Edgar McDonald, Somerset making 148 all out, Lancashire taking the honours by 125 runs.

During his first season with Somerset, Lee made 759 runs averaging 17.25, his highest score being 65. He also took 41 wickets including five for 23 against Warwickshire when *Wisden* said of him, 'he bowled an excellent length and with some variety of pace made the ball turn quickly.' They continued that he had made 'an encouraging start...' and 'may develop into a thoroughly good all-round player'.

He made his final first-class appearance on 19 August 1936 for Somerset against Essex at the County Ground, Taunton. Somerset won the toss and decided to bat. Lee made 57, the highest score of the innings, before being caught by the England test cricketer Thomas Peter Smith off the bowling of Lawrence Eastman. Somerset made 132. Lee bowled 12 overs for 50 during Essex's first innings and failed to take a wicket. Essex made 378. In his second innings Lee made 19 before being bowled by the English test cricketer Thomas Peter (TP) Smith. Somerset went on to make 180. Essex won by an innings and 66 runs.

He also played in university matches and made one appearance for the Players against the Gentlemen at the Oval in July 1934.

He made a total of 418 first-class innings, scored 7,856 runs with a high score of 193 not out against Worcestershire, made six centuries, thirty-six fifties, bowled 38,174 balls and took 495 wickets for 14,723 runs, his best figures being 7 for 45. He also made 122 catches.

At some point during his busy career he found time to meet and marry Agnes, of Highgate.

During the war Jack enlisted, becoming a private in the Pioneer Corps. On 20 June 1944, two weeks after D-Day, he was killed in an accident near Bazenville while serving with 208 company. He is buried in Ryes War Cemetery, Bazenville, grave reference V.C.3.

Batting and fielding averages

	Mat	Inns	NO	Runs	HS	Ave	100	50	Ct	St
First-class	243	418	44	7856	193*	21.00	6	36	122	0

Bowling averages

	Mat	Balls	Runs	Wkts	BBI	Ave	Econ	SR	5w	10
First-class	243	38174	14723	495	7/45	29.74	2.31	77.1	19	2

Major Charles William Christopher Packe
Leicestershire, Army
Twenty-six first-class matches
Royal Fusiliers (City of London Regiment), attached 1st
Battalion Suffolk Regiment
Died 1 July 1944, aged 35
Right-handed bat/Right arm medium

Only with his company a week

Charles Packe was born on 2 May 1909 in Pietermaritzburg. He was the son of Lieutenant Colonel Edmund Christopher Packe of the Royal Fusiliers, and Olivia, of Leicester. Returning to England from South Africa the family, which could trace its ancestors back to William the Conqueror, settled at Great Glen Hall in Leicestershire. Charles was educated at Eton where he was in the XI, later also playing for the Eton Ramblers. Deciding on a career in the army he was commissioned into the Royal Fusiliers (City of London) Regiment. He turned out for his regiment, for Colchester Garrison and the Army.

He made twenty-six first-class appearances, twenty-one for Leicestershire and five for the Army. He made his debut for Leicestershire against Essex between 24 and 27 August 1929 at South Church Park, Southend-on-Sea. Leicestershire won the toss and decided to bat making 268, Packe scoring two before being caught and bowled by the test cricketer Jack O'Connor. Essex were then all out for 163. In his second innings Packe made 14 before being stumped by Frank Gilligan again off the bowling of O'Connor, Leicestershire going on to knock up 190 before declaring. However Essex batted in and, largely thanks to an impressive 110 by O'Connor, managed to force a draw.

It took Packe two years to be selected for the first XI again, playing for Leicestershire against various counties from May 1932.

He made his debut for the Army against the South Americans (South America's tour of the British Isles which took place in May-July 1932) at the Officers' Service Ground, Aldershot, between 22 and 24 June 1932. The South Americans won the toss and decided to bat. They made an impressive 303 with Robert Stuart making 133 before being stumped by Arthur Tyler off the bowling of John Walford. Pack could only make eight in his first innings before being bowled by Cyril Ayling. The Army went on to make 208. In their second innings the South Americans made 100. During his second innings Packe made 15 before being bowled by Clement Gibson, the Army taking the honours by five wickets.

By playing for the Army and missing the Leicestershire-Nottinghamshire match he missed Leicestershire's worst defeat of the season at Trent Bridge. Larwood and Voce cut through the Leicestershire batsmen, bowling them all out twice in 160 minutes, Nottinghamshire winning by an innings and 111 runs.

Packe made his final first-class game for the Army against Cambridge University at F.P. Fenner's on 7-9 June 1939. Cambridge won the toss and decided to bat making 411. Packe bowled John Blake caught Basil Hayes for 68, then Arthur Brodhurst caught Archibald Southby for 11, and Patrick Dickinson caught off the bowling of Dunlop Manners for 40. Packe, clearly in good form, made an impressive 145 in 170 minutes with 20 fours and passing his thousand runs when he reached 132. The Army made 537. During Cambridge's second innings, Packe caught John Blake off the bowling of Peter Nelson for 46, Cambridge making 149. The match was eventually drawn.

It is worth noting that during their previous meeting in May 1938 Packe made his highest ever first-class score of 176. He did this in 135 minutes, hitting 29 fours before being caught by David Wilson off the bowling of Arthur Brodhurst. His century came in 75 minutes and was the fastest of the season until beaten by Don Bradman by two minutes three weeks later.

During his first-class career Packe made 1,013 runs, only 451 of these being in county matches at an average of 18.79. He made two centuries, five half centuries, and seventeen catches. He bowled 126 balls taking three wickets for 75 runs, his best figures being 2/33. He captained Leicestershire for part of 1932.

His brother Michael (1916-78) also made forty-one first-class appearances, for Leicestershire and Cambridge University. Another brother, Robert, also made three first-class appearances, all for Leicestershire.

Charles also made seven appearances for Leicestershire in the minor counties between 1927 and 1929, and turned out for the Free Foresters and Eton Ramblers.

Attending the Royal Military College Sandhurst as a gentlemen cadet, he was commissioned into the Royal Fusiliers (City of London Regiment) as a second lieutenant. For all but the last few weeks of his career and life he was to remain with the regiment. He was promoted to lieutenant in 1937 before being posted to Northern Command as a physical training instructor. Promoted to major he was posted to the Suffolks as second in command and was killed with them in Normandy on 1 July 1944.

The *History of the Suffolk Regiment 1928-1946* explains his death in more detail:

> The Occupation of Chateau de la Londe. For eleven days the Battalion remained under shellfire while occupying the area in and around the Chateau. It was a tense period with little rest for anybody. The enemy still occupied Lebisey to the east and were only a few hundred yards away at La Bijude and Epron to the [north] and south. There was active patrolling and continuing shelling from guns and multi-barrelled mortars with losses almost daily. One of these was Major Packe, Royal Fusiliers, the newly arrived second-in-command who was killed on 1 July from a concentration of shellfire while talking to the Adjutant and Signal Officer; he had been only a week with Battalion.

He had married Margaret Lane Fox, the youngest daughter of Lord Bingley. She gave birth to their daughter two weeks after his death.

Packe is buried in Hermanville War Cemetery, grave reference 5. E. 4.

Batting and fielding averages

	Mat	Inns	NO	Runs	HS	Ave	100	50	Ct	St
First-class	26	41	0	1013	176	24.70	2	5	17	0

Bowling averages

	Mat	Balls	Runs	Wkts	BBI	Ave	Econ	SR	5w	10
First-class	26	126	75	3	2/33	25.00	3.57	42.0	0	0

Lieut Colonel Leslie Frank Hancock OBE
Marylebone Cricket Club
Two first-class matches
Royal Engineers
Died 12 July 1944, aged 45
Right-handed bat/Medium fast

'Married a famous Hollywood actress'

Leslie Hancock was born on 25 October 1899 in Jamnagar, Gujarat, the son of Major F. de B. and Kathleen Hancock. He was educated at Cheltenham College where he was in the cricket XI.

Deciding on a career in the army he was sent to the Royal Military Academy Woolwich, turning out for the XI there (1918-21). He also played for the Royal Military College Sandhurst (1920). Joining the Royal Engineers in 1922 he remained with them for the rest of his service, rising to the rank of lieutenant colonel.

A first-rate engineer he served all over the world, including a time spent building roads in Sierra Leone. His private life was no less interesting. He married the famous actress Ellen Pollock (1902-97) who was in *Moulin Rouge* in 1928, *The Wicked Lady* in 1983 and many films in between. She was also a magnificent theatre actress and the subject of an episode of 'This is your Life' in 1992.

Hancock made two first-class appearances, both for the MCC, the first on 2-4 June 1926 at Lord's against Wales. Wales won the toss and decided to bat making 179. Hancock caught John Bell off the bowling of John Hearne for 41. He then bowled Cyril Rowland caught by Walter Franklin for one. Batting in the middle order he scored 23 before being caught by John Clay off the bowling of John Mercer. The MCC made 114 before the weather closed in and the match was drawn.

He made his second appearance against Cambridge University, again at Lord's. The MCC won the toss and decided to bat making 386. Hancock, playing lower down the order, made only one before being bowled lbw by Leonard Irvine. During Cambridge's first innings Hancock caught Edward Dawson (later an England test cricketer) off the bowling of Frederick Durston (another England test player) for 13. Cambridge only made 113 and followed on. In their second innings Hancock caught Kumas Shri Duleepsinhji (an English test player and cricketer of the year 1930) off the bowling of Eric Kidd for eight. Hancock didn't bat in the second innings, the MCC making 93 and wining the match by six wickets.

Lieutenant Colonel Hancock served throughout the war until he was killed serving with the Royal Engineers on the 12 July 1944 when the Jeep in which he was a passenger reversed over a land mine. On 1 January 1945, six months after he was killed, he was awarded the OBE for his services during the war.

He is buried in the Bayeux War Cemetery, grave reference II.G.26. He is also commemorated on the Trefoil Guild Garden Memorial at the National Memorial Arboretum, Alrewas, Staffordshire.

Curiously, his birth was registered as Frank Leslie Hancock.

Batting and fielding averages

	Mat	Inns	NO	Runs	HS	Ave	100	50	Ct	St
First-class	2	2	0	24	23	12.00	0	0	3	0

Bowling averages

	Mat	Balls	Runs	Wkts	BBI	Ave	Econ	SR	5w	10
First-class	2	54	24	1	1/4	24.00	2.66	54.0	0	0

**Lieutenant Colonel Donald William Garnham Ray
MCC
One first-class appearance
17th Battalion Royal Fusiliers (City of London Regiment)
Commanding 7th Battalion Hampshire Regiment
Died 12 July 1944, aged 41
Wicketkeeper**

*Commanded the 7th Battalion, The Hampshire Regiment
when he was killed just after D-Day*

Donald Ray was born on 2 July 1903 in Stoneleigh House, Wimborne, Dorset. Son of Walter John Orbell and Marie Estelle Ray, he attended Wellington College and while there represented the first XI, playing as wicketkeeper against Westminster, Haileybury, Charterhouse, Marlborough and Bradfield. On leaving school in 1921 and deciding on a career in the army he went up to Sandhurst where he played in the XI, captaining the side.

Ray made one first-class appearance, for the MCC against the Army on 15 August 1931 at Lord's. He played as wicketkeeper. The MCC won the toss and elected to bat making 140. Ray made zero before being clean bowled by John Walford. Walford took six wickets for 31 off 19 overs. In reply the Army made 142. Ray caught John Richard Cole off the bowling of Reginald John Covill for a duck. He also stumped Arnold Minnis off the bowling of James Alfred Powell also for a duck. Covill took five wickets for 31 off 24 overs. Powell also took five wickets for 42 off 20 overs. In their second innings the MCC made 97. Ray made two before being bowled by John Stephenson (later DSO). Minnis took seven wickets for 48 off 17 overs. In their second innings the Army made 99 for six. Ray stumped James Henry Thrale Mardall off the bowling of Powell for one. The Army won the match by four wickets.

He played two non-first-class matches for the MCC, against the Devon Club and Ground and Cornwall. He also played for the Free Foresters, the Royal Fusiliers and I Zingari.

Ray took a commission into the Royal Fusiliers. He served in India before becoming adjutant to the Ceylon Planters' Rifles. He married Marcy Marcella of Wimborne.

In 1940 he went over to France with the BEF and after seeing heavy fighting was evacuated from the Dunkirk beaches. He was later promoted to lieutenant colonel and took command of the 7th Battalion, The Hampshire Regiment. He landed with them on D-Day and was mentioned in dispatches for his work that day and in the advance that followed. He was wounded near Caen. Evacuated back to England he died on the hospital ship shortly before it docked in Southampton on 12 July 1944.

He is buried in Wimborne Minster Cemetery, 17. A. 11, grave 7377.

His brother Major Philip Orbell Clement Ray of the Worcestershire Regiment was killed in action in March 1941 serving in the Middle East. He was last seen firing a Bren gun that he picked up from a man who fell in front of him.

Batting and fielding averages

	Mat	Inns	NO	Runs	HS	Ave	100	50	4s	6s	Ct	St
First-class	1	2	0	2	2	1.00	0	0	0	0	1	2

Bowling averages

	Mat	Balls	Runs	Wkts	BBI	BBM	Ave	Econ	SR	4w	5w	10
First-class	1	-	-	-	-	-	-	-	-	-	-	-

Major Maurice Joseph Lawson Turnbull
England, Cambridge University, Glamorgan, Wales
Nine tests for England, 388 first-class matches
First Battalion Welsh Guards
Died 5 August 1944, aged 38
Right-handed bat/Right arm off break

'The finest most loyal player Glamorgan ever produced'

Maurice Turnbull was born on 16 March 1906 in Cardiff, the son of Philip Bernard (1879-1930), ship owner, and Annie Marie Hennessy Oates Turnbull (1879-1942). He was destined to have a sporting career. His father was a Welsh international hockey player taking a bronze medal at the 1908 Olympic Games and six of his eight sons played for Cardiff Rugby club.

Turnbull was educated at Downside (the sixth form bar is still named after him) where he played cricket for the first XI and rugby for the first XV. At Trinity Cambridge he got his blue for hockey and rugby and played cricket both for his college and the university.

Turnbull made his debut first-class appearance for Glamorgan (the side he was most associated with) against Lancashire in a county championship match between 13 and 15 August 1924 at St Helens Swansea and while still a pupil at Downside School. Glamorgan won the toss and decided to bat making 153 all out. Turnbull was Glamorgan's highest scorer, making 40 in the first innings before being lbw to the test player Richard Tyldesley. In the second innings Turnbull made 16 before being lbw to another test cricketer Cecil Parkin. Glamorgan won the match by 38 runs.

Turnbull continued playing for Glamorgan until 1939, being captain between 1930 and 1939, and club secretary. He played a major part in turning the fortunes of the club. He scored over a thousand runs in a season on ten occasions and made three double centuries. His highest score was 233 against Worcestershire at Swansea in 1937. However, for me personally it was the 205 he made against Nottinghamshire at the Cardiff Arms Park between 24 and 26 August 1932 that stands out, as he was batting against two of England's greatest and most dangerous bowlers, Larwood and Voce, names made famous through the bodyline series in Australia. In the end and almost inevitably he was caught by Voce off the bowling of Larwood. The match was drawn.

Turnbull was undoubtedly one of Glamorgan's most inspirational captains, almost single-handedly turning Glamorgan into a profit-making club. Besides setting numerous club records he was also their first ever test cricketer. In 1934 on Turnbull's initiative Glamorgan and Monmouthshire cricket clubs amalgamated, extending the club's catchment area and bringing in much fresh talent. He was also an English selector in 1938 and 1939.

He played for Cambridge between 1923 and 1929 while continuing to play for Glamorgan during the university summer breaks. He played his first game against Middlesex at F.P. Fenner's between 1 and 4 May 1926. He was bowled by Ernest North for one in his first innings, Cambridge going on to make a very poor 89 all out. Middlesex made 223 and the match was drawn.

Turnbull did little better in his second university match against the Australians played again at F.P. Fenner's between 19 and 21 May 1926. He was caught by John Ellis off the bowling of John Ryder for a duck in the first innings, Cambridge going on to make 212. Australia made 235 in their first innings. In the second innings Turnbull improved making 21 before being bowled by Clarence Grimmett for 21. Cambridge making 81. The match was eventually drawn.

Things did improve however. He scored his maiden first-class century, an unbeaten 106, against Worcestershire at the Cardiff Arms Park. He captained the university in 1929 and scored over 1,000 runs for them.

He went on the MCC tour of Australia and New Zealand in 1929/30 turning out for the MCC on seven occasions including the first test against New Zealand when Turnbull made seven in his only innings, England winning by eight wickets.

He went on to play in a further eight test matches against South Africa during the MCC 1930/31 tour.

In 1933 an unbeaten 200 against Northamptonshire led to his recall to the England side for the tests against the West Indies at Lord's and the Oval. His finally test appearance came against India at Lord's in 1936.

He co-authored two books, *The book of the two Maurices* (1930) and *The two Maurices again* (1931), light hearted reminisces about the tours against New Zealand and South Africa with his friend the Surrey and England player Maurice Allom, famous for being one of only three players to have taken a hat-trick on his test debut.

Turnbull made his final first-class appearance against Leicestershire at Aylestone Road, Leicester, between 26 and 29 August 1939. Clearly wanting to go out with a bang he made 156 before being caught by George Leslie Berry off the bowling of James Sperry. He was zero not out in his second innings. The match was drawn. It was a fitting end to a remarkable test and first-class career.

During his career he played in nine tests making 224 runs, made no fewer than 388 first-class appearances scoring 17,544 runs including 29 centuries and 82 half centuries, and in 1931 was *Wisden* cricketer of the year.

On the 7 September 1939 Turnbull married Elizabeth Brooke of Scunthorpe. They had three children: Sara, Simon and Georgina.

Like so many people who play sports to a high level Turnbull excelled at other sports too. He played hockey for both his university and Wales, rackets for his university, and squash for Wales being a founder member of the Cardiff Squash Rackets Club. He also won the squash rackets championship of South Wales. As if this wasn't enough he was a fine rugby player turning out for St Peters, Cardiff, Glamorgan, Cambridge University, the London Welsh and Somerset. He was selected to play for Wales twice, both during the Home Nations championship (his elder brother Bernard

had already represented Wales). He made his debut against England at Twickenham on 21 January 1933, being one of seven fresh caps brought into the Welsh side. Wales won the game 3-7 breaking the so-called 'Twickenham Bogey' (ten losses in ten visits). He was unable to play against Scotland due to an injury but was selected once again to play against Ireland in Belfast. Wales went down 10-5. It was Turnbull's last game for Wales.

During the war Turnbull was commissioned into the Welsh Guards rising to the rank of major. He was killed while commanding No. 2 Company 1st Battalion by a sniper's bullet on 5 August 1944 during the fighting for the French village of Montchamp. His body was lost for a while but later found thanks to the efforts of Sergeant Frederick Llewellyn who searched the battlefield at no small risk to himself.

Turnbull is buried in Bayeux War Cemetery, grave reference XX. C. 3. Well worth a visit and a few flowers.

Batting and fielding averages

	Mat	Inns	NO	Runs	HS	Ave	100	50	6s	Ct	St
Tests	9	13	2	224	61	20.36	0	1	2	1	0
First-class	388	626	37	17544	233	29.78	29	82		280	0

Bowling averages

	Mat	Inns	Balls	Runs	Wkts	BBI	BBM	Ave	Econ	SR	4w	5w	10
Tests	9	-	-	-	-	-	-	-	-	-	-	-	-
First-class	388		390	355	4	1/4		88.75	5.46	97.5		0	0

Edward Leslie Gibson
Rangoon Gymkhana
One first-class appearance
Civilian
Died 11 August 1944, aged 45
Right-handed bat

Murdered by the Japanese

Edward Gibson was born on 8 August 1899 in India. One of three children (Humphrey, and Marjorie d.1915) born to Edward Marriott Gibson who was Chief Engineer and Outside Manager to the Schlüsselburg Calico Printing Company in Russia. His mother was Margaret Favre (née MacCallum). Edward was sent back to England to, be like his father, educated at Winchester.

In 1915 Gibson's father committed suicide, almost certainly because of the death of his daughter. The family left Russia and moved to their home in Lausanne.

Edward left Winchester, continuing his education at the Lausanne École de Commerce (1916-19) where he received a diploma. By 1921 he had become a chartered accountant and obtained a post with the Bombay Burma Trading Corporation before moving to Rangoon.

Gibson made one first-class appearance, for the Rangoon Gymkhana against the MCC in India and Ceylon on 9 January 1927 at the Gymkhana Ground, Rangoon. The MCC won the toss and decided to bat making 381 for six declared. Gibson bowled three overs taking no wickets for 11, Jack Parsons making 160. In reply Rangoon made 173. Gibson made one before being bowled by John Mercer (*Wisden* cricketer of the year 1927). Mercer took six wickets for 39 of 21 overs. Forced to follow on, Rangoon Gymkhana made 211 for five. Gibson failed to bat. The match was drawn.

On 17 December 1927 Gibson married Charlotte Noreen Fuller-Good and they had two sons, Patrick and Jonathon. He took up a position in Thailand, travelling there with his wife. On the outbreak of the war, Bangkok fell to the rapid Japanese advance and British businesses were shut down within a few days. Gibson, together with his wife and son Jonathon, were interned. The camp, which contained around 500 men, women and children, stood on the playing fields behind Thammasat University. One inmate, Sir James Holt later wrote, 'life was not too harsh at first, since the Thais helped to pass food into the camp to supplement the inadequate rations supplied by the Japanese. Inmates had access to books, and many learned Thai or other languages to stave off boredom.'

Another inmate wrote about the air raids that had begun on 8 January 1942: 'as the alarm sounded some idiots in one of the camp buildings started to smoke, and after a warning, were shot at by the guards... Next day we discovered that the raid had hit Assumption College, a clinic at the end of Silom Road, and a row of shops on Jawarat Road. There were many Chinese casualties.'

On 11 August 1944, after surviving for two and a half years, Gibson was murdered by his captors. I have not been able to discover the reason, or what happened to his family. He was later buried in the Jewish Cemetery, Charoen Krung 72/5 Bangkok.

Batting and fielding averages

	Mat	Inns	NO	Runs	HS	Ave	100	50	4s	6s	Ct	St
First-class	1	1	0	1	1	1.00	0	0	0	0	0	0

Bowling averages

	Mat	Balls	Runs	Wkts	BBI	BBM	Ave	Econ	SR	4w	5w	10
First-class	1	-	-	-	-	-	-	-	-	-	-	-

Wing Commander (pilot) Michael Trentham Maw DFC
Cambridge University
Three first-class appearances
640 Squadron Royal Air Force
Died 13 August 1944, aged 32
Right-handed bat/Right arm medium

'The finest C/O we ever had'

Michael Maw was born on 29 September 1912 at Nutfield, Reigate, Surrey, the second son of Mowbray and Mary Maw. He was educated at Oundle (Crosby House) from 1926 where he played in the first XI. He also played football for the school and was head of house. He went up to Christ's College Cambridge in 1931 where he read engineering and in 1932 joined the Reserve of Air Force Officers as a trainee pilot.

While at Cambridge he made two first-class appearances for the university followed by representing H.D.G. Leveson-Gower's XI against Oxford. He made his debut for Cambridge on 27 May 1933 against Northamptonshire at F.P. Fenner's. Cambridge won the toss and elected to bat making 160. Maw, batting last, made zero before being caught by Arnold Cyril Payne off the bowling of the England Test cricketer Austin David George Matthews. In reply Northamptonshire made 166. Maw bowled six overs taking no wickets for 17. In their second innings Cambridge made 162. Batting last again Maw made three not out. Matthews took six wickets for 34 off 20 overs. In reply Northamptonshire made 158 for one. Northamptonshire won by nine wickets.

Maw made his second appearance against Nottinghamshire 23 May 1934, again at Fenner's ground. Cambridge won the toss and decided to bat making 245. Maw, batting last, made zero not out. Bill Voce took six wickets for 51 off 18 overs and Harold Larwood took three wickets for 68. In reply Nottingham made 223. Maw bowled 11 overs taking no wickets for 38 runs. In their second innings Cambridge made 219 for seven declared. Maw failed to bat. George Vernon Gunn took five wickets for 48 off 19 overs. In their second innings Nottinghamshire made 105 for two. Maw bowled seven overs taking one wicket for 15. The England test player William Walter Keeton (*Wisden* cricketer of the year 1940) caught Grahame Wilshaw Parker (who was also a rugby international) for 29. The match was eventually drawn.

Maw made his final first-class appearance for H.D.G. Leveson-Gower's XI against Oxford University on 4 July 1934 at Park Lane, Reigate. Oxford won the toss and decided to bat making 399, Derrick de Saram making 208. Maw bowled 15 overs taking one wicket for 45, that of Gerald Chalk (killed 17 February 1943) lbw for one. Arthur Baxter took five wickets for 105. In reply Gower's XI made 341. Maw made nine before being caught by Norman Knight off the bowling of John Anderson Darwall-Smith. In their second innings Oxford made 215. Maw bowled ten overs taking one wicket for 26, Knight for zero. In their second innings Gower's XI made 185. Maw made seven before being caught by Darwall-Smith off the bowling of Alexander Singleton. Singleton took six wickets for 44 off 19 overs. Oxford University won by 88 runs.

Maw also played in the Cambridge University Seniors' match on 28 April 1934 at F.P. Fenner's playing for A.F. Skinner's against A.G. Pelham's. The match was drawn. He also played in the Cambridge University trial match, playing for the Etceteras against the Perambulators. The Perambulators won by an innings and 76 runs. He played for the RAF twice against Nottinghamshire and Sussex, Reigate Priory against South Africa, and the West Indies and Cambridge University Crusaders against Norfolk.

On leaving Cambridge he became a director in the family business of Messrs S. Maw & Sons Ltd, chemists. He was called up at the outbreak of the Second World War and instructed at the Central Flying School, Cranwell, and later at Calgary, Alberta. In 1943 he was posted to No. 10 Squadron RAF before taking command of 640 Squadron in 1944. He was posted missing from a raid near Frankfurt on 13 August 1944 while flying a Halifax III. It was later established that he had been shot down.

He is buried in Reichswald Forest War Cemetery, collective grave 22. D. 4-8. He left a widow Joan Eleanor, of Harpenden, Hertfordshire.

Batting and fielding averages

	Mat	Inns	NO	Runs	HS	Ave	100	50	Ct	St
First-class	3	5	2	19	9	6.33	0	0	0	0

Bowling averages

	Mat	Balls	Runs	Wkts	BBI	Ave	Econ	SR	5w	10
First-class	3	294	141	3	1/15	47.00	2.87	98.0	0	0

NZ42537 Flight Sergeant (Air Gunner) Henry George Walters
Auckland
One first-class match
180 Squadron RAF
Died 25 August 1944, aged 26
Left-handed bat

'Suaviter in modo fortiter in re'
(Gentle in manner, resolute in deed)

Henry Walters was born on 6 November 1917 in Auckland, the son of William Albert and Olive May Elizabeth Walters. On leaving school he took up employment in the newsroom of the *New Zealand Herald*.

A fine cricketer he played for the North Shore Cricket Club and made one first-class appearance playing for Auckland against Wellington at Eden Park between 6 and 9 February 1942. Auckland won the toss and decided to bat. Walters did well. Opening for Auckland he made 81 before being bowled by Frederick Andrews. Auckland scored 469. Wellington made 307 runs in their first innings, following on and scoring a further 286. During Auckland's second innings Walters scored a further 39 runs before being stumped by Francis Mooney off the bowling of Alec Riddolls. Auckland scored a further 124 runs, taking the match by eight wickets. Walters was also a talented football player.

During the war Walters joined the RAF training with 34 OUT in New Brunswick Canada before joining 180 Squadron as an air gunner and being promoted to flight sergeant. 180 squadron was a medium bomber unit flying Mitchell IIs at the time and formed part of number two group, Second Tactical Air Force. On 25 August 1944, while flying with his crew en route to bomb the oil and lubricant dump at Clermont, his Mitchell II (HD316) crashed into the sea as a result of engine failure twelve miles off Beachy Head. Three other New Zealanders were also killed.

Walters is commemorated on the Takapuna War Memorial, the Takapuna Grammar School War Memorial, and on the Runnymede Memorial in Surrey, panel 264.

Batting and fielding averages

	Mat	Inns	NO	Runs	HS	Ave	100	50	Ct	St
First-class	1	2	0	120	81	60.00	0	1	0	0

Bowling averages

	Mat	Balls	Runs	Wkts	BBI	BBM	Ave	Econ	SR	4w	5w	10
First-class	1	-	-	-	-	-	-	-	-	-	-	-

**1548829 Warrant Officer Class II Battery Sergeant Major
James Grimshaw
Cambridge University, Kent, MCC
Twenty-nine first-class matches
Honourable Artillery Company, 275 Battery
Died 26 September 1944, aged 32
Right-hand bat/Slow left arm orthodox.**

Killed fighting his way through Europe

James Grimshaw was born on 17 February 1912 in Darlington, the son of Dr. W.E. Grimshaw OBE. He was educated at King William School on the Isle of Man before going up to Emmanuel College Cambridge.

He made twenty-nine first-class appearances, twenty-four for Cambridge University, two for Kent and two for the MCC, his debut being for Cambridge against Yorkshire at F.P. Fenner's on 11-13 May 1932. Cambridge won the toss and decided to bat. Grimshaw batting last made zero before being bowled by Arthur Rhodes (who took six wickets during the innings) Cambridge only managing a total of 68. Yorkshire scored 195 with Grimshaw bowling five overs for 14 and taking no wickets. The weather closed in and the match was drawn.

He next played for Cambridge on 9 May 1934 against Australia at Fenner's, when he took his first two first-class wickets, those of Stan McCabe caught by John Human for 15, and Bill Brown caught by Hugh Bartlett for 105. He also made his first first-class runs scoring five not out. Australia managed a mighty 481 in their first innings winning the match by an innings and 163 runs.

Grimshaw played in various matches before his return match against Yorkshire on 15-17 May 1935, once again at Fenner's. Grimshaw managed eight not out in the first innings and seven in the second, being lbw off the bowling of Thomas Smailes. However he took five Yorkshire wickets, including Len Hutton caught Jahangir Khan for 44, Arthur Sellers caught Grahame Parker for 50, test cricketer Arthur Mitchell caught Frank King for 66, Smailes who also played for England (1946 test) caught John Cameron for one, and finally Ellis Robinson for 12. Yorkshire still took the honours by seven runs but the improvement in James Grimshaw was clear for all to see.

He made two first-class appearances for Kent, firstly against Northamptonshire played at the County Ground, Northampton between 18 and 20 July 1934. Northamptonshire won the toss and decided to bat, making 154. Grimshaw took three wickets off 23 overs for 29, John Timms caught William Levett for 26, Arthur Cox caught Levett for four, and Harry Lamb stumped Levett for 17. Grimshaw didn't bat during Kent's first innings as they scored 426 with the England test cricketers Frank Woolley and Arthur Fagg making 176 and 99. Grimshaw failed to take a wicket during Northamptonshire's second innings but did catch Harry Lamb off the bowling of Alfred Freeman for seven. Despite Northamptonshire making 210 Kent took the match by an innings and 62 runs.

His second match for Kent was against Yorkshire played at Mote Park, Maidstone, between 21 and 24 July 1934. Kent won the toss and decided to bat making 142. This time

Grimshaw made 17 before being caught by Arthur Wood off the bowling of Thomas Smailes. In Yorkshire's first innings Grimshaw bowled 13 overs for 31 but only managed one wicket, Cyril Turner caught by Alfred Freeman for 46. In his second innings Grimshaw made 13 before being bowled by Smailes for 13. Yorkshire took the match by eight wickets.

Grimshaw made his final first-class appearance for the MCC against Kent played between 29 August and 1 September at the Cheriton Road Sports Ground, Folkstone. The MCC won the toss and elected to bat, making 96. Grimshaw scored zero being bowled by Alfred Freeman. Kent made 342 during their first innings, Grimshaw failing to take a wicket. During MCC's second innings Grimshaw was caught by William Levett off the bowling of Alan Watt once again for a duck. In Kent's second innings Grimshaw bowled two overs for 23 runs and failed to take a wicket, Kent taking the game by five wickets.

Grimshaw also made thirteen second XI appearances for Kent in the minor counties championships and turned out for the Young Professionals, Kent Young Amateurs, The Perambulators Cambridge University Trial Match, Blackheath and A.G. Pelham's XI. During his first-class career Grimshaw made 355 runs, his highest score being 40, and made 20 catches. He also took 65 wickets bowling 5,176 balls, his best figures being five for 92.

On leaving Cambridge he went into the city and became a stockbroker. In 1943 he married Florence Emily Attrill of Grove Place, South Street, Yarmouth, and they had one child.

During the war he joined the Honourable Artillery Company becoming attached to 274 (the Blue Battery) and rising to the rank of battery sergeant major WO class II.

During March 1939 the HAC formed an anti-aircraft regiment to defend London during the Blitz. This became the 86th (HAC) Heavy Anti-Aircraft Regiment RA, formed with three batteries, 273, 274 and 275. They landed in France on D-Day, 6 June 1944. The batteries fought through to Belgium and on into Germany. Over 700 men serving with HAC units and Company members serving with other units lost their lives in the war, Grimshaw was one, being killed at Nijmegen on 26 September 1944. He was buried in Jonkerbos War Cemetery, grave reference 15. B. 6.

Batting and fielding averages

	Mat	Inns	NO	Runs	HS	Ave	100	50	Ct	St
First-class	29	40	14	355	40	13.65	0	0	19	0

Bowling averages

	Mat	Balls	Runs	Wkts	BBI	Ave	Econ	SR	5w	10
First-class	29	5176	1760	65	5/92	27.07	2.04	79.6	1	0

Major William (Bill) Nicol Carson MC
Auckland
Thirty-one first-class matches
5 Field Regiment New Zealand Artillery
Died 8 October 1944, aged 28
Left-handed bat/Left arm fast medium

Set a world record for a third wicket partnership

Bill Carson was born on 16 July 1916 at Gisborne, New Zealand. He was the son of John Carson, Gisborne harbour master, and Mable Alice (née Scoullar). He was educated at the Gisborne Boys' High School 1929-33. A fine all round sportsman he was in the school's first XI and first XV.

Carson was an aggressive left-handed batsman and useful fast-medium bowler. He made thirty-one first-class appearances, nine for Auckland and twenty-two for New Zealand. He made his debut for Auckland against Canterbury in the Plunket Shield between the 25 and 29 December 1936 at Lancaster Park. Canterbury won the toss and elected to bat making 280. Carson bowled three overs and took no wickets for 13. He did however take two catches, Charles Joshua Oliver off the bowling of Henry Vivian for 35, and Ian Burns Comb again off the bowling of Vivian for two. During Auckland's first innings Carson made 12 before being caught by Charles Jackman off the bowling of Albert Roberts. Carson didn't bowl during Canterbury's second innings but did manage to catch Walter Hadlee off the bowling of Leicester Spring for 17. Canterbury managed a further 164. The match was eventually drawn.

His second first-class match was against Otago again in the Plunket Shield and played at the Carisbrook, Dunedin, between 31 December 1936 and 4 January 1937. Carson made a remarkable 290 batting with Paul Whitelaw who made 195, putting on 445 between them, a world record for a third wicket stand. Auckland won by an innings and 175 runs.

In his next match against Wellington again in the Plunket Shield played at Eden Park between 5 and 9 February 1937 Carson scored another impressive 194. This gave him an aggregate of 496 runs and an average of 165.33 after only three innings.

Carson went on to play for Auckland against Otago and Wellington (on several occasions).

His impressive performances earned him a New Zealand call-up and he was selected to play in their tour of Great Britain in 1937. He made his debut against Surrey between 8 and 11 May 1937 at the Oval during New Zealand's tour of the British Isles. Surrey won the toss and decided to bat making 149. In New Zealand's first innings Carson was their top scorer with 85 before being caught by Robert Gregory off the bowling of the test cricketer Alfred Grover, New Zealand making 233. The match was eventually drawn. After more matches in Great Britain the team returned home playing against New South Wales in Sydney on their way.

Carson made his final first-class appearance for Auckland in the Plunket Shield against Canterbury between the 5 and 9 January 1940 at Eden Park. Canterbury won the toss and decided to bat, making 227. Carson bowled five overs for 14 runs and took no wickets. In

Auckland's first innings Carson made 26 before being caught by Albert Roberts off the bowling of Ian Cromb. Auckland made 693 runs with Walter Wallace making 211 and Verdun Scott 198. During Canterbury's second innings Carson took two wickets, Walter Hadlee caught by Gordon Weir for 23, and Cromb caught by John Blandford for 15. Canterbury made 326. Auckland won by an innings and 140 runs.

Carson was also a first-class rugby player, playing for the Ponsonby Club in Auckland. During the 1936-39 seasons he made eighteen representative appearances for the union and during the 1938-39 season played for North Island. In 1938 he was selected for the All Black tour of Australia but because of an injury played in only three minor matches and failed to play in any of the tests. By playing for the All Blacks Carson became one of an elite group of seven New Zealanders to be seen as a double All Black in both rugby and cricket.

On 13 August 1940 Carson married Marie Patricia Jeffries at St Luke's Church in Auckland. The couple had no children.

Commissioned as a second lieutenant Carson served first with the 6th Field Regiment of the New Zealand Artillery, serving in Crete where he was injured in the famous charge to retake Galatos before joining his unit in North Africa. At Sidi Rezegh his battery distinguished itself by holding off a dozen German tanks for two days. Because of its efficiency his battery was often chosen for special duties. During one of these his troop was ordered to support the 1st King's Dragoon Guards, who at the time was were doing important reconnaissance for the New Zealand corps. Using armoured cars they were involved in pursuing the Desert Fox, Rommel, as he retreated across the desert. Carson received the MC for quickly positioning his guns to fire accurately against two well-equipped Italian battalions at the Battle of Mareth in June 1943. He was also later mentioned in despatches.

Leaving North Africa he was posted to Italy serving with the 5th Field Regiment and being promoted to acting major. On 29 July 1944 at San Michele, near Florence, Carson was being driven to a forward observation post to take up command of F Troop when a shell struck his scout car and he was seriously injured being wounded in his lungs, liver, thigh and ankle. The other two men in the car, Lieutenant Graves and Gunner I.H. Henry, were both killed.

Although seriously wounded he was a strong and resilient man and seemed to be making a full recovery. Preparations began to ship him home on board a hospital ship. Alas while waiting at Bari he contracted jaundice and, already in a weakened state, failed to respond to treatment. Carson finally succumbed while being evacuated to Egypt on 8 October 1944.

Carson is buried at Heliopolis military cemetery in Egypt, grave reference 4.A.16.

Major General H.K. Kippenberger, a friend and admirer of Carson's, said of him, 'How often other commanders had cause to be grateful for his skill and boldness and his sportsman's sense of anticipation I do not know, but there were many times.'

Carson's memory is honoured by several trophies named after him. The Auckland Cricket Association has a Carson Cup which is presented to a player or administrator for their contribution to the sport as a volunteer. The prestigious Roller Mills Shield rugby tournament for primary-school-age representative teams from unions in the upper half of the North Island also features a Carson Cup. It is awarded to the team displaying the best sportsmanship and behaviour on and off the field. Carson would have liked that.

Batting and fielding averages

	Mat	Inns	NO	Runs	HS	Ave	100	50	Ct	St
First-class	31	51	7	1535	290	34.88	4	3	27	0

Bowling averages

	Mat	Runs	Wkts	BBI	Ave	5w	10
First-class	31	752	35	4/20	21.48	0	0

Lieutenant Colonel John Henry Hamlyn Whitty DSO MC
Army
One first-class match
5th Battalion Queen's Own Royal West Kent Regiment
Died 23 October 1944, aged 34
Right-hand bat/Right arm (unknown style)

Described by Monty as the best field commander in the army

John Whitty was born on 4 February 1910 in New South Wales. He was the son of Hamlyn and Marguerite Louisa Whitty. Returning to England on 8 December 1922 he was educated at Clifton College, a school famous for its sporting and cricketing prowess, one of its pupils A.E.J. Collins making the highest score in cricket history, 628 not out. Being a member of the first XI he turned out for Bristol on three occasions against Rugby (won by five wickets), Cheltenham College (lost by 167 runs) and Tonbridge (lost by ten wickets).

In 1931 he took a commission in the regular army from the Supplementary Reserve joining the Queen's Own Royal West Kent Regiment. A fine all-round sportsman he played football, golf, rugby and cricket for the army. He played for his regiment on three occasions, against Band of Brothers in 1933 (losing by 110 runs), Band of Brothers again in 1934 (winning by 138 runs, Whitty taking all ten Band of Brothers wickets), and finally again in 1934 against The Mote (losing by 42 runs despite Whitty making his first half century). In 1942 he also represented Southern Command against Western Command. Playing alongside the England test player Lionel (Lord) Tennyson he scored 22. The match was drawn.

He made one first-class appearance for the Army against Cambridge University, played between 23 and 26 May 1936 at F.P. Fenner's. Cambridge won the toss and decided to bat. Whitty took two wickets, Alan White caught by Cyril Hamilton (who died serving with the RA as a major on 10 February 1941) for 21 and John Pawle caught by Francis Hugonin for three. He bowled 13 overs, Cambridge finally scoring 238. In his first innings Whitty was stumped by Billy Griffith off the bowling of John Cameron for one. The Army managed a total of 151. Whitty took two more wickets during Cambridge's second innings, Norman Yardley lbw for 18 and Hugh Bartlett for one. This time the Army kept Cambridge's score down to 109. In his second innings Whitty did much better scoring 22 before being lbw to a ball from John Cameron (later a test cricketer for the West Indies). The Army were finally all out for 191, Cambridge taking the game by a mere five runs, a near run thing.

On 20 March 1937 Whitty married Sheila Hope. They resided at Seaford, Sussex, and had two boys.

In 1938 he was posted as a lieutenant with the 2nd Battalion to Palestine to help deal with a nationalist uprising by Palestinian Arabs (the Arab Revolt) against British colonial rule and to stop Palestine becoming, as they saw it, a Jewish homeland. It was an important peace-keeping role trying to keep the Arabs and Jews from killing each other. It was during this 'policing' operation that Whitty was to receive the MC for his outstanding bravery and leadership skills:

During the night advance on Tanra on 14 May 1938 Lieut Whitty was slightly injured in the hand and leg in a car accident. In spite of this he remained at duty and during the action in the early afternoon he went forward with the attack of 'A' company and set a very fine example by his coolness and courage. When a report reached him that Private Moyes was missing, he together with Captain Kelleher R.A.M.C. and Private Parkin went forward in front of the leading troops under considerable fire to search for him, found him, and helped to carry him back to a covered position.

At the outbreak of the Second World War Whitty was sent to France with the British Expeditionary Force, 132nd Infantry Brigade. As the BEF began its retreat to the sea Whitty's battalion formed part of the rear car. His extraordinary story can be found on line but is too big for the room I have here, but I have included some extracts to give readers a taste:

'I was in a red hot spot and there seemed no way of escape…I found Major Woodhouse and spoke to him. He was in a ditch, he lifted his head no doubt to give me some orders and was instantly shot through the head. I turned to the troops behind me and ordered them to follow me through a gap in the hedge which I found; at that moment I was hit by what appeared to be a heavy calibre bullet. It knocked me out for a moment and I must say I thought I was finished, but when I came to I was able to get up and realized that it was not so bad after all.

'Not so bad' meant being hit by two machine gun bullets, one hitting him in the chest and one in the shoulder. Making for Dunkirk he was picked up by an ambulance and taken to a makeshift hospital in Dunkirk before being loaded onto a hospital ship and finally being shipped to England and the safety of a hospital in Dover with all its 'English smells'.

He later wrote, 'Those twenty-one days, since 10th May shall I ever forget them? I hardly think so. The retreating in good order, the enemy armoured vehicles, the congested and burning road, the C.C.S. eighteen hours in that ambulance, and so near and yet so far at the dock in Dunkirk, and all the rest of my life.'

On recovery he was sent to the Middle East with the 5th Battalion taking part in the Battle of El Alamein and given command of the 5th (Territorial Battalion) Royal West Kents, being promoted to lieutenant colonel. All this at the tender age of 32. None other than Field Marshal Montgomery described him as 'the best field commander in the 8th army'. After Africa and further training he was posted to Italy.

As a talented musician, he always insisted that the battalion took with it a honkytonk piano to keep up troops' morale.

Once again he led his battalion with great valour and took leave only once. Within a month of arriving in Italy he was awarded the DSO. His citation read,

On 30 November 1943 Lt-Col Whitty's battalion attacked Romagnoli. The two forward companies were held up with heavy casualties.

Lieut-Col Whitty went forward over an area swept by heavy machine gun and mortar fire, co-ordinated supporting weapons, and by deliberately exposing himself to enemy fire set such an example that his men were encouraged to leave cover and resume the advance which was finally successful and inflicted many casualties on the enemy.

After reaching his objective the unit was counter-attacked by tanks and infantry and considerable confusion caused. Lt-Col Whitty again exposed himself to heavy fire went to the scene of the possible break in and forced the enemy back with loss.

His leadership and complete indifference to danger inspired his unit throughout the action.

Just over a year later, on 23 October 1944, Whitty was killed after stepping on a mine at Vicchio, Florence.

A brother officer later wrote of him, 'He will be remembered with the greatest affection by all those who came into contact with him and by those of us who had the great honour of serving under his command.'

He is buried in the Florence War Cemetery, grave reference IV. B. 4.

Batting and fielding averages

	Mat	Inns	NO	Runs	HS	Ave	100	50	Ct	St
First-class	1	2	0	23	22	11.50	0	0	0	0

Bowling averages

	Mat	Balls	Runs	Wkts	BBI	Ave	Econ	SR	5w	10
First-class	1	126	46	4	2/19	11.50	2.19	31.5	0	0

Lieutenant John Lawson Richards
Cambridge University
One first-class match
240 Field Company Royal Engineers
Died 2 November 1944, aged 26

John Richards was born on 6 October 1918 in Williton, Somerset. He was educated at the Monmouth School between 1934 and 1938 where he was captain of the school for two years. He excelled at all sports being captain of the first XI, the first XV (he captained an unbeaten rugby team in 1936) and hockey. On leaving school in 1938 he went up to Selwyn College Cambridge where he read mathematics. While there he played cricket and rugby (scrum half) for his college but also for many other first-class representative sides. He was elected secretary of the College RUFC and played in several games for the university, gaining the LX club colours.

Richards made one first-class appearance for Cambridge University against Yorkshire between 24 and 26 May 1939 at F.P. Fenner's. Cambridge won the toss and decided to bat. Richards was stumped by Arthur Wood of the bowling of Leonard Hutton for zero in his first innings, and Cambridge made only 84 runs. Yorkshire then made 350 with Len Hutton making 102 and Norman Yardley 140 not out. Richards fared no better in his second innings being once again out for a duck off the bowling of Ellis Robinson (who took five wickets in the innings). Cambridge did better though, scoring 369 with Arthur Brodhurst making 106 not out. However it was to be Yorkshire's day. They made 104 for one in their second innings and took the game by nine wickets.

Richards must have occasionally popped back to his old university on leave because during May and June 1942 he played for them on three occasions: against D.L. Donnelly's XI (Cambridge winning by ten wickets), the Army (drawn), and for the Cambridge University Crusaders against Epsom (the Crusaders won by eight wickets).

He took a commission in the Royal Engineers for the duration of the war joining 240 Field Company and was involved in bomb disposal. He was killed with the British Liberation Army on 1 November 1944 and buried in Jonkerbos War Cemetery, Gelderland, Netherlands, grave reference 24. I. 3.

The Times of 15 May 1945 announced his death: 'It is now known that Lieutenant J.L. Richards, R.E., who played scrum-half for the Wasps, Cardiff, and Newport Rugby football clubs, was killed in action last November.'

First-class Career Batting and Fielding (1939)

	M	I	NO	Runs	HS	Ave	100	50	Ct
Cambridge University	1	2	0	0	0	0.00	0	0	0

First-class Career Bowling (1939)

	Balls	Mdns	Runs	Wkts	BB	Ave	5wI	10wM	SRate	Econ
Cambridge University	104	1	50	0	0-18					2.88

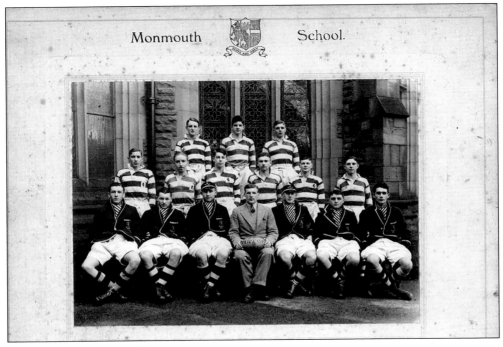

Richards standing, first on left centre row.

Captain Cedric Alfred Humphries
Worcestershire
Thirteen first-class appearances
1st Battalion Worcestershire Regiment attached 4 Battalion
Somerset Light Infantry
Died 18 November 1944, aged 30
Right-handed bat/Right arm medium

'his heart once glowed with enthusiasm for the games he loved'

Cedric Humphries was born on 26 December 1913 in Kidderminster, the son of Henry Alfred John and Ethel Eliza Humphries. He was educated at Downing College Cambridge after which in 1935 he became a teacher at the Royal Grammar School Worcestershire, becoming housemaster at Whiteladies. He was a devoted coach of the rugby and cricket teams at the school, remaining there until 1940 when he was called up.

He made thirteen first-class appearances all for Worcestershire between June 1934 and July 1935 all in the County Championships. He made his debut against Lancashire on 9 June 1934 at the County Ground, New Road, Worcestershire. Lancashire won the toss and decided to bat making 456 for six declared. Humphries caught Leonard Parkinson off the bowling of Reginald Perks for nine. The Lancashire opener Frank Watson made 148 and the England test player Edward Paynter (*Wisden* cricketer of the year 1938) made 100. Perks, the Worcestershire and England test bowler, took five wickets for 108 off 35 overs. In reply Worcestershire made 149, Humphries making the top score of 41 not out. Watson took five wickets for 57 off 16 overs. Forced to follow on, Worcestershire made 115. Humphries was run out for five. Lancashire won the match by an innings and 192 runs.

He went on to play Cambridge University (catching the Hampshire opener and England test player John Arnold off the bowling of Cyril Stanley Harrison), Sussex (he made 34), Derbyshire, Lancashire, Nottinghamshire (Humphries made 43 not out), Gloucestershire (Humphries made 11 and 35), and Somerset three times (Humphries made scores of 29 and 13 and caught Jack Lee off the bowling of Peter Jackson for one).

Humphries played his thirteenth and final first-class match against Northamptonshire on 20 July 1935 at the County Ground, Northamptonshire. Worcestershire won the toss and decided to bat making 93. Humphries made one before being stumped by Benjamin Walter Bellamy off the bowling of George Cyril Perkins. Perkins took six wickets for 54 off 15 overs. In reply Northamptonshire made 171. Frank Warne took six wickets for 51. In their second innings Worcestershire made 307. Humphries made one before being caught by Bellamy off the bowling of the England Test cricketer, Austin Matthews. In their second innings Northamptonshire made 199. Worcestershire won by 39 runs.

He also played for the Gentlemen of Worcestershire against the Gentlemen of Suffolk and for A.F. Skinners XI against A.G. Pelham's XI (Cambridge University Seniors Match). He was also a regular and outstanding player with the combined Worcestershire and Herefordshire rugby XV.

Cedric Humphries trained as an officer cadet before being commissioned as a 2nd lieutenant into the Worcestershire Regiment on the 28 December 1940. Becoming involved in training and instructional work with the army, he made three appearances for Eastern Command in July 1943.

At the time of his death Humphries had risen to the rank of captain and was attached to the 4th Somerset Light Infantry. The Somersets were holding a position at the small German village of Pannenschopp near the Dutch/German frontier. On 18 November 1944 a 105 mm enemy shell hit the slit trench he was in killing him instantly, together with 2nd Lieutenant Ken Oxland.

Captain Humphries is buried with other men of the Worcestershire Regiment at the British War Cemetery at Brunssun in Holland, grave reference II. 63.

After the war a subscription was raised and a seat, suitably inscribed, was placed in front of the old pavilion on Flagge Meadow so Humphries would be forever remembered in the green setting where his heart once glowed with enthusiasm for the games he loved.

His two brothers Gerald and Norman also played briefly for Worcestershire.

Batting and fielding averages

	Mat	Inns	NO	Runs	HS	Ave	100	50	Ct	St
First-class	13	24	3	328	44	15.61	0	0	3	0

Bowling averages

	Mat	Balls	Runs	Wkts	BBI	BBM	Ave	Econ	SR	4w	5w	10
First-class	13	-	-	-	-	-	-	-	-	-	-	-

1945

Captain Peter Ralph Cherrington DSO
Leicestershire
Ten first-class appearances
1st Battalion Northamptonshire Regiment
Died 20 January 1945, aged 27
Right-hand bat/Leg break googly

His outstanding bravery won him the DSO

Peter Cherrington was born on 20 January 1945 in Newark, Nottinghamshire, the son of George Esam and Kate Elsie Cherrington of Averham. He was educated at Wellingborough where he played in the first XI. He made ten first-class appearances all for Leicestershire and all in 1938 in the County Championship.

He made his debut against Hampshire on 14 May at the County Ground, Southampton. Hampshire won the toss and decided to bat making 221. In reply Leicestershire made 288. Cherrington made two before being bowled by William Charles Leonard Creese. The New Zealand test player Charles Stewart Dempster (*Wisden* cricketer of the year 1932) made 110. George Stuart Boyes took five wickets for 52. In their second innings Hampshire made 64 for two. The match was drawn.

He went on to play against Warwickshire, Northamptonshire, Kent (Cherrington made 18), Lancashire (he caught Norman Oldfield off the bowling of James Sperry for 73), Yorkshire, Kent (Cherrington made 33 and 10), and Glamorgan.

His final first-class match took place against Gloucestershire at the Ashley Down Ground, Bristol, on 24 August 1938. Gloucestershire won the toss and decided to bat making 160. Haydon Smith took eight wickets for 40. In reply Leicestershire made 202, Cherrington making three before being bowled by the England player Thomas Goddard. In their second innings Gloucestershire made 214. William Flamson took five wickets for 53. In their second innings Leicestershire made 160. Cherrington made zero before being bowled by Goddard. Goddard took eight wickets for 62. Gloucestershire took the game by 12 runs.

During the war Cherrington served with the 1st Battalion Northamptonshire Regiment becoming a captain. He went on to win the DSO while serving in Burma. The regimental history describes his bravery in more detail:

On the night of the 4th/5th January, 1945, Capt. Cherrington's Company was sent to capture the water supply at the village of Hlwede on the outskirts of Dudalin. This water supply was vital to the future operations of the Battalion against Budalin itself, and was defended by the enemy in dug positions. By outstanding leadership Capt.

Cherrington infiltrated his Company by night into a position from which a final charge took the enemy completely by surprise and secured all objectives at the low cost of three casualties to his company. He subsequently held all the positions gained and the essential water supply against the enemy attacks till joined by the remainder of the Battalion.

In the subsequent operations to clear Budalin, Capt. Cherrington, on the 8th January, 1945, was again sent off, this time to effect an infiltration behind the enemy's flank and to cut off one of his most valuable sources of water. In the course of 48 hours continuous fighting in a town affording ample positions and cover to the enemy, he conducted against determined opposition a series of attacks, the cumulative effect of which was to clear the whole northern environs of Budalin, deprive the enemy of valuable sources of water and, above all, force the enemy to evacuate positions from which the attack of the rest of the Battalion from the west was being held up. His manoeuvres were decisive in allowing the final successful advance of the whole Battalion to go in.

In particular, at 1700 hours on the 8th January, 1945, when he heard that a party laying cable to him and a second party carrying casualties were being attacked by the enemy, he, with one man as escort, made his way under fire to the cable party, organized a counter-attack and beat off the enemy, himself killing three Japanese and obtaining important identifications. Later in the same day, after a very hazardous personal reconnaissance by night, he succeeded in contacting a Company of Gurkhas 600 yards to his left and in guiding them to an advantageous tactical position on his own left flank. As a result of these manoeuvres the enemy was compelled to evacuate positions in the east centre of Budalin.

Throughout the whole of the five days action at Budalin, Capt. Cherrington has displayed outstanding qualities of leadership, initiative and resource. These, added to his many acts of conspicuous personal gallantry under fire and his endurance and selfless devotion to duty, have been an outstanding inspiration, not only to his Company, but to the whole Battalion, and proved a prime factor in the capture of Budalin in the face of desperate resistance.

London Gazette, 19 April 1945.

Cherrington died on 20 January 1945.

He is buried in the Taukkyan War Cemetery, grave reference 19. E. 23. There is also a memorial to him at St. Michael and All Angels Church at Averham.

Batting and fielding averages

	Mat	Inns	NO	Runs	HS	Ave	100	50	Ct	St
First-class	10	14	0	85	33	6.07	0	0	3	0

Bowling averages

	Mat	Balls	Runs	Wkts	BBI	BBM	Ave	Econ	SR	4w	5w	10
First-class	10	177	127	0	-	-	-	4.30	-	0	0	0

927033 Leading Aircraftsman Frederick Stratford Campling
Orange Free State
Five first-class matches
258 Squadron RAF Volunteer Reserve
Died 22 March 1945, aged 36
Right-handed bat/Leg break

'Victim of the Japanese Death March'

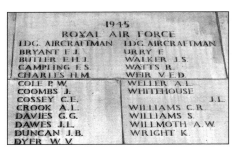

Frederick Campling was born in West Bridgford, Nottingham, on 9 June 1908. Not a great deal is known about his early life other than at some point he travelled to Kenya taking part in his first known cricket match for the Settlers against the Officials in Nairobi between the 9 and 10 October 1926. During the first innings Campling scored 34. During the Officials first innings Campling stumped Alan of the bowling of Noel Winsland, Merrick off the bowling of John Harcombe, and caught Rowe off the bowling of Harcombe. Campling scored zero not out in the second innings, but took two catches. The match was drawn.

Campling also turned out for the Europeans between 1934 and 1936.

Remaining in Africa Campling made five first-class appearances all for the Orange Free State in the Curry Cup between 1930 and 1934. He made his debut first-class appearance against Rhodesia at the Ramblers Cricket Club ground, Bloemfontein, on 13-15 January 1930. Orange Free State won the toss and elected to bat making 225. Campling made five not out before running out of partners. In Rhodesia's first innings Campling took three wickets, William Wood lbw for three, Frederick Morgan lbw for 12, and the tail-ender Edward Dollar bowled for zero. Rhodesia made 156. In his second innings Campling once again ran out of partners scoring four, Orange Free State going on to score 325. Campling took four further wickets during this innings, Thomas Symington for 23, Cecil Roberts caught by Murray Francis for one, Henry O'Reilly for nine, and Ernest Sim caught Francis for a duck. The Orange Free State won by 184 runs.

Campling went on to play for the Orange Free State against the Eastern Province (19 February 1930), Griqualand West (15 December 1933), Natal (26 December 1933) and finally Border. The match was played on 5 January 1934 at the Ramblers ground. Border won the toss and decided to bat making 250. Campling took Border's opening bat Charles Byron for 18. In Orange Free State's first innings Campling made eight before being bowled by Cecil Closenberg. Orange Free State made 164. During their second innings Campling once again took Border's opening bat, this time John Phillips for 36. This didn't stop Border making 284. In Orange Free State's second innings Campling made ten before being bowled by Ivor Gardiner. Border took the match by 118.

During his first-class career Campling scored 59 runs with a high score of 16 against Natal and took 11 wickets, his best figures being 4 for 75.

306

At some point Campling returned to England and took up residence in Ilsington, Devon, on the edge of Dartmoor. He continued to play cricket, this time for the minor counties side, Devon, making twenty-four appearances for them between 1935 and 1939.

During the Second World War Campling served as a leading aircraftman with 258 Squadron RAF Volunteer Reserve. Posted to Singapore he was taken prisoner by the Japanese and was to become one of the victims of the Sandakan Death Marches. He died on 22 March 1945.

In February 1942, Allied PoWs were shipped to North Borneo to construct a military airstrip and PoW camp at Sandakan. They were forced to work at gunpoint and received the most brutal of treatment. In January 1945 the advancing allies managed to bomb the airstrip so the commanding officers decided to move the remaining prisoners into the mountains. On the marches at least 2,300 died or were killed by the guards. Only six survived. After the war several of the Japanese officers involved were tried and either shot or hanged.

Campling's official cause of death (as recorded by the Japanese) was acute enteritis.

He is buried in the Paginatan cemetery but the precise location of his grave was never recorded. He is commemorated on the Kranji War Memorial in Singapore together with 24,000 other names, on column 453. He is also commemorated on the war memorial in Ilsington.

Batting and fielding averages

	Mat	Inns	NO	Runs	HS	Ave	100	50	Ct	St
First-class	5	9	3	59	16	9.83	0	0	0	0

Bowling averages

	Mat	Runs	Wkts	BBI	Ave	5w	10
First-class	5	243	11	4/75	22.09	0	0

1146677 Gunner Sidney Clarke Adams
Northamptonshire
Eleven first-class matches
Royal Artillery, the Worcestershire Yeomanry, Airlanding
Light Regiment
Died 24 March 1945, aged 40
Right-hand bat/Leg break

'The only man to have bowled a Nobel Laureate with his first first Class ball'

Sidney Adams was born on 17 August 1904 in Northampton the son of Albert Clarke and Norah Adams. He was educated at Northampton School for Boys where his talent for cricket first came to notice. On leaving school he became a clerk for the local council.

Samuel Beckett.

Adams made eleven first-class appearances between 1926 and 1932, his debut being against Dublin University at College Park, Dublin, between 7 and 9 June 1926. Dublin won the toss and elected to bat scoring 138 all out in their first innings. Northamptonshire went on to make 291. Together with Alfred Hawtin, Adams opened the batting. He scored 12 before being bowled by Mark Sugden. In their second innings Dublin only managed 89, Adams catching the Dublin opener John Lawrence for one off the bowling of John Nicholson. Northamptonshire won the game by an innings and 64 runs.

In their return match played between 7 and 8 July 1926 at the County Ground, Northampton, Adams scored 87 (his highest first-class score) before being caught by Samuel Barclay Beckett off the bowling of Thomas Dixon (Dixon took six wickets for 32 off seven overs, his best first-class bowling figures). Adams had his revenge, bowling Beckett for one during his second innings with his very first, first-class ball. Samuel Beckett later won the Nobel Prize for Literature (Beckett, a left-handed bat and left-arm medium pace bowler, made two first-class appearances, both for Dublin University, one in 1925, and then again against Northamptonshire when he scored 18 and 12 and failed to take a wicket). Adams bowled seven overs during the innings taking six wickets for 32, Samuel Beckett for one, Thomas Hartigan Dixon caught Kenneth James Rymill for seven, his brother Patrick O'Madigan Dixon for zero, Stephen Tempest Adair Radcliffe for 14, James Robertson Wills lbw for ten, and Hugh Thomas Baker stumped George Henry Johnson for two.

Adams went on to play against various counties, making his final first-class appearance against the Indians between 4 and 7 June 1932 at the Town Ground, Kettering. Northamptonshire won the toss and decided to bat, making 155, Adams scoring one before being caught by Janardan Navle off the bowling of Mohammed Khan. In reply the Indians made 279. Adams fared little better in his second innings scoring only two before being bowled by Syed Ali. Northamptonshire's second innings score was 151. This left the Indians only 22 to take the match, which they made quickly winning the game by ten wickets.

Adams married Gwendoline and they resided at East Haddon in Northamptonshire.

During the Second World War he served with the Royal Artillery attached to the Worcestershire Yeomanry, Airlanding Light Regiment, when he was killed near Hamminkeln crossing the Rhine on 24 March 1945. He is buried at the Reichswald Forest War Cemetery, grave reference 38. E. 2.

Batting and fielding averages

	Mat	Inns	NO	Runs	HS	Ave	100	50	Ct	St
First-class	11	16	1	158	87	10.53	0	1	5	0

Bowling averages

	Mat	Balls	Runs	Wkts	BBI	Ave	Econ	SR	5w	10
First-class	11	359	250	13	6/32	19.23	4.17	27.6	1	0

First Officer David Russell Hayward
Oxford University
Nine first-class appearances
Air Transport Auxiliary
Died 21 April 1945, aged 24
Right-handed bat /Leg break googly

Tragic waste of such a young life

David Hayward was born on 7 June 1920 in Australia. He was the son of Edwyn Walton (Jim) Hayward and his wife Eileen Frances Russell. He was educated at Harrow where he was in the first XI between 1935 and 1938 playing against Winchester, Charterhouse, Marlborough, Free Foresters and Eton. He also turned out for C.F. Tufnell's XI against a Lord's XI (Lord's won by an innings and one run) and Lord's School against The Rest (the match was drawn).

At Oxford he was selected to play in Oxford's First XI. He made his debut for the university against Gloucestershire in a university match on 29 April 1939 at the University Parks. Oxford won the toss and decided to bat making 286. Hayward made zero not out. Thomas Goddard took five wickets for 42 off 17 overs. In reply Gloucestershire made 213 for eight declared. In their second innings Oxford made 132 for eight declared. Hayward did not bat. In their second innings Gloucestershire made 206. Hayward caught the England test cricketer and Gloucestershire opener Charles Barnett (*Wisden* cricketer of the year 1937) off the bowling of Christopher Lubbock for 23. Gloucestershire won by five wickets.

He went on to play against Yorkshire, Middlesex (he took one wicket), Derbyshire (he took two wickets and caught the England test cricketer George Pope off the bowling of David Macindoe for 20), Lancashire (he took four wickets for 37 off 12 overs), and the West Indies.

Against Somerset on the 17 June 1939 at the Recreational Ground Bath he bowled 33 overs during Somerset's first innings taking six wickets for 79, and bowled 19 overs during Somerset's second innings taking three further wickets for 71. Despite Hayward's best efforts however Somerset won by 219 runs.

His final university match was played against Surrey on 21 June 1939 at the Kennington Oval. Hayward failed to bat but bowled 22 overs taking three wickets for 86. The weather closed in and the match was drawn.

Hayward's one and only county championship match was also his final first-class appearance, playing for Middlesex against Hampshire on the 24 June 1939 at the Victoria Recreation Ground, Newport. Middlesex won the toss and decided to bat making 261. Hayward made ten before being caught by Neil Thomas McCorkell off the bowling of George Stuart Boyes. Boyes took five wickets for 45 off 17 overs. The England test cricketer Bill Edrich (*Wisden* cricketer of the year 1940) made 118. In reply Hampshire made 93. Forced to follow on, Hampshire made 143. Hayward bowled three overs taking one wicket for five: Boyes caught by Jack Robertson. Middlesex won by an innings and 25 runs.

Hayward also played for the Harlequins and the Minor Counties.

During the Second World War Hayward trained as a pilot before joining the Air Transport Auxiliary as a first officer. The Air Transport Auxiliary's job was to deliver aircraft around the country so he flew a great many different types. On 21 April 1945 Hayward was piloting an Argus II HB595 at Lasham Airfield, Hampshire, in the moonlight. Soon after takeoff the aircraft's engines suddenly cut out and it crashed burning furiously not far from Lasham Hill Farm. An investigation was held to establish the cause of the crash and it was discovered the petrol cocks were only half on.

On 22 March 1941 David married Peggy Alice Georgina Farmer and they had one son, born in 1943.

Hayward is buried in Maidenhead Cemetery, grave reference section D, row W, grave 21.

Batting and fielding averages

	Mat	Inns	NO	Runs	HS	Ave	100	50	Ct	St
First-class	9	13	7	36	14	6.00	0	0	2	0

Bowling averages

	Mat	Runs	Wkts	BBI	Ave	5w	10
First-class	9	591	20	6/79	29.55	1	0

Captain Alexander Armstrong Shaw
Sussex and Bengal
Two first-class matches
11th Sikh Regiment
Died 19 July 1945, aged 37
Right-hand bat/Wicketkeeper

Took his own life

Alexander Shaw was born on 7 September 1907 in Shardlow, Derbyshire. He was one of six children (four girls and two boys) born to Philip Armstrong and Helen Ursula Shaw of Hemington Hall. He was educated at Eastbourne College (Blackwater House) where he was a house prefect. He excelled at cricket and was in the school XI in 1923, 1924 and 1925. During his last year he captained the side and made two centuries. After leaving school he played club cricket for Eastbourne Cricket Club. In 1926 *Wisden* wrote of him,

> The backbone of ECC lay in Shaw's batting. A splendid man to open the innings, and scored heavily throughout the year. He had the coolness of temperament and soundness of defense so important for that role, but he was also a fine stroke player, and some of his innings were among the best seen at Eastbourne for years. No doubt Sussex will keep an eye on him as, I am told, he will continue to live in the county.

Shaw made two first-class appearances. The first was on 15 June 1927 playing for Sussex against Cambridge University at the County Ground, Hove. Sussex won the toss and elected to bat. Batting last Shaw knocked up six before being lbw by Thomas Longfield. During Cambridge's first innings Shaw kept wicket and devastated Cambridge's batsmen making three catches and three stumpings. He stumped the England test player Edward Dawson for 54 off the bowling of Edward Bowley, he then caught Edmund Longrigg off the bowling of Albert Wensley for 20, he did the same to England test player Walter Robins off the bowling of Nazir Ali for 85, then he caught the former Eton captain Ralph Cobbold off the bowling of Reginald Hollingdale for 29. His next victim was Longfield who he stumped off the bowling of Edward Bowley for 17, before finally stumping another England test player Maurice Allom off the bowling of Bowley for a duck. Shaw didn't bat in the second innings and only took one more Cambridge wicket, catching Cobbold off the bowling of George Cox for six. The match was finally drawn.

By 1929 Shaw was in Calcutta working as a shellac broker for the firm of J. Thomas and Co. While there he played club cricket for the famous and ancient Calcutta Club. He also learned to ride with the Calcutta Light Horse, although it didn't all go well, as one article pointed out: 'he had just passed out of the riding school and was suffering severely where he sat…'

He was to wait eight years before he made his second and final first-class appearance, this time playing for Bengal against the Australians at the Eden Gardens, Calcutta, between 27 and 29 December 1935. Bengal won the toss and decided to bat. Shaw, batting in the lower orders, was stumped by John Ellis for a duck off the bowling of Charles Macartney. Shaw did little better in his second innings being out lbw off the bowling of Ronald Oxenham for one. Australia won by nine wickets.

On 1 May 1936 he married Geraldine Kingsley. On a return to England he turned out for the Stragglers of Asia against his old school. By 1937 he was living near Calcutta and was the honorary secretary of the Calcutta Cricket Club. He was also a member of the Royal Calcutta Turf Club where he acted as a timekeeper and did a little judging. His school magazine the *Eastbournian* wrote a small passage about him while tracing down their former pupils living in India:

> A. A. Shaw (BI. 19-25) J Thomas & Co., Tea Broker. A pillar of the turf who lives in a delightful house in Garie, outside Calcutta. He keeps 'tumbler pigeons' and plays lots of tennis and a little cricket. If he is as artful with his tea broking as he is at handing on jobs not unconnected with the Old Eastbournian, he has a big future.

In 1942 Shaw was granted an emergency commission into the Indian Army, being attached to the 11th Sikh Regiment's machine gun section. Serving in Burma he became a captain. At some point his wife seems to have met and run off with a brother officer, later divorcing Shaw. On 19 July 1945, in New Delhi, shortly after the divorce, Shaw committed suicide, whether as a consequence of the divorce I have no idea, but it seems likely.

He was initially buried at Dehra Dun in Northern India and later removed to the Delhi War Cemetery, grave reference 2. B. 6.

First-class Career Batting and Fielding

	M	I	NO	Runs	HS	Ave	100	50	Ct	St
Overall	2	3	0	7	6	2.33	0	0	4	3

Sub-Lieutenant Charles Henry Sutton
South America
One first-class appearance
Royal Naval Volunteer Reserve (HMS *Daedalus III*)
Died 29 July 1945, aged 38
Right-handed bat/Right arm slow

Returned from South America to fight and die for his country

Charles Sutton was born on 17 December 1906 in North Bierley, Bradford, the son of Charles Evans and Annie Gertrude Sutton. The family moved to Valparaiso, Chile, where his father went into business. He returned home in 1921 to be educated at the Leys School, Oxford. On leaving school he returned to Valparaiso, Chile, to help in his father's firm, and was also able to indulge his passion for cricket, playing successfully for several local sides.

In 1932 he was selected to play for South America during their tour of the British Isles between May and July 1932 when they played nineteen games.

On 25 June 1932 he made one first-class appearance for South America against Sir J. Cahn's XI at West Park, Nottingham. Cahn's won the toss and decided to bat making 413, the South African test cricketer Denijs Morkel making more than half their score with 251. Sutton made a total of ten runs in the match and took no wickets, but South America still managed to win by five wickets.

Sutton played for the South Americans on a further eight occasions during the tour, none of which were first-class matches. He also represented Chile twice against Argentina in 1938.

In 1942 Sutton left Chile as a volunteer and took a commission as a sub-lieutenant in the RNVR. He was later transferred to the Fleet Air Arm and stationed at HMS *Daedalus III*, where he was involved in the training of new recruits. During this time he became seriously ill, dying at Haslar, Gosport, on 29 July 1945.

He is buried at Haslar Royal Naval Cemetery, grave reference G. 11. 10.

Batting and fielding averages

	Mat	Inns	NO	Runs	HS	Ave	100	50	Ct	St
First-class	1	1	0	10	10	10.00	0	0	0	0

Bowling averages

	Mat	Balls	Runs	Wkts	BBI	BBM	Ave	Econ	SR	4w	5w	10
First-class	1	30	23	0	-	-	-	4.60	-	0	0	0

Wing Commander John Gordon Halliday
Oxford University
Twenty-six first-class matches
59 Squadron RAF Volunteer Reserve
Died 3 December 1945, aged 30
Right-handed bat/Right arm medium pace

Saw the war through only to die going home

John Halliday was born on 4 July 1915 in Cockermouth, Cumberland, the son of John and Ann Elizabeth Halliday. He was educated at the City of Oxford High School for Boys where his talent for cricket was quickly recognized.

He played for Oxfordshire in the Minor Counties Championship against Bedfordshire on 27 July 1932 scoring nine not out in his only innings with the match being drawn due to bad weather.

From school he went up to Merton College Oxford where he was soon selected for both the college and the university. He made twenty-five first-class appearances for the university between 1934 and 1937.

He made his debut against Gloucestershire at the University Parks on 2-4 May 1934. Oxford won the toss and decided to bat. Halliday made one not out in his first innings and zero not out in his second. He took the wicket of Lionel Cranfield for two and caught Victor Hopkins off the bowling of John Dyson for 24. The match was eventually drawn.

Halliday went on to play against many other teams (including a match against Yorkshire in which he was bowled by another famous casualty of the Second World War, Hedley Verity), finally appearing for Oxford against Sussex at the County Ground, Hove, between the 26 and 29 June 1937. Halliday was lbw for zero in his first innings and retired hurt after scoring three in his second, Oxford going on to win by three wickets.

Halliday also made one first-class appearance for the Minor Counties against Oxford at the University Parks between 30 May and 1 June 1934 (making his total first-class appearances twenty-six). Minor Counties won the toss and decided to bat. Halliday scored an impressive 49 before being caught by Norman Knight off the bowling of Peter Badham. During the same innings William Farrimond (later an England test cricketer) made 174. Halliday scored 33 not out in his second innings. He impressed with the ball as well, taking the wickets of Anthony Benn stumped Farrimond for five, Neville Cohen for six, and Knight for 20.

Halliday also played sixty minor counties championship matches.

He scored a total of 776 first-class runs at an average of 23.21, during which time he made five half-centuries with a top score of 87 against the Free Foresters at the

University Parks on 26 May 1934. He took 18 wickets at an average of 37.66 with his best figures being three for 11. He also made eight catches.

He was elected Oxford County Cricket Club captain in 1938 and at some point found time to meet and marry Frances Mary. The couple later lived in Aylesbury.

During the war Halliday was commissioned into the RAF, joining 59 Squadron, being promoted to pilot officer in 1940, flying officer in 1941, flight lieutenant in June 1942, and finally wing commander. The squadron departed for France in 1939 and, flying Blenheim Vs, was mainly engaged in photographic reconnaissance of harbours, bridges and convoys. After Germany defeated France in 1940 the squadron was moved to Thorney Island where they carried out escort duties on convoys, night bombing raids (ten on Cherbourg) and anti-invasion sweeps. In 1941 they became attached to Coastal Command becoming a general reconnaissance squadron taking part in anti-shipping strikes. A typical month for them (January 1941) was thirty-five sorties on a Hipper-class cruiser in dry dock at Brest, seven sorties against train ferries at Flushing, six sorties on an enemy convoy, two escorts to convoys, one recce of Boulogne, one 'moon' patrol and one 'hookos' patrol (search and rescue). These activities did not come without a cost and during the first six months of 1941 the squadron lost twelve Blenheims and their crews. It was later re-equipped with Hudsons and in 1942 took part in bomber raids on Germany. In August the squadron was again re-equipped, this time with Liberators and commenced anti-submarine and convoy escort protection duties over the Atlantic. The squadron destroyed several U-Boats including U470, U990, U292 and U844. At the end of the war it became attached to Transport Command and was given the task of flying troops home to India.

After surviving the war Halliday, while a passenger on board a Liberator B-24 on 3 December 1945, was killed together with twenty-eight other passengers and crew when their aircraft's wing broke off after being struck by lightning in severe turbulence near Rochefort in France. He is buried in Rochefort-sur-Mer Naval Cemetery, grave reference NE plot, row 4, grave 1.

Batting and fielding averages

	Mat	Inns	NO	Runs	HS	Ave	100	50	Ct	St
First-class	26	42	8	848	87	24.94	0	5	8	0

Bowling averages

	Mat	Runs	Wkts	BBI	Ave	5w	10
First-class	26	747	21	3/11	35.57	0	0

2667542 Lance Corporal Paul Wilson Brooks
Middlesex
One first-class appearance
Coldstream Guards
Died 26 January 1946, aged 25
Left-handed bat/Left arm fast medium

When 16 years of age in 1938 he became famous by bowling Don Bradman

Paul Brooks was born on 28 May 1921 in Marylebone, the son of William James and Mabel of Maida Hill. A fine cricketer as a County of London schoolboy he headed the batting averages and played against both Eton and Harrow for selected schoolboy teams. He became a member of the Lord's ground staff and it was while in this position he first gained a reputation and some fame. In 1938 when the Australian touring side came to Lord's for practice, the young Paul Brooks was told to go down to the nets at the Old Nursery to bowl for Don Bradman. You can imagine the young cricketer's excitement. In front of the viewing press, his left arm fast-medium bowling caught Bradman out. Hooking at a left-hand delivery, Bradman missed the ball, which knocked down Bradman's middle wicket. The papers were full of it and it earned young Brooks an interview on British Movietone News:

> *Paul Wilson Brooks, 17-year-old youth, who created a sensation by bowling Bradman at the Australians' first practice at Lord's Cricket Ground. Brooks is a left-hand medium-pace bowler, and is a member of Lord's ground staff.*

Brookes turned out for Middlesex Second XI against Kent second XI. It wasn't a glorious start: he failed to make a run or take a wicket.

Brooks only made one first-class match, for Middlesex against Warwickshire on 30 August 1939 in the County Championship at Lord's. Middlesex won the toss and decided to bat making 525. Batting with Dennis Compton, Brooks made 44 not out. Jack Robertson made 154 and Bill Edrich 101. In reply Warwickshire made 194. Following on, Warwickshire made 131. Middlesex won by an innings and 200 runs.

Compton later remembered his encounter with the young Brooks: 'When he joined me at the wicket,' Compton wrote, 'I knew, from the look on his face, that he was enjoying the happiest moment of his life … he "wallowed" in his batting, and with me as his partner, cracked up a wonderful unbeaten 45.' One of the Warwickshire players went so far as to say, "You've a big find there." There was general agreement among the Middlesex dressing room.

Brookes served in London and Coventry with the National Fire Service during the height of the Blitz.

Later, after joining the Coldstream Guards and reaching the rank of lance corporal, he played for the British Empire XI in 1943 and 1944 and the Combined Services in 1944. None of these matches were rated first-class.

FRIDAY. DAILY EXPRESS

BRADMAN IS BOWLED BY A 17-YEAR-OLD 'UNKNOWN'

Glory—then back to boot-cleaning

By WILLIAM POLLOCK

A DARK-HAIRED youth, Paul Wilson Brooks by name, had the thrill of bowling Don Bradman at Lord's yesterday. Then he returned to his job of boot-cleaning in the members' dressing-room.

Brooks, aged seventeen, unknown in big cricket, is a left-hander on the ground staff. When he knocked the Don's castle over he tried not to smile—but he did.

"I think Mr. Bradman must have been 'mucking about'," he said. "No one was more surprised than me that a plain ball took his middle stump.

"I thought he would send it sailing into the road; but he tried to hook it and missed it completely.

"The funny thing is I am supposed to be a batsman and not a bowler."

PUBLIC PAY TO SEE PRACTICE

Brooks played for London schoolboys a year ago, and after writing to Lord's for a trial was given a ground staff engagement.

It was the Australians' first practice—the first time that half the team had ever seen Lord's—and a large number of people paid their shillings at the gate to watch.

A shilling admission to see net practice is a new one to me.

It wasn't a very serious occasion, of course. Bradman was having a crack. Most of his fifteen minutes' batting, and his wicket went several times. Chipperfield once bowled him with a beauty.

When he had batted, Don trotted round the practice ground, with Hassett and Barnett. Then he had a bowl.

He says that as a bowler he is a cross between Arthur Mailey and Walter Robins. A bit quicker off the bat, perhaps.

The injured Barnes, with his wrist strapped up, did not practise, but the efficient invalid, Stan McCabe, both batted and bowled.

THE LIGHT PUZZLES THEM

The wickets took plenty of spin, and the grey afternoon London light puzzled some of the players. One who did a lot of catching practice said that the ball was in a fog to him.

Sturdy little Jackie Badcock, who is a cricket ball harder than almost any one in the game, made some fierce hooks; and Jack Fingleton, who usually bats his head down and plays strictly in and down the line of the ball, "went up" during his turn in the net, and hit violently.

Bowler Fleetwood-Smith was satisfied with the two wicketkeepers, Walker and Barnett, to bowl to him.

It was an overcast afternoon for those of us who looked on—and we were slightly surprised to find that the Lord's score board has apparently already begun the season with a boundary. Underneath "Total" there was "4."

TRAINING for the "other Cup Final" as the Rugby League event at Wembley—this year between Salford and Barrow on May 7—is known. Left: Don Bradman, opening his shoulders at Lord's yesterday, was bowled by seventeen-year-old Paul Brooks—and middle stump, too. Paul could hardly believe it. Right: Grandpa Sandy Herd, seventy years old on Sunday, "burned up the course" in doing nine holes in 30 strokes at Moor Park. Leo Munro tells the story below.

Grandpa Herd does nine holes in 30: best ever in senior golf

By LEO MUNRO

OLD champion Sandy Herd was the star of the £1,000 golf tournament at Moor Park, yesterday.

He had a wonderful second round score of sixty-seven on the West course—and Sandy, a grandfather, will be seventy years old next Sunday.

He did not lead the field. First place, with two rounds played, was shared by two of the younger school stalwarts, Dick Burton and Alf Perry, each having an aggregate of 135.

Nor could Herd claim the best single round of a sensationally low-scoring day. Perry put in an amazing record 64 on the West course, for which the scratch score is 73.

But ruddy-faced, clear-eyed Sandy, the oldest man among nearly 200 competitors, set up records of his own.

He thrilled the crowd by reeling off the first nine holes in a total of thirty strokes. No other player, old or young, has equalled that in a major tournament in this country.

A grand performance by an old-timer. Something for the moderns to think about. Herd was handicapped. He felt when he went round the West course splendidly in 67.

But Perry overhauled Burton, had a spot of revenge on Herd in the thunderstealing business.

Perry's 64 made the West course look easy. Out in 33, length, accuracy, confident putting all employed. Home amazingly in 31, with six 3's included.

Henry Cotten, James Adams and Eddie Whitcombe are all well up at aggregate 137, with two rounds still to be played by the sixty-one qualifiers.

RED WINGS BEATEN

MONTREAL CANADIENS beat Detroit Red Wings 5 goals to 4...

Tragically while fighting with the Coldstream Guards in Italy in April 1945, Brooks was wounded in the spine by a sniper's bullet. Invalided home he never recovered and was bedridden, dying of his injuries on the night of 26 January 1946 at St Mary's Hospital, Paddington.

The local paper covered his death:

> "Boy Who Bowled Bradman" dies of war injuries
> LONDON, Monday. -- Paul Wilson
> Brookes (24), who in 1938 made cricket
> news as "the boy who bowled Brad-
> man," died on Saturday night in St.
> Mary's Hospital, Paddington.
> Brookes was 16 when he bowled Brad-
> man at the practice nets at Lord's. He
> was wounded in Italy in April, 1945, and
> was brought back to St. Mary's, where
> he had been bedridden ever since.
> During the war he served in the fire
> services in the London and Coventry
> blitzes and the Surrey dock fires. He
> joined the R.A.F. and later transferred
> to the Coldstream Guards, with which
> he was serving when he was wounded.

He is buried in Brompton Cemetery, grave reference plot N (Guards plot), grave 194035.

I'll let Denis Compton have the last word: 'But Paul Brooks – God bless him! Never lived to enjoy the success he had earned, for after lying three months in a hospital bed in England, after receiving a spine wound while fighting in Italy, he passed away.'

Batting and fielding averages

	Mat	Inns	NO	Runs	HS	Ave	100	50	Ct	St
First-class	1	1	1	44	44*	-	0	0	0	0

Bowling averages

	Mat	Balls	Runs	Wkts	BBI	BBM	Ave	Econ	SR	4w	5w	10
First-class	1	-	-	-	-	-	-	-	-	-	-	-

Captain Ralph Alexander Spitteler
Europeans (India), Madras
Four first-class matches
10th Gurkha Rifles (3rd Battalion)
Died 14 March 1946, aged 30
Left-handed bat/Right arm fast medium

Survived the war but not his wounds

Ralph Spitteler was born on 16 November 1915 in Cannanore (now Kannur), Kerala. He was the son of Charles and Daisy Spitteler of Fern Dell, Yercaud, India, and educated at Madras University.

He made four first-class appearances, between January 1939 and January 1941. His debut came against India in the Madras Presidency match played 13-15 January 1939 at Madras Cricket Club ground. The Europeans won the toss and decided to bat. Spitteler was bowled for zero by Morappakam Joysam Gopalan, the entire team being dismissed for 155. Spitteler's failure with the bat was more than made up for with the ball. In India's first innings he took the wickets of Krishnaswami for four, Doraiswami for three, Lakshmanan for 16, and Jagannatha for 41. He also made three catches taking the wickets of Gopalan (who had just bowled him for a duck), Deenan and Rangachari. In the second innings he scored one before running out of partners, the Europeans making 123 all out. During India's second innings Spitteler was once again impressive taking the wickets of Doraiswami for four, Deenan for five, Bhadradri for 26, Ram Singh for 46, and finally Krishnaswami for zero. Despite Spitteler's best efforts, the Europeans lost by four wickets.

He made his second first-class appearance a few weeks later, this time in the Ranji Trophy playing for Madras against Bengal. The match was played at the Eden Gardens, Calcutta, 21-23 January 1939. Bengal won the toss and decided to bat. During Bengal's first innings Spitteler took the wicket of A. Jabbar (caught Gopalan) for 46. He failed to score in Madras's first innings, again running out of partners. Bengal won by an innings and 285 runs.

Spitteler next turned out for the Europeans against the Indians in a Madras Presidency match at the Madras Cricket Club 12-14 January 1940. The Europeans won the toss and decided to bat. This time Spitteler achieved his best innings with a bat making 11 not out. He went on to do well with the ball taking five wickets in 29 overs, Krishnaswami for twenty, Ramaswami caught Coldwell for 105, Parthasarathi caught Ward for six, Gopalan for 32, and Chari for nine. During the second innings he managed a further eight runs not out and took one further wicket, that of Ramaswami for zero. Again Spitteler was on the losing side, the Indians winning by four wickets.

Spitteler made his final first-class appearance for the Europeans against India in the Madras Presidency match played between 12 and 14 January 1941 at the Madras Cricket Club ground. India won the toss and decided to bat. Spitteler took two wickets off 24 overs, Swaminathan caught Johnstone for 44, and Parthasarathi for 32. In the second innings he was not out for zero and took the wicket of BS Krishna Rao for two. Spitteler was once again on the losing side, Indian winning by 97 runs. Alas Spitteler was never on the winning side in a first-class match.

Jakarta War Cemetery.

During the war Spitteler enlisted into the ranks of the 10th Gurkha Rifles becoming a corporal before being commissioned into the third battalion on 12 February 1942 rising to the rank of lieutenant.

He was seriously wounded with the 3rd Gurkha Rifles while fighting the Japanese at Scraggy Hill and Shenam Pass, the soldiers often using their kukris in fierce hand-to-hand combat. Spitteler died of his wounds on 14 March 1946.

He is buried in Jakarta War Cemetery, grave reference 6. K. 12.

Batting and fielding averages

	Mat	Inns	NO	Runs	HS	Ave	100	50	Ct	St
First-class	4	8	6	24	11*	12.00	0	0	5	0

Bowling averages

	Mat	Runs	Wkts	BBI	Ave	5w	10
First-class	4	407	19	5/29	21.42	2	0

Lieutenant Colonel William Murray Leggatt DSO
Kent/Army
Eleven first-class appearances
11 (HAC) Field Regiment Royal Horse Artillery
Died 13 August 1946, aged 45
Right-hand batsman/Right arm fast

His health broken down by service

William (Bill) Leggatt was born on 2 September 1900, in Crail, Fife. He was the second son of Ernest Hugh Every Leggatt of the Indian Civil Service, and Jesse, daughter of the banker Andrew Murray. He was educated at Mr A.V. Pott's School, Parkside, Ewell, before going up to Winchester, joining Mr Little's House in September 1914 (he was a contemporary of Douglas Jardine). A first-class athlete he was in both the school's first XV and XI.

Deciding on a career in the army he went up to the Royal Military Academy Woolwich in 1919. While there he was captain of their football squad and their cricket XI.

Commissioned into the Royal Artillery he played several matches for them against the Royal Engineers, MCC and Quidnuncs, later going on to play for the Army.

Leggatt made eleven first-class appearances, five in the County Championship for Kent and the Army between July 1926 and August 1933. He made his debut on 3 July 1926 at the Rectory Field, Blackheath. Yorkshire won the toss and decided to bat making an impressive 428. In reply Kent made 225. Leggatt made 30 before being caught by the England test cricketer Percy Holmes (*Wisden* cricketer of the year 1920) off the bowling of another England test cricketer Wilfred Rhodes (cricketer of the year 1899). Forced to follow on, Kent made 42 for zero. The match was eventually drawn.

His next match for Kent in the County Championship was against Gloucestershire. Leggatt made 51 and 92, Kent winning by four wickets.

He made his debut for the Army on 17 July 1926 against the Royal Navy at Lord's. The Royal Navy won the toss and decided to bat making 249. Leggatt caught Edwin Llewellyn Pain off the bowling of Philip Davies for 17. In their first innings the Army made 376. Leggatt made 29 before being bowled by Pain. In their second innings the Royal Navy made 151, Robert George William Melsome taking six wickets for 44. In their second innings the Army made 26 for no wicket. Leggatt failed to bat. The Army won by ten wickets.

His next four first-class matches were played in the County Championship, all in 1926.

In 1931 he played against the RAF (the Army won by an innings and 37 runs), and in 1932 he played against the RAF once again (the Army won by an innings and 130 runs).

He made his final first-class appearance for the Army against the West Indies in England on 26 August 1933 at the Officers' Club Services Ground, Aldershot. The Army won the toss and decided to bat making a solid 472. Leggatt made 18 before being bowled by George Copeland Grant. Reginald Hudson made 181 and Cyril Hamilton 121. In their first innings the West Indies made 346, Benjamin James Sealey making 106 not out. In their second innings the Army made 149. Leggatt failed to bat. In their second innings the West Indies made 181 for four. The match was drawn.

During his career Leggatt made 479 runs including three fifties, his highest score being 92 against Gloucestershire. He also made nine catches.

On 29 July 1929 he married Connel Auld, daughter of T. Ogilvie Mathieson. They had a son and lived at Hinton Place, Hinton St. George.

In 1933 Bill was promoted to captain serving as an instructor with the Royal Marines between 1931 and 1935. He was later promoted to adjutant of 16 Field Brigade. In 1938 he was promoted to major. He then served as a brigade major in Egypt until the outbreak of war. During this time he was mentioned in dispatches twice (*London Gazette* 30-12-41 and 9-9-42). He attended the Middle East Staff School in Haifa, which had been opened to provide staff training for officers unable to return to the Staff College in Camberley. He was given command of the 11 (HAC) Field Regiment RHA with whom he saw service at the battle of El Alamein and was awarded the DSO (*LG* 28-01-43). In August 1943 he took command of 83 Anti-Tank Regiment Royal Artillery and was promoted to lieutenant colonel in 1944. Due to his years at the front his health began to fail and he was returned to England in 1945 and put in command of the 3rd Royal Artillery Reserve Regiment. His health never recovered and he died from a heart attack in the smoking room of the Cavalry Club, Piccadilly, on 13 August 13 1946.

His funeral was held on 17 August 1946 and he rests in St George's churchyard, Hinton St George. Worth a visit if your passing and perhaps a few flowers.

Batting and fielding averages

	Mat	Inns	NO	Runs	HS	Ave	100	50	Ct	St
First-class	11	16	0	479	92	29.93	0	3	9	0

Alphabetical List

A

Adams S.C., Northamptonshire
Alexander E.M., Bengal
Alexander L.A., Europeans (India)
Alexander R., Ireland
Anderson M.H., Cambridge University, Free Foresters
Arkwright F.G.B., Hampshire
Ashton C.T., Cambridge University, Free Foresters, Essex, England

B

Bairnsfather Cloete P.H., Western Province
Baker G.G., Queensland
Balance T.G.L., Oxford University
Baldock W.F., Somerset
Barker C.M., Transvaal
Barnardo F., Cambridge University, Middlesex
Barnes J.H.B., Ireland
Behrend S.W.M., Bengal/Europeans (India)
Bennett M.V., Minor Counties
Bevan T., Army
Blagg P.H., Oxford University
Blake J.P.B., Cambridge University, Hampshire
Blount C.H.B., RAF
Bowell N.H., Hampshire, Northamptonshire
Briscoe A.W., South Africa, Transvaal
Brooks P.W., Middlesex
Bruce-Jones J., Scotland
Burke A.O.L., Europeans (India)
Butterworth J.C., Oxford University, Middlesex
Butterworth R.E.C., Oxford University, Middlesex, Sir J. Cahn's XI, H.D.G. Leveson-Gower's XI

C

Campbell A.K., Hampshire
Campling F.S., Orange Free State
Carr H.L., Glamorgan, H.D.G. Leveson-Gower's XI
Carson W.N., Auckland
Chalk F.G.H., Oxford University, Kent, MCC, Gentlemen, England, Gentlemen of England, Sir P.F. Warner's XI
Cherrington P.R., Leicestershire
Chiodetti V.A., Hyderabad

Cobden A.P., Canterbury New Zealand
Cocks A.D.B., Army
Cokayne-Frith C., Army
Connaughton J.M.F., Oxford University, Middlesex
Cressall E.F., British Guiana
Crook R.C., Wellington
Cruickshanks G.L., Eastern Province

D

Day D.A.S., Europeans (India)
Dixon E.J.H., Oxford University, Northamptonshire
Dobs H.W., Minor Counties, Sir T.E.W. Brinckman's XI
Doyle C., Orange Free State
Dunbar H.C.F.V., Europeans (India)

E

Eastman. L. C., Essex Otago
Eckersley P.T., Lancashire
Edwards A.J., Otago
Evans R.J., Border
Everett D.T., Western Australia

F

Fairbairn S.G., MCC
Farnes K., England, Cambridge University, Essex.
Fenton G.G.J., Viceroy's XI
Fletcher G.E., Oxford University, Somerset
Francois C.M., South Africa, Griqualand West, J.M.M. Commaille's XI
Freakes H.D., Eastern Province, The Rest

G

Gartly J.D.E., Transvaal
Gasson E.A., Canterbury
Gerrard R.A., Somerset
Gibson E.L., Rangoon Gymkhana
Gregory R.G., Australia, Victoria
Grimshaw J.W.T., Cambridge University, Kent, MCC
Grove L.T., Army, Combined Services
Groves G.J., Nottinghamshire

H

Halliday J.G., Oxford University
Hamilton C.P., Army, Kent
Hamilton E.P., City of Transvaal, Transvaal
Hancock L.F., MCC

Hart-Davis G.C., Natal
Hayward D.R., Oxford University
Hodder F.S., RAF
Hodges A.D., MCC
Howie A.D., Army (India)
Howlett B., Europeans (India), Kent, MCC, Bombay
Human R.H.C., Berkshire, Cambridge University, Oxfordshire, Worcestershire
Humphries C.A., Worcestershire

J

Jameson H.G., Cambridge University
Jeffreys J.A., Western Australia
Jose G.E., South Australia

K

Kemp-Welch G.D., Warwickshire, Cambridge University, MCC, LH Tennyson's XI
Kerr F.B., Otago
King S.P., Victoria

L

Langton A.C.B., South Africa, Transvaal
Lee J.W., Middlesex, Somerset, Players
Leggatt W.M., Kent, Army
Legge G.B., England, Kent, Oxford University
Longfield G.P., RAF

M

Macaulay G.G., England, Yorkshire
Magill M.D.P., Oxford and Cambridge Universities
Matthews M.H., Oxford University
Maw M.T., Cambridge University
Mayo C.T.W., Somerset
McMillan N.H., Auckland
McNeil A.S.B., Scotland
McRae F.M., Somerset
Merry D., Trinidad and Tobago
Miller R.A.T., Sussex
Moloney D.A.R., New Zealand, Canterbury, Otago, Wellington
Monaghan D.W., South Island Army
Monteath A.P.J., Otago
Moss E.H., Oxford University, H.D.G. Leveson-Gower's XI
Moyle E.J.R., South Australia
Musson R.G., Combined Services
Myles H.F., Western Province, Rhodesia

Alphabetical List

N

Nelson R.P., Middlesex, Cambridge University, MCC, Northamptonshire

O

Orton C.T., Army, Europeans (India)

P

Packe C.W.C., Leicestershire, Army
Papenfus C.F.B., Orange Free State
Parry W.J., Rhodesia, Natal
Pearsall A.L., Tasmania
Pershke W.J., Oxford
Philpot-Brookes R.F.H., Europeans (India)
Price D., Western Province

R

D.W.G. Ray, MCC
Richards J.L., Cambridge University
Ridings K.L., South Australia
Roach W.A., Western Australia
Rucker P.W., Oxford University

S

Scott K.B., Oxford University, Free Foresters, Sussex
Scott P.M.R., Oxford University
Seeley G.H., Worcestershire
Shadwell C.R., Europeans (India)
Shaw A.A., Sussex, Bengal
Sides F.W., Queensland, Victoria
Spencer C.R., Oxford University, Glamorgan
Spitteler R.A., Europeans (India), Madras
Stephenson R.H., Royal Navy
Sutton C.H., South America

T

Talbot G.L., Canterbury
Thorn F.L.O., Victoria
Thorne G.C., Army
Tindall R.G., Oxford University
Titley E.G., Cambridge University
Turnbull M.J.L., England, Cambridge University, Glamorgan, Wales

V

Verity H., England, Yorkshire, MCC, Players, H.D.G. Leveson-Gowers XI

W

Walker C.W., South Australia
Walker Donald F., Hampshire
Walker David F., Oxford University, MCC, Sir P.F. Warner's XI
Walters H.G., Auckland
Wareham C.P.S., Wellington
Warren G.M., Roshanara Club
Watson D.J.F., Oxford University
Welch W.M., Free Foresters
Whetherly R.E., Oxford University
Whitehouse P.M.W., Kent, Oxford University
Whitty J.H.H., Army
Wilkinson K., Cambridge University
Wills A.P.S., Combined services
Winlaw R.de W.K., Cambridge University, Surrey
Witherington D.M., Cambridge University
Wood P.B., West Australia

By Club and Country

Test cricketers

Briscoe A.W. (South Africa)
Farnes K. (England)
Francois C.M. (South Africa)
Gregory R.G. (Australia)
Langton A.C.B. (South Africa)
Legge G.B. (England)
Macaulay G.G. (England)
Moloney D.A.R. (New Zealand)
Turnbull M.J.L. (England)
Verity H. (England)

First-class cricketers by team

Northamptonshire
Adams C.C.
Bowell N. H.
Dixon E.J.H.
Nelson R.P.

Nottinghamshire
Groves G.J.

Hampshire
Arkwright F.G.B.
Blake J.P.B.
Bowell N.H.
Campbell A.K.
Walker Donald F.

Essex
Ashton C.T.
Eastman. L. C.
Farnes K.

Somerset
Baldock W.F.
Fletcher G.E.
Gerrard R.A.
Lee J.W.
Mayo C.T.W.

McRae F.M.
Whetherly R.E.

Middlesex
Barnardo F.
Brooks P.W.
Butterworth J.C.
Butterworth R.E.C.
Connaughton J.F.M.
Lee J.W.
Nelson R.P.

Berkshire
Human R.H.C.

Worcestershire
Human R.H.C.
Humphries C.A.
Seeley G.H.

Glamorgan
Carr H.L.
Spencer C.R.
Turnbull M.J.L.

Sussex
Scott K.B.
Shaw A.A.
Miller R.A.T.

Leicestershire
Cherrington P.R.
Packe C.W.C.

Kent
Chalk F.G.H.
Grimshaw J.W.T.
Hamilton C.P.
Howlett B.
Leggatt W.M.

Legge G.B.
Whitehouse P.M.W.

Warwickshire
Kemp-Welch G.D.

Surrey
Winlaw R.de W.K.

Lancashire
Eckersley P.T.

Yorkshire
Macaulay G.G.
Verity H.

Minor Counties
Bennett M.V.
Dobs H.W.

Gentlemen/Gentlemen of England
Chalk F.G.H.

Players
Lee J.W.
Verity H.

The Rest
Freakes H.D.

England XI
Chalk F.G.H.

Ireland
Alexander R.
Barnes J.H.B.

Scotland
Bruce-Jones J.
McNeil A.S.B.

Wales
Turnbull M.J.L.

MCC
Chalk F.G.H.
Fairbairn S.G.
Grimshaw J.W.T.
Hancock L.F.
Hodges A.D.
Howlett B.
Kemp-Welch G.D.
Nelson R.P.
Ray D.W.G.
Verity H.
Walker David F.

Free Foresters
Anderson M.H.
Ashton C.T.
Scott K.B.
Welch W.M.

England XI
Ashton C.T.

Cambridge University
Anderson M.H.
Ashton C.T.
Barnardo F.
Blake J.P.B.
Farnes K.
Grimshaw J.W.T.
Human R.H.C.
Jameson H.G.
Kemp-Welch G.D.
Magill M.D.P.
Maw M.T.
Nelson R.P.
Richards J.L.
Titley E.G.
Turnbull M.J.L.
Wilkinson K.
Winlaw R.de W.K.
Witherington D.M.

Oxford University
Ballance T.G.L.
Blagg P.H.

By Club and Country

Butterworth J.C.
Butterworth R.E.C.
Chalk F.G.H.
Connaughton J.F.M.
Dixon E.J.H.
Fletcher G.E.
Halliday J.G.
Hayward D.R.
Human R.H.C.
Legge G.B.
Magill M.D.P.
Matthews M.H.
Moss E.H.
Pershke W.J.
Rucker P.W.
Scott K.B.
Scott P.M.R.
Spencer C.R.
Tindall R.G.
Walker David F.
Watson D.J.F.
Whetherly. R. E.
Whitehouse. P.M.W.

Army/Army (India)
Bevan T.
Cocks A.D.B.
Cokayne-Frith C.
Grove L.T.
Hamilton C.P.
Howie A.D.
Leggatt W.M.
Magill. M.D.P.
Monaghan D.W. (South Island Army)
Orton C.T.
Packe C.W.C.
Thorne G.C.
Whitty J.H.H.

RAF
Blount C.H.B.
Hodder F.S.
Longfield G.P.

Royal Navy
Stephenson R.H.

Combined Services
Grove L.T.
Musson R.G.
Willis A.P.S.

India

Europeans (India)
Alexander L.A.
Behrend S.W.M.
Burke A.O.L.
Day D.A.S.
Dunbar H.C.F.V.
Howlett B.
Orton C.T.
Philpot-Brookes R.F.H.
Shadwell C.R.
Spitteler R.A.

Bengal
Alexander E.M.
Behrend S.W.M.
Shaw F.W.

Bombay
Howlett B.

British Guiana
Cressall E.F.

Hyderabad
Chiodetti V.A.

Viceroy's XI
Fenton G.G.J.

Madras
Spitteler R.A.

Rangoon Gymkhana
Gibson E.L.

Roshanara Club
Warren G.M.

Australia

Queensland
Baker G.G.
Sides F.W.
Whitehouse P.M.W.

Tasmania
Pearsall A.L.

South Australia
Jose G.E.
Moyle E.J.R.
Ridings K.L.
Walker C.W.

Western Australia
Everett. D.T.
Jeffreys J.A.
Roach W.A.
Wood P.B.

Victoria
Gregory R.G.
King S.P.
Sides F.W.
Thorn F.L.O

South America
Sutton C.H.

South Africa

Western Province
Bairnsfather Cloete P.H.
Price D.

Transvaal/City of Transvaal
Barker C.M.
Briscoe A.W.
Gartly J.D.E.
Hamilton E.P.
Langton A.C.B.

Orange Free State
Campling F.S.

Doyle C.
Papenfus C.F.B

Eastern Province
Cruickshanks G.L.
Freakes H.D.

Griqualand West
Francois C.M.

Rhodesia
Myles H.F.
Parry W.J.

Natal
Hart-Davis G.C.
Parry W.J.

Western Province
Myles H.F.

Border
Evans R.J.

New Zealand

Auckland
Carson W.N.
McMillan N.H.
Walters H.G.

Canterbury
Cobden A.P.
Gasson E.A.
Moloney D.A.R.
Talbot G.L.

Wellington
Crook R.C.
Moloney. D.A.R.
Wareham C.P.S.

Otago
Eastman. L.C.
Edwards A.J.
Kerr F.B.

Moloney D.A.R.
Monteath A.P.J.

Various

Sir J. Cahn's XI
Butterworth R.E.C.

J.M.M. Commaille's XI
Francois C.M.

H.D.G. Leveson-Gower's XI
Butterworth R.E.C.
Carr H.L.
Moss E.H.
Verity H.

Sir P.F. Warner's XI
Chalk F.G.H.
Walker David F.

Sir T.E.W. Brinckman's XI
Dobs H.W.

L.H. Tennyson's XI
Kemp-Welch G.D.

Trinidad and Tobago
Merry D.

South Island Army
Monaghan D.W.